RHODE ISLAND COLLEGE EDITION

Axelrod & Cooper's
CONCISE
GUIDE
TO WRITING

RHODE ISLAND COLLEGE EDITION

Axelrod & Cooper's CONCISE GUIDE TO WRITING

FOURTH EDITION

Rise B. Axelrod
UNIVERSITY OF CALIFORNIA, RIVERSIDE

Charles R. Cooper
UNIVERSITY OF CALIFORNIA, SAN DIEGO

BEDFORD/ST. MARTIN'S
Boston • New York

Manufactured in the United States of America.

3   2   1   0   9   8
f   e   d   c   b   a

For information, write: Bedford/St. Martin's, 75 Arlington Street, Boston, MA 02116
(617-399-4000)

ISBN: 0-312-53925-8
EAN: 978-0-312-53925-2

Acknowledgments
Donna Britt, "A Kiss May Not Still Be a Kiss." Copyright © 1996 by Washington Post Writers Group. Reprinted with permission.
Alfred Eisenstaedt, "VJ Day Times Square 1945." Alfred Eisenstaedt, Life Magazine © Time Inc. Used with permission.
Stephen King, "Why We Crave Horror Movies," originally appeared in *Playboy*. Copyright © 1982 by Stephen King. Reprinted with permission.
Anne Lamott, "Shitty First Drafts," from *Bird by Bird* by Anne Lamott. Copyright © 1994 by Anne Lamott. Used by permission of Pantheon Books, a division of Random House, Inc.
Mike Rose, from *Lives on the Boundary: The Struggle and Achievements of America's Underprepared.* Copyright © 1989 by Mike Rose. All rights reserved. Reprinted with permission of The Free Press, a division of Simon & Schuster Adult Publishing Group.

Acknowledgments and copyrights continue at the back of the book on page 349, which constitutes an extension of the copyright page.

Acknowledgments

This special edition of *Axelrod and Cooper's Concise Guide to Writing* is a collaborative project with Bedford/St. Martin's Custom Publishing and the English Department of Rhode Island College. The coordinating committee—Marjorie Roemer, Jenn Cook, Karen Pfeil, and Claudine Griggs—worked closely with Nancy Perry of Bedford/St.Martin's, as well as her colleagues Maureen McLaughlin, Brian Donnellan, and Jane Smith. Many thanks to Rhode Island College for providing funding for this project, and especially to the FAS Dean, Rich Weiner, and Associate Dean, Earl Simson. The committee also appreciates the enthusiastic support of Maureen Reddy, the Rhode Island College English Department Chair, and the English Department faculty who attended preliminary discussions in Spring and Fall 2007 to help shape the textual concepts. Thanks to the faculty who contributed material for the book; to Eugene St. Pierre, the College Photographer; and to the students who offered sample essays. And finally, the committee wishes to thank the faculty and staff of the Rhode Island College Writing Program for their continuing efforts, year by year, to guide students through the magic of writing and rhetoric. Thank you, all.

Letter from Maureen Reddy, Chair of the English Department

A recent prompt for a standardized writing test asked whether the goal of education should be to teach facts or to have an open mind. If those are the only options, then most Rhode Island College faculty would probably choose the latter, on the grounds that stuffing minds full of facts cannot truly be called education and that open minds are crucial for learning of any kind to take place. However, I think we would prefer a third option: the goal of education is to nurture in our students the capacity to think critically, which is the essential skill for an involved, productive, and satisfying life in a participatory democracy.

Writing is all about thinking: to write well, we must think clearly. And thinking is all about writing: to think clearly, we often must write, and rewrite, and rewrite again, trying to discover and then to explain our ideas to ourselves and to others. As the novelist E. L. Doctorow once said, "Writing is an exploration. You start from nothing and learn as you go." But if "nothing" is what we start from, how do we learn how to "go" from there? How, exactly, do we learn to explore? That's where Writing 100: *Writing and Rhetoric* comes in.

Writing and Rhetoric is the most important course you will take in your college career, for in this course you will learn strategies for that exploration that you will draw on throughout your undergraduate coursework and beyond. This book, compiled by experienced instructors and specially tailored to meet the needs of Rhode Island College students, is an invaluable resource for your journey toward the goal of becoming an educated person. We all look forward to reading your writing and to helping you to "learn as you go."

—Maureen Reddy
Chair, English Department

Contents

Description of People and Places ∎ Information about the Subject ∎ A Topical or Narrative Plan ∎ A Role for the Writer ∎ A Perspective on the Subject

Supplementary Readings

Student Essays

An Introduction to Writing and Rhetoric for Rhode Island College Students

Writing and Rhetoric (or Writing 100) is a course required of all undergraduates at Rhode Island College. Why? Why do we think this course is so important? Only a handful of courses are required of all our students. What makes this one special? In a real way, this course opens your passage to the rest of your college career. We know that you have taken English courses for many years. We know that you have written essays in high school and even in the earlier grades. In Writing 100, however, we want to help you take a different place in relation to your own writing. We want you to think of yourself as in control. Writing gives you agency; it should allow you to speak your mind, to explain exactly why you feel as you do. It should help you to integrate your past experience with new things you are learning and new ideas you are trying out. It should help you to think things through.

When we study students' transcripts, we see that good grades in Writing 100 are the best predictors of success at Rhode Island College. Why is that? Learning how to write in a variety of genres enables you to adjust your style, your tone, your capacity for examining things in a variety of ways. It lets you be flexible as a thinker and observer. We have designed this course to help you understand and perfect your own processes for exploring the things you study. We are particularly interested in making this text work for our students at this college. For that reason, we are focusing only on six kinds of writing tasks, ones that you will be using in many of your other courses. The first two involve **remembering, observing, describing, interviewing, narrating, and reflecting**. The third involves **explaining** a concept. The fourth involves **arguing** a position. The fifth involves **proposing** a solution, and the sixth focuses on **making and supporting an evaluation**. Together, these cover most of the activities that you will be engaged in as a student and a writer. These are practical tasks, ones that are used in the world all the time—sometimes in formal writing, sometimes in less formal conversation. The design of our program will allow you to take your time with these tasks, to build these projects in increments, so that you can observe the processes you use as you gather materials, focus your thoughts, and shape your writing.

Students at Rhode Island College, like students in most other places, come with varied speech and writing backgrounds. Some think of themselves as writers already and have significant degrees of skill and expertise. Others have struggled with writing. Some are speakers of many languages but not native speakers of English. Some speak in

1

forms that match up well with the "standard" English required in more formal writing, and some speak most naturally in more colloquial patterns. We expect our classes to accommodate all our students and to offer a place for them all to expand their linguistic capacities. We want to offer opportunities for exploration and creative play in a wide variety of genres, forms, levels of formality, even in visual communication. The Writing Program is not about invoking "the grammar police." It is about providing models that expand the range of all. Rhetoric describes "the art, or technique of persuasion," but it depends very much on a clear understanding of audience and expectation. So, in this course, we are very interested in rhetorical situation, in understanding what forms suit what occasions, when to be formal and when to be informal.

We hope in this course to engage your best thoughts and energies. We are not trying to get you to write "canned" essays that say what you think we want to hear. Rather, we want to help you to express yourself effectively for a wider audience. We know that a lot of writing starts from a "felt sense," a vague, not yet verbal, feeling about something. Writing is often the process of putting that vague, undifferentiated feeling into words—and into words that someone outside your head can understand. How do we do that? What can we learn about that process that can make it easier for us to do? How can we help one another in that process?

Many students tell us that "creative" writing is fun and free and something they do for themselves, at least occasionally. In contrast, "academic" writing is dry and dull, a formula, sometimes a sandwich that they put together according to the instructions given. We want to re-examine that. Creative writing can have its own constraints and shaping rules, and academic writing can have much more creativity than some earlier exposure might lead you to suppose. Formulas are like training wheels; we have to get beyond using them if we are really going to ride. In this course, we hope to help you take off the training wheels and start your ride. Part of that ride involves having new models for what academic writing is and can be. Most of us don't really read academic writing before we get to college. The closest example we might have is a textbook. Textbooks are notoriously dull, distanced, and most often voiceless. We don't think they are a good model for what you will be writing as novice scholars. So, one of our projects has to be broadening the examples of academic writing. In every chapter of this text you will find models of more accessible academic writing. You will also see an appendix filled with essays written by Rhode Island College students from previous years, so that you will get an idea of how students like you have responded to these assignments.

—MARJORIE ROEMER
DIRECTOR OF COMPOSITION

What Is Writing and Rhetoric? *Faculty Voices*

Writing is not about language itself. It's about using language to express ideas, tell a story, make a claim. My cat sometimes communicates without uttering a single word. But English provides options beyond a growl, purr, or hiss. Grammar, punctuation, vocabulary, organization, artistry, evidence, quotation, and anecdote are some of the available mechanisms of written communication, but they do not guarantee success. For example, in a speculative essay about World War III, one novice high school writer insists, "The end is as near as far can see." This vainglorious nonsense came from me, forty years ago, when I believed that the sentence was so cool, so John Lennon and William Shakespeare, that it would inevitably earn me an "A," stop the war in Vietnam, and encourage unilateral disarmament. World peace would follow. Yet the sentence (and most of the essay) made no sense to others—my teacher, my peers, or present-day me. In hindsight, if I had substituted my entire tenth grade nuclear holocaust masterpiece with the Stephen King word-clause "fuhgeddaboudit," I would have delivered a better paper. So my contemporary advice to student writers is: Toss every highfalutin, indecipherable aphorism into the nearest wastebasket, which is the inevitable repository of first drafts. Strive for clarity above all things. And then make sure others understand what you've put down on paper. That said, Get Ready! Aim! Write! Or else, fuhgeddaboudit.

—CLAUDINE GRIGGS

The advice I often give my students is, "Begin with something that personally interests you; let yourself tell a story." From the vantage point of familiarity, student writers can often see their way into an essay. Once inside the project, the next step is to be curious and explore beyond the frame of firsthand knowledge. We must ask how and why. It is important, as learners, to challenge ourselves, to delve beneath the surface layer of understanding, to add on to what we already know. This is how we make new meanings. This is how we compose work that dances across the page.

—Joyce Cote

As an English 010 teacher, I feel that my main job is to communicate the message that *writing requires revision*. I explain to students that writing is like sculpting. When one writes, new thoughts emerge, and discoveries and mistakes are made, just as when stone is carved or clay manipulated. The writer must accept the fact that as layers are probed, the unexpected may surface. It's important to let time pass in between drafts, so that new ideas percolate. Present steps determine future directions. Writing involves risk, practice, and patience. Most English 010 students don't start the class with this view. They've been taught from previous school experiences that they must write perfect prose from the get-go—or their grades will suffer. They've been told that their ideas must be fully formulated once they submit their outline. Basic writing students are surprised when they're given the opportunity to revise papers three or more times after responses from different readers. Several students have told me that this new perspective about writing has improved their overall experience at Rhode Island College since they spend a huge amount of their time at college producing papers. This is the beauty of English 010. It helps students to succeed in all of their classes. Students are encouraged—and not punished—to think, to explore, to interact, and to change, which is key to a creative educational process.

—Susan Sklar

Perhaps the most valuable lesson the students of Writing 100 have taught me is simply to remember that I cannot always judge effort by the quality of work I receive; especially, I need to be wary of judging student work hastily and without first attempting to understand the students' motives behind what they write. This can only be achieved by one-on-one conferences with students. Just because I enjoy writing does not mean many of my students do, and certain writing exercises that may seem simple to me can at times frustrate and appear insurmountable to them. I have learned to take more pleasure in their progress and individual triumphs than in a perfect finished piece, and the result of that shift in attitude makes for a more pleasant learning environment for all of us.

—STEPHANIE WHEELER

Eudora Welty once said, "If you haven't surprised yourself, you haven't written." It's a simple statement, but I can't resist including this quote on my syllabi for *Writing and Rhetoric* courses that I teach here at Rhode Island College. Reading and writing, processes of learning and discovery, should be surprising. In a similar way, I think, so should teaching. My favorite part about teaching *Writing and Rhetoric* is the storytelling; I like the stories students tell in class, the topics they write about, the way stories (personal and otherwise) are shaped into drafts and then into essays that convey meaning. Rhode Island College has the advantage of being a truly diverse and multicultural campus yet somehow feeling small and local—very Rhode Island, so to speak—at the same time. Students' story lines, therefore, intertwine with one another in an interesting way, and with the stories of my own life, too. Always, I am surprised by what students in this course are capable of writing by the end of it. Always, I hope they are also surprised by the meanings they make and the voices they find to convey these meanings.

—KAREN PFEIL

We don't trust writers who don't read any more than we trust skinny cooks. Nor should we. The nonreader's writing is inevitably shallow, awkward, and, quite literally, uninspired. Think about it: when's the last time you came across a good essay written by someone who only reads cell texts or video game guides? There is only one surefire way to improve your writing, and that is to first improve your reading. Reading feeds writing every bit as much as living and thinking do, especially in the beginning when the medium can sometimes seem mysterious, if not downright arbitrary. For it is only by reading sensitively and voraciously that you can ever hope to get a feel for the tricky sentence structures, unworn-out words, and surprising but solid arguments that will ultimately help you to make complex points as simply as possible.

—MAX WINTER

When I speak about my own development as a Rhode Island College student, I often include the story about the professor I had in a freshmen-level English course. This was long before a course in writing was a requirement. After every writing assignment, she would ask me to meet her after class to go over my work. She would tell me that my ideas were good, but that they were lost in my poor sentence structure and grammar. She would go through my written work line by line. At first I thought I would never get through college if I had to spend this much time after class going over my writing. But the more I met with this professor, the more respect I had for the written word. It became more and more important for me to do better the next time she assigned something—not only because I wanted to write better but because I wanted to show my respect for the teacher who spent so much time helping me. If she spent that much time with all of her students, she must have never left campus.

Over the last thirty-four years of working with students at Rhode Island College, I have noted that, with very few exceptions, students who perform at the minimum level of competency in Writing 100 have difficulty with their other subjects in their first year. I have come to believe that the work done in English 010 and Writing 100 sets a tone or provides a context for the kinds of skills we are trying to teach throughout the coursework included in the first-year experience. Being able to express oneself well in written format is fundamental to the college experience and beyond.

—DOLORES A. PASSARELLI, DIRECTOR
OFFICE OF ACADEMIC SUPPORT AND
INFORMATION SERVICES

After four years at Rhode Island College, I still consider Writing 100 my favorite course to teach. One of the reasons the course remains my favorite is that the teaching situation is so ideal: I get to teach writing to incoming college students, and I get to teach writing like a writer, using a workshop approach to encourage writing, talking, and revising in my classes. My love of this course also stems from the students; their wide-eyed enthusiasm for college and their willingness to shake off the dust of high school works to their advantage in a course where we ask them to take risks and to explore the unexplored. It's exciting for me, and for the students, to discover each new semester that *Writing and Rhetoric* at Rhode Island College is more than just a writing course. It is a course that speaks to our intellectual, emotional, and social con-

nections to one another and to texts. It is a course that invites our students into the ongoing conversation so that they can question, investigate, illuminate, and synthesize ideas and different points of view. It is a course that welcomes them into an academic community of practice, providing a safe space where they can "try on" their academic voices and gain confidence as critical thinkers and composers.

—JENNIFER COOK

What Is Writing and Rhetoric? *Student Voices*

If I were to take away only one lesson from *Writing and Rhetoric*, it would be to revise anything and everything. Revision has never come too easily to me. In fact, at times it is almost painful for me to take my first draft and change it into something completely different. This fall, I learned the real difference between revising and editing. To revise a paper is to change it, add new material, take away unnecessary information, move entire paragraphs to a place where they will better flow, and reword sentences to strengthen an idea. To edit is to merely correct format and grammatical errors. When we wrote our narrative essays at the beginning of September, I was reluctant to alter my first draft at all. Nevertheless, by December, revision was becoming almost natural. Over the course of three drafts of my final research paper, I had deleted entire sentences, changed my idea, and written completely new paragraphs. I have finally understood the importance of the revision process, which is that until fresh ideas and different word choices are explored, a piece of writing cannot reach its full potential.

—Katherine Lucock

Taking *Writing and Rhetoric* this semester has changed my views about writing. After a bad experience with a high school teacher, I just about gave up on writing altogether. This class has taught me to enjoy writing all over again and has definitely changed how I will approach writing assignments in the future. Sometimes I need to remind myself that I'm not going to write a brilliant paper 100 percent of the time, but that's okay because I know I can learn from where I went wrong. I also learned to take time in picking my topic because I can't write a good paper if I'm writing about something I have no interest in. As the semester ends, I am one step closer to becoming an English teacher. Next year, I will start student teaching and that scares me. But I've learned many valuable lessons from this writing class. I loved workshopping our drafts, and I think that when I teach, it will definitely be something that I'll use, along with some of the writing projects. This class has made me grow not only as a writer but as a person.

—Brianne Kuras

In *Writing and Rhetoric*, I learned that writing is a process and not a one-shot thing. You have to brainstorm, write drafts, and do revisions. I learned that writing is a skill that you have to build and that it's not just a gift that some people have. To become a better writer, you have to write more and more. While doing research, I learned that you have to give enough time to it in order to get the best information. As a student who has gone through his first semester of college, I am at a point that I know nothing will come easily to me. I know if I want something in this world, I will have to fight for it. For example, before I started college, I couldn't write to save my life. My writing wasn't something that I could be proud of, but that is not so anymore. Even though I'm not the best writer in the world, I can go into assignments with confidence, knowing that I will be able to handle them.

—Anthony Moore

In *Writing and Rhetoric*, I have significantly improved not only my own writing but my understanding of writing styles as well. These are important skills that I will need throughout my life. I am also thankful for the "ice-breaking" activities we were forced to do in the beginning of the semester in this class. I can honestly say this is the only class I've had at Rhode Island College in which I know every student's name. I must say that because of this, I have also made new friends.

—Brian Plante

I feel that I have grown immensely as a writer through this course. Whether it is through an interview, research, or personal opinion paper, I feel that my writing skills and techniques have sharpened. I have never been a terrible writer, but this course has helped me understand more of the fundamental techniques that can be used to form a paper. Surprisingly enough, it has helped me in other classes as well. I have been able to apply the skills learned in this writing class to the essays of my Western History course, and the results have shown.

—Jovan Zuniga

One thing that changed for me as a writer was my entire view on rough drafts. Unfortunately, sometimes I can be a bit of a perfectionist, and I feel I need to get things absolutely right on the first go, so my first draft usually ended up being the only draft, which became the final one. However, after exploring this semester and especially after reading that "Shitty First Drafts" essay in the book, something seemed to have been lifted from my shoulders. Even though I still get those perfectionist urges, even when it comes to my artwork, I just take a step back and say, "Hold on. I'm the only one who's going to see this for a little while, so I can mess it up as much as I need to."

That feels so good, especially when it's a particularly long piece of writing or an in-depth piece of creative work. I hope I'll be able to remember that essay during the rest of my college days, for it helps with reducing my stress levels a little bit.

—Amanda Tellier

When we moved into our I-Search essays, I was very excited. I could do it on a topic that I was interested in, and all I had to do was write about my journey as a researcher. Perhaps the most important thing I learned in doing this paper was how much the library had to offer. I tended to stay away from libraries in previous times, because they were just so confusing to me. After getting our personal class lesson on the Adams Library from the librarian, Dr. Brennan, I realized that I was missing out on some great sources and techniques I could be using to research both online and off. I not only learned that there were an incredible number of books, magazines, newspapers, and other periodicals that were available to me, but also learned that there were many useful Internet tools I could use, such as Google Scholar. In using these in my research, I had great success and will undoubtedly use these throughout the remainder of my college career.

—Katie Traut-Savino

At first, I thought *Writing and Rhetoric* would be a class filled with commas, scrutiny, and tedious essays. I assumed the class would be dedicated to MLA style and perfect grammar, blended together with a boring, monotonous teacher who would assign fifty-page papers every week. Because Writing 100 was my first college class, I was very nervous about what to expect. But I was mostly scared about working with seasoned college writers who would laugh at my writing abilities. Consequently, I wasn't excited to go to class that first Wednesday morning. Looking back, I didn't notice how day-to-day changes became apparent in my writing; it's satisfying to see that I've changed a lot. The way I look at an assignment with a level head; the way I start and end an assignment with assurance; the way I peer edit efficiently; the way I address my peers in class and pay attention to my writing styles and processes. But the thing I am taking out of Writing 100 that is most satisfying is my newfound mature writer's voice. I've found out that academic writing doesn't need to be boring, tedious, or uneventful; it can be fresh, exciting, and stimulating. I've learned that an academic essay can have a writer's voice while still addressing the topic.

—Michael Savoca

The Writing Center at Rhode Island College

Craig-Lee 225

(401) 456-8141

We invite you to use the Rhode Island College Writing Center not only during your composition course but all through your college career. The service is included in your tuition, so there's no extra charge, no matter how many times you visit. We work with writers in just about every course on campus, and sometimes people ask us to talk with them about their personal writing as well. We can give you a number of strategies for getting started, for developing your ideas, for organizing your thoughts, and for editing. We can even talk to you about some of the different ways people write in history, English, psychology, and a number of other disciplines.

Who uses the Writing Center?

First-year students as well as graduate students, faculty members who are interested in using writing more effectively in their classes, some administrators (especially if they're writing to a student audience), and the tutors themselves all come to the Writing Center.

What happens during a visit?

Sometimes all writers, both beginners and professionals, become so close to their own work that they might not notice if they've left anything out. Professionals have conversations with their editors and/or reviewers, and that's really what tutors do for the writers who come to the Center. They have conversations with you. Together, the writer and tutors explore the ideas that are at the heart of the writing, how those ideas are presented, and what might be done differently. Every session is unique, but here are some questions that might initiate those conversations:

Is the main idea clear?

What kind of evidence is necessary? Should some be eliminated?

Are there connections between/among ideas?

How many ways might the material be organized? Which works best?

Usually, the last things that writer and tutor work on are editing and format issues. Sometimes an additional appointment is necessary, since it would be wasting your time to concentrate on, say, comma splices before you've had a chance to really develop your ideas.

Who are the tutors?

They're undergraduate and graduate students who come from a variety of academic backgrounds and have written the same kind of papers you're writing now and will write during your time here at the College. They've also spent a great deal of time thinking, reading, and writing *about* writing and learning. Each tutor has taken at least one 10-week summer course, Workshop in Writing Center Theory and Practice, and everyone meets every other week during the rest of the year to continue that coursework.

How do I make an appointment?

Sometimes you can walk in and get an appointment on the spot, but when the semester gets going, you need to plan a few days in advance. The appointments are fifty minutes long and are scheduled on the hour. The first one is at 9:00 a.m., and many nights we're open until 7:00 (the last appointment is at 6:00). It's a good idea, particularly if you want to get to the editing stage of your paper, to plan more than one meeting. We can also schedule you for a regular time each week with the same tutor.

When you come, bring your assignment with you, since part of the conversation with your tutor might be about what the assignment is asking for. Finally, if you're going to be late or you need to cancel an appointment, please give us a call so that we can give someone else your time. If you're fifteen minutes late, we may give your appointment to someone who comes in last minute.

Why are snacks for sale in the Writing Center?

Every Tuesday, we have pastries and fresh-brewed coffee. The rest of the week we have instant coffee and snacks. We've found that food serves an important purpose. First of all, lots of people begin conversations about writing while they're choosing a snack; second, when people get stuck, a cup of coffee or tea often gets them going again; third, our snack and breakfast business brings in enough money to send tutors to regional and sometimes national conferences where they present workshops and papers and have a chance to learn, and bring back to you, what other writing centers are doing around the world (yes, there are centers in Europe and Asia as well as at just about every college and university throughout the United States!).

—THE WRITING CENTER TUTORS AND MEG CARROLL

The James P. Adams Library at Rhode Island College

Adams Library represents a gateway into the world of scholarly communication. We're holding the door open for you into an ongoing conversation among scholars, intellectuals, and others about action and ideas, about politics and people, about theory and research, and about information that may pique your curiosity or that your professors may ask you to find.

Although you can eavesdrop on some of that "conversation" by searching for freely accessible resources on the Web, a large proportion of information produced for academic audiences is available only through a variety of printed and online information resources that are purchased for you by your college library. Books, scholarly journals, videos, music scores, sound recordings, and other materials all form part of the Adams Library collections, both physically in our beautiful building on campus and "virtually" as links from our home page (www.ric.edu/adamslibrary). The library home page is your starting point for access to this broad array of information resources, including a link labeled "Ask-a-Librarian." If you have a question, use the contact information you find there to get our help.

To support your academic work, the HELIN Library Catalog, which you can search via our home page, gives you access to over five million—yes million—circulating items; and Rhode Island College students can use our Periodicals List or Online Resources indexes to gain access to more than twenty thousand paper and electronic journals, magazines, and newspapers.

The reference librarians at the James P. Adams Library invite you to consult with us—we are here to support your intellectual inquiry wherever it may take you. Everything else may change—the design and contents of the Adams Library home page, the material on the shelves, the way you gain access to our online materials—but that opportunity to ask questions and receive research support will never change. And this offer of support will remain open to you throughout your time at Rhode Island College and in the alumni years to follow.

Go forth and ask good questions.

—Patricia B. M. Brennan
Associate Professor and Head of Reference
James P. Adams Library

Computer Resources at Rhode Island College

Rhode Island College has two walk-in computing facilities for students, the Horace Mann Technology Center and Whipple 102. The Horace Mann Technology Center houses about eighty-five computers, Dells and Apples, for students. The Horace Mann Center is open until midnight on Sunday through Thursday and until 5:00 p.m. on Friday. Whipple 102 is a slightly smaller walk-in computer lab housing about sixty student computers. Each of the walk-in labs has high-end multimedia workstations for video editing. Whipple 102 is open until 10:00 p.m. weeknights and until 5:00 p.m. on Friday and Saturday. Lab monitors are on hand in both locations to assist Rhode Island College students with basic computing tasks using supported software applications such as the Microsoft Office suite, email, and WebCT, the College's Learning Management System. Students should expect to find every software application that is required in a Rhode Island College course installed on the computers in the walk-in computing labs.

—PAT HAYS, DIRECTOR
USER SUPPORT SERVICES

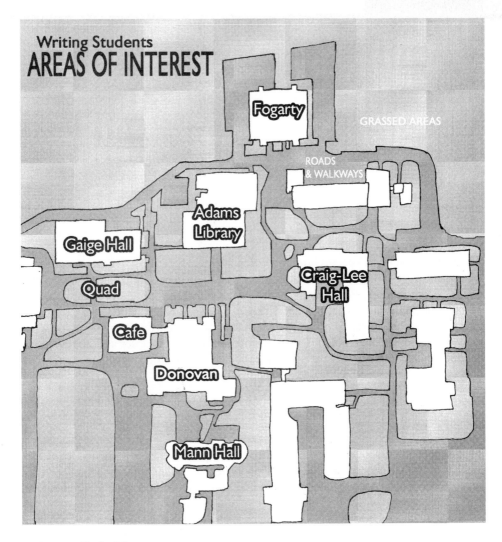

Writing Students
AREAS OF INTEREST

Fogarty

GRASSED AREAS

ROADS & WALKWAYS

Adams Library

Gaige Hall

Craig-Lee Hall

Quad

Cafe

Donovan

Mann Hall

Guide to This Map

Craig-Lee Hall: English Department (Room 263) and mailboxes for all writing instructors

Writing Center (Room 225)

Full-time faculty offices

English Department adjunct faculty office (Room 227)

Adams Library: Support with research; books, journals, and other resources

Horace Mann Hall: Computer lab (Write and print your papers here!)

Café and Donovan Dining Center: Good places to write if you like to have food and coffee close at hand

The Quad: A great place to write and people watch during good weather

Artwork by Rhode Island College student artist Julian Robinson.

1

Using This Book

Axelrod & Cooper's Concise Guide to Writing presents writing assignments for six important genres: autobiographical events, profile, explanation, position paper, proposal, and evaluation. Each of these writing assignment chapters provides readings that demonstrate how written texts of that genre work and a Guide to Writing that will help you write an effective essay in the genre for your particular purpose and audience. Each chapter also includes a discussion of possible purposes and audiences for the genre and a summary of the genre's basic features and strategies. A section titled Reflecting on Your Writing concludes each of these chapters.

■ THE READINGS

Each chapter includes readings, some written by professional writers and others by students who have used earlier editions of this book. All of the readings have been selected to reflect a wide range of topics and strategies. If you read these selections with a critical eye, you will see many different ways writers use a genre.

Each reading selection is accompanied by the following groups of questions, activities, and commentary to help you learn how essays in that genre work:

Connecting to Culture and Experience invites you to explore with other students an issue or question raised by the reading.

Analyzing Writing Strategies helps you examine closely the reading's basic features or writing strategies.

Commentary points out important features of the genre and strategies the writer uses in the essay.

Considering Topics for Your Own Essay suggests subjects related to the reading that you might write about in your own essay.

Most of the assignments in this book provide opportunities to explore your connections to the world. When you are choosing a topic to write about, you might consider suggestions listed under Identity and Community and under Work and Career in the Guides to Writing. These topics enable you to explore your personal connections to the various communities of which you are a part, visit and learn more about places in your community, debate issues important to your community, examine your ideas and attitudes about work, and consider issues related to your future career.

■ THE GUIDES TO WRITING

Each chapter provides detailed suggestions for thinking about your subject and purpose as well as your readers and their expectations. These Guides to Writing will help you develop a truly recursive process of discovery that will enable you to write an effective essay in the genre for your particular purpose and audience.

To make the process manageable, the Guide to Writing is divided into sections: The Writing Assignment, Invention and Research, Planning and Drafting, a Critical Reading Guide, Revising, and Editing and Proofreading. The "menu" preceding the Writing Assignment shows you at a glance the sections and the headings under each section. But to understand how the activities in the Guide to Writing will help you do the kinds of thinking you need to do, you must look closely at the types of activities included in each section.

The Writing Assignment.   Each Guide to Writing begins with an assignment that defines the general purpose and basic features of the genre you have been studying in the chapter. The assignment does not tell you what subject to write about or who your readers will be. You will have to make these decisions, guided by the invention activities in the next section.

Invention and Research.   Every Guide to Writing includes invention activities, and most also include suggestions for observational, library, or Internet research. The Invention and Research activities are designed to help you find a topic, discover what you already know about it, consider your purpose and audience, research the subject further to see what others have written about it, explore and develop your ideas, and compose a tentative thesis statement to guide your planning and drafting.

Remember that invention is not a part of the writing process you can skip. It is the basic, ongoing preoccupation of all writing. As writers, we cannot choose *whether* to invent; we can only decide *how*.

You can use the Invention activities before, during, and after you have written a first draft. However, the sequence of invention activities can be especially helpful before drafting because it focuses systematically on the basic genre features and writing strategies. The sequence reminds you of questions you need to think about as you collect, analyze, and synthesize ideas and information in light of your particular subject, purpose, and readers. A sequence of invention activities may take only two or three hours to complete. But it works best when spread over several days, giving yourself time to think. So if at all possible, begin the invention process far enough ahead of the deadline to let your thinking develop fully. Here is some general advice to keep in mind as you do the invention activities:

Use Writing to Explore Your Ideas. You can use writing to gather your thoughts and see where they lead. As you approach each invention activity, try to refrain from censoring yourself. Simply try writing for several minutes. Explore your ideas freely, letting one idea lead to another. Later, you can reread what you have written and select the most promising ideas to develop.

Focus on One Issue at a Time. Explore your topic systematically by dividing it into its component parts and exploring them one at a time. For example, instead of trying to think of your whole argument, focus on one reason and the support you would give for it, or focus on how you might refute one objection to your argument.

Planning and Drafting. To get you started writing the first draft of your essay, each Guide to Writing includes suggestions for planning. You set goals and try to implement them as you plan and write the draft. While drafting, you may make notes about new ideas or additional information you need to research, but you try to keep your focus on the ideas and information you have already discovered in order to work out their meanings.

The section is divided into four parts:

Seeing What You Have involves reviewing what you have discovered about your subject, purpose, and audience.

Setting Goals helps you think about your overall purpose as well as your goals for the various parts of your essay.

Outlining suggests some of the ways you might organize your essay.

Drafting launches you on the writing of your first draft.

As you begin your first draft, keep in mind the following practical points, many of which assist professional writers as they begin drafting:

Choose the Best Time and Place. You can write a draft anytime and anyplace. As you probably already know, people write under the most surprising or arduous conditions. Drafting is likely to go smoothly, however, if you choose a time and place ideally suited for sustained and thoughtful work. Many professional writers have a place where they can concentrate for a few hours without repeated interruptions. Writers often find one place where they write best, and they return there whenever they have to write. Try to find such a place for yourself.

Make Revision Easy. If possible, compose your draft on a word processor. If you usually write with pen or pencil and paper, consider making the change to word processing for the ease of drafting and revising, as well as for the sake of long-term speed and efficiency. Even if you do not touch-type or if it seems strange at first, you may find, like most students, that you adjust relatively quickly to writing directly on the keyboard. If you do choose to compose on paper, leave plenty of space in the margins to make notes and revisions.

Do the Easy Parts First.   Divide your task into manageable portions and do the easy parts first. Just aim to complete a small part of the essay—one section or paragraph—at a time. Try not to agonize over difficult parts, such as the first paragraph or the right word. Start with the part you understand best.

Lower Your Expectations—for the Time Being.   Be satisfied with less than perfect writing in a first draft, and do not be overly critical of what you are getting down on paper at this stage. Remember, you are working on a draft that you will revise later. For now, try things out. Follow digressions. Let your ideas flow. Later you can go back and cross out a sentence, rework a section, or make other changes. Now and then, of course, you will want to reread what you have written, but do not reread obsessively. Return to drafting new material as soon as possible. Avoid editing or proofreading during this stage.

Take Short Breaks—and Reward Yourself.   Drafting can be hard work, and you may need to take a break to refresh yourself. But be careful not to wander off for too long, or you may lose momentum. By setting small goals and rewarding yourself regularly, you will make it easier to complete the draft.

Critical Reading Guide.   Each Guide to Writing includes a Critical Reading Guide that will help you get a good critical reading of your draft as well as help you read others' drafts. Once you have finished drafting your essay, you will want to make every effort to have someone else read the draft and comment on how to improve it. Experienced writers often seek out such advice from critical readers to help them see their drafts as others do.

Ask whether your critical reader would prefer an electronic version of your draft or a hard copy. Even a reader who is going to comment on the draft electronically may prefer to read a hard copy.

When you are asked to evaluate someone else's draft, you need to read it with a critical eye. You must be both positive and skeptical—positive in that you want to identify what is workable and promising in the draft, skeptical in that you need to question the writer's assumptions and decisions.

Here is some general advice on reading any draft critically:

Make a Written Record of Your Comments.   Although talking with the writer about your reading of the draft can be useful and even fun, you will be most helpful if you put your ideas into writing. When you write down your comments and suggestions—either within an electronic or hard copy of the draft or in a separate electronic or paper document—you leave a record that can be used later when the writer revises the material.

Read First for an Overall Impression.   On first reading, try not to be distracted by any errors in spelling, punctuation, or word choice. Look at the big issues: clear focus, compelling presentation, forcefulness of argument, novelty and quality of ideas. What seems particularly good? What problems do you see? Focus on the overall goal of the draft and how well it is met. Write just a few sentences expressing your initial reaction.

Read Again to Analyze the Draft.   For this second reading, focus on individual parts of the draft, bringing to bear what you know about the genre and the subject.

When you read the draft at this level, you must shift your attention from one aspect of the essay to another. Consider how well the opening paragraphs introduce the essay and prepare the reader for what follows. Pay attention to specific writing strategies, like narration or argument. Notice whether the parts seem logically sequenced. Look for detailing, examples, or other kinds of support.

As you analyze, you are evaluating as well as describing, but a critical reading involves more than criticism of the draft. A good critical reader helps a writer see how each part of an essay works and how all the parts work together. By describing what you see, you help the writer view the draft more objectively, a perspective that is necessary for thoughtful revising.

Offer Advice, but Do Not Rewrite.   As a critical reader, you may be tempted to rewrite the draft—to change a word here, correct an error there, add your ideas everywhere. Resist the impulse. Your role is to read carefully, to point out what you think is or is not working, to make suggestions and ask questions. Leave the revising to the writer.

In turn, the writer has a responsibility to listen to your comments but is under no obligation to do as you suggest. "Then why go to all the trouble?" you might ask. There are at least two good reasons. First, when you read someone else's draft critically, you learn more about writing—about the decisions writers make, about how a thoughtful reader reads, about the constraints of particular kinds of writing. Second, as a critical reader you embody for the writer the abstraction called "audience." By sharing your reactions with the writer, you complete the circuit of communication.

Revising.   Each Guide to Writing includes a Revising section to help you get an overview of your draft, chart a plan for revision, consider critical comments, and carry out the revisions. Productive invention and smooth drafting rarely result in the essay a writer has imagined. Experienced writers are not surprised or disappointed, however, because they expect revision to be necessary. They know that revising will bring them closer to the essay they really want to write. When writers read their drafts thoughtfully and critically—and perhaps reflect on the advice of critical readers—they are able to see many opportunities for improvement. They may notice sentence-level problems such as misspelled words or garbled syntax, but more important, they discover ways to delete, move, rephrase, and add material in order to develop their ideas and say what they want to say more clearly.

Here is some general advice on revising:

Reflect on Your Purpose and Audience.   Remind yourself of what you are trying to accomplish in this essay. If someone has read and responded to your draft, you may now have a better understanding of your readers' likely interests and concerns. You may also have refined your purpose. Keep your purpose and audience in mind as you reread the essay and revise in stages. Do not try to do everything at once.

Look at Major Problems First.   Identify any major problems preventing the draft from achieving its purpose. Major problems might include a lack of awareness of your audience, inadequate development of key parts, missing sections, or the need for further invention or research. Trying to solve these major problems will probably lead to some substantial rethinking and rewriting, so do not get diverted by sentence-level problems at this time.

Focus Next on Organization and Coherence.   Look at the introductory section of the essay to see how well it prepares readers for the parts that follow. It may help to make a paragraph-by-paragraph scratch outline to help you see at a glance what each paragraph does in the essay. If you have difficulty identifying the function of any paragraph, you may need to add an appropriate transition to clarify the paragraph's connection to the previous paragraphs or write a new topic sentence that better announces the subject of the paragraph. Or you may need to do some more extensive rewriting or reorganization.

Then Consider the Details.   As the saying goes, the devil is in the details. The details have to be selected for a specific purpose, such as to convey significance, support an argument, or provide a concrete example of an abstract idea. If any details seem unrelated to your larger purpose, you need to make the connections explicit. If your essay lacks details, you can review your invention notes or do some additional research to come up with the details you need.

Editing and Proofreading.   Once you have finished revising your essay, your next step is to edit and proofread it carefully. You want to make sure that every word, phrase, and sentence is clear and correct. Using language and punctuation correctly is an essential part of good writing. Errors will distract readers and lessen your credibility as a writer.

Be sure to save editing until the end — after you have planned and worked out a revision. Too much editing too early in the writing process can limit, or even block, invention and drafting.

Here are some other suggestions:

Proofread on Hard Copy.   If your essay exists only in electronic form, print out a copy and proofread that version. Electronic text is difficult and fatiguing to read, and you can easily miss errors that are obvious on the printed page.

Keep a List of Your Common Errors.   Note the grammatical and spelling errors you discover in your own writing. You will probably start to recognize error patterns to check for as you edit your work. Many word processor grammar checkers allow you to customize, to some extent, what kinds of errors they call your attention to. If you find that you consistently make a particular error, cultivate the habit of using your word processor's Find function to locate instances of that error in the late stages of every piece of writing.

Begin Proofreading with the Last Word.   To focus your attention on word errors, it may help to read backward word for word, beginning with the last word of your essay. When you read backward, it is harder to pay attention to content and thus easier to recognize spelling and keying errors.

Exchange Drafts with Another Student.   Because it is usually easier to see errors in someone else's writing than in your own, consider trading essays with a classmate and proofreading one another's writing. If you do this, check whether your classmate would prefer an electronic version of your essay or a hard copy.

Reflecting on Your Writing.   Each chapter concludes with a set of activities to help you consider how you solved problems writing that particular kind of essay. If you are compiling a portfolio of your coursework that will be assessed at the end of the term, these activities may help you decide what to include in your portfolio as well as help you write a reflective essay on the work you select for the portfolio.

Remembering Events

2

When you write about remembered events in your life, you produce autobiography, a genre of writing that is very popular with both readers and writers. Autobiography is popular because reading as well as writing it leads people to reflect deeply on their own lives. When you reflect on the meaning of experience, you examine the forces within yourself and within society that have shaped you into the person you have become.

When you write about a remembered event, your purpose is to present yourself to readers by telling a story that discloses something significant about your life. Autobiographical writers do not just pour out their memories and feelings. Instead, they shape those memories into a compelling story that conveys the meaning and importance of an experience — what can be called its autobiographical significance.

Writing about your life for others to read is not the same as writing for yourself. As a writer, you must remember that autobiography is public, not private. While it requires self-presentation, it does not require you to make unwanted self-disclosures. You choose the event to write about and decide how you will portray yourself.

As you work through this chapter, you will learn to tell a story that entertains readers and lets them know something important about how you came to be the person you are now. You also will learn to describe people and places vividly so that readers can see what makes them memorable for you. As you learn to write well about a remembered event, you will be practicing two of the most basic writing strategies — narration and description. These strategies can play a role in almost every kind of writing. As you will see in Chapters 3–7, narration and description can contribute to explanatory reports and persuasive arguments, in addition to playing an essential role in the remembered-event assignment for this chapter.

You will encounter writing about a remembered event in many different contexts, as the following examples suggest.

Writing in Your Other Courses

- For an assignment in a psychology course, a student tests against her own experience an idea from the developmental psychologist Erik Erikson: "[Y]oung people... are sometimes preoccupied with what they appear to be in the eyes of others as compared with what they feel they are." The student recounts a time when she cared tremendously about what the other members of her high school soccer team thought about her. Then she explains how her teammates' reactions influenced her feelings and sense of self.

- For a linguistics course, a student is asked to write about current research on men's and women's conversational styles. One researcher, Deborah Tannen, has reported that women and men have different expectations when they talk about problems. Women expect to spend a lot of time talking about the problem itself, especially about their feelings. Men, in contrast, typically want to cut short the analysis of the problem and the talk about feelings; they would rather discuss solutions to the problem. Applying Tannen's findings to her own experience, the student recounts a conversation about a family problem with her brother, who is one year older. She reconstructs as much of the conversation as she can remember and explains which parts constitute feelings talk and which indicate problem-solving talk. She concludes that her conversation with her brother well illustrates Tannen's findings.

Writing in the Community

- As part of a local history project in a small western ranching community, a college student volunteers to help an elderly rancher write about some of his early experiences. One experience seems especially dramatic and significant—a time in the winter of 1938 when a six-foot snowstorm isolated the rancher's family for nearly a month. The student tape-records the rancher talking about how he and his wife made preparations to survive and ensure the health of their infant sons and how he snowshoed eight miles to a logging train track, stopped the train, and gave the engineer a message to deliver to relatives in the nearest town explaining that they were going to be okay. On a second visit, the student and the rancher listen to the tape recording and afterward talk about further details that might make the event more complete and dramatic for readers. The rancher then writes a draft of the remembered event, and the student later helps him revise and edit the essay. The student copies an old snow-day photograph from the nearby town's newspaper files, and the rancher selects a photograph of his young family from a family photo album. The essay and photographs are published in a special supplement to the newspaper.

- To commemorate the retirement of the city's world-famous symphony orchestra conductor, a radio program director invites the conductor to talk about his early experiences with the orchestra. Aware of his tendency to ramble and digress in interviews, the conductor decides to write down a story about the first time he asked the orchestra members to play a never-before-performed modern composition noted for its lack of familiar tones, progressions, and rhythms. He describes how he tried to prepare the orchestra members for this experience and how they went about the hard, slow work of mastering the difficult music. The conductor expresses regret over posing this challenge so early in his experience of working with the orchestra members, but he proudly asserts that their great success with the music gave them the confidence to master any music they played together. For the radio program, he alternates reading this remembered event aloud with playing brief recorded excerpts from the orchestra's polished performance.

Writing in the Workplace

- As part of an orientation manual for new employees, the founder of a highly successful computer software company describes the day she spent with the Silicon Valley venture capitalists who lent her the money to start the company. She describes how other venture capitalists had turned her down and how desperately anxious she was for this group to fund her company. The meeting had barely begun when she spilled her coffee across the top of the gleaming conference table. She describes some of the questions and her answers and traces her rising and falling hopes during the discussion. She left dejected and resigned to giving up the dream of founding her own company. The next morning a member of the group who had not asked any questions at the meeting phoned her to praise her proposal and announce that his group would fund her company. He invited her to a celebratory lunch with the group at the best restaurant in town, where she was careful not to tip over her long-stemmed wine glass.

- The highway department offices of a large midwestern state have recently been the site of violence and threats of violence. One worker has killed another, and several managers have been threatened. To keynote a statewide meeting of highway department managers seeking solutions to this problem, a manager writes a speech that describes an incident when he was confronted in his office by an employee who was unhappy about an overtime assignment. The employee came into the manager's office without knocking and would not sit down. He talked loudly, waved his arms, and threatened to harm the manager and his family. He would not leave when asked to. The manager reflects on his fear and on his frustration about not knowing what to do when the employee finally left. The department's published procedures seemed not to apply to this case. He acknowledges his reluctance to report the incident to the state office because he did not want to appear to be ineffective and indecisive.

Practice Remembering an Event: A Collaborative Activity	The preceding scenarios suggest some occasions for writing about events in one's life. Think of an event in your life that you would feel comfortable describing to others in your class. The only requirements are that you remember the event well enough to tell the story and that the story lets your classmates learn something about you. Your instructor may schedule this

collaborative activity as a face-to-face in-class discussion or ask you to conduct an online real-time discussion in a chat room. Whatever the medium, here are some guidelines to follow:

Part 1. Consider several events, and choose one you feel comfortable telling in this situation. Then, for two or three minutes, make notes about how you will tell your story.

Now, get together with two or three other students, and take turns telling your stories. Be brief: Each story should take only a few minutes.

Part 2. Take ten minutes to discuss what happened when you told about a remembered event:

- Tell each other how you chose your particular story. What did you think about when you were choosing an event? How did your purpose and audience—what you wanted your classmates to know and think about you—influence your choice?

- Review what each of you decided to include in your story. Did you plunge right into telling what happened, or did you first provide some background information? Did you decide to leave any of the action out of your story? If so, what did you leave out and why? Did you include a physical description of the scene? Did you describe any of the people, including yourself, or mention any specific dialogue? Did you tell your listeners how you felt at the time the event occurred, or did you say how you feel now looking back on it?

- What was the easiest part of telling a story about a remembered event in your life? What was the most difficult part?

READINGS

No two essays remembering an event are alike, and yet they share defining features. Together, the three readings in this chapter reveal a number of these features, so you will want to read as many of them as possible. If time permits, complete the activities in the Analyzing Writing Strategies section that follows each selection, and read the Commentary. Following the readings is a section called Basic Features: Remembering Events (p. 42), which offers a concise description of the features of writing about remembered events and provides examples from the three readings.

Annie Dillard won the Pulitzer Prize for nonfiction writing with her first book, Pilgrim at Tinker Creek *(1974). Since then, she has written nine books in a variety of genres, including the essay collections* Teaching a Stone to Talk *(1988) and* For the Time Being *(1999); a novel,* The Living *(1993); poetry,* Mornings like This *(1996); literary theory,* Living by Fiction *(1988); and an account of her work as a writer,* The Writing Life *(1990). Dillard also wrote an autobiography of her early years,* An American Childhood *(1987), from which the following reading comes.*

Dillard is a professor of English and writer in residence at Wesleyan College. In The Writing Life, *she describes her writing as a process of discovery: "When you write, you lay out a line of words. The line of words is a miner's pick, a woodcarver's gouge, a surgeon's probe. You wield it, and it digs a path you follow. Soon you find yourself in new territory." Through this process, she explains, the writing "changes from an expression of your notions to an epistemological tool." In other words, the very act of writing helps her learn more about herself and others.*

The reading that follows relates an event that occurred one winter morning when the seven-year-old Dillard and a friend were chased relentlessly by an adult stranger at whom they had been throwing snowballs. Dillard admits that she was terrified at the time, and yet she asserts that she has "seldom been happier since." As you read, think about how this paradox helps you grasp the autobiographical significance of this experience for Dillard.

From *An American Childhood*

Annie Dillard

Some boys taught me to play football. This was fine sport. You thought up a new strategy for every play and whispered it to the others. You went out for a pass, fooling everyone. Best, you got to throw yourself mightily at someone's running legs. Either you brought him down or you hit the ground flat out on your chin, with your arms empty before you. It was all or nothing. If you hesitated in fear, you would miss and get hurt: you would take a hard fall while the kid got away, or you would get kicked in the face while the kid got away. But if you flung yourself wholeheartedly at the back of his knees—if you gathered and joined body and soul and pointed them diving fearlessly—then you likely wouldn't get hurt, and you'd stop the ball. Your fate, and your team's score, depended on your concentration and courage. Nothing girls did could compare with it. 1

Boys welcomed me at baseball, too, for I had, through enthusiastic practice, what was weirdly known as a boy's arm. In winter, in the snow, there was neither baseball nor football, so the boys and I threw snowballs at passing cars. I got in trouble throwing snowballs, and have seldom been happier since. 2

On one weekday morning after Christmas, six inches of new snow had just fallen. We were standing up to our boot tops in snow on a front yard on trafficked Reynolds Street, waiting for cars. The cars traveled Reynolds Street slowly and evenly; they were targets all but wrapped in red ribbons, cream puffs. We couldn't miss. 3

I was seven; the boys were eight, nine, and ten. The oldest two Fahey boys were there—Mikey and Peter—polite blond boys who lived near me on Lloyd Street, and who already had four brothers and sisters. My parents approved Mikey and Peter Fahey. Chickie McBride was there, a tough kid, and Billy Paul and Mackie Kean too, from across Reynolds, where the boys grew up dark and furious, grew up skinny, knowing, and skilled. We had all drifted from our houses that morning looking for action, and had found it here on Reynolds Street. 4

It was cloudy but cold. The cars' tires laid behind them on the snowy street a complex trail of beige chunks like crenellated castle walls. I had stepped on some earlier; they 5 squeaked. We could not have wished for more traffic. When a car came, we all popped it one. In the intervals between cars we reverted to the natural solitude of children.

I started making an iceball—a perfect iceball, from perfectly white snow, perfectly   6
spherical, and squeezed perfectly translucent so no snow remained all the way through. (The Fahey boys and I considered it unfair actually to throw an iceball at somebody, but it had been known to happen.)

I had just embarked on the iceball project when we heard tire chains come clanking   7
from afar. A black Buick was moving toward us down the street. We all spread out, banged together some regular snowballs, took aim, and, when the Buick drew nigh, fired.

A soft snowball hit the driver's windshield right before the driver's face. It made a   8
smashed star with a hump in the middle.

Often, of course, we hit our target, but this time, the only time in all of life, the   9
car pulled over and stopped. Its wide black door opened; a man got out of it, running. He didn't even close the car door.

He ran after us, and we ran away from him, up the snowy Reynolds sidewalk. At the   10
corner, I looked back; incredibly, he was still after us. He was in city clothes: a suit and tie, street shoes. Any normal adult would have quit, having sprung us into flight and made his point. This man was gaining on us. He was a thin man, all action. All of a sudden, we were running for our lives.

Wordless, we split up. We were on our turf; we could lose ourselves in the neighbor-   11
hood backyards, everyone for himself. I paused and considered. Everyone had vanished except Mikey Fahey, who was just rounding the corner of a yellow brick house. Poor Mikey, I trailed him. The driver of the Buick sensibly picked the two of us to follow. The man apparently had all day.

He chased Mikey and me around the yellow house and up a backyard path we knew   12
by heart: under a low tree, up a bank, through a hedge, down some snowy steps, and across the grocery store's delivery driveway. We smashed through a gap in another hedge, entered a scruffy backyard and ran around its back porch and tight between houses to Edgerton Avenue; we ran across Edgerton to an alley and up our own sliding woodpile to the Halls' front yard; he kept coming. We ran up Lloyd Street and wound through mazy backyards toward the steep hilltop at Willard and Lang.

He chased us silently, block after block. He chased us silently over picket fences,   13
through thorny hedges, between houses, around garbage cans, and across streets. Every time I glanced back, choking for breath, I expected he would have quit. He must have been as breathless as we were. His jacket strained over his body. It was an immense discovery, pounding into my hot head with every sliding, joyous step, that this ordinary adult evidently knew what I thought only children who trained at football knew: that you have to fling yourself at what you're doing, you have to point yourself, forget yourself, aim, dive.

Mikey and I had nowhere to go, in our own neighborhood or out of it, but away from   14
this man who was chasing us. He impelled us forward; we compelled him to follow our route. The air was cold; every breath tore my throat. We kept running, block after block; we kept improvising, backyard after backyard, running a frantic course and choosing it

simultaneously, failing always to find small places or hard places to slow him down, and discovering always, exhilarated, dismayed, that only bare speed could save us—for he would never give up, this man—and we were losing speed.

He chased us through the backyard labyrinths of ten blocks before he caught us by our jackets. He caught us and we all stopped. 15

We three stood staggering, half blinded, coughing, in an obscure hilltop backyard: a man in his twenties, a boy, a girl. He had released our jackets, our pursuer, our captor, our hero: he knew we weren't going anywhere. We all played by the rules. Mikey and I unzipped our jackets. I pulled off my sopping mittens. Our tracks multiplied in the backyard's new snow. We had been breaking new snow all morning. We didn't look at each other. I was cherishing my excitement. The man's lower pants legs were wet; his cuffs were full of snow, and there was a prow of snow beneath them on his shoes and socks. Some trees bordered the little flat backyard, some messy winter trees. There was no one around: a clearing in a grove, and we the only players. 16

It was a long time before he could speak. I had some difficulty at first recalling why we were there. My lips felt swollen; I couldn't see out of the sides of my eyes; I kept coughing. 17

"You stupid kids," he began perfunctorily. 18

We listened perfunctorily indeed, if we listened at all, for the chewing out was redundant, a mere formality, and beside the point. The point was that he had chased us passionately without giving up, and so he had caught us. Now he came down to earth. I wanted the glory to last forever. 19

But how could the glory have lasted forever? We could have run through every backyard in North America until we got to Panama. But when he trapped us at the lip of the Panama Canal, what precisely could he have done to prolong the drama of the chase and cap its glory? I brooded about this for the next few years. He could only have fried Mikey Fahey and me in boiling oil, say, or dismembered us piecemeal, or staked us to anthills. None of which I really wanted, and none of which any adult was likely to do, even in the spirit of fun. He could only chew us out there in the Panamanian jungle, after months or years of exalting pursuit. He could only begin, "You stupid kids," and continue in his ordinary Pittsburgh accent with his normal righteous anger and the usual common sense. 20

If in that snowy backyard the driver of the black Buick had cut off our heads, Mikey's and mine, I would have died happy, for nothing has required so much of me since as being chased all over Pittsburgh in the middle of winter—running terrified, exhausted—by this sainted, skinny, furious redheaded man who wished to have a word with us. I don't know how he found his way back to his car. 21

Connecting to Culture and Experience: Childhood Play

"The point," Dillard tells us near the end, "was that he had chased us passionately without giving up" (paragraph 19). What seems to fascinate her is not that the man chased the kids to bawl them out, but that an adult could still do what she thought only children knew how to do: "you have to fling yourself at what you're doing, you have to point yourself, forget yourself, aim, dive" (paragraph 13). In fact, she explains at the beginning of the essay that in teaching her to play football, the neighborhood boys taught her something that few girls learned about: the joy of flinging yourself wholeheartedly, fearlessly, into play or, indeed, into anything you do in life.

With other students in your class, discuss what you have learned from childhood play about how to live your life. You might begin by telling one another about a particular kind of play you enjoyed as a child—something you did with others or alone such as team sports, computer games, playing a musical instrument, dancing, listening to music, or reading. Then, explore together what the kinds of play you enjoyed taught you about being yourself, facing challenges, getting along with others, or understanding your own body and mind or your attitude toward life.

Analyzing Writing Strategies

1. At the beginning of this chapter, we make several assertions about remembered-event essays. Consider which of these are true of Dillard's essay:

   • It tells an entertaining story.

   • It is vivid, letting readers see what makes the event as well as the people and places memorable for the writer.

   • It is purposeful, trying to give readers an understanding of why this particular event was significant in the writer's life.

   • It includes self-presentation but not unwanted self-disclosures.

   • It can lead readers to think in new ways about their own experiences or about how other people's lives differ from their own.

2. Visual description—naming objects and detailing their colors, shapes, sizes, textures, and other qualities—is an important writing strategy in remembered-event essays. To see how writers use naming and detailing to create vivid word pictures or images, let us look closely at Dillard's description of an iceball: "I started making an iceball—a perfect iceball, from perfectly white snow, perfectly spherical, and squeezed perfectly translucent so no snow remained all the way through" (paragraph 6). Notice that she names two things: *iceball* and *snow*. She adds to these names descriptive details—*white* (color), *spherical* (shape), and *translucent* (appearance)—that help readers imagine more precisely what an iceball looks like. She also repeats the words *perfect* and *perfectly* to emphasize the color, shape, and appearance of this particular iceball.

   To analyze Dillard's use of naming and detailing to present scenes and people, reread paragraphs 10–13, where she describes the man and the neighborhood through which he chases her and Mikey. As you read these paragraphs, underline the names of objects and people (nearly always nouns), and put brackets around all of the words and phrases that modify the nouns they name. Here are two examples from paragraph 10 to get you started: "[snowy] Reynolds sidewalk" and "[city] clothes."

Notice first how frequently naming and detailing occur in these paragraphs. Notice also how many different kinds of objects and people are named. Then consider these questions: Does naming sometimes occur without any accompanying detailing? How do you think the naming helps you as a reader visualize the scene and people? What do you think the detailing contributes?

Commentary: Organizing a Well-Told Story

An American Childhood is a well-told story. It provides a dramatic structure that arouses readers' curiosity, builds suspense, and concludes the action in a rather surprising way.

Writers of remembered-event essays usually begin at the beginning or even before the beginning. That is how Annie Dillard organizes *An American Childhood*—opening with two introductory paragraphs that give readers a context for the event and prepare them to appreciate its significance. Readers can see at a glance, by the space that separates the second paragraph from the rest of the essay, that the first two paragraphs are meant to stand apart as an introduction. They also are general, broad statements that do not refer to any particular incident.

In contrast, paragraph 3 begins by grounding readers in specifics. It is not any "weekday morning" but "one" in particular, one morning "after Christmas" and after a substantial snowfall. Dillard goes on to locate herself in a particular place "on a front yard on trafficked Reynolds Street," engaged in a particular set of actions with a particular group of individuals. She has not yet begun to tell what happened but is giving us the cast of characters (the "polite blond" Fahey boys, "tough" Chickie McBride) and setting the scene ("cloudy but cold"). The narrative, up to this point, has been moving slowly, like the cars making their way down Reynolds Street. But in paragraph 9, when the driver of the Buick "got out of it, running," Dillard's narrative itself suddenly springs into action, moving at breakneck speed for the next seven paragraphs until the man catches up with the kids in paragraph 15.

We can see this simple narrative organization in the following paragraph-by-paragraph scratch outline:

1. explains what she learned from playing football
2. identifies other sports she learned from boys in the neighborhood
3. sets the scene by describing the time and place of the event
4. describes the boys who were playing with her
5. describes what typically happened: a car would come down the street, they would throw snowballs, and then they would wait for another car
6. describes the iceball-making project she had begun while waiting
7. describes the Buick's approach and how they followed the routine
8. describes the impact of the snowball on the Buick's windshield
9. describes the man's surprising reaction: getting out of the car and running after them

10. narrates the chase and describes the man

11. explains how the kids split up and the man followed her and Mikey

12. narrates the chase and describes how the neighborhood looked as they ran through it

13. continues the narration, describing the way the man threw himself into the chase

14. continues the narration, commenting on her thoughts and feelings

15. narrates the ending or climax of the chase, when the man caught the kids

16. describes the runners trying to catch their breath

17. describes her own physical state

18. relates the man's words

19. explains her reactions to his words and actions

20. explains her later thoughts and feelings

21. explains her present perspective on this remembered event

From this simple scratch outline, we can see that Dillard's essay focuses on the chase. This focus on a single incident that occurred in a relatively short span of time is the hallmark of the remembered-event essay. A chase is by nature dramatic because it is suspenseful: Readers want to know whether the man will catch the kids and, if he does, what will happen. Dillard heightens the drama in a couple of ways. One strategy she uses is identification: She lets us into her point of view, helping us to see what she saw and feel what she felt. In addition, she uses surprise. In fact, Dillard surprises us from beginning to end. The first surprise is that the man gets out of the car. But the fact that he chases the kids and that he continues to chase them beyond the point that any reasonable person would do so ratchets up the suspense. We simply cannot know what such a man is capable of doing. Finally, the story reaches its climax when the man catches Mikey and Dillard. Even then, Dillard surprises readers by what the man says and doesn't say or do. All he says is, "You stupid kids" (paragraph 18). Moreover, Dillard tells us, he says it "perfunctorily," as if it is something he is supposed to say as an adult "in his ordinary Pittsburgh accent with his normal righteous anger and the usual common sense" (paragraph 20). Dillard's language here is ironic because it is obvious that she feels that the man's behavior was anything but *ordinary, normal,* or *usual*— which is, of course, precisely what Dillard wants us to appreciate.

Considering Topics for Your Own Essay

Dillard writes about throwing yourself body and soul into a sport, a chase, or whatever you are doing. Dillard explains that she learned "concentration and courage" (paragraph 1) from the boys who taught her to play football. What do you think you learned from playing or watching other kids play? Recall your own experiences at play as a child and as a young adult. List any sports events, school projects, musical performances, computer games, or other occasions that would enable you to reflect on your own ideas about play, commitment, or working with others or working alone to achieve a goal.

Tobias Wolff is probably best known for his short-story collections Back in the World *(1985),* In the Garden of the North American Martyrs *(1981), and* The Night in Question *(1996) and for his novel* The Barracks Thief *(1984), which won the PEN/Faulkner Award in 1985. Wolff has also written two autobiographies. The first,* A Boy's Life *(1989), won the* Los Angeles Times Book Award *for biography and was made into a movie (1993) in which Wolff was played by Leonardo DiCaprio. The second autobiography,* In Pharaoh's Army: Memories of the Lost War *(1994), about his experience serving as a Green Beret in the Vietnam War, was a finalist for a National Book Award and a* Los Angeles Times *Award for biography. In addition to his fiction and autobiography, Wolff has also edited several short-story collections, including* The Best American Short Stories. *Wolff has taught creative writing at Syracuse University and is currently the Ward W. and Priscilola B. Woods Professor at Stanford University, where he also has directed the creative writing program.*

In this selection from A Boy's Life, *Wolff tells the story of an experience he had when he was ten years old. He and his mother had just moved west from Florida to Salt Lake City, followed by Roy, his divorced mother's boyfriend. "Roy was handsome," Wolff writes, "in the conventional way that appeals to boys. He had a tattoo. He'd been to war and kept a silence about it that was full of heroic implication." As you read, notice how the young Wolff is motivated, at least in part, by a desire to be the kind of self-sufficient man he associates with soldiers and cowboys.*

On Being a Real Westerner
Tobias Wolff

Just after Easter Roy gave me the Winchester .22 rifle I'd 1
learned to shoot with. It was a light, pump-action, beautifully balanced piece with a walnut stock black from all its oilings. Roy had carried it when he was a boy and it was still as good as new. Better than new. The action was silky from long use, and the wood of a quality no longer to be found.

The gift did not come as a surprise. Roy was stingy, and slow to take a hint, but I'd 2 put him under siege. I had my heart set on that rifle. A weapon was the first condition of self-sufficiency, and of being a real Westerner, and of all acceptable employment—trapping, riding herd, soldiering, law enforcement, and outlawry. I needed that rifle, for itself and for the way it completed me when I held it.

My mother said I couldn't have it. Absolutely not. Roy took the rifle back but promised 3 me he'd bring her around. He could not imagine anyone refusing him anything and treated the refusals he did encounter as perverse and insincere. Normally mute, he became at these times a relentless whiner. He would follow my mother from room to room, emitting one ceaseless note of complaint that was pitched perfectly to jelly her nerves and bring her to a state where she would agree to anything to make it stop.

After a few days of this my mother caved in. She said I could have the rifle if, and only 4 if, I promised never to take it out or even touch it except when she and Roy were with me. Okay, I said. Sure. Naturally. But even then she wasn't satisfied. She plain didn't like the fact of me owning a rifle. Roy said he had owned several rifles by the time he was my age, but this did not reassure her. She didn't think I could be trusted with it. Roy said now was the time to find out.

For a week or so I kept my promises. But now that the weather had turned warm Roy   5
was usually off somewhere and eventually, in the dead hours after school when I found
myself alone in the apartment, I decided that there couldn't be any harm in taking the rifle
out to clean it. Only to clean it, nothing more. I was sure it would be enough just to break
it down, oil it, rub linseed into the stock, polish the octagonal barrel and then hold it up to
the light to confirm the perfection of the bore. But it wasn't enough. From cleaning the rifle
I went to marching around the apartment with it, and then to striking brave poses in front
of the mirror. Roy had saved one of his army uniforms and I sometimes dressed up in
this, together with martial-looking articles of hunting gear: fur trooper's hat, camouflage
coat, boots that reached nearly to my knees.

The camouflage coat made me feel like a sniper, and before long I began to act like   6
one. I set up a nest on the couch by the front window. I drew the shades to darken the
apartment, and took up my position. Nudging the shade aside with the rifle barrel, I followed people in my sights as they walked or drove along the street. At first I made shooting sounds—kyoo! kyoo! Then I started cocking the hammer and letting it snap down.

Roy stored his ammunition in a metal box he kept hidden in the closet. As with every-   7
thing else hidden in the apartment, I knew exactly where to find it. There was a layer of
loose .22 rounds on the bottom of the box under shells of bigger caliber, dropped there by
the handful the way men drop pennies on their dressers at night. I took some and put
them in a hiding place of my own. With these I started loading up the rifle. Hammer
cocked, a round in the chamber, finger resting lightly on the trigger, I drew a bead on
whoever walked by—women pushing strollers, children, garbage collectors laughing
and calling to each other, anyone—and as they passed under my window I sometimes
had to bite my lip to keep from laughing in the ecstasy of my power over them, and at
their absurd and innocent belief that they were safe.

But over time the innocence I laughed at began to irritate me. It was a peculiar kind   8
of irritation. I saw it years later in men I served with, and felt it myself, when unarmed Vietnamese civilians talked back to us while we were herding them around. Power can be
enjoyed only when it is recognized and feared. Fearlessness in those without power is
maddening to those who have it.

One afternoon I pulled the trigger. I had been aiming at two old people, a man and a   9
woman, who walked so slowly that by the time they turned the corner at the bottom of the
hill my little store of self-control was exhausted. I had to shoot. I looked up and down the
street. It was empty. Nothing moved but a pair of squirrels chasing each other back and
forth on the telephone wires. I followed one in my sight. Finally it stopped for a moment
and I fired. The squirrel dropped straight into the road. I pulled back into the shadows and
waited for something to happen, sure that someone must have heard the shot or seen
the squirrel fall. But the sound that was so loud to me probably seemed to our neighbors
no more than the bang of a cupboard slammed shut. After a while I sneaked a glance into
the street. The squirrel hadn't moved. It looked like a scarf someone had dropped.

When my mother got home from work I told her there was a dead squirrel in the   10
street. Like me, she was an animal lover. She took a cellophane bag off a loaf of bread

and we went outside and looked at the squirrel. "Poor little thing," she said. She stuck her hand in the wrapper and picked up the squirrel, then pulled the bag inside out away from her hand. We buried it behind our building under a cross made of popsicle sticks, and I blubbered the whole time.

I blubbered again in bed that night. At last I got out of bed and knelt down and did an imitation of somebody praying, and then I did an imitation of somebody receiving divine reassurance and inspiration. I stopped crying. I smiled to myself and forced a feeling of warmth into my chest. Then I climbed back in bed and looked up at the ceiling with a blissful expression until I went to sleep.   11

For several days I stayed away from the apartment at times when I knew I'd be alone there.   12

Though I avoided the apartment, I could not shake the idea that sooner or later I would get the rifle out again. All my images of myself as I wished to be were images of myself armed. Because I did not know who I was, any image of myself, no matter how grotesque, had power over me. This much I understand now. But the man can give no help to the boy, not in this matter nor in those that follow. The boy moves always out of reach.   13

Connecting to Culture and Experience: Role Playing

Wolff shows us that he took great delight in playing the role of a soldier—looking at himself in the mirror dressed in camouflage and "striking brave poses" (paragraph 5). The word *brave* suggests that the young Wolff wanted to see himself as possessing certain traits, like bravery, that we often associate with soldiers. Another part of the attraction of playing soldier, he admits, is the sense of power he experienced holding a rifle.

With other students in your class, discuss the roles you played as children. What personal and cultural factors influenced the roles that you and your classmates imagined for yourselves? You might begin by comparing your own childhood imaginings with Wolff's desire to play soldier. In addition to having firsthand experience with Roy, a soldier who impressed him with his masculine authority and power, Wolff grew up during World War II, when children were bombarded by media images of brave soldiers fighting heroic wars and lone cowboys bringing justice to the Wild West. What media images—from television, film, the Internet, and computer games—do you think influenced the kinds of role play that you engaged in as a child or young adult?

Analyzing Writing Strategies

1. Writers convey the significance of autobiographical events by telling how they felt at the time the event occurred and by telling how they feel now as they look back on the event. Skim paragraphs 7, 8, and 13, noting where Wolff expresses his

feelings and thoughts about the event. Try to distinguish between what he remembers thinking and feeling at the time and what he thinks and feels as he looks back on the event. What impression do you get of the young Wolff? What does the adult Wolff seem to think about his younger self?

2. Good stories show people in action—what we call specific narrative action— people moving or gesturing. Analyze paragraphs 7 and 9 by underlining the narrative actions and then putting brackets around the verb or verbal in each narrative action that specifically names the action. (A verbal is the *-ing* or *to* form of a verb: *laughing*, *to laugh*.) For example, here are the narrative actions (underlined) with their action verbs or verbals (in brackets) in paragraph 6:

   [set up] a nest, [drew] the shades, [took up] my position, [nudging] the shade aside, [followed] people, [walked] or [drove], [made] shooting sounds—kyoo! kyoo!, [started cocking] the hammer, [letting] it [snap] down.

   Now that you have completed your analysis of paragraphs 7 and 9, how do you think specific narrative action contributes to autobiographical stories?

3. Like other autobiographers, Wolff sometimes uses relatively short sentences. To understand why he might do so, compare the short and long sentences in the most dramatic and revealing action in the event. Begin by underlining every sentence of nine words or fewer (in paragraph 9). Then put brackets around the relatively long sentence at the end of paragraph 7 and the three relatively long sentences beginning "I had been aiming," "I pulled back," and "But the sound" in paragraph 9. Compare what the long and short sentences contribute to the action. How do their contents differ? What effect do the short sentences have on you as a reader? For more on the role of short sentences in remembered-event essays, turn to Sentence Strategies, pp. 54–55.

Commentary: Narrative Cueing in a Well-Told Story

This is a gripping story. The subject makes it inherently dramatic: Putting a rifle in a child's hands immediately alerts readers to the possibility that something dreadful could happen. Thus the potential for suspense is great. Contributing to the drama is Wolff's use of narrative strategies that move the action through time and help readers keep track of what happened.

If we look closely at Wolff's narration, we can see how two narrating strategies— verb tenses and temporal transitions—create the impression of time passing. These strategies serve as cueing devices because, like road signs, they enable readers to follow the action.

Verb Tenses. Verb tenses signal when the action occurred—in the past, present, or future. Because remembered-event essays tell about past events, most of the verbs are in the past tense. Looking at the verbs in Wolff's essay, we can find several different kinds of past tense. In the first sentence of the essay, for example, Wolff shows an action that occurred at one point in the past (underlined) together with an action that was already completed (in brackets): "Just after Easter Roy <u>gave</u> me the Winchester .22 rifle [I'd learned to shoot with]." ("I'd learned" is a shortened form of "I had learned.") A second example shows an earlier action that was still going on (in brackets) when the more recent action occurred (underlined): "One afternoon I <u>pulled</u> the trigger. I [had been aiming] at two old people..." (paragraph 9).

Our final example is a little more complicated: "Roy <u>took</u> the rifle back but <u>promised</u> me [he'd bring] her around" (paragraph 3). This example presents three past actions. Whereas the first two actions (underlined) occurred at roughly the same time, the third (in brackets) predicts a future action that occurred after the first two actions were completed. (Here "he'd" is a short form of "he would.")

You probably do not know the technical names for these tenses, nor do you need to know them. However, you do need to know what the different verb tenses mean and how to use them. In your remembered-event essay, you will want to be sure that the verb tenses you use accurately indicate the time relations among various actions in your story.

Temporal Transitions. In addition to using verb tense to show time, writers use transitions to move the narrative action forward in time and thereby keep readers oriented. Wolff uses many transitional words and phrases to locate an action at a particular point in time or to relate an action at one point in time to an action at another time. He uses four in the first paragraph alone: *just after, when, still,* and *no longer.* Time markers may appear at the beginning of a sentence or within a sentence. Notice how many paragraphs in Wolff's story include such a transition in the opening sentence: "Just after" (paragraph 1), "After a few days" (4), "For a week or so" (5), "before long" (6), "One afternoon" (9), "When" (10), "again" (11), and "For several days" (12). This extensive use of temporal transitions is not unusual in remembered-event essays. You will want to use them liberally in your own essay to orient readers and propel your narrative through time.

Considering Topics for Your Own Essay

In this selection, Wolff describes experiencing what he calls the "ecstasy of my power" to inflict harm on others (paragraph 7). Try to recall two or three incidents when you were in a position to exercise power over another person or when you were subject to someone else's power. You may have been in such relationships for long periods of time, but select only those relationships that can be well illustrated by one key incident that occurred within a day or two. Pick one such incident. Think about how you would present it, explaining what you did and how you felt.

Jean Brandt wrote this essay as a first-year college student. In it, she tells about a memorable event that occurred when she was thirteen. Reflecting on how she felt at the time, Brandt writes, "I was afraid, embarrassed, worried, mad." As you read, look for places where these tumultuous and contradictory remembered feelings are expressed.

Calling Home
Jean Brandt

As we all piled into the car, I knew it was going to be a fabulous day. My grandmother was visiting for the holidays; and she and I, along with my older brother and sister, Louis and Susan, were setting off for a day of last-minute Christmas shopping. On the way to the mall, we sang Christmas carols, chattered, and laughed. With Christmas only two days away, we were caught up with holiday spirit. I felt light-headed and full of joy. I loved shopping—especially at Christmas. 1

The shopping center was swarming with frantic last-minute shoppers like ourselves. We went first to the General Store, my favorite. It carried mostly knickknacks and other useless items which nobody needs but buys anyway. I was thirteen years old at the time, and things like buttons and calendars and posters would catch my fancy. This day was no different. The object of my desire was a 75-cent Snoopy button. Snoopy was the latest. If you owned anything with the Peanuts on it, you were "in." But since I was supposed to be shopping for gifts for other people and not myself, I couldn't decide what to do. I went in search of my sister for her opinion. I pushed my way through throngs of people to the back of the store where I found Susan. I asked her if she thought I should buy the button. She said it was cute and if I wanted it to go ahead and buy it. 2

When I got back to the Snoopy section, I took one look at the lines at the cashiers and knew I didn't want to wait thirty minutes to buy an item worth less than one dollar. I walked back to the basket where I found the button and was about to drop it when suddenly, instead, I took a quick glance around, assured myself no one could see, and slipped the button into the pocket of my sweatshirt. I hesitated for a moment, but once the item was in my pocket, there was no turning back. I had never before stolen anything; but what was done was done. A few seconds later, my sister appeared and asked, "So, did you decide to buy the button?" 3

"No, I guess not." I hoped my voice didn't quaver. As we headed for the entrance, my heart began to race. I just had to get out of that store. Only a few more yards to go and I'd be safe. As we crossed the threshold, I heaved a sigh of relief. I was home free. I thought about how sly I had been and I felt proud of my accomplishment. 4

An unexpected tap on my shoulder startled me. I whirled around to find a middle-aged man, dressed in street clothes, flashing some type of badge and politely asking me to empty my pockets. Where did this man come from? How did he know? I was so sure that no one had seen me! On the verge of panicking, I told myself that all I had to do was give this man his button back, say I was sorry, and go on my way. After all, it was only a 75-cent item. 5

Next thing I knew, he was talking about calling the police and having me arrested and thrown in jail, as if he had just nabbed a professional thief instead of a terrified kid. I couldn't believe what he was saying. 6

"Jean, what's going on?" 7

The sound of my sister's voice eased the pressure a bit. She always managed to get   8
me out of trouble. She would come through this time too.

"Excuse me. Are you a relative of this young girl?"   9

"Yes, I'm her sister. What's the problem?"   10

"Well, I just caught her shoplifting and I'm afraid I'll have to call the police."   11

"What did she take?"   12

"This button."   13

"A button? You are having a thirteen-year-old arrested for stealing a button?"   14

"I'm sorry, but she broke the law."   15

The man led us through the store and into an office, where we waited for the police offi-   16
cers to arrive. Susan had found my grandmother and brother, who, still shocked, didn't say
a word. The thought of going to jail terrified me, not because of jail itself, but because of the
encounter with my parents afterward. Not more than ten minutes later, two officers arrived
and placed me under arrest. They said that I was to be taken to the station alone. Then, they
handcuffed me and led me out of the store. I felt alone and scared. I had counted on my sister being with me, but now I had to muster up the courage to face this ordeal all by myself.

As the officers led me through the mall, I sensed a hundred pairs of eyes staring at   17
me. My face flushed and I broke out in a sweat. Now everyone knew I was a criminal. In
their eyes I was a juvenile delinquent, and thank God the cops were getting me off the
streets. The worst part was thinking my grandmother might be having the same thoughts.
The humiliation at that moment was overwhelming. I felt like Hester Prynne being put on
public display for everyone to ridicule.

That short walk through the mall seemed to take hours. But once we reached the   18
squad car, time raced by. I was read my rights and questioned. We were at the police
station within minutes. Everything happened so fast I didn't have a chance to feel
remorse for my crime. Instead, I viewed what was happening to me as if it were a movie.
Being searched, although embarrassing, somehow seemed to be exciting. All the movies
and television programs I had seen were actually coming to life. This is what it was really
like. But why were criminals always portrayed as frightened and regretful? I was having
fun. I thought I had nothing to fear—until I was allowed my one phone call. I was trembling
as I dialed home. I didn't know what I was going to say to my parents, especially my mother.

"Hi, Dad, this is Jean."   19

"We've been waiting for you to call."   20

"Did Susie tell you what happened?"   21

"Yeah, but we haven't told your mother. I think you should tell her what you did and   22
where you are."

"You mean she doesn't even know where I am?"   23

"No, I want you to explain it to her."   24

There was a pause as he called my mother to the phone. For the first time that night,   25
I was close to tears. I wished I had never stolen that stupid pin. I wanted to give the phone
to one of the officers because I was too ashamed to tell my mother the truth, but I had no
choice.

"Jean, where are you?"   26

"I'm, umm, in jail."   27

"Why? What for?"   28

"Shoplifting."   29

"Oh no, Jean. Why? Why did you do it?"   30

"I don't know. No reason. I just did it."   31

"I don't understand. What did you take? Why did you do it? You had plenty of money   32
with you."

"I know but I just did it. I can't explain why. Mom, I'm sorry."   33

"I'm afraid sorry isn't enough. I'm horribly disappointed in you."   34

Long after we got off the phone, while I sat in an empty jail cell, waiting for my par-   35
ents to pick me up, I could still distinctly hear the disappointment and hurt in my mother's
voice. I cried. The tears weren't for me but for her and the pain I had put her through. I felt
like a terrible human being. I would rather have stayed in jail than confront my mom right
then. I dreaded each passing minute that brought our encounter closer. When the officer
came to release me, I hesitated, actually not wanting to leave. We went to the front desk,
where I had to sign a form to retrieve my belongings. I saw my parents a few yards away
and my heart raced. A large knot formed in my stomach. I fought back the tears.

Not a word was spoken as we walked to the car. Slowly, I sank into the back seat   36
anticipating the scolding. Expecting harsh tones, I was relieved to hear almost the opposite from my father.

"I'm not going to punish you and I'll tell you why. Although I think what you did was   37
wrong, I think what the police did was more wrong. There's no excuse for locking a thirteen-year-old behind bars. That doesn't mean I condone what you did, but I think you've
been punished enough already."

As I looked from my father's eyes to my mother's, I knew this ordeal was over.   38
Although it would never be forgotten, the incident was not mentioned again.

Connecting to Culture and Experience: Shame and Social Disapproval

In paragraph 17, Brandt gives us a vivid portrait of how excruciating the feeling of shame can be: "I sensed a hundred pairs of eyes staring at me. My face flushed and I broke out in a sweat." Shame, as this description indicates, involves a desire for people's approval or a dread of their disapproval. (The words *shame* and *guilt* are often used interchangeably, but they have different connotations: Shame involves anxiety about social acceptance, whereas guilt is a more private, inward-looking emotion associated with morality.) We know that Brandt is feeling shame because of her emphasis on other people's opinions of her.

Identify one occasion when you felt ashamed. With other students, take turns briefly explaining what happened, who was ashamed of you, and why you felt shame. Then, keeping in mind that the social goal of shame is to constrain individuals' behavior, discuss what you think groups—families, friends, teams, employees—gain from creating fear of social disapproval among their members. Consider also what individuals might lose from undue pressure of social disapproval.

Analyzing Writing Strategies

1. Reread the essay, paying particular attention to Brandt's use of dialogue—reconstructed conversation from the time of the event. What do you learn about the author from what she says and how she says it? What do you learn about her relationship with her parents?

2. The story begins and ends in a car, with the two car rides framing the story. Framing, a narrative device, echoes something from the beginning in the ending. Review what happens in each car ride. The writer assumes that you might think of the beginning as you are reading the ending. What effect might this awareness have on your response to the ending car ride?

Commentary: A Vivid Presentation of Places and People

To present the people involved in the event and especially to dramatize her relationship with her parents, Brandt depends on dialogue. We can see from her use of dialogue the two ways that writers typically present remembered conversations: quoting and summarizing. Compare the two examples that follow. In the first example, Brandt quotes a brief exchange between herself and her sister as they were leaving the store (paragraphs 3 and 4):

> A few seconds later, my sister appeared and asked, "So, did you decide to buy the button?"
> "No, I guess not." I hoped my voice didn't quaver.

In this second example, Brandt summarizes what the store manager said to her as she left the store (paragraphs 5 and 6):

> An unexpected tap on my shoulder startled me. I whirled around to find a middle-aged man, dressed in street clothes, flashing some type of badge and politely asking me to empty my pockets....
> Next thing I knew, he was talking about calling the police and having me arrested....

As these examples indicate, writers usually summarize rather than quote when they need to give only the gist of what was said. Brandt apparently decides that the manager's actual words and way of speaking are not important for her purpose. However, presenting her response to her sister's question is important because it shows how she felt at the time. When you write a remembered-event essay, you too will have to decide in light of your overall purpose what to summarize and what to quote.

Considering Topics for Your Own Essay

Think of a few occasions when you did something uncharacteristic. Perhaps you acted on impulse or took a chance you would not ordinarily take. The events do not have to be reckless, dangerous, or illegal; they can be quite harmless or even pleasant. Pick one occasion you might like to write about. What would you want your readers to recognize about you on the basis of reading your story?

■ PURPOSE AND AUDIENCE

Writing autobiography, writers relive moments of pleasure and pain, and they also gain insight, learning who they are now by examining who they used to be and the forces that shaped them. Because autobiographers write to be read, though, they are as much concerned with self-presentation as with self-discovery. Writers present themselves to readers in the way they want to be perceived. The rest they keep hidden, though readers may read between the lines.

We read about others' experiences for much the same reason that we write about our own—to learn how to live our lives. Reading autobiography can validate our sense of ourselves, particularly when we see our own experience reflected in another's life. Reading about others' lives can also challenge our complacency and help us appreciate other points of view.

BASIC FEATURES: REMEMBERING EVENTS

A Well-Told Story

An essay about a remembered event should tell an interesting story. Whatever else the writer may attempt to do, he or she must shape the experience into a story that is entertaining and memorable. This is done primarily by building suspense, leading readers to wonder, for example, whether the driver of the Buick will catch Annie Dillard, Tobias Wolff will shoot the rifle, or Jean Brandt will get caught for shoplifting. The principal technique for propelling the narrative and heightening suspense is specific narrative action with its action verbs and verbals. Suspense increases, for instance, when Wolff gives a detailed close-up of his play with the rifle. In addition, writers use temporal transitions to cue readers and move the narrative through time, as when Tobias Wolff begins paragraphs with "Just after Easter," "For a week or so," and "One afternoon." Finally, writers often use dialogue to convey immediacy and drama, as Brandt does to dramatize her confrontation with her mother on the phone.

A Vivid Presentation of Places and People

Instead of giving a generalized impression, skillful writers attempt to re-create the place where the event occurred and let us hear what people said. Vivid language and specific details make the writing memorable. By moving in close, a writer can name specific objects at a place, such as when Brandt catalogs the store's knickknacks, calendars, and buttons. A writer may also provide details about some of the objects, as when Brandt describes the coveted "75-cent Snoopy button." Finally, writers use similes and metaphors to draw comparisons and thereby help readers understand the point. For example, when Brandt says she felt "like Hester Prynne being put on public display" (paragraph 17), readers familiar with *The Scarlet Letter* can imagine how embarrassed Brandt must have felt.

To present people who played an important role in a remembered event, autobiographers often provide some descriptive details and a snatch of dialogue. They may detail the person's appearance, as Annie Dillard does by describing the man who chased her "in city clothes: a suit and tie, street shoes" as "a thin man, all action" (paragraph 10). Dialogue can be an especially effective way of giving readers a vivid impression of someone. Wolff, for example, describes his mother by combining specific narrative actions with her empathetic words: "She took a cellophane bag off a loaf of bread and we went outside and looked at the squirrel. 'Poor little thing,' she said. She stuck her hand in the wrapper and picked up the squirrel, then pulled the bag inside out away from her hand" (paragraph 10).

An Indication of the Event's Significance

There are two ways a writer can communicate an event's autobiographical significance: by showing us that the event was important or by telling us directly what it meant. Most writers do both. Showing is necessary because the event must be dramatized for readers to appreciate its importance and understand the writer's feelings about it. Seeing the important scenes and people from the writer's point of view naturally leads readers to identify with the writer. We can well imagine what that "unexpected tap on [the] shoulder" (paragraph 5) must have felt like for Brandt and how Dillard felt when the man chased her and Mikey "silently over picket fences, through thorny hedges, between houses, around garbage cans, and across streets" (paragraph 13).

Telling also contributes to a reader's understanding, so most writers comment on the event's meaning and importance. Readers expect to understand the significance of the event, but they do not expect the essay to begin with the kind of thesis statement typical of argumentative writing. Instead, as the story moves along, writers tell us how they felt at the time or how they feel now as they look back on the experience. Often writers do both. Wolff, for example, tells us some of his remembered feelings when he recalls feeling "like a sniper" and delighting in the "ecstasy" of power. He also tells us what he thinks looking back on the experience: "Because I did not know who I was, any image of myself, no matter how grotesque, had power over me. This much I understand now" (paragraph 13). Telling is the main way that writers interpret the event for readers, but skillful writers are careful not to append these reflections artificially, like a moral tagged on to a fable.

GUIDE TO WRITING
Remembering Events

THE WRITING ASSIGNMENT

Write an essay about an event in your life that will be engaging for readers and that will, at the same time, help them understand the significance of the event. Tell your story dramatically and vividly.

◄ **THE WRITING ASSIGNMENT**

INVENTION

| Finding an Event to Write About |
| Describing the Place |
| Recalling Key People |
| Sketching the Story |
| Testing Your Choice |
| Exploring Memorabilia |
| Reflecting on the Event's Significance |
| Defining Your Purpose for Your Readers |
| Formulating a Tentative Thesis Statement |

INVENTION ►

PLANNING & DRAFTING

| Seeing What You Have |
| Setting Goals |
| Outlining |
| Drafting |

◄ **PLANNING AND DRAFTING**

CRITICAL READING GUIDE ►

| CRITICAL READING GUIDE |
| First Impression |
| Storytelling |
| Vivid Description |
| Autobiographical Significance |
| Memorabilia |
| Organization |
| Final Thoughts |

REVISING

| A Well-Told Story |
| A Vivid Presentation of Places and People |
| Autobiographical Significance |
| Organization |

◄ **REVISING**

EDITING & PROOFREADING

| Checking for Missing Commas after Introductory Elements |
| Checking for Fused Sentences |
| Checking Your Use of the Past Perfect |
| A Common ESL Problem |

EDITING AND PROOFREADING ►

■ THE WRITING ASSIGNMENT

Write an essay about an event in your life that will be engaging for readers and that will, at the same time, help them understand the significance of the event. Tell your story dramatically and vividly.

■ INVENTION

The following invention activities will help you choose an appropriate event, recall specific details, sketch out the story, test your choice, and explore the event's autobiographical significance. Each activity is easy to do and takes only a few minutes. If you can spread out the activities over several days, it will be easier for you to recall details and to reflect deeply on the event's meaning in your life. Keep a written record of your invention work to use when you draft the essay and later when you revise it.

Finding an Event to Write About

To find the best possible event to write about, consider several possibilities rather than choosing the first event that comes to mind.

Listing Remembered Events.   *Make a list of significant events from your past. Include only those events about which you can recall detail about what happened, where and when it happened, and the people involved.* Begin your list now, and add to it over the next few days. Include possibilities suggested by the Considering Topics for Your Own Essay activities following each reading in this chapter. Make your list as complete as you can. The following categories may give you some more ideas:

- An occasion when you realized you had a special skill, ambition, or problem
- A time when you became aware of injustice, selflessness, heroism, sexism, racism
- A difficult situation, such as when you had to make a tough choice, when someone you admired let you down (or you let someone else down), or when you struggled to learn or understand something hard
- An occasion when things did not turn out as expected, such as when you expected to be praised but were criticized or ignored or when you were convinced you would fail but succeeded
- An incident charged with strong emotion, such as love, fear, anger, embarrassment, guilt, frustration, hurt, pride, happiness, or joy
- An incident that you find yourself thinking about frequently or occasionally or one you know you will never forget

Listing Events Related to Identity and Community. Whenever you write about events in your life, you are likely to reveal important aspects of your sense of identity and your relationships with others. The suggestions that follow, however, will help you recall events that are particularly revealing of your efforts to know yourself and to discover your place in the communities to which you belong.

- An event that shaped you in a particular way or revealed an aspect of your personality you had not seen before, such as your independence, insecurity, ambitiousness, or jealousy
- An incident that made you reexamine one of your basic values or beliefs, such as when you were expected to do something that went against your better judgment or when your values conflicted with someone else's values
- An occasion when others' actions led you to consider seriously a new idea or point of view
- An incident that made you feel the need to identify yourself with a particular community, such as an ethnic group, a political or religious group, or a group of coworkers
- An event that made you realize that the role you were playing did not conform to what was expected of you as a student, as a male or female, as a parent or sibling, as a believer in a particular religious faith, or as a member of a particular community
- An incident in which a single encounter with another person changed the way you view yourself or changed your ideas about how you fit into a particular community

Listing Events Related to Work and Career. The following suggestions will help you think of events involving your work experiences as well as your career aspirations.

- An event that made you aware of your capacity for or interest in a particular kind of work or career or an event that convinced you that you were not cut out for a particular kind of work or career
- An incident of harassment or mistreatment at work
- An event that revealed to you other people's assumptions, attitudes, or prejudices about you as a worker, your fitness for a particular job, or your career goals
- An incident of conflict or serious misunderstanding with a customer, a fellow employee, a supervisor, or someone you supervised

Finding an Event to Write About: An Online Activity   Exploring Web sites where other people write about their own life experiences might inspire you by triggering memories of similar events in your own life and by suggesting a broad range of possibilities for the kinds of remembered events people find significant.

- If you do a search for remembered-event essays in Google (www.google.com) or Yahoo! Directory (http://dir.yahoo.com), you will find essays written by students in other composition classes throughout the country.
- Sites such as citystories.com and storypreservation.com where people post brief stories about their lives may suggest significant events in your own life.

Add to your list of possibilities any events suggested by your online research. But do not be disappointed if other people's stories do not help you think of events in your own life that you could write about.

Choosing an Event. *Look over your list of possibilities, and choose one event that you think will make an interesting story.* You should be eager to explore the significance of the event and comfortable about sharing the event with your instructors and classmates, who will be your first readers. You may find the choice easy to make, or you may have several equally promising possibilities from which to choose.

It may help you in choosing an event if you tentatively identify your ultimate readers, the people with whom you most want to share the story. They could include, for example, your personal friends, members of your family, people you work with, members of a group with which you identify or of an organization to which you belong, your classmates, an instructor, or even the public at large.

Make the best choice you can now. If this event does not work out, you can try a different one later.

Describing the Place

The following activities will help you decide which places are important to your story and what you remember about them. Take the time now to explore your memory and imagination. This exploration will yield descriptive language you can use in your essay.

Listing Key Places. *Make a list of all the places where the event occurred, skipping some space after each entry on your list.* Your event may have occurred in one or more places. For now, list all the places you remember without worrying about whether they should be included in your story.

Describing Key Places. *In the space after each entry on your list, make some notes describing each place.* As you remember each place, what do you see (excluding people for the moment)? What objects stand out? Are they large or small, green or brown, square or oblong? What sounds do you hear? Do you detect any smells? Does any taste come to mind? Do you recall anything soft or hard, smooth or rough?

Recalling Key People

These activities will help you remember the people who played a role in the event—what they looked like, did, and said.

Listing Key People. *List the people who played more than a casual role in the event.* You may have only one person to list, or you may have several.

Describing Key People. *Write a brief description of the people who played major roles in the event.* For each person, name and detail a few distinctive physical features or items of dress. Describe the person's way of talking or gesturing.

Re-Creating Conversations. *Reconstruct any important conversations you had during the event.* Also try to recall any especially memorable comments, any unusual choice of words, or any telling remarks that you made or were made to you. You may not remember exactly what was said during an entire conversation, but try to re-create it so that readers will be able to imagine what was going on.

Sketching the Story

Write for a few minutes, telling what happened. You may find it easier to outline what happened rather than writing complete sentences and paragraphs. Any way you can put the main action into words is fine. Over the next few days, you may want to add to this rough sketch.

Testing Your Choice

Now you need to decide whether you recall enough detail to write a good story about this particular event. Reread your invention notes to see whether your initial memories seem promising. If you can recall clearly what happened and what the important scenes and people were like, then you have probably made a good choice. If at any point you lose confidence in your choice, return to your list, and choose another event.

Testing Your Choice: A Collaborative Activity

At this point, you will find it useful to get together with two or three other students to try out your story. Your instructor may ask you to do this collaborative activity in class or online using a chat room. Their reactions to your story will help you determine whether you have chosen an event you can present in an interesting way.

Storytellers: Take turns telling your story briefly. Try to make your story dramatic (by piquing your listeners' curiosity and building suspense) and vivid (by briefly describing the place and key people).

Listeners: Briefly tell each storyteller what you found most intriguing about the story. For example, were you eager to know how the story would turn out? Were you curious about any of the people? Were you able to identify with the story-teller? Could you imagine the place? Could you understand why the event is so memorable and significant for the storyteller?

Exploring Memorabilia

Memorabilia are visual images, sounds, and objects that can help you remember details and understand the significance of an event. Examples include photographs, newspaper or magazine clippings, recordings of popular music, souvenirs, medals or trophies, and even items not necessarily designated as mementoes (restaurant menus and movie, theater, or concert stubs and programs). *If you can obtain access to relevant memorabilia, take time to do so now. Add to your invention notes any details about the period, places, or people the memorabilia suggest.*

Consider including one or more pieces of memorabilia in your essay. You can simply append photographs or other items to your printed-out essay, or if you have the capability, you can scan them into your electronic document. If you include visual memorabilia in your essay, you should label and number them as Figure 1, Figure 2, and so on, and include captions identifying them.

Reflecting on the Event's Significance

You should now feel fairly confident that you can tell an interesting story about the event you have chosen. The following activities will help you to understand the meaning that the event holds in your life and to develop ways to convey this significance to your readers.

Recalling Your Remembered Feelings and Thoughts. *Write for a few minutes about your feelings and thoughts during and immediately after the event.* The following questions may help stimulate your memory:

- What were my expectations before the event?
- What was my first reaction to the event as it was happening and right after it ended?
- How did I show my feelings? What did I say?
- What did I want the people involved to think of me? Why did I care what they thought of me?
- What did I think of myself at the time?
- How long did these initial feelings last?
- What were the immediate consequences of the event for me personally?

Pause now to reread what you have written. *Then write another sentence or two about the event's significance to you at the time it occurred.*

Exploring Your Present Perspective. *Write for a few minutes about your current feelings and thoughts as you look back on the event.* These questions may help you get started:

- Looking back, how do I feel about this event? If I understand it differently now than I did then, what is the difference?
- What do my actions at the time of the event say about the kind of person I was then? How would I respond to the same event if it occurred today?
- Can looking at the event historically or culturally help explain what happened? For example, did I upset gender expectations? Did I feel torn between two cultures or ethnic identities? Did I feel out of place?
- Do I now see that there was a conflict underlying the event? For example, did I struggle with contradictory desires within myself? Did I feel pressured by others or by society in general? Were my desires and rights in conflict with someone else's? Was the event about power or responsibility?

Pause now to reflect on what you have written about your present perspective. *Then write another sentence or two, commenting on the event's significance as you look back on it.*

Defining Your Purpose for Your Readers

Write a few sentences, defining your purpose in writing about this particular event for your readers. Use these questions to focus your thoughts:

- Who are my readers? (Remember that in choosing an event, you considered several possible readers: your personal friends, members of your family, people you work with, members of a group with which you identify or of an organization to which you belong, your classmates, an instructor, even the public at large.)
- What do my readers know about me?
- What do my readers expect when they read autobiography?
- How do I expect my readers to understand or react to the event?
- How do I want my readers to feel about what happened? What is the dominant impression or mood I want my story to create?
- What specifically do I want my readers to think of me? What do I expect or fear they might think?

It is unlikely, but you may decide at this point that you feel uncomfortable disclosing this event. If so, choose another event to write about.

Formulating a Tentative Thesis Statement

Review what you wrote for Reflecting on the Event's Significance, and add another two or three sentences, not necessarily summarizing what you already have written but extending your insights into the significance of the event, what it meant to you at the time, and what it means now. These sentences must necessarily be speculative and tentative because you may not fully understand the event's significance in your life.

Keep in mind that readers do not expect you to begin your essay with the kind of explicit thesis statement typical of argumentative or explanatory writing. If you do decide to tell readers explicitly why the event was meaningful or significant, you will most likely do so as you tell the story, by commenting on or evaluating what happened, instead of announcing it at the beginning. Keep in mind that you are not obliged to tell readers the significance, but you should show it through the way you tell the story.

■ PLANNING AND DRAFTING

This section will help you review your invention writing and get started on your first draft.

Seeing What You Have

You have now done a lot of thinking and writing about the basic elements of a remembered-event essay: what happened, where it happened, who was involved, what was said, and how you felt. You have also begun to develop your understanding of why the event is so important to you. If you have done your invention writing on the computer, you may have sentences or whole paragraphs that can be copied and pasted into your draft. Reread what you have written so far to see what you have. Watch for specific narrative actions, vivid descriptive details, choice bits of dialogue. Note also any language that resonates with feeling or that seems especially insightful. Highlight any writing you think could be used in your draft.

Then ask yourself the following questions:

- Do I remember enough specific details about the event to describe it vividly?
- Do I understand how the event was significant to me?
- Does my invention material provide what I need to convey that significance to my readers?
- Does my present perspective on this event seem clear to me?
- Does the dominant impression I want to create in my essay seem relevant?

If you find little that seems promising, you are not likely to be able to write a good draft. Consider starting over with another event.

If, however, your invention writing offers some promising material, the following activities may help you develop more:

- To remember more of what actually happened, discuss the event with someone who was there or who remembers having heard about it at the time.

- To recall additional details about a person who played an important role in the event, look at any available photographs or letters, talk with the person, or talk with someone who remembers the person. If that is impossible, you might imagine having a conversation with the person today about the event: What would you say? How do you think the person would respond?

- To remember how you felt at the time of the event, try to recall what else was happening in your life during that period. What music, television shows, movies, sports, books, and magazines did you like? What concerns did you have at home, school, work, play?

- To develop your present perspective on the event, try viewing your experience as a historical event. If you were writing a news story or documentary about the event, what would you want people to know?

- To decide on the dominant impression you want your story to have on readers, imagine that you are making a film based on this event. What would your film look like? What mood or atmosphere would you try to create? Alternatively, imagine writing a song or poem about the event. Think of an appropriate image or refrain. What kind of song would you write—blues, hip-hop, country, ranchera, rock?

Setting Goals

Before starting to draft, set goals that will help you make decisions and solve problems as you draft and revise. Here are some questions that will help you set your goals:

Your Purpose and Readers

- What do I want my readers to think of me and my experience? Should I tell them how I felt and what I thought at the time of the event, as Dillard does? Should I tell them how my perspective has changed?

- If my readers are likely to have had a similar experience, how can I convey the uniqueness of my experience or its special importance in my life? Should I tell them more about my background or the particular context of the event? Should I give them a glimpse, as Dillard does, of its impact years later?

- If my readers are not likely to have had a similar experience, how can I help them understand what happened and appreciate its importance? Should I reveal the cultural influences acting on me, as Wolff does?

The Beginning

- What can I do in the opening sentences to arouse readers' curiosity? Should I begin with a surprising announcement, as Wolff does, or should I establish the setting and situation, as Dillard and Brandt do?

- How can I get my readers to identify with me? Should I tell them a few things about myself?

- Should I do something unusual, such as begin in the middle of the action or with a funny bit of dialogue?

The Story

- What should be the climax of my story—the point that readers anticipate with trepidation or eagerness?

- What specific narrative actions or dialogue would intensify the drama of the story?

- Should I follow strict chronological order? Or would flashback (referring to an event that occurred earlier) or flashforward (referring to an event that will occur later) make the narrative more interesting?

- How can I use vivid descriptive detail to dramatize the story?

The Ending

- If I conclude with some reflections on the meaning of the experience, how can I avoid tagging on a moral or being too sentimental?

- If I want readers to think well of me, should I conclude with a philosophical statement, as Wolff does? Should I end with a paradoxical statement, like Dillard? Should I be satirical? Should I be self-critical to avoid seeming smug?

- If I want to underscore the event's continuing significance in my life, can I show that the conflict was never fully resolved, as Brandt does? Could I contrast my remembered and current feelings and thoughts?

- Should I frame the essay by echoing something from the beginning to give readers at least a superficial sense of closure, as Brandt does by setting the last scene, like the first, in a car?

Outlining

The goals you have set should help you draft your essay, but first you might want to make a quick scratch outline to refocus on the basic story line. (For an example of a paragraph scratch outline, turn to the Commentary following Annie Dillard's essay on p. 31.) You could use the outlining function of your word processing program. In your outline, list the main actions in order, noting where you plan to describe the place, introduce particular people, present dialogue, and insert remembered or current feelings and thoughts. Use this outline to guide your drafting, but do not feel tied to it. As you draft, you may find a better way to sequence the action and integrate these features.

Drafting

General Advice.   Start drafting your essay, keeping in mind the goals you have set for yourself, especially the goal of telling the story dramatically. Turn off your grammar checker and spelling checker at this stage if you find them distracting. Don't be afraid to skip around in your story. Jump back and fill in a spontaneous idea, or leap ahead and write a later section first if you find that easier. Refer to your outline to help you sequence the action. If you get stuck while drafting, either make a note of what you need to fill in later or see if you can use something from your invention writing.

As you read over your first draft, you may see places where you can add new material to make the story dramatic. Or you may even decide that after this first draft you can finally see the story you want to write and set out to do so in a second draft.

Sentence Strategies.   As you draft a remembered-event essay, you will be trying to help readers feel the suspense of your story and recognize its significance. You will also need to orient readers to the time sequence of all the various actions in your narrative. In thinking about how to achieve these goals, you can often benefit by paying attention to how long your sentences are and where you place references to time.

Use short sentences to heighten the drama or suspense, point out autobiographical significance, and summarize action. Experienced writers of autobiography usually use both short and long sentences, as a glance at any reading in this chapter demonstrates. They write short sentences not to relieve the monotony or effort of writing long sentences but to achieve certain purposes they cannot achieve as easily with long sentences.

To dramatize actions or heighten suspense:

He caught us and we all stopped. (Annie Dillard, paragraph 15)

To emphasize the significance of the event to the writer:

I wanted the glory to last forever. (Annie Dillard, paragraph 19)
The humiliation at that moment was overwhelming. (Jean Brandt, paragraph 17)

To summarize actions:

One afternoon, I pulled the trigger. (Tobias Wolff, paragraph 9)

Short sentences are not the only way to achieve these purposes, but they do so notably well. Note, though, that most of these writers use short sentences infrequently. Because short sentences are infrequent, they attract the reader's attention: They seem to say, "Pay close attention here." But short sentences achieve this effect only in relation to long sentences, in context with them. (Some of the Sentence

Strategies presented in other chapters of this book illustrate ways that writers construct and purposefully deploy relatively long, complex sentences.) See how Dillard uses a series of longer sentences to build suspense that she brings to a peak with a short one:

> On one weekday morning after Christmas, six inches of new snow had just fallen. We were standing up to our boot tops in snow on a front yard on trafficked Reynolds Street, waiting for cars. The cars traveled Reynolds Street slowly and evenly; they were targets all but wrapped in red ribbons, cream puffs. We couldn't miss. (paragraph 3)

Place references to time toward the front of your sentences. Because your remembered-event essay is organized narratively—that is, it tells readers a story—you must regularly give them cues about when various actions occur. Without these time cues, readers may not know in which decade, year, or season the event occurred; whether it unfolded slowly or quickly; or in what sequence the various actions took place. When experienced writers of autobiography use these cues, they nearly always place them at the beginnings of sentences (or main clauses), as Annie Dillard does in this sentence from *An American Childhood:*

> *On one weekday morning after Christmas,* six inches of new snow had just fallen. (paragraph 3)

Placing these two important time cues—day of the week and time of the year—at the beginning of a sentence may not seem noteworthy, but in fact time cues can usually be placed nearly anywhere in a sentence. Consequently, Dillard might have written

> Six inches of new snow had just fallen *on one weekday morning after Christmas.*

Or she could have written

> *After Christmas,* six inches of new snow had just fallen *one weekday morning.*

Why might Dillard decide to locate these time cues at the beginning of the sentence, as she does with nearly all the time cues in her essay? Why not begin the sentence with the subject or main idea, in this case *six inches of snow?* The answer is that experienced writers of autobiography give highest priority to keeping readers oriented to time, specifically to the time of each action in the sequence of actions that make up a remembered event. To do so, they can rely on words, phrases, or clauses:

> Slowly, . . . (Jean Brandt, paragraph 36)
>
> For a week or so . . . (Tobias Wolff, paragraph 5)
>
> A few seconds later, . . . (Jean Brandt, paragraph 3)

In addition to using short sentences and locating explicit time cues at the beginning of sentences, you can strengthen your autobiographical writing with a kind of sentence that is important in observational writing—absolute phrases (p. 102).

CRITICAL READING GUIDE

Now is the time to get a good critical reading of your draft. Your instructor may schedule readings of drafts as part of your coursework—in class or online. If not, ask a classmate, friend, or family member to read your draft. You could also seek comments from a tutor at your campus writing center. The guidelines in this section can be used by anyone reviewing an essay about a remembered event. (If you are unable to have someone read your draft, turn ahead to the Revising section on p. 58, where you will find guidelines for reading your own draft critically.)

If you read another student's draft online, you may be able to use a word processing program to insert suggested improvements directly into the text of the draft or to write them out at the end of the draft. If you read a printout of the draft, you may write brief comments in the margins and lengthier suggestions on a separate page. When the writer sits down to revise, your thoughtful, extended suggestions written at the end of the draft or on separate pages will be especially helpful.

If You Are the Writer. To provide focused, helpful comments, your reader must know your essay's intended audience, your purpose, and a problem in the draft that you need help solving. Briefly write out this information at the top of your draft.

- *Readers:* Identify the intended readers of your essay.

- *Purpose:* What do you hope to achieve in writing this remembered-event essay? What features of your story do you hope will most interest readers? What do you want to disclose about yourself?

- *Problem:* Ask your reader to help you solve the single most important problem with your draft. Describe this problem briefly.

If You Are the Reader. Use the following guidelines to help you give critical comments to others on remembered-event essays.

1. *Read for a First Impression.* Read first to enjoy the story and to get a sense of its significance. Then, in just a few sentences, describe your first impression. If you have any insights about the meaning or importance of the event, share your thoughts. Next, consider the problem the writer identified, and respond briefly to that concern now. (If you find that the problem is covered by one of the other guidelines listed below, respond to it in more detail there if necessary.)

2. *Analyze the Effectiveness of the Storytelling.* Review the story, looking at the way the suspense builds and resolves itself. Point to any places where the

drama loses intensity—perhaps where the suspense slackens, where specific narrative action is sparse or action verbs are needed, where narrative transitions would help readers, or where dialogue could be added to dramatize people's interactions.

3. *Consider How Vividly the Places and People Are Described.* Point to any descriptive details, similes, or metaphors that are especially effective. Note any places or people that need more specific description. Also indicate any descriptive details that seem unnecessary. Identify any quoted dialogue that might be summarized instead or any dialogue that does not seem relevant.

4. *Assess Whether the Autobiographical Significance Is Clear.* Explain briefly what you think makes this event significant for the writer. Point out any places in the draft where the significance seems so overstated as to be sentimental or so understated as to be vague or unclear. If the event seems to lack significance, speculate about what you think the significance could be. Then point to one place in the draft where you think the significance could be made clearer by telling the story more fully or dramatically or by stating the significance.

5. *Assess the Use of Memorabilia.* If the writer makes use of memorabilia, evaluate how successfully each item is used. How is it relevant? Does it seem integrated into the narrative or merely appended? Is it placed in the most appropriate location? Does it make a meaningful contribution to the essay?

6. *Analyze the Effectiveness of the Organization.* Consider the overall plan, perhaps by making a scratch outline. Pay special attention to temporal transitions and verb tenses so that you can identify any places where the order of the action is unclear. Also indicate any places where you think the description or background information interrupts the action. If you can, suggest other locations for this material.

   - *Look at the beginning.* If it does not arouse curiosity, point to language elsewhere in the essay that might serve as a better opening—for example, a bit of dialogue, a striking image, or a remembered feeling.

   - *Look at the ending.* Indicate whether the conflict in the story is too neatly resolved at the end, whether the writer has tagged on a moral, or whether the essay abruptly stops without really coming to a conclusion. If there is a problem with the ending, try to suggest an alternative ending, such as framing the story with a reference to something from the beginning or projecting into the future.

7. *Give the Writer Your Final Thoughts.* What is the draft's strongest part? What part is most in need of further work?

■ REVISING

Now you have the opportunity to revise your essay. Your instructor or other students may have given you advice. You may have begun to realize that your draft requires not so much revising as rethinking. For example, you may recognize that the story you told is not the story you meant to tell. Or maybe you realize only now why the incident is important to you. Consequently, you may need to reshape your story radically or draft a new version of it, instead of working to improve the various parts of your first draft. Many students—and professional writers—find themselves in this situation. Often a writer produces a draft or two and gets advice on them from others and only then begins to see what might be achieved.

However, if instead you feel satisfied that your draft mostly achieves what you set out to do, you can focus on refining the various parts of it. Very likely you have thought of ways to improve your draft, and you may even have begun revising it. This section will help you get an overview of your draft and revise it accordingly.

Getting an Overview

Consider the draft as a whole, following these two steps:

1. *Reread.* If at all possible, put the draft aside for a day or two. When you do reread it, start by reconsidering your purpose. Then read the draft straight through, trying to see it as your intended readers will.
2. *Outline.* Make a quick scratch outline on paper, or use the headings and outline or summary functions of your word processor.

Planning for Revision.   Resist the temptation to dive in and start changing your text until you have a comprehensive view of what needs to be done. Using your outline as a guide, move through the document, using the change-highlighting or commenting tools of your word processor to note comments received from others and problems you want to solve (or mark on a hard copy if you prefer).

Analyzing the Basic Features of Your Own Draft.   Turn to the Critical Reading Guide on the preceding pages (pp. 56–57). Using this guide, reread the draft to identify problems you need to solve. Note the problems on your draft.

Studying Critical Comments.   Review all of the comments you have received from other readers and add to your notes any that you intend to act on. For each comment, refer to the draft to see what might have led the reader to make that particular point. Try to be objective about any criticism. Ideally, these comments will help you to see your draft as others see it (rather than as you hoped it would be) and to identify specific problems.

Carrying Out Revisions

Having identified problems in your draft, you now need to figure out solutions and—most important—to carry them out. Basically, there are three ways to find solutions:

1. Review your invention and planning notes for material you can add to your draft.
2. Do additional invention writing to provide material you or your readers think is needed.
3. Look back at the readings in this chapter to see how other writers have solved similar problems.

The following suggestions, which are organized according to the basic features of remembered-event essays, will get you started solving some writing problems that are common in them.

A Well-Told Story

- **Is the climax difficult to identify?** Check to be sure your story has a climax. Perhaps it is the point when you get what you were striving for (Dillard), when you do what you were afraid you might do (Wolff), or when you get caught (Brandt). If you cannot find a climax in your story or reconstruct your story so that it has one, then you may have a major problem. If this is the case, you should discuss with your instructor the possibility of starting over with another event.

- **Does the suspense slacken instead of building to the climax?** Try showing people moving or gesturing, adding narrative transitions to propel the action, or substituting quoted dialogue for summarized dialogue. Remember that writers of autobiography often use short sentences to summarize action and heighten suspense, as when Dillard writes "We couldn't miss" and "He didn't even close the car door."

A Vivid Presentation of Places and People

- **Do any places or people need more specific description?** Try naming objects and adding sensory details to help readers imagine what the objects look, feel, smell, taste, or sound like. For people, describe a physical feature or mannerism that shows the role the person plays in your story.

- **Does any dialogue seem irrelevant or poorly written?** Eliminate any unnecessary dialogue, or summarize quoted dialogue that has no distinctive language or dramatic purpose. Liven up quoted dialogue with faster repartee to make it more dramatic. Instead of introducing each comment with the dialogue cue "he said," describe the speaker's attitude or personality with phrases like "she gasped" or "he joked."

- **Do any descriptions weaken the dominant impression?** Omit extraneous details or reconsider the impression you want to make. Add similes and metaphors that strengthen the dominant impression you want your story to have.

- *Do readers question any visuals you used?* Might you move a visual to a more appropriate place or replace an ineffective visual with a more appropriate one? Could you make clear the relevance of a visual by mentioning it in your text?

An Indication of the Event's Significance

- *Are readers getting a different image of you from the one you want to create?* Look closely at the language you use to express your feelings and thoughts. If you project an aspect of yourself you did not intend to, reconsider what the story reveals about you. Ask yourself again why the event stands out in your memory. What do you want readers to know about you from reading this essay?

- *Are your remembered or current feelings and thoughts about the event coming across clearly and eloquently?* If not, look in your invention writing for more expressive language. If your writing seems too sentimental, try to express your feelings more directly and simply, or let yourself show ambivalence or uncertainty.

- *Do readers appreciate the event's uniqueness or special importance in your life?* If not, consider giving them more insight into your background or cultural heritage. Also consider whether they need to know what has happened since the event took place to appreciate why it is so memorable for you.

The Organization

- *Is the overall plan ineffective or the story hard to follow?* Look carefully at the way the action unfolds. Fill in any gaps. Eliminate unnecessary digressions. Add or clarify temporal transitions. Fix confusing verb tenses. Remember that writers of autobiography tend to place references to time at the beginnings of sentences — "*When a car came,* we all popped it one" — to keep readers on track as the story unfolds.

- *Does description or other information disrupt the flow of the narrative?* Try integrating this material by adding smoother transitions. Or consider removing the disruptive parts or placing them elsewhere.

- *Is the beginning weak?* See whether there is a better way to start. Review the draft and your notes for an image, a bit of dialogue, or a remembered feeling that might catch readers' attention or spark their curiosity.

- *Does the ending work?* If not, think about a better way to end — with a memorable image, perhaps, or a provocative assertion. Consider whether you can frame the essay by referring back to something in the beginning.

Checking Sentence Strategies Electronically. To check your draft for a sentence strategy especially useful in remembered-event essays, use your word processor's highlighting function to mark references to time. Then look at where each one appears in its sentence, and think about whether moving any of them closer to the beginning of the sentence would make it easier for readers to follow the sequence of actions in your narrative. For more on placement of time references, see p. 55.

■ EDITING AND PROOFREADING

Now is the time to check your revised draft for errors in grammar, punctuation, and mechanics and to consider matters of style. Our research has identified several errors that occur often in essays about remembered events: missing commas after introductory elements, fused sentences, and misused past-perfect verbs. The following guidelines will help you check your essay for these common errors. This book's Web site also provides interactive online exercises to help you learn to identify and correct each of these errors; to access the exercises for a particular error, go to the URL listed after each set of guidelines.

Checking for Missing Commas after Introductory Elements.   Introductory elements in a sentence can be words, phrases, or clauses. A comma tells readers that the introductory information is ending and the main part of the sentence is about to begin. If there is no danger of misreading, you can omit the comma after single words or short phrases or clauses, but you will never be wrong to include the comma. Remembered-event essays require introductory elements, especially those showing time passing. The following sentences, taken from drafts written by college students using this book, show several kinds of introductory sentence elements that should have a comma after them.

▶ Through the nine-day run of the play ͵ the acting just kept getting better and better.

▶ Knowing that the struggle was over ͵ I felt through my jacket to find tea bags and cookies the robber had taken from the kitchen.

▶ As I stepped out of the car ͵ I knew something was wrong.

For practice, go to bedfordstmartins.com/conciseguide/comma.

Checking for Fused Sentences.   Fused sentences occur when two independent clauses are joined with no punctuation or connecting word between them. When you write about a remembered event, you try to re-create a scene. In so doing, you might write a fused sentence like this one:

▶ Sleet glazed the windshield the wipers were frozen stuck.

There are several ways to edit fused sentences:

• Make the clauses separate sentences.

 The
▶ Sleet glazed the windshield ⊙the wipers were frozen stuck.

• Join the two clauses with a comma and *and, but, or, nor, for, so,* or *yet.*

 ͵ and
▶ Sleet glazed the windshield the wipers were frozen stuck.

- Join the two clauses with a semicolon.

  ▶ Sleet glazed the windshield; the wipers were frozen stuck.

- Rewrite the sentence, subordinating one clause.

  As sleet   *became*
  ▶ ~~Sleet~~ glazed the windshield; the wipers ~~were~~ frozen stuck.

For practice, go to bedfordstmartins.com/conciseguide/csplice.

Checking Your Use of the Past Perfect.   Verb tenses indicate the time an action takes place. As a writer, you will generally use the present tense for actions occurring at the time you are writing (we *see*), the past tense for actions completed in the past (we *saw*), and the future tense for actions that will occur in the future (we *will see*). When you write about a remembered event, you will often need to use various forms of the past tense: the past perfect to indicate an action that was completed at the time of another past action (she *had finished* her work when we saw her) and the past progressive to indicate a continuing action in the past (she *was finishing* her work). One common problem in writing about a remembered event is the failure to use the past perfect when it is needed. For example:

  had
  ▶ I had three people in the car, something my father told me not to do on
  several occasions.

In the following sentence, the meaning is not clear without the past perfect:

  had run
  ▶ Coach Kernow told me I ~~ran~~ faster than ever before.

For practice, go to bedfordstmartins.com/conciseguide/verbs.

A Common ESL Problem.   It is important to remember that the past perfect is formed with *had* followed by a past participle. Past participles usually end in *-ed*, *-d*, *-en*, *-n*, or *-t*: *worked, hoped, eaten, taken, bent.*

  spoken
  ▶ Before Tania went to Moscow last year, she had not really ~~speak~~ Russian.

For practice, go to bedfordstmartins.com/conciseguide/everb.

A Note on Grammar and Spelling Checkers.   These tools are good at catching certain types of errors, but currently there's no replacement for a good human proofreader. Grammar checkers in particular are extremely limited in what they can usually find, and often they only give you summary information that isn't helpful if you don't already understand the rule in question. They are also prone to give faulty advice for fixing problems and to flag correct items as wrong. Spelling checkers cause fewer problems but can't catch misspellings that are themselves words, such as *to* for *too*.

REFLECTING ON YOUR WRITING

Now that you have worked extensively in autobiography—reading it, talking about it, writing it—take some time for reflection. Reflecting on your writing process will help you gain a greater understanding of what you learned about solving the problems you encountered writing about an event.

Write a page or so telling your instructor about a problem you encountered in writing your essay and how you solved it. Before you begin, gather all of your writing—invention and planning notes, outlines, drafts, critical comments, revision plans, and final revision. Review these materials as you complete this writing task.

1. *Identify one problem you needed to solve as you wrote about a remembered event.* Do not be concerned with grammar and punctuation; concentrate on problems unique to writing a story about your experience. For example: Did you puzzle over how to present a particular place or person? Was it difficult to structure the narrative so it held readers' interest? Did you find it hard (or uncomfortable) to convey the event's autobiographical significance?

2. *Determine how you came to recognize the problem.* When did you first discover it? What called it to your attention? Did you notice it yourself, or did another reader point it out? Can you now see hints of it in your invention writing, your planning notes, or an earlier draft? If so, where specifically?

3. *Reflect on how you went about solving the problem.* Did you work on a particular passage, cut or add details, or reorganize the essay? Did you reread one of the essays in the chapter to see how another writer handled similar material? Did you look back at the invention guidelines? Did you discuss the problem with another student, a tutor, or your instructor? If so, how did talking about it help, and how useful was the advice you got?

4. *Write a brief explanation of the problem and your solution.* Be as specific as possible in reconstructing your efforts. Quote from your invention notes or early drafts, from readers' comments, from your revision plan, and from your final revision to show the various changes your writing underwent as you worked to solve the problem. Taking the time now to think about how you recognized and solved a real writing problem will help you become more aware of what works and does not work, making you a more confident writer.

3

Writing Profiles

Profiles tell about people, places, and activities. Some profile writers try to reveal the unapparent inner workings of places or activities we consider familiar. Other profile writers introduce us to the exotic places or people — peculiar hobbies, unusual places of business, bizarre personalities.

Whatever their subject, profile writers strive most of all to enable readers to imagine the person, place, or activity that is the focus of the profile. Writers succeed only by presenting many specific and vivid details: how the person dresses, gestures, and talks; what the place looks, sounds, and smells like; what the activity requires of those who participate in it. Not only must the details be vivid, but they also must help to convey a writer's perspective — some insight, idea, or interpretation — on the subject.

Because profiles share many features with essays about remembered events — such as description, narration, and dialogue — you may use many of the strategies learned in Chapter 2 when you write your profile. Yet profiles differ from writing that reflects on personal experience in that profiles present newly acquired knowledge gained from your observations. In acquiring this knowledge, you practice observing, interviewing, and notetaking. These field research activities are important in many areas of academic study, including anthropology, sociology, psychology, education, and business.

The scope of your profile may be large or small, depending on your assignment and your subject. You could attend a single event such as a parade, dress rehearsal for a play, or city council meeting and write your observations of the place, people, and activities. Or you might conduct an interview with a person who has an unusual occupation and write a profile based on your interview notes. If you have the time to do more extensive research, you might write a more complete profile based on several visits and interviews with various people.

Writing in Your Other Courses

- For an education course, a student who has been studying collaborative learning principles profiles a group of sixth-grade students working together on an Internet project. The student observes and takes extensive notes on the collaboration. To learn what the sixth graders think about working together, the student interviews them individually and as a group. She also talks with the classroom teacher about how students were prepared to do this kind of work and how their collaboration will be evaluated. She organizes the profile narratively, telling the story of one erratic but ultimately productive group meeting. She interweaves interpretive comments based on collaborative learning principles. From her descriptions and comments emerges a perspective that group work is unlikely to succeed unless the students together with the teacher frequently reflect on what they are learning and how they can work together more productively.

- For an anthropology assignment, a student plans to research and write an ethnography (somewhat like an in-depth profile) about the football program and team at a local high school. He interviews coaches, players, parents, a few teachers not directly involved in the football program, the school principal, and a sports reporter for the local newspaper. He attends several practices and games. His detailed description of the football program alternates observational details with his own perspective on what football means to this particular high school community, particularly the way it confers status on the players, their parents, and their friends.

Writing in the Community

- An art history student profiles a local artist recently commissioned to paint an outdoor mural for the city. The student visits the artist's studio and talks with him about the process of painting murals. The artist invites the student to spend the following day with a team of local art students and neighborhood volunteers working on the mural under his direction. This firsthand experience helps the student describe the process of mural painting almost from an insider's point of view. She organizes her profile around the main stages of this collaborative mural project, from conception to completion. As she describes each stage, she weaves in details about the artist, his helpers, and the site of their work, seeking to capture the civic spirit that pervades the mural project.

- For a small-town newspaper, a writer profiles a community activist who appears regularly at city council meetings to speak on various problems in his neighborhood. The writer interviews the activist as well as two of the council members. He also observes the activist speaking at one council meeting on the problem of trash being dumped in unauthorized areas. At this meeting, the activist describes an all-night vigil he made to capture on videotape a flagrant act of illegal dumping in an empty lot near his home. The writer uses the activist's appearance at this meeting as a narrative framework for the profile; he also integrates details of the activist's public life along with images from the videotape.

Writing in the Workplace

- To help a probation court judge make an informed decision about whether to jail a teenager convicted of a crime or return him to his family, a social worker prepares to write a report and make a recommendation to the court. She interviews the teenager and his parents and observes the interactions among the family members. Her report describes in detail what she saw and heard, concluding with a recommendation that the teenager be allowed to return to his parents' home.

- For a company newsletter, a public-relations officer profiles a day in the life of the new CEO. He follows the CEO from meeting to meeting—taking photographs, observing her interactions with others, and interviewing her between meetings about her management philosophy and her plans for handling the challenges facing the company. The CEO invites the writer to visit her at home and meet her family. He stays for dinner, helps clear the table, and then watches the CEO help her daughter with homework. He takes more photographs. The published profile is illustrated by two photographs, one showing the CEO engaged in an intense business conference and the other showing her helping her daughter with homework.

Practice Choosing a Profile Subject: A Collaborative Activity

The preceding scenarios suggest some occasions for writing profiles. Imagine that you have been assigned to write a profile of a person, a place, or an activity on your campus, in your community, or at your workplace. Think of subjects that you would like to know more about. Your instructor may schedule this collaborative activity as a classroom discussion or ask you to conduct an online discussion in a chatroom.

Part 1. List three to five subjects you are curious about. Choose subjects you can imagine yourself visiting and learning more about. If possible, name a specific subject—a particular musician, day-care center, or local brewery. Consider interesting *people* (for example, store owners, distinguished teachers, accomplished campus or community musicians or sports figures, newspaper columnists, public defenders, CEOs, radio talk show hosts), *places* (for example, a college health center or student newspaper office, day-care center, botanical garden, community police department, zoo, senior citizen center, farmer's market, artist's studio, museum or sculpture garden, historic building, public transportation center, or garage), and *businesses* or *activities* (for example, a comic-book store, wrecking company, motorcycle dealer, commercial fishing boat, local brewery or winery, homeless shelter, building contractor, dance studio, private tutoring service, or dog kennel).

Now get together with two or three other students, and take turns reading your lists of subjects to one another. The other group members will tell you which item on your list they personally find most interesting and why they chose that item and ask you any questions they have about it.

Part 2. After you have all read your lists and received responses, discuss these questions as a group:

- What surprised you most about group members' choices of interesting subjects from your list?

- If you were now choosing a subject from your list to write about, how would group members' comments and questions influence your choice?
- How might their comments and questions influence your approach to learning more about this subject?

READINGS

No two profiles are alike, and yet they share defining features. Together, the three readings in this chapter reveal a number of these features, so you will want to read as many of them as possible. If time permits, complete the activities in the Analyzing Writing Strategies section that follows each reading, and read the Commentary. Following the readings is a section called Basic Features: Profiles (p. 85), which offers a concise description of the features of profiles and provides examples from the three readings.

John T. Edge directs the Southern Foodways Symposium, which is part of the Center for the Study of Southern Culture at the University of Mississippi. He coordinates an annual conference on southern food. Food writer for the national magazine Oxford American, *he has also written for* Cooking Light, Food & Wine, *and* Gourmet. *He has published several books, including* A Gracious Plenty: Recipes and Recollections from the American South *(1999);* Southern Belly *(2000), a portrait of southern food told through profiles of people and places; and, with photographer Robb Helfrick,* Compass Guide Georgia *(2001), a collection of new and archival photographs, literary excerpts, and practical travel information.*

This reading (and the photograph shown on p. 68) first appeared in a 1999 issue of Oxford American *and was reprinted in 2000 in* Utne Reader. *Edge profiles an unusual manufacturing business, Farm Fresh Food Supplier, in a small Mississippi town. He introduces readers to its pickled meat products, which include pickled pig lips. Like many other profile writers, Edge participates in his subject, in his case not by joining in the activities undertaken at Farm Fresh but by attempting to eat a pig lip at Jesse's Place, a nearby "juke" bar. You will see that the reading begins and ends with this personal experience.*

As you read, enjoy Edge's struggle to eat a pig lip, but notice also how much you are learning about this bar snack food as Edge details his discomfort in trying to eat it. Be equally attentive to the information he offers about the history and manufacturing of pig lips at Farm Fresh.

I'm Not Leaving Until I Eat This Thing

John T. Edge

It's just past 4:00 on a Thursday afternoon in June at Jesse's Place, a country juke 17 miles south of the Mississippi line and three miles west of Amite, Louisiana. The air conditioner hacks and spits forth torrents of Arctic air, but the heat of summer can't be kept at bay. It seeps around the splintered doorjambs and settles in, transforming the

squat particleboard-plastered roadhouse into a sauna. Slowly, the dank barroom fills with grease-smeared mechanics from the truck stop up the road and farmers straight from the fields, the soles of their brogans thick with dirt clods. A few weary souls make their way over from the nearby sawmill. I sit alone at the bar, one empty bottle of Bud in front of me, a second in my hand. I drain the beer, order a third, and stare down at the pink juice spreading outward from a crumpled foil pouch and onto the bar.

I'm not leaving until I eat this thing, I tell myself.

Half a mile down the road, behind a fence coiled with razor wire, Lionel Dufour, proprietor of Farm Fresh Food Supplier, is loading up the last truck of the day, wheeling case after case of pickled pork offal out of his cinder-block processing plant and into a semi-trailer bound for Hattiesburg, Mississippi.

His crew packed lips today. Yesterday, it was pickled sausage; the day before that, pig feet. Tomorrow, it's pickled pig lips again. Lionel has been on the job since 2:45 in the morning, when he came in to light the boilers. Damon Landry, chief cook and maintenance man, came in at 4:30. By 7:30, the production line was at full tilt: six women in white smocks and blue bouffant caps, slicing ragged white fat from the lips, tossing the good parts in glass jars, the bad parts in barrels bound for the rendering plant. Across the aisle, filled jars clatter by on a conveyor belt as a worker tops them off with a Kool-Aid-red slurry of hot sauce, vinegar, salt, and food coloring. Around the corner, the jars are capped, affixed with a label, and stored in pasteboard boxes to await shipping.

Unlike most offal—euphemistically called "variety meats"—lips belie their provenance. Brains, milky white and globular, look like brains. Feet, the ghosts of their cloven hoofs protruding, look like feet. Testicles look like, well, testicles. But lips are different. Loosed from the snout, trimmed of their fat, and dyed a preternatural pink, they look more like candy than like carrion.

At Farm Fresh, no swine root in an adjacent feedlot. No viscera-strewn killing floor lurks just out of sight, down a darkened hallway. These pigs died long ago at some Midwestern abattoir. By the time the lips arrive in Amite, they are, in essence, pig Popsicles, 50-pound blocks of offal and ice.

"Lips are all meat," Lionel told me earlier in the day. "No gristle, no bone, no nothing. They're bar food, hot and vinegary, great with a beer. Used to be the lips ended up in sausages, headcheese, those sorts of things. A lot of them still do."

Lionel, a 50-year-old father of three with quick, intelligent eyes set deep in a face the color of cordovan, is a veteran of nearly 40 years in the pickled pig lips business. "I started out with my daddy when I wasn't much more than 10," Lionel told me, his shy smile framed by a coarse black mustache flecked with whispers of gray. "The meatpacking business he owned had gone broke back when I was 6, and he was peddling out of the back of his car, selling dried shrimp, napkins, straws, tubes of plastic cups, pig feet, pig lips, whatever the bar owners needed. He sold to black bars, white bars, sweet shops, snowball stands, you name it. We made the rounds together after I got out of school, sometimes staying out till two or three in the morning. I remember bringing my toy cars to this one joint and racing them around the floor with the bar owner's son while my daddy and his father did business."

For years after the demise of that first meatpacking company, the Dufour family sold someone else's product. "We used to buy lips from Dennis Di Salvo's company down in Belle Chasse," recalled Lionel. "As far as I can tell, his mother was the one who came up with the idea to pickle and pack lips back in the '50s, back when she was working for a company called Three Little Pigs over in Houma. But pretty soon, we were selling so many lips that we had to almost beg Di Salvo's for product. That's when we started cooking up our own," he told me, gesturing toward the cast-iron kettle that hangs from the rafters by the front door of the plant. "My daddy started cooking lips in that very pot."

Lionel now cooks lips in 11 retrofitted milk tanks, dull stainless-steel cauldrons shaped like oversized cradles. But little else has changed. Though Lionel's father has passed away, Farm Fresh remains a family-focused company. His wife, Kathy, keeps the books. His daughter, Dana, a button-cute college student who has won numerous beauty titles, takes to the road in the summer, selling lips to convenience stores and wholesalers. Soon, after he graduates from business school, Lionel's younger son, Matt, will take over operations at the plant. And his older son, a veterinarian, lent his name to one of Farm Fresh's top sellers, Jason's Pickled Pig Lips.

"We do our best to corner the market on lips," Lionel told me, his voice tinged with 11 bravado. "Sometimes they're hard to get from the packing houses. You gotta kill a lot of pigs to get enough lips to keep us going. I've got new customers calling every day; it's all I can do to keep up with demand, but I bust my ass to keep up. I do what I can for my family—and for my customers.

"When my customers tell me something," he continued, "just like when my daddy told 12 me something, I listen. If my customers wanted me to dye the lips green, I'd ask, 'What shade?' As it is, every few years we'll do some red and some blue for the Fourth of July. This year we did jars full of Mardi Gras lips—half purple, half gold," Lionel recalled with a chuckle. "I guess we'd had a few beers when we came up with that one."

Meanwhile, back at Jesse's Place, I finish my third Bud, order my fourth. *Now,* I tell 13 myself, my courage bolstered by booze, *I'm ready to eat a lip.*

They may have looked like candy in the plant, but in the barroom they're carrion once 14 again. I poke and prod the six-inch arc of pink flesh, peering up from my reverie just in time to catch the barkeep's wife, Audrey, staring straight at me. She fixes me with a look just this side of pity and asks, "You gonna eat that thing or make love to it?"

Her nephew, Jerry, sidles up to a bar stool on my left. "A lot of people like 'em with 15 chips," he says with a nod toward the pink juice pooling on the bar in front of me. I offer to buy him a lip, and Audrey fishes one from a jar behind the counter, wraps it in tinfoil, and places the whole affair on a paper towel in front of him.

I take stock of my own cowardice, and, following Jerry's lead, reach for a bag of 16 potato chips, tear open the top with my teeth, and toss the quivering hunk of hog flesh into the shiny interior of the bag, slick with grease and dusted with salt. Vinegar vapors tickle my nostrils. I stifle a gag that rolls from the back of my throat, swallow hard, and pray that the urge to vomit passes.

With a smash of my hand, the potato chips are reduced to a pulp, and I feel the cold 17 lump of the lip beneath my fist. I clasp the bag shut and shake it hard in an effort to ensure chip coverage in all the nooks and crannies of the lip. The technique that Jerry uses—and I mimic—is not unlike that employed by home cooks mixing up a mess of Shake 'n Bake chicken.

I pull from the bag a coral crescent of meat now crusted with blond bits of potato 18 chips. When I chomp down, the soft flesh dissolves between my teeth. It tastes like a flaccid cracklin', unmistakably porcine, and not altogether bad. The chips help, providing texture where there was none. Slowly, my brow unfurrows, my stomach ceases its fluttering.

Sensing my relief, Jerry leans over and peers into my bag. "Kind of look like Frosted 19 Flakes, don't they?" he says, by way of describing the chips rapidly turning to mush in the pickling juice. I offer the bag to Jerry, order yet another beer, and turn to eye the pig feet floating in a murky jar by the cash register, their blunt tips bobbing up through a pasty white film.

Connecting to Culture and Experience: Gaining Firsthand Experience

Undoubtedly, Edge believed that he should visit a place where Farm Fresh Food Supplier's most popular product is consumed. He went further, however: He decided to experience the product firsthand by handling, smelling, and tasting it. Except for his own squeamishness, nothing prevented him from gaining the firsthand experience he sought. Aside from experiences in family and personal relationships, think about times when you have sought to gain firsthand experience and either succeeded or failed. Perhaps you yearned to sing but never took lessons, challenged yourself to go beyond watching basketball or soccer on television and won a spot on a school team, dreamed of an internship at a certain workplace but never could find the time to arrange it, imagined visiting a natural or historic site you had only read about and found a way to do so, or thought about joining others to protest a social injustice but never took action.

Identify one longed-for personal experience you missed out on and one you achieved, and think about why you failed in one case and succeeded in the other. At the time, how ready and able were you to gain access to the experience? What part did your personal decisiveness and effort play? Did you feel timid or bold about seeking what you wanted? Did you try to be accommodating, or did you have to be challenging or even disruptive? What roles did other people play? Who supported you, and who attempted to silence or exclude you? With whom did you have to negotiate? How did your gender or age affect the outcome? How important was money or other resources?

With two or three other students, discuss your attempts to gain longed-for personal experience. Begin by telling each other about one experience, explaining briefly what drew you to it, what happened, how you felt about the outcome, and why you think you succeeded or failed. Then, as a group, discuss what your stories reveal about what motivates and helps young Americans and what frustrates them as they try to gain longed-for experiences that may open new opportunities to them.

Analyzing Writing Strategies

1. The introduction to this chapter makes several generalizations about profile essays. Consider which of these assertions apply to Edge's essay:
   - It is based on the writer's newly acquired observations.
   - It takes readers behind the scenes of familiar places or introduces them to unusual places and people.
   - It is informative and entertaining.
   - It presents scenes and people vividly through description, action, and dialogue.
   - It suggests or asserts the writer's perspective on the subject—an idea about the subject or an insight into it.
2. Edge focuses on one of Farm Fresh's products, pickled pig lips. He probably assumes that most of his readers have never seen a pickled pig lip, much less eaten

one. Therefore, he describes this product carefully. To see how he does so, under-line in paragraphs 4, 5, 7, 14, and 18 every detail of a pickled pig lip's appearance, size, texture or consistency, smell, and taste. If you have never seen a pickled pig lip, what more do you need to know to imagine what it looks like? Which details make a lip seem appealing to you? Which ones make it seem unappealing? Edge scatters the details across the profile, rather than collecting them in one place. For you as one reader, how did this scattering help or hinder your attempts to fully understand what a pig lip is like?

3. To present their subjects, profile writers occasionally make use of a sentence strat-egy that relies on a sentence structure known as an *absolute phrase*. To discover what absolute phrases contribute, underline these absolutes in Edge's profile: in paragraph 1, sentence 4, from "the soles" to the end of the sentence, and sen-tence 6, from "one empty bottle" to the end; in paragraph 8, sentence 2, from "his shy smile" to the end; and in paragraph 19, sentence 3, from "their blunt tips" to the end. Make notes in the margin about how the absolute phrase seems to be related to what comes before it in the sentence. Given that Edge's goal is to help readers imagine what he observes, what does each absolute contribute toward that goal? How are these four absolutes alike and different in what they add to their sentences? (To learn more about how absolute phrases contribute to profiles, see Sentence Strategies, p. 101.)

Commentary: A Topical Plan

A profile may be presented narratively, as a sequence of events observed by the writer during an encounter with the place, person, or activity; or it may be presented topi-cally, as a series of topics of information gathered by the writer about the person, place, or activity. Though Edge frames (begins and ends) his profile with the narrative or story about attempting to eat a pig lip, he presents the basic information about Farm Fresh Food Supplier topically.

The following scratch outline of Edge's profile shows at a glance the topics he chose and how they are sequenced:

loading meat products on a truck (paragraph 3)

an overview of the production process, with a focus on that day's pig lips (4)

pig lips' peculiarity in not looking like where they come from on the pig (5)

the origin of Farm Fresh's materials—shipped frozen from the Midwest (6)

some characteristics of a pig lip (7)

Lionel's introduction to marketing food products and services (8)

Lionel's resurrection of the family meatpacking business (9)

family involvement in the business (10)

Lionel's marketing strategy (11)

Lionel's relations with customers (12)

Reviewing his interview and observation notes taken while he was at Farm Fresh, Edge apparently decided to organize them not as a narrative in the order in which he took them but as topics sequenced to be most informative for readers. He begins with the finished product, with Lionel loading the truck for shipment. Then he outlines the production process and mentions the various products. From there, he identifies the source of the products and briefly describes a pig lip, his main interest. Then he offers a history of Farm Fresh and concludes with Lionel's approach to his business. When you plan your profile essay, you will have to decide whether to organize your first draft topically or chronologically.

Considering Topics for Your Own Essay

Consider writing about a place that serves, produces, or sells something unusual, perhaps something that, like Edge, you could try yourself for the purpose of further informing and engaging your readers. If such places do not come to mind, you could browse the Yellow Pages of your local phone directory. There are many possibilities: producer or packager of a special ethnic or regional food or a local café that serves it, licensed acupuncture clinic, caterer, novelty and toy balloon store, microbrewery, chain saw dealer, boat builder, talent agency, manufacturer of ornamental iron, bead store, nail salon, pet fish and aquarium supplier, detailing shop, tattoo parlor, scrap metal recycler, fly fishing shop, handwriting analyst, dog or cat sitting service, photo restorer, burglar alarm installer, Christmas tree farm, wedding specialist, reweaving specialist, wig salon. You need not evaluate the quality of the work provided at a place as part of your observational essay. Instead, keep the focus on informing readers about the service or product the place offers. Relating a personal experience with the service or product is a good idea but not a requirement for a successful essay.

Trevor B. Hall *runs a Boston nonprofit company, The Call Academy, that provides enrichment programs for low-income urban high school students. Program participants study literature, practice the documentary arts (writing, video and film, photography), and take part in adventure travel. DoubleTake, a magazine for the documentary arts, published Hall's "A Documentary Classroom," a profile of one teacher's efforts to bring documentary into the English classroom, in 2001. The following profile was published in* DoubleTake *in 2000. As you read, notice how Hall goes about presenting the Edison Café as an irreplaceable social asset to Skagit Valley, Washington.*

The Edison Café
Trevor B. Hall

It is almost 6 A.M. in the town of Edison, Washington, and Julie Martin's headlights are cutting through fog and darkness. Julie is the cook and owner of the Edison Café. When she pulls up behind the small, crooked, fire-engine-red building, her first customer is waiting for her. Few words are passed as she opens the doors and begins to ready the kitchen. Soon the local farmers will begin to pour in.

1

They are tall, hearty men with weathered baseball caps or cowboy hats, earned dirt under every fingernail. Their entrance is always the same: the door creaks open; everyone looks at the new arrival, who swings around the lunch counter to the coffee machine.

"Mornin'," shouts Julie from the kitchen.   2

The new arrival quietly replies: "How-do?" The regulars each grab a mug, fill it, then   3
top off everyone else's cup. It's an unwritten rule that no one's coffee gets low or cold.

Outside it's still pitch black, and the only light in Edison comes from the café—the   4
fluorescent red EAT sign in the window and the dim yellow glow of the interior lights. Some mornings, there is playful banter; at times they all hold comfortable stares and listen quietly to the faux-antique, turquoise radio.

Edison is set in Washington State's Skagit Valley, some twenty-three thousand   5
square acres of the most plush, fertile farmland one can imagine. The valley has the look of a dark-green down comforter, creased by the water that travels down from the Cascade Mountains on its way to the Pacific Ocean. Dotting the horizon to the west are the rounded San Juan Islands. Directly to the east, the ten-thousand-foot volcanic Mount Baker stands watch (when, on occasion, the winter clouds split to allow its appearance). It is from this mountain that rainwater begins the journey down through the foothills and into the Samish River and its tributaries, creating a wetlands on this valley floor.

The valley gives life to a wide variety of birds: waterfowl (mostly ducks), eagles, blue   6
herons, huge flocks of sparrows, occasionally an exotic snowy egret or a mysterious Egyptian hawk. The valley is home to some of the best winter hawk-watching in the country. It is an active, lively place where nature and its doings are never far from the eye.

Most of Skagit Valley is farmland, and Edison is one of the only towns with remnants   7
of a main street (though Edison is no longer officially recognized by a postal zip code of its own). Established in 1869 and named after the inventor Thomas Alva Edison, the town enjoyed a heyday in the late 1880s, when it boasted three hotels, two churches, three grocery stores, a hardware store, a bank, a cheese factory, and four thirst-quenching establishments. For the most part, individually owned farms have since been pushed out

Mt. Baker's clouds over Edison, 2000

Early-rise breakfast, 2000

by larger industry, and the logging and fishing businesses have slowed to a near stand-still. The town has learned to be grateful for its two remaining bars and, of course, the Edison Café.

As the day progresses, the café will see three waves of customers: the early-morning farmers; the gamy, dice-wielding "shakers and rollers"; and the Edison Elementary School's rear-window gang.   8

The first crew is mostly men (and two of their wives, Rosie and Lucille) in their fifties   9
or sixties. They are people who have, in one way or another, worked the land of Skagit Valley: dairy farmers, potato farmers, fishermen, construction workers. The Edison Café is home for them—a combination dining room and kitchen.

One local asserts that while an estimated twenty-seven people have actually owned   10
the café since its beginnings in 1944, life in the café hasn't changed much over the years. Some of the owners have tried to fancy the place up a bit, but the changes were always met with either indifference or outright scorn by its customers. Julie understands: "It needs to be a place where people can come in with cow dung on their boots. You can't change that."

Julie is an attractive woman in her early forties, her blond hair usually pulled back for   11
cooking—a woman who knows what people around here like, to the point that almost no one actually places a food order. Customers sit down, chat with whoever is around, and eventually some food shows up—their meal, which is a day's selection of certain familiar possibilities: two pieces of bacon, a pancake, and a sausage; two eggs, a piece of bacon, and hash browns; an egg, two pancakes, and toast. The bill arrives on time. Everyone pays for the food (though some on mentally kept accounts), but if you're lucky, you can drink coffee for free.

"They roll me double or nothin' for the coffee," Julie declares. With five dice, in three   12
rolls, you must get a six, a five, a four, then the highest total of the remaining two dice wins. Those are the basic rules, but time has built many nuances into this game. Before people head out the door, they call to Julie, "Come roll me for this coffee." Julie emerges from the kitchen, dries her hands on her white apron, straightens her shoulders, peers at her competition, and grabs the dented leather dice cup. When Julie is on one of her winning streaks, she gets her fair share of suspicious looks, but it's part of the deal.

"Now, don't you bad mouth me for that one," she gently warns a loser as she makes   13
way back to the griddle.

By about 7:30 A.M., the first wave of customers is off to work, and the dice cup has   14
moved to the corner table, where the next wave will hit. It's not the last Julie will see of the morning crew, though; most will return periodically throughout the day (some of them four or five times). A little bit of light comes into the valley, and Julie can step out back for a moment's break.

Other than the arrival of her two waitresses—the sharp-tongued Roxy and the   15
charming woman known as Bear—or one of Julie's two high-school-aged daughters, the midmorning quiet lasts until about ten o'clock, when the shakers and rollers—a group of eight to ten local residents, mostly retired couples—show up, as they do every day, for The Game. The first half-hour or so is spent rolling for coffee, until someone rises to

Morning dice, 2000

the top as the day's winner. That person then rolls one-on-one against Julie, double or nothing, for the entire table's coffee. Talk of the weather, the nation, and town gossip rumble through the café. Then, promptly at 10:45, the usual breakfasts are delivered for everyone.

The meals are the standard fare—eggs, toast, hash browns, bacon—except in the case of Peter Menth, who is in his late sixties and whose well-trimmed gray beard and black captain's hat give him the authority of a fishing-boat captain at sea. His meal commands an equally grand respect and even has its own name on the menu: the Peter Pan Hotcake. This is no ordinary hotcake, and is surely the mark of a man who "won't grow up." Simply put, it is huge—so big that Peter bought his own larger-than-life plate to accommodate it—but the hotcake still falls over the sides. Julie respectfully keeps the plate in back.

16

Yet the usual stack is nothing to ignore—especially when ordered as part of the farmer's breakfast special: two eggs, two sausage links, two strips of bacon, hash browns, and two pancakes, all for $7.25. Many adolescent appetites have made an attempt at this one and come close—until the pancakes arrived, thudding on the counter under their own weight.

In his book *Blue Highways,* William Least Heat-Moon offers that the measure of an American café can be taken by the number of calendars on its wall; five calendars earns his top rating. The Edison Café tops that by three, and I would add one twist to Least Heat-Moon's measuring stick: if one of the calendars features pictures of tractors... loosen your belt. This café offers such a calendar, and a meal for two, really, all for under $10; a customer is hard pressed to spend more than $5, and further pressed not to leave the Edison Café teetering, completely full. Nonetheless, at noon a gang of students from the Edison Elementary School certainly tries their hand at this. (The café sits on the school's property, always has, which is why the elementary-school students are allowed to run over for lunch.) One local, Duane, recalls the café's presence in his life during his days as a student in the late 1940s: "I remember being beat up in this café in 1947—by my dad," he says with a smile—then explains: "I brought a white-face bull right in the front door, did a one-eighty-degree turn with it, and headed out. They banned me for a month." The school cafeteria food soon helped him mend his ways, and today's students are quick to tell you that Julie's food is an "awesome" option.

The madness begins quietly enough as two of the students, Emma and Kyla, arrive before the crowds. Through good grades, they have earned the right to "work the window" and get a free lunch in exchange. Moments after their arrival, the rush is on. From the back window of the café, it looks like a mob running in panic from a fire: backpacks bouncing off of shoulders, sneakers squeaking across the wet pavement, eyes wide with anticipation.

"We keep them under control," Emma says. "They give us their order, we shout it out to Julie, then we make sure everyone gets the right food. It's not too hard, and we get a free lunch, which is great!" Julie loves her two helpers, referring to them as "my girls."

This last rush is usually over by twelve-thirty; then Julie can take a well-earned rest on the bench out back. The sun is most likely to show its face about this time of the day, and she leans against the café wall, her face aimed at the warmth. One of her waitresses likely joins her, and the gossip begins. If it's her daughter, she often prods, "Didn't I fire you this morning for being late?" Leaning on her mom's shoulder, the daughter shoots back, "Mom, you fire me every morning."

So it has gone for years and years—a community tradition born of the need for food, comfort, and ritual. Everyday service to others is willingly and eagerly offered as a café owner's privilege—a service tendered with love, not because it promotes good corporate culture or because it will bolster profits, but because these are Julie's day husbands, her shakers and rollers, her girls. The Edison Café is a town's reliable home away from home, where personal politics and pettiness must be checked at the door. From the dark, foggy mornings to the breaks of sunshine in the afternoon, Julie knows that day in and day out, for better and for worse, in Edison, Washington, she "gets 'em fed."

Connecting to Culture and Experience: Community Social Life

You belong to several communities: your college, your neighborhood if you live off campus, perhaps a church or other spiritual community. You can see that communities are small-scale, local, and somewhat intimate, in that people at least recognize and greet each other and perhaps even talk casually. Besides these occasional brief, casual interactions, people in a community are likely to seek more substantial social interactions and look for places to find it, like the customers at the Edison Café.

Think about the communities you have belonged to or now belong to, and identify one place where you occasionally met or meet now to talk informally with others. These would be meetings, indoors or out, with two or more people you consider friends or perhaps only acquaintances. The meetings recur, at least for a few weeks. There is typically no agenda or purpose for the meeting, even though you might eat together, play cards, or watch a sports event on television. It may be scheduled, or it may occur spontaneously. There could be a different mix of people at each meeting.

With two or three other students, describe in turn this place, detailing where you meet, who typically shows up, how frequently and for how long you talk, and what you talk about. Then together explore the social meanings of these informal meetings. That is, what is your motive for meeting? What sustains your interest in meeting? What do you gain as individuals and as a group from these meetings? What do you think holds together groups like this, and what dissolves them?

Analyzing Writing Strategies

1. A profile writer attempts to convey a perspective on a subject—a point of view on it, an insight into it, an idea about it, an interpretation of it, or even a judgment about its worth. This perspective can be stated or implied, and all the details and information in the profile must be consistent with this perspective. Hall states his perspective quite directly in paragraph 22. In that paragraph, underline phrases that identify the role of the Edison Café in the community. Also underline relevant phrases in paragraphs 7, 9, and 15. From these various statements, write a sentence of your own that concisely expresses your understanding of Hall's perspective on his subject.

2. Photographs seem a natural partner to the written text of a profile. Hall includes three with his text. With film or digital camera, you can create visual images to combine with the text of your profile. Any images you choose to include should complement the information your text offers and be consistent with your perspective on the subject.

   Consider Hall's images in relation to his text, and make notes about what the images contribute to your understanding of the Edison Café. Try to think about the text without the images. What do the images add that you could not imagine or infer about the café from the text itself? How do the images support Hall's perspective on the café?

Commentary: A Role for the Writer

Depending on their subjects and personal inclinations, profile writers usually adopt one of two roles: participant observer or detached observer. In the participant-observer role, the writer reports his personal involvement and engagement in the subject. John T. Edge adopts this role in profiling Farm Fresh Food Supplier by narrating his personal experience with a real pig lip, oozing red-dyed vinegar and other unidentified juices, caked with soggy crushed potato chips, soft and yielding to the touch. He inserts himself in a vivid and humorous way into his profile. In contrast, Trevor B. Hall adopts the detached-observer role in profiling the Edison Café. He remains invisible, merely a reporter of what he observes. Although most readers would assume that Hall had eaten a meal at the café, he offers no clues that he did so. His chosen role as a writer may not correspond to his role as a researcher, however. Sitting quietly at the counter, sipping his coffee, not talking to anyone — only observing — he could have learned much of what he presents in the profile. He could have remained a cool observer of activities. Instead, it is evident that he interviewed owner Julie Martin, two or three of the adult customers, and two of the elementary school students. It seems very likely that he ate at least one, maybe two, meals, since he was at the café from before 6 A.M. to after 12:30 P.M. Even though Hall almost certainly initiated conversations, drank many cups of coffee, and ordered a meal or two, he nevertheless adopts a detached-observer role in writing the profile.

Considering Topics for Your Own Essay

Consider writing about places or activities that fulfill a major — or even essential — social function in your community, just as the Edison Café does for many people who live in Edison, Washington. You might visit a place where people, perhaps of different ages, gather occasionally and informally, like a senior citizens' center, local park, bowling alley, campaign headquarters, public library reading room, coffee house, café, or bar. Or you might profile an activity with a community purpose, such as a parade, Little League game, church youth group, college informal study group, benefit walk-athon or marathon, gallery opening, bake sale, or jazz festival.

Brian Cable wrote the following selection when he was a first-year college student. Cable's profile of a mortuary combines both seriousness and humor. He lets readers know his feelings as he presents information about the mortuary and the people working there. As you read, notice how Cable manages to inform you about the business of a mortuary while taking you on a guided tour of the premises. Notice also how he expresses his lack of seriousness about a serious place, a place of death and grief.

The Last Stop

Brian Cable

Let us endeavor so to live that when we come to die even the undertaker will be sorry.

—MARK TWAIN

Death is a subject largely ignored by the living. We don't discuss it much, not as children (when Grandpa dies, he is said to be "going away"), not as adults, not even as senior citizens. Throughout our lives, death remains intensely private. The death of a loved one can be very painful, partly because of the sense of loss but also because someone else's mortality reminds us all too vividly of our own. 1

Thus did I notice more than a few people avert their eyes as they walked past the dusty-pink building that houses the Goodbody Mortuaries. It looked a bit like a church — tall, with gothic arches and stained glass — and somewhat like an apartment complex — low, with many windows stamped out of red brick. 2

It wasn't at all what I had expected. I thought it would be more like Forest Lawn, serene with lush green lawns and meticulously groomed gardens, a place set apart from the hustle of day-to-day life. Here instead was an odd pink structure set in the middle of a business district. On top of the Goodbody Mortuaries sign was a large electric clock. "What the hell," I thought, "Mortuaries are concerned with time, too." 3

I was apprehensive as I climbed the stone steps to the entrance. I feared rejection or, worse, an invitation to come and stay. The door was massive, yet it swung open easily on well-oiled hinges. "Come in," said the sign. "We're always open." Inside was a cool and quiet reception room. Curtains were drawn against the outside glare, cutting the light down to a soft glow. 4

I found the funeral director in the main lobby, adjacent to the reception room. Like most people, I had preconceptions about what an undertaker looked like. Mr. Deaver fulfilled my expectations entirely. Tall and thin, he even had beady eyes and a bony face. A low, slanted forehead gave way to a beaked nose. His skin, scrubbed of all color, contrasted sharply with his jet black hair. He was wearing a starched white shirt, gray pants, and black shoes. Indeed, he looked like death on two legs. 5

He proved an amiable sort, however, and was easy to talk to. As funeral director, Mr. Deaver ("Call me Howard") was responsible for a wide range of services. Goodbody Mortuaries, upon notification of someone's death, will remove the remains from the hospital or home. They then prepare the body for viewing, whereupon features distorted by illness or accident are restored to their natural condition. The body is embalmed and then placed in a casket selected by the family of the deceased. Services are held in one of three chapels at the mortuary, and afterward the casket is placed in a "visitation room," where family and friends can pay their last respects. Goodbody also makes arrangements for the purchase of a burial site and transports the body there for burial. 6

All this information Howard related in a well-practiced, professional manner. It was obvious he was used to explaining the specifics of his profession. We sat alone in the lobby. His desk was bone clean, no pencils or paper, nothing — just a telephone. He did all his paperwork at home; as it turned out, he and his wife lived right upstairs. The phone rang. As he listened, he bit his lips and squeezed his Adam's apple somewhat nervously. 7

"I think we'll be able to get him in by Friday. No, no, the family wants him cremated." 8

His tone was that of a broker conferring on the Dow Jones. Directly behind him was a 9 sign announcing "Visa and Master Charge Welcome Here." It was tacked to the wall, right next to a crucifix.

"Some people have the idea that we are bereavement specialists, that we can 10 handle the emotional problems which follow a death: Only a trained therapist can do that. We provide services for the dead, not counseling for the living."

Physical comfort was the one thing they did provide for the living. The lobby was 11 modestly but comfortably furnished. There were several couches, in colors ranging from earth brown to pastel blue, and a coffee table in front of each one. On one table lay some magazines and a vase of flowers. Another supported an aquarium. Paintings of pastoral scenes hung on every wall. The lobby looked more or less like that of an old hotel. Nothing seemed to match, but it had a homey, lived-in look.

"The last time the Goodbodys decorated was in '59, I believe. It still makes people 12 feel welcome."

And so "Goodbody" was not a name made up to attract customers but the owner's 13 family name. The Goodbody family started the business way back in 1915. Today, they do over five hundred services a year.

"We're in *Ripley's Believe It or Not,* along with another funeral home whose owners' 14 names are Baggit and Sackit," Howard told me, without cracking a smile.

I followed him through an arched doorway into a chapel that smelled musty and old. 15 The only illumination came from sunlight filtered through a stained glass ceiling. Ahead of us lay a casket. I could see that it contained a man dressed in a black suit. Wooden benches ran on either side of an aisle that led to the body. I got no closer. From the red roses across the dead man's chest, it was apparent that services had already been held.

"It was a large service," remarked Howard. "Look at that casket—a beautiful work of 16 craftsmanship."

I guess it was. Death may be the great leveler, but one's coffin quickly reestablishes 17 one's status.

We passed into a bright, fluorescent-lit "display room." Inside were thirty coffins, lids 18 open, patiently awaiting inspection. Like new cars on the showroom floor, they gleamed with high-gloss finishes.

"We have models for every price range." 19

Indeed, there was a wide variety. They came in all colors and various materials. 20 Some were little more than cloth-covered cardboard boxes, others were made of wood, and a few were made of steel, copper, or bronze. Prices started at $400 and averaged about $1,800. Howard motioned toward the center of the room: "The top of the line."

This was a solid bronze casket, its seams electronically welded to resist corrosion. 21 Moisture-proof and air-tight, it could be hermetically sealed off from all outside elements. Its handles were plated with 14-karat gold. The price: a cool $5,000.

A proper funeral remains a measure of respect for the deceased. But it is expensive. 22 In the United States the amount spent annually on funerals is about $2 billion. Among ceremonial expenditures, funerals are second only to weddings. As a result, practices are changing. Howard has been in this business for forty years. He remembers a time when everyone was buried. Nowadays, with burials costing $2,000 a shot, people often opt instead for cremation—as Howard put it, "a cheap, quick, and easy means of disposal." In some areas of the country, the cremation rate is now over 60 percent. Observing this trend, one might wonder whether burials are becoming obsolete. Do burials serve an important role in society?

For Tim, Goodbody's licensed mortician, the answer is very definitely yes. Burials will remain in common practice, according to the slender embalmer with the disarming smile, because they allow family and friends to view the deceased. Painful as it may be, such an experience brings home the finality of death. "Something deep within us demands a confrontation with death," Tim explained. "A last look assures us that the person we loved is, indeed, gone forever." 23

Apparently, we also need to be assured that the body will be laid to rest in comfort and peace. The average casket, with its inner-spring mattress and pleated satin lining, is surprisingly roomy and luxurious. Perhaps such an air of comfort makes it easier for the family to give up their loved one. In addition, the burial site fixes the deceased in the survivors' memory, like a new address. Cremation provides none of these comforts. 24

Tim started out as a clerk in a funeral home but then studied to become a mortician. "It was a profession I could live with," he told me with a sly grin. Mortuary science might be described as a cross between pre-med and cosmetology, with courses in anatomy and embalming as well as in restorative art. 25

Tim let me see the preparation, or embalming, room, a white-walled chamber about the size of an operating room. Against the wall was a large sink with elbow taps and a draining board. In the center of the room stood a table with equipment for preparing the arterial embalming fluid, which consists primarily of formaldehyde, a preservative, and phenol, a disinfectant. This mixture sanitizes and also gives better color to the skin. Facial features can then be "set" to achieve a restful expression. Missing eyes, ears, and even noses can be replaced. 26

I asked Tim if his job ever depressed him. He bridled at the question: "No, it doesn't depress me at all. I do what I can for people and take satisfaction in enabling relatives to see their loved ones as they were in life." He said that he felt people were becoming more aware of the public service his profession provides. Grade-school classes now visit funeral homes as often as they do police stations and museums. The mortician is no longer regarded as a minister of death. 27

Before leaving, I wanted to see a body up close. I thought I could be indifferent after all I had seen and heard, but I wasn't sure. Cautiously, I reached out and touched the skin. It felt cold and firm, not unlike clay. As I walked out, I felt glad to have satisfied my curiosity about dead bodies, but all too happy to let someone else handle them. 28

Connecting to Culture and Experience: Death

"Death," Cable announces in his opening sentence, "is a subject largely ignored by the living. We don't discuss it much, not as children (when Grandpa dies, he is said to be 'going away'), not as adults, not even as senior citizens." Yet when a family member dies, every family is forced to mark death in some way.

With two or three other students, discuss how your families and friends prepare for and arrange a funeral or memorial service. Think of a funeral you have attended, or ask a family member to describe how your family traditionally marks the death of a loved one. Consider the following questions, for example: Is there a formal service? If so, where does it take place — in a house of worship, a funeral home, a private home, a cemetery, or somewhere else? Who typically attends? Do people dress formally or informally? Who speaks, and what kinds of things are said? What kind of music, if any, is played? Is the body cremated or buried? Is there usually a gathering after the formal service? If so, what is its purpose compared to the formal service?

Then, together, compare the different family traditions revealed in the services described by the members of your group. Try to answer these questions: What do you think the funeral or memorial service accomplishes for each family? What did it accomplish for you personally?

Analyzing Writing Strategies

1. How does the opening quotation from Mark Twain shape your expectations as a reader? Compare Cable's opening (the quotation and paragraphs 1 and 2) against the openings of the two other profile essays in this chapter. What can you conclude about the opening strategies of these profile writers? Given each writer's subject, materials, and purpose, which opening do you find most effective and why?

2. During his visit to the mortuary, Cable focuses on four rooms: the lobby (paragraph 11), the chapel where funeral services are conducted (15), the casket display room (18–21), and the embalming room (26). Reread Cable's descriptions of these four rooms, and then underline the details he uses to describe each room. What impression do you get of each room? What might Cable gain by contrasting them so sharply? How do these descriptions work together to convey Cable's perspective on the mortuary?

Commentary: Conveying a Perspective

By deciding to present himself as a participant in his profile, Cable can readily convey his perspective, his ideas and insights, by telling readers directly what he thinks and feels about the mortuary and the people who work there. He begins with some general ideas about death and the way that people tend to deal with death basically by ignoring it. Then, in paragraphs 3 and 4, he discusses his expectations and confesses his apprehensions about the initial visit.

Cable quotes Howard and Tim and summarizes their words, describing them and commenting on what the funeral director and mortician said. His descriptions and comments express his insights into these people and the kinds of work they do. For example, when Cable introduces Howard Deaver, the funeral director, in paragraphs 5–10, he begins by comparing Deaver to his preconceptions about what an

undertaker looks like. Then he describes Deaver, no doubt emphasizing his stereotyp-
ical features:

> Tall and thin, he even had beady eyes and a bony face. A low, slanted forehead gave
> way to a beaked nose. His skin, scrubbed of all color, contrasted sharply with his jet
> black hair. He was wearing a starched white shirt, gray pants, and black shoes. Indeed,
> he looked like death on two legs. (5)

The description creates an image that reinforces the stereotype of an undertaker. But
that is apparently not the perspective he wants to convey because Cable quickly re-
places this stereotype with a different one when he describes Howard's tone on the
telephone with a client as "that of a broker conferring on the Dow Jones" (paragraph 9).
To make sure readers get the idea that mortuaries are a big business, Cable points out
that on the wall directly behind Howard "was a sign announcing 'Visa and Master
Charge Welcome Here.'" Skillfully combining direct comment and concise description (sometimes called telling and showing), Cable conveys a perspective on mortuaries as efficient, profit-seeking businesses that nevertheless understand that their
services provide clients with what they want and need at a difficult time.

Considering Topics for Your Own Essay

Try to list at least two or three places or activities that you have strong preconceptions
about, and add a few notes to each one describing the preconception. For example,
you might think that fast-food places are popular because their customers have few
other choices of places to eat, that counselors will put pressure on you to conform if
you ask for help with a personal problem at the student counseling center, that car
repair shops regularly perform unnecessary repairs and overcharge customers, or that
college librarians are too busy to help students find sources for their essays. Choose
one such place or activity, and think about how you would go about profiling it. How
would you test your preconception? How might you use your preconception to
heighten readers' interest in your profile?

■ PURPOSE AND AUDIENCE

A profile writer's primary purpose is to inform readers about the subject of the profile.
Readers expect a profile to present information in an engaging way, however. Whether
profiling people, places, or activities, the writer must engage as well as inform readers.
Readers of profiles expect to be surprised by unusual subjects. If the subject is familiar,
they expect it to be presented from an unusual perspective. When writing a profile,
you will have an immediate advantage if your subject is a place, an activity, or a person
that is likely to surprise and intrigue your readers. For example, the writer of "I'm Not
Leaving Until I Eat This Thing" (pp. 67–70) has the triple advantage of being able to
describe an unusual snack food, a little-known production process, and a colorful bar
in which he can try out the unusual snack. Even when your subject is familiar, how-

ever, you can still engage your readers by presenting it in a way they have never before considered. For example, the writer of "The Last Stop" describes a mortuary owner as an ordinary, efficient businessman and not a "bereavement specialist."

A profile writer has one further concern: to be sensitive to readers' knowledge of a subject. Since readers must imagine the subject profiled and understand the new information offered about it, the writer must carefully assess what readers are likely to know already. For a profile of a pig-products processor, the decisions of a writer whose readers have likely never seen a pickled pig lip or foot will be quite different from those of a writer whose readers occasionally hang out in jukes and other bars where pickled pig products are always visible floating in a bottle of garish-colored vinegar. Given Edge's attention to detail, he is clearly writing for a general audience that has never before seen a pickled pig lip or foot, much less considered eating one.

BASIC FEATURES: PROFILES

Description of People and Places

Successful profile writers master the strategies of description. The profiles in this chapter, for example, evoke all the senses: *sight* ("the pink juice pooling on the bar in front of me," Edge, paragraph 15); *touch* ("slick with grease," Edge, 16; "the skin...felt cold and firm, not unlike clay," Cable, 28); *smell* ("Vinegar vapors tickle my nostrils," Edge, 16); *taste* ("hot and vinegary," Edge, 7); *hearing* ("[plates] thudding on the counter under their own weight," Hall, 17; "sneakers squeaking across the wet pavement," Hall, 19); and *physical sensation* ("a gag that rolls from the back of my throat," Edge, 16; "my stomach ceases its fluttering," Edge, 18). *Similes* (elementary school students "like a mob running in panic from a fire," Hall, 19) and *metaphors* ("the air conditioner hacks and spits forth torrents of Arctic air," Edge, 1) appear occasionally.

Profile writers often describe people in graphic detail ("his shy smile framed by a coarse black mustache," Edge, 8; "beady eyes and a bony face," Cable, 5). They show people moving and gesturing ("he bit his lips and squeezed his Adam's apple," Cable, 7; "I poke and prod the six-inch arc of pink flesh," Edge, 14). Writers rely on dialogue to reveal character ("Look at that casket—a beautiful work of craftsmanship," Cable, 16; "You gonna eat that thing or make love to it?," Edge, 14).

Information about the Subject

Profile writers give much thought to how and where to introduce information to their readers. After all, readers expect to be informed—to learn something surprising or useful. To meet this expectation, profile writers' basic strategy is to interweave information with descriptions of the subject (as Cable does profiling a mortuary) and with narratives of events (as Edge does when he struggles to eat a pig lip). Throughout their profiles, writers make good use of several strategies relied on by all writers of explanation: classification, example or illustration, comparison and contrast, definition, process narration, and cause and effect.

Edge classifies information about Farm Fresh when, in one part of his profile, he divides information about the business into four categories: rebirth of the family business, family involvement, marketing strategies, and customer relations. Hall gives several examples of the kinds of food served at the Edison Café. Cable defines the terms "mortuary science" and "embalming fluid." Edge narrates the process of preparing and bottling pig lips and, after receiving instruction, of eating one. Edge presents the causes of Farm Fresh's failure as a business and of its rebirth, and he discloses frankly the effects of his attempts to eat a pig lip.

A Topical or Narrative Plan

Profile writers rely on two basic plans for reporting their observations: *topical*, with the information grouped into topics; and *narrative*, with the information interwoven with elements of a story. The profiles by Hall and Cable are organized narratively. In each, the narrative is a story of a single visit to a place. For Hall, the visit is a long morning from 6:30 A.M. to 12:30 P.M. spent at the Edison Café; even the long chunk of information about Skagit Valley that Hall presumably acquired at a different time (paragraphs 5–7) is inserted into the morning narrative. For Cable, the visit is one of indeterminate length, probably two or three hours, to Goodbody Mortuaries. (Some profile writers present information gathered from several visits as though it was learned in a single visit.)

In the central segment of his profile of a southern pig-products producer, Edge organizes the information topically: He creates topics out of the many bits of information he gathers on the tour of Farm Fresh led by the owner, Lionel Dufour, and then sequences them in the profile in a way that he thinks will be most informative to readers. Yet Edge frames the information about Farm Fresh with a narrative of his attempts to eat one of its products, illustrating that a profile can be organized topically in some parts and narratively in others. Usually, however, one plan or the other predominates. Which plan you adopt will depend on your subject, the kinds of information you collect, and your assessment of what might be most engaging and informative for your readers.

A Role for the Writer

Profile writers must adopt a role or stance for themselves when they present their subjects. There are two basic options: detached observer and participant observer. Hall remains a detached and invisible observer throughout his profile. There is no evidence that he participates in any of the activities or conversations at the Edison Café. In the central part of his profile, where he presents what he learned on his visit to Farm Fresh Food Supplier, Edge, too, is a detached observer. We can easily infer that he asked questions and made comments, but he decides not to report any of them; instead, he focuses unwaveringly on the equipment, canning process, workers, and Dufour family members. By contrast, Cable adopts a participant-observer role. Even before he enters the mortuary, he inserts himself personally into the profile, reflecting on death, expressing his disappointment in the appearance of the place, admitting his apprehension about entering, revealing his sense of humor. Readers know where he is at all times as his tour of the building proceeds, and he seems as much a participant in the narrative of his visit as Deaver and Tim are. Before he leaves the mortuary, he touches a corpse, to satisfy his curiosity. Edge adopts a participant-observer role when he tries to eat a pig's lip in the juke.

A Perspective on the Subject

Profile writers do not simply present their observations of a subject; they also offer insights into the person, place, or activity being profiled. They may convey a perspective on their subjects by stating it explicitly, by implying it through the descriptive details and other information they include, or both. Cable shares his realization that Americans seem to capitalize on death as a way of coping with it. Hall comes to understand that the warm, civil social interactions he observes at the Edison Café are more than merely pleasurable for the patrons: They are essential to social cohesion in Skagit Valley. Edge's perspective on pig products is less explicit, but perhaps, as a specialist in southern cooking, he hopes to convey the impression that regional foods remain important to many of the people who live in a region. In small southern towns, bar patrons are not satisfied by peanuts, pretzels, and packaged cheese and crackers. They want a soft, pink, vinegary pig lip shaken in a bag of crushed potato chips.

GUIDE TO WRITING
Profiles

THE WRITING ASSIGNMENT

Write an essay about an intriguing person, place, or activity in your community. Observe your subject closely, and then present what you have learned in a way that both informs and engages readers.

THE WRITING ASSIGNMENT

INVENTION & RESEARCH

Finding a Subject to Write About

Exploring Your Preconceptions

Planning Your Project

Posing Some Preliminary Questions

Discovering a Perspective

Considering Your Own Role

Defining Your Purpose for Your Readers

Formulating a Tentative Thesis Statement

Considering Document Design

INVENTION AND RESEARCH

PLANNING & DRAFTING

Seeing What You Have

Setting Goals

Outlining

Drafting

PLANNING AND DRAFTING

CRITICAL READING GUIDE

First Impression

Organization

The Writer's Role

Description

Quality and Presentation of Information

The Writer's Perspective

Final Thoughts

CRITICAL READING GUIDE

REVISING

A Description of People and Places

Information about the Subject

A Topical or Narrative Plan

A Role for the Writer

A Perspective on the Subject

REVISING

EDITING & PROOFREADING

Checking the Punctuation of Quotations

A Common ESL Problem: Adjective Order

EDITING AND PROOFREADING

■ THE WRITING ASSIGNMENT

Write an essay about an intriguing person, place, or activity in your community. Observe your subject closely, and then present what you have learned in a way that both informs and engages readers.

■ INVENTION AND RESEARCH

Preparing to write a profile involves several activities, such as finding a subject, exploring your preconceptions about it, planning your project, and posing some preliminary questions. Each step takes no more than a few minutes, yet together these activities will enable you to anticipate problems likely to arise in a complex project like a profile, to arrange and schedule your interviews wisely, and to take notes and gather materials in a productive way. There is much to learn about observing, interviewing, and writing about what you have learned, and these activities will support your learning.

Finding a Subject to Write About

When you choose a subject, you consider various possibilities, select a promising one, and check that particular subject's accessibility.

Listing Subjects. *Make a list of subjects to consider for your profile.* Even if you already have a subject in mind, take a few minutes to consider some other possibilities. The more possibilities you consider, the more confident you can be about your choice. Do not overlook the subjects suggested by the Considering Topics for Your Own Essay activities following each reading in this chapter.

Before you list possible subjects, consider realistically the time you have available and the amount of observing and interviewing you will be able to accomplish. Whether you have a week to plan and write up one observational visit or interview or a month to develop a full profile will determine what kinds of subjects will be appropriate for you. Consult with your instructor if you need help defining the scope of your profile project.

Here we present some ideas you might use as starting points for a list of subjects. Try to extend your list to ten or twelve possibilities. Consider every subject you can think of, even unlikely ones. People like to read about the unusual.

People

- Anyone with an unusual or intriguing job or hobby — a private detective, bee-keeper, classic-car owner, or dog trainer

- A prominent local personality—a parent of the year, labor organizer, politician, consumer advocate, television or radio personality, or community activist
- A campus personality—a coach, distinguished teacher, or ombudsman
- Someone recently recognized for outstanding service or achievement—a volunteer, mentor, or therapist

Places

- A weight-reduction clinic, martial arts studio, body-building gym, or health spa
- A small-claims court, juvenile court, or consumer fraud office
- A used-car lot, old movie house, used-book store, antique shop, historic site, auction hall, flower or gun show, or farmers' or flea market
- A hospital emergency room, hospice, birthing center, or psychiatric unit
- A local diner; the oldest, biggest, or quickest restaurant in town; or a coffeehouse
- A campus radio station, computer center, agricultural research facility, student center, faculty club, museum, newspaper office, or health center
- A book, newspaper, or Internet publisher; florist shop, nursery, or greenhouse; pawnshop; boatyard; or automobile restorer or wrecking yard
- A recycling center; fire station; airport control tower; theater, opera, or symphony office; refugee center; orphanage; or convent or monastery

Activities

- A citizens' volunteer program—a voter registration service, public television auction, meals-on-wheels project, tutoring program, or election campaign
- A sports event—a marathon, Frisbee tournament, chess match, or wrestling or boxing meet
- A hobby—folk dancing, roller blading, rock climbing, or poetry reading

Listing Subjects Related to Identity and Community.   Writing a profile about a person or a place in your community can help you learn more about particular individuals in your community and about institutions and activities fundamental to community life. By *community* we mean both geographic communities, such as towns and neighborhoods, and institutional and temporary communities, such as religious congregations, college students majoring in the same subject, volunteer organizations, and sports teams. The following suggestions will enable you to list several possible subjects.

People

- Someone who has made or is currently making an important contribution to a community

- Someone who is a prominent member of one of the communities you belong to and can help you define and understand that community
- Someone in a community who is generally tolerated but is not liked or respected, such as a homeless person, a gruff store owner, or an unorthodox church member, or someone who has been or is in danger of being shunned or exiled from a community
- Someone who has built a successful business, overcome a disability or setback, supported a worthy cause, served as a role model, or won respect from coworkers or neighbors

Places

- A facility that provides a needed service in a community, such as a legal advice bureau, child-care center, medical clinic, or shelter offering free meals
- A place where people of different ages, genders, ethnic groups, or some other attribute have formed a kind of ongoing community, such as a chess table in the park, political or social action headquarters, computer class, local coffeehouse, or barber or beauty shop
- A place where people come together because they are of the same age, gender, or ethnic group, such as a seniors-only housing complex, a boathouse for a men's crew team, a campus women's center, or an African American or Asian American student center
- An Internet site where people form a virtual community, such as a chat room, game parlor, or bulletin board

Activities

- A team practicing a sport or other activity (one you can observe as an outsider, not as a participant)
- A community improvement project, such as graffiti cleaning, tree planting, house repairing, church painting, or highway litter pickup
- A group of researchers working collaboratively on a project

Listing Subjects Related to Work and Career. The following categories will help you consider work- and career-related subjects. Writing a profile on one of these possibilities can help you learn more about your attitudes toward your own work and career goals by examining how others do their work and pursue their careers.

People

- A college senior or graduate student in a major you are considering
- Someone working in the career you are thinking of pursuing
- Someone who trains people to do the kind of work you would like to do

Places

- A place on campus where students work—the library, computer center, cafeteria, bookstore, office, or tutoring or learning center
- A place where you could learn more about the kind of career you would like to pursue—a law office, medical center, veterinary hospital, research institute, television station, newspaper, school, software manufacturer, or engineering firm
- A place where people do a kind of work you would like to know more about—a clothing factory, coal mine, dairy farm, racetrack, restaurant, bakery, commercial fishing boat, gardening nursery, nursing home, or delicatessen
- A place where people are trained for a certain kind of work or career—a police academy, cosmetology program, video repair course, or truck drivers' school

Activities

- The actual activities performed by someone doing a kind of work represented on television, such as that of a police detective, judge, attorney, newspaper reporter, taxi driver, novelist, or emergency room doctor
- The activities involved in preparing for a particular kind of work, such as a boxer preparing for a fight, an attorney preparing for a trial, a teacher or professor preparing a course, an actor rehearsing a role, or a musician practicing for a concert

Choosing a Subject.   *Look over your list of possibilities, and choose a subject that you find you want to know more about and that your readers will find interesting.* Note, too, that most profile writers report the greatest satisfaction and the best results when they profile an unfamiliar person, place, or activity. If you choose a subject with which you are somewhat familiar, try to study it in an unfamiliar setting. For example, if you are a rock climber and decide to write a profile on rock climbing, do not rely exclusively on your own knowledge of and authority on the subject. Seek out other rock-climbing enthusiasts, even interview some critics of the sport to get another perspective, or visit a rock-climbing event or training class where you can observe without participating. By adopting an outsider's perspective on a familiar subject, you can make writing your profile a process of discovery for yourself as well as for your readers.

Stop now to focus your thoughts. *In a sentence or two, identify the subject you have chosen, and explain why you think it is a good choice for you and your readers.*

Checking on Accessibility.   *Take steps to ensure that your subject will be accessible to you.* Having chosen a subject, you need to be certain you will be able to make observations and conduct interviews to learn more about it. Find out who might be able to give you information by making some preliminary phone calls. Explain that you need information for a school research project. You will be surprised how helpful people can be when they have the time. If you are unable to contact knowledgeable people or get access to the place you need to observe, you may not be able to write on this subject. Therefore, try to make these initial contacts early.

Exploring Your Preconceptions

Explore your initial thoughts and feelings about your subject in writing before you begin observing or interviewing. Write for a few minutes about your thoughts, using the following questions as a guide:

What I already know about this subject

- How can I define or describe it?
- What are its chief qualities or parts?
- Do I associate anyone or anything with it?
- What is its purpose or function?
- How does it compare with other, similar subjects?

My attitude toward this subject

- Why do I consider it intriguing?
- What about it most interests me?
- Do I like it? Respect it? Understand it?

My own and my readers' expectations

- How do my preconceptions of this subject compare with my readers'?
- What might be unique about my preconceptions?
- What attitudes about this subject do I share with my readers?
- How is this subject represented in the media?
- What values and ideas are associated with subjects of this kind?

Testing Your Choice: A Collaborative Activity

At this point, you will find it useful to get together with two or three other students and describe the subject you have chosen to profile. Your instructor may ask you to do this collaborative activity either in class or online, using a chat room for your real-time discussion. It will help you decide whether you have chosen a good subject to write about, one that will allow you to proceed confidently as you develop your profile.

Presenters: Take turns identifying your subjects. Explain your interest in the subject, and speculate about why you think it will interest your readers.

Listeners: Briefly tell each presenter what you already know about his or her subject, if anything, and what would make it interesting to readers.

Planning Your Project

Set up a tentative schedule for your observational and interview visits. Whatever the scope of your project—a single observation, an interview with one follow-up exchange, or multiple observations and interviews—you will want to get the most out of your time with your subject.

Take time now to figure out the amount of time you have to complete your essay, and then decide what visits you will need to make, whom you will need to interview, and what library or Internet research you might want to do, if any. Estimate the time necessary for each. You might use a chart like the following one:

Date	Time Needed	Purpose	Preparation
10/23	1 hour	Observe	Bring map, directions, paper
10/25	2 hours	Library research	Bring references, change or copycard for copy machine
10/26	45 minutes	Interview	Read brochure and prepare questions
10/30	3 hours	Observe and interview	Confirm appointment; bring questions and extra pen

You will probably have to modify your plan once you actually begin work, but it is a good idea to keep some sort of schedule in writing.

If you are developing a full profile, your first goal is to get your bearings. Some writers begin by observing; others start with an interview. Many read up on the subject before doing anything else to get a sense of its main elements. You may also want to read about other subjects similar to the one you have chosen. Save your notes.

Researching Your Profile Subject: An Online Activity

One way to get a quick initial overview of the information available on the subject of your profile is to search for the subject online. Use Google (www.google.com) or Yahoo! Directory (http://dir.yahoo.com) to discover possible sources of information about the subject:

- For example, if you are profiling a beekeeper, you could get some useful background information to guide you in planning your interview by entering "bee keeping."
- If you are profiling a person, enter the full name to discover whether he or she has a personal Web site. If you are profiling a business or institution, the chances are even better that it offers a site. Either kind of site would orient and inform you prior to your interview or first visit.

Bookmark or keep a record of promising sites. After your interview with or visit to the subject, download any materials, including visuals, you might consider including in your own essay. If you find little or no information about your subject online, do not lose confidence in your choice. All of the information you need to develop your profile can come from your observations and interviews when you visit your subject.

Posing Some Preliminary Questions

Write questions to prepare for your first visit. Before beginning your observations and interviews, try writing some questions for which you would like to find answers. These questions will orient you and allow you to focus your visits. As you work, you will find answers to many of these questions. Add to this list as new questions occur to you, and delete any that come to seem irrelevant.

Each subject invites its own special questions, and every writer has particular concerns. Consider, for example, how one student prepares interview questions for her profile of a local office of the Women's Health Initiative, a nationwide fifteen-year study of women's health established by the National Institutes of Health in 1991. After reading about the long-term health study in her local newspaper, the student calls the local WHI office to get further information. The administrator faxes her a fact sheet on the study and her office's special part in it. The student knows that she will need to mention the study in her profile of the local office and the people who work there. She also hopes to interview women who volunteer to participate in the research. Consequently, she devises the following questions to launch her research and prepare for her interview of the local director:

- Why has so little research been done until recently on women's health?
- How did the study come about, and what is the role of the National Institutes of Health?
- Why does the study focus only on women between the ages of fifty and eighty?
- Will women from all income levels be involved?
- Why will it take fifteen years to complete the study?
- When was this office established, and what role does it play in the national study?
- Does the office simply coordinate the study, or does it also provide health and medical advice to women participating in the study?
- Who works at the office, and what are their qualifications to work there?
- Will I be able to interview women who volunteer to participate in the research?
- Will I be permitted to take photographs at the office?
- Would it be appropriate to take photographs of the researchers and participants, if they give their consent?

Discovering a Perspective

After you have completed your observations and interviews, write for a few minutes, reflecting on what you now think is interesting and meaningful about the person, place, or activity you have chosen for your profile. Consider how you would answer these questions about your subject:

- What visual or other sensory impression is most memorable?
- What does this impression tell me about the person, place, or activity?
- What mood do I associate with my subject?
- What about my subject is most striking and likely to surprise or interest my readers?
- What is the most important thing I have learned about my subject? Why is it important?
- If I could find out the answer to one more question about my subject, what would that question be? Why is this question important?
- What about my subject says something larger about our culture and times?
- Which of my ideas, interpretations, or judgments do I most want to share with readers?

Considering Your Own Role

Decide tentatively whether you will adopt a detached-observer or participant-observer role to present your profile. As a detached observer, you would focus solely on the place and people, keeping yourself invisible to readers. As a participant-observer, you would insert yourself personally into the profile by reporting what you said or thought during interviews and commenting on the activities you observe.

Defining Your Purpose for Your Readers

Write a few sentences, defining your purpose in writing about this particular person, place, or activity for your readers. Use these questions to focus your thoughts:

- Who are my readers? Apart from my instructors and classmates, who would be interested in reading an essay about this particular subject? If I were to try to publish my essay, what magazine, newspaper, newsletter, or Web site might want a profile on this particular subject? Would people who work in a particular kind of business or who pursue certain kinds of hobbies or sports be interested in the essay?
- What do I want my readers to learn about the person, place, or activity from reading my essay?
- What insight can I offer my readers about the person, place, or activity?

Formulating a Tentative Thesis Statement

Review what you wrote for Discovering a Perspective (p. 96), and add another two or three sentences that will help you tell readers what you understand about the person, place, or activity on which you are focusing. Try to write sentences that extend your insights and interpretations and that do not simply summarize what you have already written.

Keep in mind that readers do not expect you to begin a profile essay with the kind of explicit thesis statement typical of argumentative essays. If you decide to tell readers your perspective on the person, place, or activity, you will most likely do so through interpretive or evaluative comments as you describe people and places, present dialogue, and narrate what you observed. You are not obliged to tell readers your perspective, but you should show it through the way you profile the subject.

Considering Document Design

Think about whether visual or audio elements—photographs, postcards, menus, or snippets from films, television programs, or songs—would strengthen your profile. These are not at all a requirement of an effective profile, but they sometimes are helpful. Consider also whether your readers might benefit from design features such as headings, bulleted or numbered lists, or other typographic elements that can make an essay easier to follow.

■ PLANNING AND DRAFTING

This section will help you review your invention writing and research notes and get started on your first draft.

Seeing What You Have

Read over your invention materials to see what you have. You probably have a great deal of material—notes from observational and interview visits or from library research, some idea of your preconceptions, a list of questions, and perhaps even some answers. You should also have a tentative perspective on the subject, some idea about it or insight into it. Your goals at this point are to digest all of the information you have gathered; to pick out the promising facts, details, anecdotes, and quotations; and to see how it all might come together to present your subject and your perspective on it to readers.

If you have done your invention writing on the computer, you may have sentences or whole paragraphs that can be copied and pasted into your draft. Whether your material is on screen or on paper, highlight key words, phrases, and sentences, and either make annotations in the margins or use your computer's annotating function.

As you sort through your material, try asking yourself the following questions to help clarify your focus and interpretation:

- How do my preconceptions of the subject contrast with my findings about it?
- Can I compare or contrast what different people say about my subject? Do I see any discrepancies between people's words and their behavior?
- How do my reactions compare with those of the people directly involved?
- How could I consider the place's appearance in light of the activity that occurs there?
- If I examine my subject as an anthropologist or archaeologist would, what evidence could explain its role in society at large?
- Could I use a visual or other graphic to complement the text?

Setting Goals

The following questions will help you establish goals for your first draft. Consider each question briefly now, and then return to them as necessary as you draft and revise.

Your Purpose and Readers

- Are my readers likely to be familiar with my subject? If not, what details do I need to provide to help them understand and visualize it?
- If my readers are familiar with my subject, how can I present it to them in a new and engaging way? What information do I have that is likely to be unfamiliar or entertaining to them?
- What design elements might make my writing more interesting or easier for readers to understand?

The Beginning

The opening is especially important in a profile. Because readers are unlikely to have any particular reason to read a profile, the writer must arouse their curiosity and interest. The best beginnings are surprising and specific; the worst are abstract. Here are some strategies you might consider:

- Should I open with a brief anecdote, as Edge does, or an intriguing epigraph, as Cable does? Or can I open with an emphatic statement?
- Should I simply begin at the beginning, as Hall does?
- Can I start with an amazing fact, anecdote, or question that would catch readers' attention?

Description of People and Places

- How might I give readers a strong visual image of people and places?
- Can I think of a simile or metaphor that would help me present an evocative image?

- Which bits of dialogue would convey information about my subject as well as a vivid impression of the speaker?
- What specific narrative actions can I include to show people moving and gesturing?

Information about the Subject

- How can I fully satisfy readers' needs for information about my subject?
- How can I manage the flow of information so that readers do not lose interest?
- What special terms will I need to define for my readers?
- Would comparisons or contrasts make the information clearer and more memorable?

A Narrative or Topical Plan

Profile writers use two basic methods of organizing information, arranging it narratively like a story or topically by grouping related materials.

If You Use a Narrative Plan

- How can I make the narrative interesting, perhaps even dramatic?
- What information should I present through dialogue, and what information should I interrupt the narrative to present?
- How much space should I devote to describing people and places and to telling what happened during a visit?
- If I have the option of including design elements, how might I use them effectively — to clarify the sequence of events, highlight a dramatic part of the narrative, or illustrate how the people and places in the profile changed over time?

If You Use a Topical Plan

- Which topics will best inform my readers and hold their interest?
- How can I sequence the topics to bring out significant comparisons or contrasts?
- What transitions will help readers make connections between topics?
- If I have the option of including design elements, are there ways I can use them effectively to reinforce the topical organization?

A Perspective on the Subject

- How can I convey a perspective on the subject that seems original or at least fresh?
- Should I state my perspective or leave readers to infer it from the details of my presentation?

The Ending

- Should I try to frame the essay by repeating an image or phrase from the beginning or by completing an action begun earlier in the profile?
- Would it be effective to end by stating or restating my perspective?
- Should I end with a telling image, anecdote, or bit of dialogue or with a provocative question or connection?

Outlining

If you plan to arrange your material narratively, plot the key events on a timeline. If you plan to arrange your material topically, you might use clustering or topic outlining to help you divide and group related information.

The following outline suggests one possible way to organize a narrative profile of a place:

Begin by describing the place from the outside.

Present background information.

Describe what you see as you enter.

Introduce the people and activities.

Tour the place, describing what you see as you move from one part to the next.

Fill in information, and comment about the place or the people.

Conclude with reflections on what you have learned about the place.

Here is a suggested outline for a topical profile about a person:

Begin with a vivid image of the person in action.

Use dialogue to present the first topic.

Narrate an anecdote or a procedure to illustrate the first topic.

Present the second topic.

Describe something related to it.

Evaluate or interpret what you have observed.

Present the third topic, etc.

Conclude with a bit of action or dialogue.

All of the material for these hypothetical essays would come from observations, interviews, and background reading. The plan you choose should reflect the possibilities in your material as well as your purpose and readers. At this point, your decisions must be tentative. As you begin drafting, you will almost certainly discover new ways of organizing your material. Once you have written a first draft, you and others may see better ways to organize the material for your particular audience.

Drafting

General Advice.   Start drafting your essay, keeping in mind the goals you set while you were planning. As you write, try to describe your subject in a way that conveys your perspective on it. Turn off your grammar checker and spelling checker at this stage if you find them distracting. Don't be afraid to skip around in your draft. Jump back and fill in a spontaneous idea, or leap ahead and write a later section first if you find that easier. If you get stuck while drafting, explore the problem by using some of the writing activities in the Invention and Research section of this chapter (pp. 89–97).

As you read over your first draft, you may see places where you can add new material to reveal more about the person, place, or activity. You may even decide that after this first draft, you can finally understand the complexity of your subject and set out to convey it more fully in a second draft.

Sentence Strategies.   As you draft a profile, you will need to present what people have said to you and others during your observations and interviews and to help your readers imagine the actions, people, and objects you have encountered. Two sentence strategies called *speaker tags* and *absolute phrases* are useful for these purposes.

Use general and specific speaker tags along with other words and phrases to present what people say. When you directly quote (rather than paraphrase or summarize) what someone has said, you will usually need to identify the speaker. The principal way to do so is to create what is called a *speaker tag*.

You may rely on a *general* or all-purpose speaker tag, using forms of *say* and *tell:*

"We keep them under control," Emma *says*. (Trevor B. Hall, paragraph 20)

"It was a large service," *remarked* Howard. (Brian Cable, paragraph 16)

Other speaker tags may be more *specific* or precise:

"We used to buy lips from Dennis Di Salvo's company down in Belle Chasse," *recalled* Lionel. (John T. Edge, paragraph 9)

"Mornin'," *shouts* Julie from the kitchen. (Trevor B. Hall, paragraph 2)

As you draft your profile, consider using specific speaker tags. They give readers more help with imagining speakers' attitudes and personal styles. In addition, to any speaker tag you may add a word or phrase to identify or describe the speaker or to reveal more precisely *how, where, when,* or *why* the speaker speaks:

"We're in *Ripley's Believe It or Not,* along with another funeral home whose owners' names are Baggit and Sackit," Howard told me, *without cracking a smile.* (Brian Cable, paragraph 14)

"We do our best to corner the market on lips," Lionel told me, *his voice tinged with bravado.* (John T. Edge, paragraph 11)

"Now, don't you bad mouth me for that one," *she gently warns* a loser as she makes way back to the griddle. (Trevor B. Hall, paragraph 13)

Even though all of these sentence resources are available to help you make speaker tags more precise and revealing, keep in mind that experienced writers rely on general speaker tags using forms of *say* and *tell* without any added material for most of their sentences with quotations. Also keep in mind that some dialogue can be introduced without speaker tags, if it is likely the reader can infer from the context who is speaking. Turn to Brian Cable's essay for examples in paragraphs 8 and 10.

Use absolute phrases to help readers better imagine actions and people or objects. In profiling a subject, an unusual but very effective kind of sentence enables you to show simultaneous parts of a complex action or to detail observations of a person or object. Such a sentence relies on a grammatical structure known as an *absolute phrase,* which adds meaning to a sentence but does not modify any particular word in the rest of the sentence. (You need not remember its name or the grammatical explanation for it to use the absolute phrase effectively in your writing.) Here is an example, with the absolute phrase in italics:

> Slowly, the dank barroom fills with grease-smeared mechanics from the truck stop up the road and farmers straight from the fields, *the soles of their brogans thick with dirt clods.* (John T. Edge, paragraph 1)

Edge could have presented his observations of the farmers' shoes in a separate sentence, but the sentence he actually wrote helps to make more concrete and vivid the general idea that the customers who frequent Jesse's Place are working people arriving "straight from" their labors. Absolute phrases nearly always are attached to the end of a main clause, adding various kinds of details to it to create a more complex, informative sentence. They are usually introduced by a noun or a possessive pronoun like *his* or *their.* Here are three further examples of absolute phrases from this chapter's readings:

> This was a solid bronze casket, *its seams electronically welded to resist corrosion.* (Brian Cable, paragraph 21)

> Inside were thirty coffins, *lids open,* patiently awaiting inspection. (Brian Cable, paragraph 18)

> I offer the bag to Jerry, order yet another beer, and turn to eye the pig feet floating in a murky jar by the cash register, *their blunt tips bobbing up through a pasty white film.* (John T. Edge, paragraph 19)

Absolute phrases are certainly not required for a successful profile — experienced writers use them only occasionally — yet they do offer writers an effective sentence option. Try them out in your own writing.

In addition to using specific speaker tags and absolute phrases, you can strengthen your profile with other kinds of sentences as well, and you may want to turn to the discussions of sentences that place references to time at the beginning (p. 55).

CRITICAL READING GUIDE

Now is the time to get a good critical reading of your draft. Writers usually find it helpful to have someone else read and comment on their drafts, and all writers know how much they learn about writing when they read other writers' drafts. Your instructor may schedule readings of drafts as part of your coursework—in class or online. If not, you can ask a classmate, friend, or family member to read your draft. You could also seek comments from a tutor at your campus writing center. The guidelines in this section can be used by *anyone* reviewing a profile. (If you are unable to have someone else read your draft, turn ahead to the Revising section on p. 105, where you will find guidelines for reading your own draft critically.)

If you read another student's draft online, you may be able to use a word processing program to insert suggested improvements directly into the text of the draft or to write them out at the end of the draft. If you read a printout of the draft, you may write brief comments in the margins and lengthier suggestions on a separate page. When the writer sits down to revise, your thoughtful, extended suggestions written at the end of the draft or on separate pages will be especially helpful.

If You Are the Writer. To provide comments that are focused and helpful, your reader must know your essay's intended audience, your purpose, and a problem in the draft that you need help solving. Briefly write out this information at the top of your draft.

- *Readers:* Identify the intended readers of your essay.
- *Purpose:* What do you hope your readers will see and learn about your subject?
- *Problem:* Ask your draft reader to help you solve the most important problem you see with your draft. Describe this problem briefly.

If You Are the Reader. The following guidelines can be useful for approaching a draft with a well-focused, questioning eye.

1. *Read for a First Impression.* Read first to get a general impression. Then briefly write about the profile's perspective on its subject or main insight into it, as you best understand it. Next, consider the problem the writer identified, and respond briefly to that concern now. (If you find that the problem is covered by one of the other guidelines listed below, respond to it in more detail there if necessary.)

2. *Analyze the Effectiveness of the Organization.* Consider the overall plan, perhaps by making a scratch outline. Keep in mind that the plan may be narrative or topical or a combination of the two. If the plan narrates a visit (or visits) to a place, point out places where the narrative slows unnecessarily or

shows gaps. Point out where time markers and transitions would help. Let the writer know whether the narrative arouses and holds your curiosity. Where does dialogue fall flat, and where does it convey immediacy and drama? If the plan is organized topically, note whether the writer presents too much or too little information for a topic and whether topics might be sequenced differently or connected more clearly. Finally, decide whether the writer might strengthen the profile by reordering any of the parts or the details.

- *Look again at the beginning* of the essay to see whether it captures your attention. If not, is there a quotation, a fact, or an anecdote elsewhere in the draft that might make a better opening?

- *Look again at the ending* to see whether it leaves you hanging, seems too abrupt, or oversimplifies the subject. If it does, suggest another way of ending, possibly by moving a part or a quotation from elsewhere in the essay.

- *Look again at any visuals.* Tell the writer how well the visuals—headings, lists, tables, photographs, drawings, video—are integrated into the profile. Advise the writer about any visuals that seem misplaced or unnecessary.

3. *Evaluate the Writer's Role.* Decide whether the writer has adopted the participant-observer or detached-observer role or a combination of the two roles to present the profile subject. The writer has likely chosen one role or the other, but if both roles are visibly present, evaluate whether the writer really needs both roles or whether the alternation between the two is too frequent or confusing in any way. If the writer remains throughout in a participant-observer role, look for places where the writer is perhaps too prominent, dominating rather than featuring the subject. Point out where the writer-participant is most appealing and informative and also, perhaps, most distracting and tiresome. If the writer remains throughout in the detached-observer role, notice whether the writer consistently directs you where and how to look at the subject, keeping you confidently moving through the profile.

4. *Analyze the Description of People and Places.* Begin by pointing out two or three places in the profile where the description of people, places, and activities or processes is most vivid for you, where your attention is held and you can readily imagine who or what is being described. Identify places where you would like more descriptive details. Also indicate where you need to see people in action—moving, talking, gesturing—to understand what is going on.

5. *Assess the Quality and Presentation of the Information about the Subject.* Show the writer where you learned something truly interesting, surprising, or useful. Point out where the information is too complex, coming at you

too quickly, or incomplete. Ask for definitions of words you do not understand or clarification of definitions that do not seem immediately clear. Ask for a fuller description of any activity or process you cannot readily understand. Assess the clarity and informativeness of all visuals and design features. If there are parts of the information about the subject that you think could be better presented or complemented by visuals, let the writer know. Show the writer where the interweaving of description and information seems out of balance—too much of one or the other for too long.

6. *Question the Writer's Perspective on the Subject.* Begin by trying to state briefly what you believe to be the writer's perspective on the subject—some idea or insight the writer wants to convey. (This perspective statement may differ from the one you wrote at the beginning of your critical reading of this draft.) Then look for and underline one or two places where the writer explicitly states or implies a perspective. If the perspective is stated, tell the writer whether you fully understand or would welcome some elaboration. If the perspective is only implied, let the writer know whether you are content with the implication or whether you would prefer to have the perspective explicitly stated. With the writer's perspective in mind, skim the draft one last time looking for unneeded or extraneous description and information.

7. *Give the Writer Your Final Thoughts.* What is the draft's strongest part? What part is most memorable? What part is weakest or most in need of further work?

■ REVISING

This section will help you get an overview of your draft and revise it accordingly.

Getting an Overview

Consider your draft as a whole, following these two steps:

1. *Reread.* If at all possible, put the draft aside for a day or two. When you do reread it, start by reconsidering your purpose. Then read the draft straight through, trying to see it as your intended readers will.

2. *Outline.* Make a quick scratch outline on paper, or use the headings and outline/summary functions of your word processor.

Planning for Revision.   Resist the temptation to dive in and start changing your text until after you have a comprehensive view of what needs to be done. Using your outline as a guide, move through the document, using the change-highlighting or commenting tools of your word processor to note comments received from others and problems you want to solve (or mark on a hard copy if you prefer).

Analyzing the Basic Features of Your Own Draft. Turn to the Critical Reading Guide on pp. 103–5. Using this guide, reread the draft to identify problems you need to solve. Note the problems on your draft.

Studying Critical Comments. Review all of the comments you have received from other readers. For each comment, look at the draft to determine what might have led the reader to make that particular point. Try to be objective about any criticism. Ideally, these comments will help you see your draft as others see it (rather than as you hoped it would be) and to identify specific problems. Add to your notes any problems readers have identified.

Carrying Out Revisions

Having identified problems in your draft, you now need to figure out solutions and carry them out. Basically, you have three options for finding solutions:

1. Review your observation or interview notes for other information and ideas.
2. Do additional observations or interviews to answer questions that you or other readers raised.
3. Look back at the readings in this chapter to see how other writers have solved similar problems.

The following suggestions, which are organized according to the basic features of profiles, will get you started solving some problems common to this kind of writing.

A Description of People and Places

- *Should people be described briefly?* Consider naming and detailing a few physical features of each person. Recall, for example, Hall's descriptive phrases: "the local farmers...tall, hearty men with weathered baseball caps or cowboy hats, earned dirt under every fingernail" (paragraph 1); "Julie is an attractive woman in her early forties, her blond hair usually pulled back for cooking" (paragraph 11). Add comparisons, as Cable does when he says Howard Deaver "looked like death on two legs" (paragraph 5). Also consider adding specific narrative action. Think of Deaver again, on the phone: "As he listened, he bit his lips and squeezed his Adam's apple" (paragraph 7).

- *Can you enliven the description of the place?* Add other senses to visual description. Recall, for example, these sensory descriptions from the readings: sound (plates thudding on a countertop), texture (the soft flesh of a pig lip, a cold and firm cadaver), smell (vinegar vapors), and taste (a pig lip that tastes porcine).

- *Do readers have difficulty seeing people in action or imagining what is involved in the activity?* Add specific narrative actions to show people moving, gesturing, or talking. For example, recall Edge's description of the production line: "six women in white smocks and blue bouffant caps, slicing ragged white fat from the lips, tossing the good parts in glass jars, the bad parts in barrels bound for the rendering plant" (paragraph 4).

Information about the Subject

- *Do readers feel bogged down by information?* Look for ways to reduce information or to break up long blocks of informational text with description of scenes or people, narration of events, lists, or other design elements. Consider presenting information through dialogue, as Edge does.

A Topical or Narrative Plan

- *Does your narratively arranged essay seem to drag or ramble?* Try adding drama through dialogue or specific narrative action. Try using comparison and contrast.

- *Does your topically arranged essay seem disorganized or out of balance?* Try rearranging topics to see if another order makes more sense. Add clearer, more explicit transitions or topic sentences. Move or condense information to restore balance.

- *Does the opening fail to engage readers' attention?* Consider alternatives. Think of questions you could open with, or look for an engaging image or dialogue later in the essay to move to the beginning. Go back to your observation or interview notes for other ideas. Recall how the writers in this chapter open their profile essays: Cable combines a quote by Mark Twain with comments about how people try to ignore death, Edge sits at a juke bar staring at a pig lip, Hall stands in the dark outside the Edison Café waiting for Julie to arrive.

- *Are transitions between stages in the narrative or between topics confusing or abrupt?* Add appropriate words or phrases, or revise sentences to make transitions clearer or smoother.

- *Does the ending seem weak?* Consider ending at an earlier point or moving something striking to the end. Review your invention and research notes to see if you overlooked something that would make for a strong ending. Consider ending your essay with a quotation, as several writers in this chapter do.

- *Are the design features effective?* Consider adding textual references to any visual elements in your essay or positioning visuals more effectively. Think of other possible design features you might incorporate to enhance your profile. Use images, as do Hall and Edge.

A Role for the Writer

- *Do readers want to see more of you in the profile?* Consider revealing yourself participating in some part of the activity. Add yourself to one of the conversations you participated in, re-creating dialogue for yourself.

- *Do readers find your participation so dominant that you seem to eclipse other participants?* Bring other people forward into more prominent view by adding material about them, reducing the material about yourself, or both.

A Perspective on the Subject

- *Are readers unsure what your perspective is?* Try stating it more directly. Be sure that the descriptive and narrative details reinforce the perspective you want to convey.

- *Are your readers' ideas about the person, place, or activity being profiled different from yours?* Consider whether you can incorporate any of their ideas into your essay or use them to develop your own ideas.

- *Do readers point to any details that seem especially meaningful?* Consider what these details suggest about your own perspective on the person, place, or activity.

Checking Sentence Strategies Electronically. To check your draft for a sentence strategy especially useful in profiles, use your word processor's highlighting function to mark sentences that include direct quotations. Then look at each sentence to see whether and, if so, how you have identified the speaker. Where you have not identified the speaker, think about whether you need to do so by adding a speaker tag. Also consider whether you could help your readers better imagine speakers' attitudes and personal styles by making any speaker tags more specific, either by using a verb other than *say* or *tell* or by adding a phrase that tells how, where, when, or why the speaker spoke. For more on using speaker tags, see pp. 101–2.

■ EDITING AND PROOFREADING

Now is the time to check your revised draft for errors in grammar, punctuation, and mechanics. Our research has identified several errors that occur often in profiles, including problems with the punctuation of quotations and the order of adjectives. The following guidelines will help you check your essay for these common errors. This book's Web site also provides interactive online exercises to help you learn to identify and correct each of these errors; to access the exercises for a particular error, go to the URL listed after each set of guidelines.

Checking the Punctuation of Quotations. Because most profiles are based in part on interviews, you probably have quoted one or more people in your essay. When you quote someone's exact words, you must enclose those words in quotation marks and observe strict conventions for punctuating quotations. Check your revised draft for your use of the following specific punctuation marks.

All quotations should have quotation marks at the beginning and the end.

▶ "What exactly is civil litigation?ˇI asked.

Commas and periods go *inside* quotation marks.

▶ "I'm here to see Anna Post,", I replied nervously.

▶ Tony explained, "Fraternity boys just wouldn't feel comfortable at the Chez Moi Café."

Question marks and exclamation points go *inside* closing quotation marks if they are part of the quotation, *outside* if they are not.

▶ After a pause, the patient asked, "Where do I sign?".

▶ Willie insisted, "You can *too* learn to play Super Mario!".

▶ When was the last time someone you just ticketed said to you, "Thank you, Officer, for doing a great job."?

Use commas with speaker tags (*he said, she asked,* etc.) that accompany direct quotations.

▶ "This sound system costs only four thousand dollars," Jorge said.

▶ I asked, "So where were these clothes from originally?"

For practice, go to bedfordstmartins.com/conciseguide/quote.

A Common ESL Problem: Adjective Order.   In trying to present the subject of your profile vividly and in detail, you probably have included many descriptive adjectives. When you include more than one adjective in front of a noun, you may have difficulty sequencing them. For example, do you write *a large old ceramic pot* or *an old large ceramic pot?* The following list shows the order in which adjectives are ordinarily arranged in front of a noun.

1. *Amount:* a/an, the, a few, six
2. *Evaluation:* good, beautiful, ugly, serious
3. *Size:* large, small, tremendous
4. *Shape, length:* round, long, short
5. *Age:* young, new, old
6. *Color:* red, black, green
7. *Origin:* Asian, Brazilian, German
8. *Material:* wood, cotton, gold
9. *Noun used as an adjective:* computer (as in *computer program*), cake (as in *cake pan*)
10. *The noun modified*

For practice, go to bedfordstmartins.com/conciseguide/order.

A Note on Grammar and Spelling Checkers.   These tools are good at catching certain types of errors, but currently there's no replacement for a good human proofreader. Grammar checkers in particular are extremely limited in what they can usually find, and often they only give you summary information that isn't helpful if you don't already understand the rule in question. They are also prone to give faulty advice for fixing problems and to flag correct items as wrong. Spelling checkers cause fewer problems but can't catch misspellings that are themselves words, such as *to* for *too*.

REFLECTING ON YOUR WRITING

Now that you have spent several days discussing profiles and writing one of your own, take some time for reflection. Reflecting on your writing process will help you gain a greater understanding of what you learned about solving the problems you encountered in writing a profile.

   Write a one-page explanation, telling your instructor about a problem you encountered in writing your profile and how you solved it. Before you begin, gather all of your writing invention material, planning and interview notes, drafts, critical comments, revision notes and plans, and final revision. Review these materials as you complete this writing task.

1. *Identify one writing problem you needed to solve as you worked on your profile.* Do not be concerned with grammar or punctuation; concentrate instead on problems unique to developing a profile. For example: Did you puzzle over how to organize your diverse observations into a coherent essay? Was it difficult to convey your own perspective? Did you have any concerns about presenting your subject vividly or controlling the flow of information?

2. *Determine how you came to recognize the problem.* When did you first discover it? What called it to your attention? If someone else pointed out the problem to you, can you now see hints of it in your invention writings? If so, where specifically? When you first recognized the problem, how did you respond?

3. *Reflect on how you went about solving the problem.* Did you work on the wording of a passage, cut or add details about your subject, or move paragraphs or sentences around? Did you reread one of the essays in this chapter to see how another writer handled a similar problem, or did you look back at the invention suggestions? If you talked about the problem with another student, your instructor, or someone else, did talking about it help? How useful was the advice you received?

4. *Write a brief explanation of the problem and your solution.* Reconstruct your efforts as specifically as possible. Quote from your invention notes or draft essay, others' critical comments, your revision plan, or your revised essay to show the various changes your writing underwent as you tried to solve the problem. When you have finished, consider how explaining what you have learned about solving this writing problem can help you solve future writing problems.

4

Explaining a Concept

Explanatory writing serves primarily to inform readers. Successful explanatory writing presents information confidently and efficiently, usually with the purpose of educating the reader about a subject. College students, however, are required to write explanations not primarily to teach others but to demonstrate what they have learned. Whether the explanation is researched or written from memory, the writer must analyze and evaluate a variety of kinds of information and then organize and synthesize the information to make a coherent presentation. This type of writing—which includes much of what we find in newspapers, magazines, and research reports—may be based on firsthand observations and interviews (as in Chapter 3) as well as on library and Internet research. Although writers of explanation may be experts on a subject, more often they are people who study what experts have discovered to convey that knowledge to others, as in the essays in the chapter.

This chapter focuses on one important kind of explanatory writing—explanations of concepts. The chapter readings explain the concepts of romantic love, indirect aggression, and cannibalism. These concepts name processes and phenomena like those you are studying in your college courses or using at work. Every field of study has its concepts: Physics has entropy, mass, and fission; literature has irony, romanticism, and postmodernism; music has harmony; art has perspective; mathematics has probability; and so on. You can see from this brief list that concepts are central to the understanding of virtually every subject. Moreover, when you begin to study a new field, you are expected to learn a new set of concepts. That is why introductory courses and their textbooks teach a whole new vocabulary of technical terms and specialized jargon. When you read the opening chapter of this textbook, for example, you were introduced to many concepts important to the study of writing, such as genre, writing process, invention, and revision.

Learning to explain a concept is especially important to you as a college student. It will help you read explanatory writing, a staple of academic discourse; it will prepare you to write a common type of exam and paper assignment; it will acquaint you with the basic strategies common to all types of explanatory writing—definition, classification, comparison and contrast, cause and effect, and process narration; and it will sharpen your skill in researching and using sources, abilities essential for success in college, whatever your major.

You will encounter writing that explains concepts in many different contexts, as the following examples suggest:

Writing in Your Other Courses

- For a linguistics course, a student writes a term paper tracing children's gradual control of sentences—or syntax, as linguists say—from about eighteen months to five or six years of age. The student first explains how researchers go about studying children's syntax, using several well-known studies as examples. Then he presents the widely accepted classification of stages that children go through as they gain control of syntax. As he presents each stage, he gives examples of children's syntax in their monologues and conversations in different situations, examples chosen from many possibilities in the published research studies. Even though he writes for his instructor, who is an expert in child language development, he carefully defines key terms to show that he understands what he is writing about.

- For a history of religion course, a student writes a research paper on religious fundamentalism. To explain this concept, she relies primarily on a book by a noted religious scholar. She follows the scholar's classification of the ways that fundamentalist religious groups are similar and organizes her paper around these similarities, which include a sense of threat and an organized reaction to the threat, a reliance on authoritative texts, a resistance to ambiguity and ambivalence, an inclination to behave aggressively toward unbelievers, an allegiance to a grand past, and a belief in a bright future. She illustrates each of these features of fundamentalism with examples from the beliefs and histories of fundamentalist groups around the world. She concludes by pointing out that religious fundamentalism began to be a major political force in the late twentieth century.

Writing in the Community

- Community policing has just been adopted by the police department in a mid-sized city, and a writer in the department's public relations division has been assigned to write and produce a brochure explaining the new approach. The brochure will be mailed to all homes in the city. The writer designs a small, fold-out, six-panel, two-sided brochure that will feature both text and photographs. The text briefly explains the major features of community policing, including the involvement of neighborhood residents and businesses in police decisions about crime-control priorities, the long-term assignment of officers to particular neighborhoods, increased reliance on foot and bicycle patrols rather than on car patrols, and the establishment of neighborhood police mini-stations. Working with a photographer, the brochure writer arranges to have photographs taken that represent the different features of community policing explained in the text.

- As part of her firm's plan to encourage managers to volunteer in the community for a few hours each month, a manager at a marketing research firm has been tutoring fifth-grade students in math. Learning about the manager's expertise in surveys, the teacher encourages her to plan a presentation to the class about surveying, an important research method in the social sciences. The manager agrees to do so and begins her lesson by having students fill out a brief questionnaire on their television-watching habits. She explains that she is not collecting data for marketing purposes but rather introducing them to surveys. With the students helping, she tabulates the results on a computer, separating the results by sex, time of week (weekdays or weekends), and kinds of television shows. Using a PowerPoint program, she projects the data onto a large screen so that everyone can see how the tables represent the survey results. The manager first guides a brief discussion of the survey and the results, helping students understand its purpose, form, and graphic representation. Then she shows them on the screen examples of questions from other surveys and explains who does such surveys, what they hope to learn, and how they report and use the results. She explains that the state tests that the students take every year are a form of survey. Finally, she passes out a short-answer quiz so that she and each student can find out how much has been learned about surveys.

Writing in the Workplace

- Returning from a small invitational seminar on the national security implications of satellite photography, the CEO of a space-imaging company prepares a report to his employees on the international debate about symmetrical transparency, the concept of using satellite photography to make everything on the planet visible to everyone on the planet at one-meter resolution—enough detail to reveal individual cars in parking lots, small airplanes on runways, backyard swimming pools, and individual shrubs and trees planted in parks. Aware of the financial implications for his company of the outcome of the debate, the executive carefully organizes his information and prepares a written text to read aloud to his employees, a one-page handout that lists key issues in the debate, and a transparency to project on a large screen during his presentation. He begins by reminding employees that the company's cameras already provide high-resolution images to government and corporate purchasers. Addressing the question of whether symmetrical transparency and the multinational monitoring that it makes possible compromise national security—or promise greater worldwide security and peace—the CEO gives a brief overview of key issues in the debate. These issues include how closed societies (like that of North Korea) will be affected differently from more open ones, whether global terrorism will be reduced or become more prevalent or more effective, and whether the chance of a nuclear standoff will be lessened. He concludes by pointing out that the big question for the U.S. government to answer soon is whether to attempt to control space or insist that it be open to everyone.

- Legislation in a western state defines a new concept in tourism—agritourism. To explain the concept, a state senator invites farmers, vineyard owners, and ranchers in his part of the state to an informal meeting. To prepare for the meeting, he writes a four-page summary of the legislation and prepares a one-page list of the main points in his presentation for everyone to pick up and read before the meeting begins. Assuming that his listeners have all visited a bed and breakfast inn, the senator compares the rules in the new law with the rules governing B&Bs. He emphasizes that in agritourism, guests tour a farm or ranch and participate in supervised chores. Meals must be offered three times a day and prepared and served by people who have been certified through coursework at a community college. He also explains that the greatest beneficiaries of agritourism will be small and medium-sized farms and ranches, where income is relatively low and varies greatly from year to year.

Practice Explaining a Concept: A Collaborative Activity

The preceding scenarios suggest some occasions for writing about concepts. Think of concepts you are currently studying or have recently studied or concepts connected to a job, sport, or hobby you know a lot about. Here are some possibilities: hip-hop, squeeze play, critical thinking, ambition, hypertext, interval training, photosynthesis, civil rights, manifest destiny, postcolonialism. Your instructor may schedule this collaborative activity as a face-to-face in-class discussion or ask you to conduct an online real-time discussion in a chat room. Whatever the medium, here are some guidelines to follow:

Part 1. Choose one concept to explain to two or three other students. When you have chosen your concept, think about what others in the group are likely to know about it and how you can inform them about it in two or three minutes. Consider how you will define the concept and what other strategies you might use — description, comparison, and so on — to explain it in an interesting, memorable way.

Get together with two or three other students, and explain your concepts to one another. You might begin by indicating where you learned the concept and in what area of study or work or leisure it is usually used.

Part 2. When all group members have explained their concepts, discuss what you learned from the experience of explaining a concept. Begin by asking one another a question or two that elicits further information that you need to understand each concept more fully. Then consider these questions:

- How did you decide what to include in your explanation and what to leave out?
- What surprised you in the questions that readers asked about your presentation?
- If you were to repeat your explanation to a similar group of listeners, what would you add, subtract, or change?

READINGS

No two essays that explain concepts are much alike, and yet they share defining features. Together, the three readings in this chapter reveal a number of these features, so you will want to read as many of them as possible. If time permits, complete the activities in the Analyzing Writing Strategies section that follows each selection, and read the Commentary. Following the readings is a section called Basic Features: Explaining Concepts (p. 136), which offers a concise description of the features of concept explanations and provides examples from the three readings.

Anastasia Toufexis has been an associate editor of Time, senior editor of Discover, and editor in chief of Psychology Today. She has written major reports, including some best-selling cover stories, on subjects as diverse as medicine, health and fitness, law, environment, education, science, and national and world news. Toufexis received a bachelor's degree from Smith College in 1967 and spent several years reporting for medical and pharmaceutical magazines. She has won a number of awards for her writing, including a Knight-Wallace Fellowship at the University of Michigan and an Ocean Science Journalism Fellowship at Woods Hole Oceanographic Institution. She has also lectured on science writing at Columbia University, the University of North Carolina, and the School of Visual Arts in New York.

The following essay was originally published in 1993 in Time magazine. As you read, notice how Toufexis brings together a variety of sources of information to present a neurochemical perspective on love.

Love: The Right Chemistry

Anastasia Toufexis

Love is a romantic designation for a most ordinary biological — or, shall we say, chemical? — process. A lot of nonsense is talked and written about it.

— GRETA GARBO to Melvyn Douglas in *Ninotchka*

O.K., let's cut out all this nonsense about romantic love. Let's bring some scientific precision to the party. Let's put love under a microscope.

When rigorous people with Ph.D.s after their names do that, what they see is not some silly, senseless thing. No, their probe reveals that love rests firmly on the foundations of evolution, biology and chemistry. What seems on the surface to be irrational, intoxicated behavior is in fact part of nature's master strategy — a vital force that has helped humans survive, thrive and multiply through thousands of years. Says Michael Mills, a psychology professor at Loyola Marymount University in Los Angeles: "Love is our ancestors whispering in our ears."

It was on the plains of Africa about 4 million years ago, in the early days of the human species, that the notion of romantic love probably first began to blossom or at least that the first cascades of neurochemicals began flowing from the brain to the bloodstream to produce goofy grins and sweaty palms as men and women gazed deeply into each other's eyes. When mankind graduated from scuttling around on all fours to walking on two legs, this change made the whole person visible to fellow human beings for the first time. Sexual organs were in full display, as were other characteristics, from the color of eyes to the span of shoulders. As never before, each individual had a unique allure.

When the sparks flew, new ways of making love enabled sex to become a romantic encounter, not just a reproductive act. Although mounting mates from the rear was, and still is, the method favored among most animals, humans began to enjoy face-to-face couplings; both looks and personal attraction became a much greater part of the equation. 4

Romance served the evolutionary purpose of pulling males and females into long-term partnership, which was essential to child rearing. On open grasslands, one parent would have a hard—and dangerous—time handling a child while foraging for food. "If a woman was carrying the equivalent of a 20-lb. bowling ball in one arm and a pile of sticks in the other, it was ecologically critical to pair up with a mate to rear the young," explains anthropologist Helen Fisher, author of *Anatomy of Love.* 5

While Western culture holds fast to the idea that true love flames forever (the movie *Bram Stoker's Dracula* has the Count carrying the torch beyond the grave), nature apparently meant passions to sputter out in something like four years. Primitive pairs stayed together just "long enough to rear one child through infancy," says Fisher. Then each would find a new partner and start all over again. 6

What Fisher calls the "four-year itch" shows up unmistakably in today's divorce statistics. In most of the 62 cultures she has studied, divorce rates peak around the fourth 7

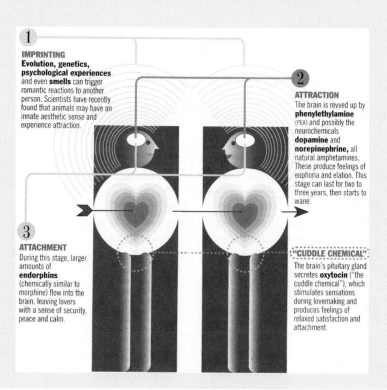

1 IMPRINTING
Evolution, genetics, psychological experiences and even **smells** can trigger romantic reactions to another person. Scientists have recently found that animals may have an innate aesthetic sense and experience attraction.

2 ATTRACTION
The brain is revved up by **phenylethylamine** (PEA) and possibly the neurochemicals **dopamine** and **norepinephrine,** all natural amphetamines. These produce feelings of euphoria and elation. This stage can last for two to three years, then starts to wane.

3 ATTACHMENT
During this stage, larger amounts of **endorphins** (chemically similar to morphine) flow into the brain, leaving lovers with a sense of security, peace and calm.

"CUDDLE CHEMICAL"
The brain's pituitary gland secretes **oxytocin** ("the cuddle chemical"), which stimulates sensations during lovemaking and produces feelings of relaxed satisfaction and attachment.

year of marriage. Additional youngsters help keep pairs together longer. If, say, a couple have another child three years after the first, as often occurs, then their union can be expected to last about four more years. That makes them ripe for the more familiar phenomenon portrayed in the Marilyn Monroe classic *The Seven-Year Itch.*

If, in nature's design, romantic love is not eternal, neither is it exclusive. Less than 5% of mammals form rigorously faithful pairs. From the earliest days, contends Fisher, the human pattern has been "monogamy with clandestine adultery." Occasional flings upped the chances that new combinations of genes would be passed on to the next generation. Men who sought new partners had more children. Contrary to common assumptions, women were just as likely to stray. "As long as prehistoric females were secretive about their extramarital affairs," argues Fisher, "they could garner extra resources, life insurance, better genes and more varied DNA for their biological futures...." 8

Lovers often claim that they feel as if they are being swept away. They're not mistaken; they are literally flooded by chemicals, research suggests. A meeting of eyes, a touch of hands or a whiff of scent sets off a flood that starts in the brain and races along the nerves and through the blood. The results are familiar: flushed skin, sweaty palms, heavy breathing. If love looks suspiciously like stress, the reason is simple: the chemical pathways are identical. 9

Above all, there is the sheer euphoria of falling in love—a not-so-surprising reaction, considering that many of the substances swamping the newly smitten are chemical cousins of amphetamines. They include dopamine, norepinephrine and especially phenylethylamine (PEA). Cole Porter knew what he was talking about when he wrote, "I get a kick out of you." "Love is a natural high," observes Anthony Walsh, author of *The Science of Love: Understanding Love and Its Effects on Mind and Body.* "PEA gives you that silly smile that you flash at strangers. When we meet someone who is attractive to us, the whistle blows at the PEA factory." 10

But phenylethylamine highs don't last forever, a fact that lends support to arguments that passionate romantic love is short-lived. As with any amphetamine, the body builds up a tolerance to PEA; thus it takes more and more of the substance to produce love's special kick. After two to three years, the body simply can't crank up the needed amount of PEA. And chewing on chocolate doesn't help, despite popular belief. The candy is high in PEA, but it fails to boost the body's supply. 11

Fizzling chemicals spell the end of delirious passion; for many people that marks the end of the liaison as well. It is particularly true for those whom Dr. Michael Liebowitz of the New York State Psychiatric Institute terms "attraction junkies." They crave the intoxication of falling in love so much that they move frantically from affair to affair just as soon as the first rush of infatuation fades. 12

Still, many romances clearly endure beyond the first years. What accounts for that? Another set of chemicals, of course. The continued presence of a partner gradually steps up production in the brain of endorphins. Unlike the fizzy amphetamines, these are soothing substances. Natural pain-killers, they give lovers a sense of security, peace and calm. "That is one reason why it feels so horrible when we're abandoned or a lover dies," notes Fisher. "We don't have our daily hit of narcotics." 13

Researchers see a contrast between the heated infatuation induced by PEA, along 14
with other amphetamine-like chemicals, and the more intimate attachment fostered and prolonged by endorphins. "Early love is when you love the way the other person makes you feel," explains psychiatrist Mark Goulston of the University of California, Los Angeles. "Mature love is when you love the person as he or she is." It is the difference between passionate and compassionate love, observes Walsh, a psychobiologist at Boise State University in Idaho. "It's Bon Jovi vs. Beethoven."

Oxytocin is another chemical that has recently been implicated in love. Produced by 15 the brain, it sensitizes nerves and stimulates muscle contraction. In women it helps uterine contractions during childbirth as well as production of breast milk, and seems to inspire mothers to nuzzle their infants. Scientists speculate that oxytocin might encourage similar cuddling between adult women and men. The versatile chemical may also enhance orgasms. In one study of men, oxytocin increased to three to five times its normal level during climax, and it may soar even higher in women....

Chemicals may help explain (at least to scientists) the feelings of passion and com- 16 passion, but why do people tend to fall in love with one partner rather than a myriad of others? Once again, it's partly a function of evolution and biology. "Men are looking for maximal fertility in a mate," says Loyola Marymount's Mills. "That is in large part why females in the prime childbearing ages of 17 to 28 are so desirable." Men can size up youth and vitality in a glance, and studies indeed show that men fall in love quite rapidly. Women tumble more slowly, to a large degree because their requirements are more complex; they need more time to check the guy out. "Age is not vital," notes Mills, "but the ability to provide security, father children, share resources and hold a high status in society are all key factors."

Still, that does not explain why the way Mary walks and laughs makes Bill dizzy with 17 desire while Marcia's gait and giggle leave him cold. "Nature has wired us for one special person," suggests Walsh, romantically. He rejects the idea that a woman or a man can be in love with two people at the same time. Each person carries in his or her mind a unique subliminal guide to the ideal partner, a "love map," to borrow a term coined by sexologist John Money of Johns Hopkins University.

Drawn from the people and experiences of childhood, the map is a record of what- 18 ever we found enticing and exciting—or disturbing and disgusting. Small feet, curly hair. The way our mothers patted our head or how our fathers told a joke. A fireman's uniform, a doctor's stethoscope. All the information gathered while growing up is imprinted in the brain's circuitry by adolescence. Partners never meet each and every requirement, but a sufficient number of matches can light up the wires and signal, "It's love." Not every partner will be like the last one, since lovers may have different combinations of the characteristics favored by the map.

O.K., that's the scientific point of view. Satisfied? Probably not. To most people— 19 with or without Ph.D.s—love will always be more than the sum of its natural parts. It's a commingling of body and soul, reality and imagination, poetry and phenylethylamine. In our deepest hearts, most of us harbor the hope that love will never fully yield up its secrets, that it will always elude our grasp.

Connecting to Culture and Experience: Love Maps

The chemistry of love is easily summarized: Amphetamines fuel romance; endorphins and oxytocin sustain lasting relationships. As Toufexis makes clear, however, these chemical reactions do not explain why specific people are initially attracted to each other. Toufexis observes that an initial attraction occurs because each of us carries a "unique subliminal guide" or "love map" (paragraph 17) that leads us unerringly to a partner. Moreover, she explains that men look for maximal fertility, whereas women look for security, resources, status, and a willingness to father children.

Discuss these explanations for attraction between the sexes. Consider where your love map comes from and how much it may be influenced by your family, your ethnicity, or images in the media or advertising. Consider whether it is possible for an individual's love map to change over time — from adolescence to adulthood, for example.

Analyzing Writing Strategies

1. At the beginning of this chapter, we made several generalizations about essays explaining concepts. Consider which of these assertions are true of Toufexis's essay:

   - It seeks to inform readers about a specific subject.
   - It presents information confidently and efficiently.
   - It relies almost exclusively on established information.

2. To explain a concept, you have to classify the information; that is, group or divide it into meaningful categories. Otherwise, you struggle to write about a jumble of information, and your readers quickly give up trying to make sense of it. For example, a writer setting out to explain testing in American colleges to a college student in Thailand would first try to classify the subject by dividing it into categories like the following: short-answer, essay, multiple-choice, lab demonstration, artistic performance.

   To understand more about how Toufexis classifies her information, make a scratch outline of paragraphs 9–15, where she presents the centrally important information on specific chemicals. How is the information divided and sequenced in these paragraphs? What cues does Toufexis provide to help you follow the sequence? What do you find most and least successful about the division?

Commentary: A Focused Concept and Careful Use of Sources

Unless they are writing entire books, writers explaining concepts must focus their attention on particular aspects of concepts. For instance, Toufexis focuses in her relatively brief magazine article on the chemistry of love between adult human heterosexual mates. She excludes homosexual love, parents' love for their children, dogs' love for their masters, views on love by various religions, the history of romance as revealed in literature, courtship rituals through time, and dozens of other possible subjects related to love. Toufexis holds to her chemical focus throughout the essay, except for a brief but relevant digression about "love maps" toward the end. When they finish the essay, readers have learned nothing new about love in general, but they are well informed about the neurochemistry of love. By keeping to this narrow focus, Toufexis is able to present information that is likely to be new to most readers and therefore is more likely to hold readers' attention.

Besides maintaining a focus on a specific aspect of a concept, concept explanations rely on authoritative, expert sources, on established material gleaned from reputable publications or interviews. Toufexis uses both these kinds of sources. She apparently arranged telephone or in-person interviews with six different professors specializing in diverse academic disciplines: psychology, anthropology, psychiatry, and sexology. (She does not immediately identify the discipline of one professor—Walsh, in paragraph 10—but from the title of his book, we might guess that he is a biochemist, and in paragraph 14 we are not surprised to learn that he is a psychobiologist.) We assume that Toufexis read at least parts of the two books she names in paragraphs 5 and 10, and perhaps she also read other sources, which may have led her to some of the professors she interviewed.

What is most notable about Toufexis's use of sources is that she does not indicate precisely where she obtained all the information she includes. For example, she does not cite the source of the anthropological information in paragraphs 3–5, although a reader might guess that she summarized it from *Anatomy of Love,* cited at the end of paragraph 5. We cannot be certain whether the quote at the end of paragraph 5 comes from the book or from an interview with its author. As long as she gives general indications of where her information comes from, Toufexis can safely assume that her readers will not fault her for failing to provide exact bibliographical information. These liberties in citing sources are expected by experienced readers of magazines and newspapers, including the leading ones that educated readers count on to keep them up to date on developments in various fields. Readers would be surprised to find footnotes or works cited lists in popular publications.

In most college writing, however, sources must be cited. Moreover, college writers—whether students or professors—are expected to follow certain styles for citing and acknowledging their sources, such as MLA style in English and APA style in psychology. Academic writers cite sources because credit must be given to the authors of any work that contributes to a new piece of work.

Observing a third important requirement of essays that explain concepts, Toufexis provides several different kinds of cues to keep readers on track. In addition to paragraph-opening transitions, Toufexis carefully forecasts the topics and direction of her essay in her second paragraph: "their probe reveals that love rests firmly on the foundations of evolution, biology and chemistry." This forecast helps readers anticipate the types of scientific information Toufexis has selected for her special focus on love and the sequence that she will use to introduce them.

Considering Topics for Your Own Essay

Like Toufexis, you could write an essay about love or romance, but you could choose a different focus: on its history (how and when did it develop as an idea in the West?), its cultural characteristics (how is love regarded currently among different American ethnic groups or world cultures?), its excesses or extremes, its expression between parent and child, or the phases of falling in and out of love. Also consider writing about other concepts involving personal relationships, such as jealousy, codependency, idealization, stereotyping, or homophobia.

Natalie Angier studied English, physics, and astronomy in college and "dreamed of starting a popular magazine about science for intelligent lay readers who wanted to know more about what's going on across the great divide of C. P. Snow's two cultures"—the sciences and the humanities. At the age of twenty-two, she realized her dream when she joined the founding staff of Discover *magazine. Since then, she has worked as a science writer for newspapers (winning a Pulitzer Prize for her* New York Times *writing on biology and medicine), magazines (such as* Time, *the* Atlantic Monthly, *and* Reader's Digest*), and television (Fox and the Canadian Broadcasting Corporation). In addition to the Pulitzer, Angier has won other distinguished honors for science writing, including the Lewis Thomas Award and recognition from the American Association for the Advancement of Science (AAAS). She also has taught science writing at New York University's Graduate Program in Science and Environmental Reporting and edited* The Best American Science and Nature Writing 2002. *Angier has written four books, including* Natural Obsessions: Striving to Unlock the Deepest Secrets of the Cancer Cell *(1988);* The Beauty of the Beastly: New Views on the Nature of Life *(1995); and* Woman: An Intimate Geography *(1999), a National Book Award finalist, from which the following selection explaining the concept of indirect aggression is excerpted.*

Like Toufexis writing for Time *magazine, Angier is writing for a popular audience, the "intelligent lay readers" she dreamed of writing for when she was still a college student. As an experienced popularizer or translator of scientific research, Angier knows that she needs to present information authoritatively and show readers that she has done her research so that they will have confidence in the credibility of the information she is presenting. As you read, consider how well she succeeds in convincing you to accept her authority.*

Indirect Aggression

Natalie Angier

This study has been done many times. If you take a group of babies or young toddlers and dress them in nondescript, non-sex-specific clothes—yellow is always a good color!—and make sure that their haircuts don't give them away, and if you put them in a room with a lot of adults watching, the adults will not be able to sex the children accurately. The adults will try, based on the behaviors of each child, but they will be right no more often than they would be if they flipped a coin. This has been shown again and again, but still we don't believe it. We think we can tell a boy or a girl by the child's behavior, specifically by its level of aggressiveness. If you show a person a videotape of a crying baby and tell her the baby is a boy, the observer will describe the baby as looking angry; if you tell the person the baby is a girl, she will say the child is scared or miserable.

I am at a party with my daughter, who is sixteen months old. A boy who is almost eighteen months comes into the room and takes a toy away from my daughter. I say something humorous to her about how she's got to watch out for those older kids, they'll always try to push you around. And the boy's mother says, "It's also because he's a boy." That's what happens at this age, she says. The boys become very boyish. A little while later, a girl who is almost eighteen months old takes my daughter's cup of milk away from her. The mother of the other girl doesn't say, "It's because she's a girl, she's becoming girlish." Of course she doesn't say that; it would make no sense, would it? An older girl taking a cup away from a younger girl has nothing to do with the girlness of either party. But taking the toy away is viewed as inherent to the older boy's boyness.

I felt very aggressive about the whole thing; alas, not being a toddler, I couldn't go and kick anybody in the kneecap. Which is the sort of thing that toddlers do, whatever their sex. They kick, they hit, they scream, they throw objects around, they act like pills past their expiration date. And we adults put up with it, and we subscribe to the myth of the helpless, innocent child, and it's a good thing we do and that children are cute, because otherwise we might well see the truth: that our children are born with astonishing powers, and with brains that seem by default to counsel aggression.

"Young children are like animals," says Kaj Björkqvist, of Turku Akademi University in Finland. "Before they have language, they have their bodies. And through their bodies they can be aggressive, and so that is what they do, that is how they are. They are physically aggressive — boys, girls, all of them." Björkqvist studies female aggression. He has done cross-cultural comparisons of children in Europe, North America, the Middle East, and Asia. Everywhere he has found that young children are physically aggressive, and that before the age of three, there are no significant differences between girl aggression and boy aggression.

We grow into our sex-specific aggressions. We own the code of aggression from birth, and we perfect its idiom through experience and experimentation.... When the mind comes into its own and the child starts speaking fluently, purposefully, adults become less tolerant of physical aggression. Today, in most cultures, acceptance of physical aggression declines as the child gets older; by the time a person reaches puberty, the tendency to use physical force to wrest a desired object or behavior from another is considered frankly pathological. This is true for both sexes, but particularly for girls. Physical aggression is discouraged in girls in manifold and aggressive ways. Not only are they instructed against offensive fighting; they are rarely instructed in defensive fighting. Girls don't learn how to throw a punch. Humor is another form of aggression, and until recently humor has been used to squelch the very notion of a warrior female. Just the thought of a girl-fight, and people snicker and rub their hands with glee. Cat fight! Scratching, screeching, pulling hair, and falling on butt with skirt hiked in the air! Happily, the smirky parody of girl-fights has gotten a bit paunchy and dated of late, and instead we've been treated to images of GI Janes and bodiced Xenas wielding swords and Klingon women with brickbat fists, though whether the mass media's revisionist fighting female has been driven by attitudinal change or by the need to jolt a bored and distracted audience is unclear.

Whatever the media moment may be, girls still do not often engage in physical fights. 6 The older children get, the less physically aggressive they become—though not always, and not everywhere—but the dropoff rate for the use of physical aggression in girls is much sharper than it is for boys. At least in the developed West, by the time girls and boys are in third grade, boys are about three times as likely as girls to kick or strike at somebody who makes them mad. What then do girls do with that aggressiveness, which in the bliss of preverbalism could speak through hands and feet? It does not go away. It finds a new voice. It finds words. Girls learn to talk hornet talk. Mastering curse words and barbed insults is an essential task of childhood. Girls also learn to use their faces as weapons. Expressions like sticking out your tongue or rolling your eyes or curling your lip all seem funny to adults, but studies show that they aren't funny to children, and that they can be effective in conveying anger and dislike or in ostracizing an undesirable. Aggression researchers initially thought that girls had the edge over boys in verbal aggression and that they were more likely than boys to belittle their peers with words and facial flexions, but a series of Finnish studies of eight- and eleven-year-olds suggested otherwise. The researchers sought to determine how children responded when they were angry. They asked the children to describe themselves and their reactions to being roused to rage; they asked teachers and parents to describe how the children reacted in conflict; and they asked children to talk about each other, to rate each other's rileability and behaviors in a squall. The scientists found that boys and girls were equally likely to use verbal aggression against their cohorts, to call them nasty names to their faces, to yell, to mock, to try to make the despised ones look stupid. And so boys kick and fight more than girls do, and the sexes argue and chide in equal amounts. We might then conclude that boys are more aggressive, for they shout with their mouths and on occasion with their bodies, while the girls keep their fists to themselves.

There are other ways in which rage emerges among girls, though, ways that are 7 roughly girl-specific. A girl who is angry often responds by stalking off, turning away, snubbing the offender, pretending she doesn't exist. She withdraws, visibly so, aggressively so. You can almost hear the thwapping of her sulk. Among eleven-year-olds, girls are three times more likely than boys to express their anger in the form of a flamboyant snub. In addition, girls at this age, more than boys, engage in a style of aggression called indirect aggression.

I'll admit up front that I dislike this form of aggression, and that to mention it is to rein- 8 force clichés about female treachery and female conniving. Yet it is an aggression that we gals know, because we grew up as girls and we saw it and struggled against it and hated it and did it ourselves. Indirect aggression is anonymous aggression. It is backbiting, gossiping, spreading vicious rumors. It is seeking to rally others against the despised but then denying the plot when confronted. The use of indirect aggression increases over time, not just because girls don't generally use their fists to make their point, but because the effectiveness of indirect aggression is tied to the fluency of a person's social intelligence; the more sophisticated the person, the cleverer her use of the dorsal blade. In this sense, then, a girl's supposed head start over boys in verbal fluency may give her an edge in applying an indirect form of aggression. But the advantage, such as it is, doesn't last, for males catch up, and by the time we reach adulthood we have all become political animals, and men and women are, according to a number of studies, equally likely to express their aggression covertly. Despite rumors to the contrary, systematic eavesdroppings have revealed that men and women gossip an equal amount about their friends, families, colleagues, and celebrities. Adults of both sexes go to great lengths to express their antipathy toward one another indirectly, in ways that mask their hostile intent while still getting the jab done. For example, a person might repeatedly interrupt an opponent during an office meeting, or criticize the antagonist's work, rather than attacking his or her character—even though the source of the aggressor's ire has nothing to do with the quality of the opponent's performance.

Indirect aggression is not pretty, nor is it much admired. To the contrary it is universally condemned. When children and adults are asked to describe their feelings about the various methods of expressing anger, backstabbing behavior ranks at the bottom, below a good swift kick to the crotch. Yet there it is, with us, among us, not exclusively female by any means, but a recognizable hazard of girlhood. Part of the blame lies with the myth of the good-girl, for the more girls are counseled against direct forms of aggression and the more geniality of temperament is prized, the greater is the likelihood that the tart girls will resort to hidden machinations to get what they want. In cultures where girls are allowed to be girls, to speak up and out, they are in fact more verbally, directly aggressive and less indirectly aggressive than in cultures where girls and women are expected to be demure. In Poland, for example, a good smart mouth is considered a female asset, and girls there rag each other and pull no punches and report feeling relatively little threat of intragroup skullduggery. Among female Zapotec Indians in Mexico, who are exceedingly subordinate to men, indirect aggression prevails. Among the Vanatinai of Papua New Guinea, one of the most egalitarian and least stratified societies known to anthropologists, women speak and move as freely as they please, and they sometimes use their fists and feet to demonstrate their wrath, and there is no evidence of a feminine edge in covert operations.

Another reason that girls may resort to indirect aggression is that they feel such extraordinary aggression toward their friends—lashing, tumbling, ever-replenishing aggression. Girl friendships are fierce and dangerous. The expression "I'll be your best friend" is not exclusively a girl phrase, but girls use it a lot. They know how powerful the words are, how significant the offer is. Girls who become good friends feel a compulsion to define the friendship, to stamp it and name it, and they are inclined to rank a close friend as a best friend, with the result that they often have many best friends. They think about their friends on a daily basis and try to figure out where a particular friend fits that day in their cosmology of friendships. Is the girl her best friend today, or a provisional best friend, pending the resolution of a minor technicality, a small bit of friction encountered the day before? The girl may want to view a particular girl as her best friend, but she worries how her previous best friend will take it—as a betrayal or as a potential benefit, a

9

10

bringing in of a new source of strength to the pair. Girls fall in love with each other and feel an intimacy for each other that is hard for them to describe or understand.

When girls are in groups, they form coalitions of best friends, two against two, or two in edgy harmony with two. A girl in a group of girls who doesn't feel that she has a specific ally feels at risk, threatened, frightened. If a girl who is already incorporated into the group decides to take on a newcomer, to sponsor her, the resident girl takes on a weighty responsibility, for the newcomer will view her as (for the moment) her best friend, her only friend, the guardian of her oxygen mask. 11

When girls have a falling-out, they fall like Alice down the tunnel, convinced that it will never end, that they will never be friends again. The Finnish studies of aggression among girls found that girls hold grudges against each other much longer than boys do. "Girls tend to form dyadic relationships, with very deep psychological expectations from their best friends," Björkqvist said. "Because their expectations are high, they feel deeply betrayed when the friendship falls apart. They become as antagonistic afterwards as they had been bonded before." If a girl feels betrayed by a friend, she will try to think of ways to get revenge in kind, to truly hurt her friend, as she has been hurt. Fighting physically is an unsatisfactory form of punishing the terrible traitor. It is over too quickly. To express anger might work if the betrayer accepts the anger and responds to it with respect. But if she doesn't acknowledge her friend's anger or sense of betrayal, if she refuses to apologize or admit to any wrongdoing, or if she goes further, walking away or mocking or snubbing her friend, at that point a girl may aim to hurt with the most piercing and persistent tools for the job, the psychological tools of indirect, vengeful aggression, with the object of destroying the girl's position, her peace of mind, her right to be. Indirect aggression is akin to a voodoo hex, an anonymous but obsessive act in which the antagonist's soul, more than her body, must be got at, must be penetrated, must be nullified. 12

Connecting to Culture and Experience:
Gender and Aggression

Angier makes the point that although both boys and girls use both direct and indirect aggression, adolescent boys are more likely to use direct aggression and girls of the same age are more likely to use indirect aggression. Try to recall one experience from your adolescent and teenage years of each kind of aggression — indirect and direct — when you were either the aggressor or the victim of aggression.

With two or three other students, discuss your experience with these two kinds of aggression. For each of the experiences you recall, tell what happened, who was involved, and what was said and done. Then discuss whether your experience supports the research Angier cites showing that adolescent boys use direct aggression more often than girls, and girls use indirect aggression more often than boys. Also discuss your attitudes toward these two kinds of aggression. Note that Angier states that she personally dislikes indirect aggression and that it is "universally condemned" (paragraph 9). Which kind of aggression, if any, do you think is more acceptable, and by whom? If you think that one kind of aggression tends to be preferred or relied on more than the other, how would you explain the preference?

Analyzing Writing Strategies

1. Reread paragraphs 1–3 to see how Angier begins this concept explanation. Focus first on paragraph 1. What is the point of this paragraph? Having already read the rest of the selection, how do you think this first paragraph prepares readers for the explanation that follows? What does it lead readers to expect will follow?

   Now focus on paragraphs 2 and 3. What is the point of these paragraphs? How do they prepare readers for the explanation that follows?

   Finally, speculate on why Angier chose to begin her essay with these two different openings. How effective for you is this way of beginning? If you were to choose, which opening would you keep, and why? If you think they work together well, comment on why you think so.

2. In paragraphs 9–12, Angier presents two causes for girls' apparent preference for indirect over direct aggression. Reread these paragraphs to identify the two causes and to notice that Angier is not arguing for her own speculations about why girls prefer indirect aggression. Instead, she has decided that for readers to understand the concept of indirect aggression, they need to know what researchers have determined to be the causes for girls' reliance on indirect aggression. Therefore, she devotes several paragraphs to reporting the causes established by field and experimental research studies. Review these paragraphs, and highlight the passages where she is referring to sources she has read in the library and possibly on the Internet.

   Notice also that Angier explains one cause rather quickly but spends several paragraphs elaborating her explanation of the other cause. How well do you think she explains each of these causes? Why do you think she decided to go into more detail about one cause and not the other?

3. To explain indirect aggression, Angier makes effective use of a sentence strategy that relies on a grammatical structure known as an *appositive*. Underline these appositives: in paragraph 10, sentence 1, from *lashing* to the end; paragraph 10, sentence 8, from *bringing in* to the end; paragraph 11, sentence 1, from *two against two* to the end; paragraph 12, the second from last sentence, from *psychological* through *aggression;* paragraph 12, the last sentence, from *an anonymous* to the end. Now compare each appositive to what comes before in its sentence. Make notes in the margin about how the appositive and what comes before seem to be related to each other. What does each appositive contribute? How are the five of them alike and different in what they add to the sentence? (For more on sentence strategies important to writers explaining concepts, turn to Sentence Strategies, p. 150.)

Commentary: Using Comparison/Contrast to Explain Concepts

As a writer experienced in explaining new concepts, Angier knows that perhaps the best way to explain something unfamiliar is to relate it to something familiar. Comparing and contrasting seeks to make clear how the unfamiliar is like or unlike the familiar. In this selection, Angier sets up three kinds of comparisons: between indirect aggression and other kinds of aggression, between girls and boys, and between different age groups.

Let us look first at the comparison of indirect aggression to other types of aggression. Although her readers are unlikely to know what indirect aggression is, Angier can assume they will know other types of aggression with which she can compare it. In the opening paragraphs, she discusses the most common type of aggression — physical aggression. She lists many examples of physical aggression, including kicking, hitting, and throwing objects. In paragraph 6, she brings up a second type of aggression: "hornet talk" or verbal aggression. This kind of aggression is exemplified by cursing, belittling, insulting, yelling, and mocking. In paragraph 7, Angier introduces a third type of aggression, which she identifies at the end of the paragraph as "indirect aggression" and contrasts with the other kinds of aggression. In contrast to the confrontation and body contact associated with physical aggression, she tells us that indirect aggression involves withdrawing or turning away. In contrast to calling people "nasty names to their faces" (paragraph 6), which is typical of verbal aggression, indirect aggression includes backstabbing behaviors such as gossiping, spreading rumors, and plotting (paragraph 8). These contrasts help readers understand that indirect aggression has both physical and verbal elements but differs from physical and verbal aggression chiefly by being indirect or by masking its "hostile intent," as Angier explains in paragraph 8.

In addition to comparing indirect aggression to other types of aggression, Angier also compares boys and girls in terms of which type of aggression they use. At the same time, she compares aggressive behaviors at different ages. In paragraphs 1–3, she shows that people assume there is a difference between girls and boys as toddlers. In paragraph 4, however, she summarizes the research finding that "before the age of three, there are no significant differences between girl aggression and boy aggression." In paragraph 5, she makes explicit the idea that "sex-specific aggressions" change through time. This point is developed in subsequent paragraphs where she contrasts girls' and boys' preferences at different ages. She explains that as children grow older, girls become less physically aggressive and more verbally aggressive and boys become both more physically and more verbally aggressive. In paragraph 8, she explains that although girls develop indirect aggression earlier, by the time they are adults both sexes are equally adept at this covert form of aggression.

Comparison and contrast are important explanatory writing strategies that you may want to consider using in your own concept explanation.

Considering Topics for Your Own Essay

Angier mentions several concepts associated with behavior that you might consider explaining, such as hostility, aggression, obsession, grudge, coalition, friendship, intimacy, betrayal, and rileability. She also refers to kinds of communication such as gossip and rumor. Other kinds of communication you could write about include body language, metaphor, instant messaging, sign language, and semiotics.

Linh Kieu Ngo *wrote this essay as a first-year college student. In it, he defines a concept that is of importance in anthropology and of wide general interest—cannibalism, the eating of human flesh by other humans. Most Americans know about survival cannibalism—eating human flesh to avoid starvation—but Ngo also explains the historical importance of dietary and ritual cannibalism in his essay. As you read, notice how he relies on examples to illustrate the types.*

Cannibalism: It Still Exists

Linh Kieu Ngo

Fifty-five Vietnamese refugees fled to Malaysia on a small fishing boat to escape communist rule in their country following the Vietnam War. During their escape attempt, the captain was shot by the coast guard. The boat and its passengers managed to outrun the coast guard to the open sea, but they had lost the only person who knew the way to Malaysia, the captain. [1]

The men onboard tried to navigate the boat, but after a week fuel ran out, and they drifted farther out to sea. Their supply of food and water was gone; people were starving, and some of the elderly were near death. The men managed to produce a small amount of drinking water by boiling salt water, using dispensable wood from the boat to create a small fire near the stern. They also tried to fish but had little success. [2]

A month went by, and the old and weak died. At first, the crew threw the dead overboard, but later, out of desperation, they turned to human flesh as a source of food. Some people vomited as they attempted to eat it, while others refused to resort to cannibalism and see the bodies of their loved ones sacrificed for food. Those who did not eat died of starvation, and their bodies in turn became food for others. Human flesh was cut out, washed in salt water, and hung to dry for preservation. The liquids inside the cranium were drunk to quench thirst. The livers, kidneys, hearts, stomachs, and intestines were boiled and eaten. [3]

Five months passed before a whaling vessel discovered the drifting boat, looking like a graveyard of bones. There was only one survivor. [4]

Cannibalism, the act of human beings eating human flesh (Sagan 2), has a long history and continues to hold interest and create controversy. Many books and research reports offer examples of cannibalism, but a few scholars have questioned whether it actually was ever practiced anywhere, except in cases of ensuring survival in times of famine or isolation (Askenasy 43–54). Recently, some scholars have tried to understand why people in the West have been so eager to attribute cannibalism to non-Westerners (Barker, Hulme, and Iversen). Cannibalism has long been a part of American popular culture. For example, Mark Twain's "Cannibalism in the Cars" tells a humorous story about cannibalism by well-to-do travelers on a train stranded in a snowstorm, and cannibalism is still a popular subject for jokes ("Cannibal Jokes"). [5]

If we assume there is some reality to the reports about cannibalism, how can we best understand this concept? Cannibalism can be broken down into two main categories: exocannibalism, the eating of outsiders or foreigners, and endocannibalism, the eating of members of one's own social group (Shipman 70). Within these categories are several functional types of cannibalism, three of the most common being survival cannibalism, dietary cannibalism, and religious and ritual cannibalism.

6

Survival cannibalism occurs when people trapped without food have to decide "whether to starve or to eat fellow humans" (Shipman 70). In the case of the Vietnamese refugees, the crew and passengers on the boat ate human flesh to stay alive. They did not kill people to get human flesh for nourishment but instead waited until the people had died. Even after human carcasses were sacrificed as food, the boat people ate only enough to survive. Another case of survival cannibalism occured in 1945, when General Douglas MacArthur's forces cut supply lines to Japanese troops stationed in the Pacific Islands. In one incident, Japanese troops were reported to have sacrificed the Arapesh people of northeastern New Guinea for food in order to avoid death by starvation (Tuzin 63). The most famous example of survival cannibalism in American history comes from the diaries, letters, and interviews of survivors of the California-bound Donner Party, who in the winter of 1846 were snowbound in the Sierra Nevada Mountains for five months. Thirty-five of eighty-seven adults and children died, and some of them were eaten (Hart 116–117; Johnson).

7

Unlike survival cannibalism, in which human flesh is eaten as a last resort after a person has died, in dietary cannibalism humans are purchased or trapped for food and then eaten as a part of a culture's traditions. In addition, survival cannibalism often involves people eating other people of the same origins, whereas dietary cannibalism usually involves people eating foreigners.

8

In the Miyanmin society of the west Sepik interior of Papua, New Guinea, villagers do not value human life over that of pigs or marsupials because human flesh is part of their normal diet (Poole 7). The Miyanmin people observe no differences in "gender, kinship, ritual status, and bodily substance"; they eat anyone, even their own dead. In this respect, then, they practice both endocannibalism and exocannibalism; and to ensure a constant supply of human flesh for food, they raid neighboring tribes and drag their victims back to their village to be eaten (Poole 11). Perhaps, in the history of this society, there was at one time a shortage of wild game to be hunted for food, and because people were more plentiful than fish, deer, rabbits, pigs, or cows, survival cannibalism was adopted as a last resort. Then, as their culture developed, the Miyanmin may have retained the practice of dietary cannibalism, which has endured as a part of their culture.

9

Similar to the Miyanmin, the people of the Leopard and Alligator societies in South America eat human flesh as part of their cultural tradition. Practicing dietary exocannibalism, the Leopard people hunt in groups, with one member wearing the skin of a leopard to conceal the face. They ambush their victims in the forest and carry their victims back to their village to be eaten. The Alligator people also hunt in groups, but they hide them-

10

selves under a canoelike submarine that resembles an alligator, then swim close to a fisherman's or trader's canoe to overturn it and catch their victims (MacCormack 54).

Religious or ritual cannibalism is different from survival and dietary cannibalism in that it has a ceremonial purpose rather than one of nourishment. Sometimes only a single victim is sacrificed in a ritual, while at other times many are sacrificed. For example, the Bangala tribe of the Congo River in central Africa honors a deceased chief or leader by purchasing, sacrificing, and feasting on slaves (Sagan 53). The number of slaves sacrificed is determined by how highly the tribe members revered the deceased leader. 11

Ritual cannibalism among South American Indians often serves as revenge for the dead. Like the Bangalas, some South American tribes kill their victims to be served as part of funeral rituals, with human sacrifices denoting that the deceased was held in high honor. Also like the Bangalas, these tribes use outsiders as victims. Unlike the Bangalas, however, the Indians sacrifice only one victim instead of many in a single ritual. For example, when a warrior of a tribe is killed in battle, the family of the warrior forces a victim to take the identity of the warrior. The family adorns the victim with the deceased warrior's belongings and may even force him to marry the deceased warrior's wives. But once the family believes the victim has assumed the spiritual identity of the deceased warrior, the family kills him. The children in the tribe soak their hands in the victim's blood to symbolize their revenge of the warrior's death. Elderly women from the tribe drink the victim's blood and then cut up his body for roasting and eating (Sagan 53–54). The people of the tribe believe that by sacrificing a victim, they have avenged the death of the warrior and the soul of the deceased can rest in peace. 12

In the villages of certain African tribes, only a small part of a dead body is used in ritual cannibalism. In these tribes, where the childbearing capacity of women is highly valued, women are obligated to eat small, raw fragments of genital parts during fertility rites. Elders of the tribe supervise this ritual to ensure that the women will be fertile. In the Bimin-Kuskusmin tribe, for instance, a widow eats a small, raw fragment of flesh from the penis of her deceased husband in order to enhance her future fertility and reproductive capacity. Similarly, a widower may eat a raw fragment of flesh from his deceased wife's vagina along with a piece of her bone marrow; by eating her flesh, he hopes to strengthen the fertility of his daughters borne by his dead wife, and by eating her bone marrow, he honors her reproductive capacity. Also, when an elder woman of the village who has shown great reproductive capacity dies, her uterus and the interior parts of her vagina are eaten by other women who hope to benefit from her reproductive power (Poole 16–17). 13

Members of developed societies in general practice none of these forms of cannibalism, with the occasional exception of survival cannibalism when the only alternative is starvation. It is possible, however, that our distant-past ancestors were cannibals who through the eons turned away from the practice. We are, after all, descended from the same ancestors as the Miyanmin, the Alligator, and the Leopard people, and survival cannibalism shows that people are capable of eating human flesh when they have no other choice. 14

Works Cited

Askenasy, Hans. *Cannibalism: From Sacrifice to Survival.* Amherst, NY: Prometheus, 1994.

Barker, Francis, Peter Hulme, and Margaret Iversen, eds. *Cannibalism and the New World.* Cambridge: Cambridge UP, 1998.

Brown, Paula, and Donald Tuzin, eds. *The Ethnography of Cannibalism.* Washington: Society of Psychological Anthropology, 1983.

"Cannibal Jokes." *The Loonie Bin of Jokes.* 22 Sept. 1999 <http://www.looniebin.mb.ca/cannibal.html>

Hart, James D. *A Companion to California.* Berkeley: U of California P, 1987.

Johnson, Kristin. "New Light on the Donner Party." 28 Sept. 1999 <http://www.metrogourmet.com/crossroads.KJhome.htm>.

MacCormack, Carol. "Human Leopard and Crocodile." Brown and Tuzin 54–55.

Poole, Fitz John Porter. "Cannibals, Tricksters, and Witches." Brown and Tuzin 11, 16–17.

Sagan, Eli. *Cannibalism.* New York: Harper, 1976.

Shipman, Pat. "The Myths and Perturbing Realities of Cannibalism." *Discover* Mar. 1987: 70+.

Tuzin, Donald. "Cannibalism and Arapesh Cosmology." Brown and Tuzin 61–63.

Twain, Mark. "Cannibalism in the Cars." *The Complete Short Stories of Mark Twain.* Ed. Charles Neider. New York: Doubleday, 1957. 9–16.

Connecting to Culture and Experience: Taboos

The author of a respected book on the Donner Party has this to say about the fact that some members of the party ate other members after they had died:

> Surely the necessity, starvation itself, had forced them to all they did, and surely no just man would ever have pointed at them in scorn, or assumed his own superiority.... Even the seemingly ghoulish actions invoked in the story may be rationally explained. To open the bodies first for the heart and liver, and to saw apart the skulls for the brain were not acts of perversion. We must remember that these people had been living for months upon the hides and lean meat of half-starved work oxen; their diet was lacking not only in mere quantity, but also in all sorts of necessary vitamin and mineral constituents, even in common salt. Almost uncontrollable cravings must have assailed them, cravings which represented a real deficiency in diet to be supplied in some degree at least by the organs mentioned.
>
> — GEORGE R. STEWART, *Ordeal by Hunger*

With two or three other students, discuss this author's argument and his unwillingness to pass judgment on the Donner Party's cannibalism. Individually, are you inclined to agree or disagree with the author? Give reasons for your views. Keep in mind that no one, perhaps with one exception toward the very end of the Donner Party's isolation, was murdered to be eaten. Therefore, the issue is not murder but the eating of human flesh and body parts by other humans to remain alive. Humans do eat many other animals' flesh and body parts for nourishment. Where do you think the taboo against cannibalism comes from in our society? What are your views on whether the taboo should be observed in all circumstances? What do you think about extending the taboo to the consumption of animal flesh?

Analyzing Writing Strategies

1. At the end of paragraph 6, Ngo names three types of cannibalism, which he defines in the subsequent paragraphs. Find where these types are defined in paragraphs 7, 8, and 12, and underline the definitions. Some definitions are given in a single phrase, and others are made up of several phrases, not always contiguous. Exclude the examples from your underlining. Then look over the definitions you have underlined with the following questions in mind: What makes these definitions easy or hard for you to understand? In what ways does the example that begins the essay (paragraphs 1–4) prepare you to understand the definitions? How do the examples that follow the definitions help you understand each concise definition?

2. As he explains the different types of cannibalism, Ngo makes good use of examples in paragraphs 7–13. Choose one of the longer examples in paragraph 9, 12, or 13, and analyze how it is put together and how effective it is. What kinds of information does it offer? What sources does the writer rely on? What seems most memorable or surprising to you in the example? How does it help you understand the type of cannibalism being illustrated? In general, how effective does it seem to you in explaining the concept?

Commentary: A Logical Plan

Writers face special challenges in planning essays that explain concepts. First they gather a lot of information about a concept. Then they find a focus for the explanation. With the focus in mind, they research the concept further, looking for information to help them develop the focus. At this point, they have to find a way to arrange the information into logically related topics. This process is known formally as *classifying*. Sometimes, as in Ngo's research, one of the sources provides the classification, but sometimes the writer has to create it. This borrowing or creation allows writers to plan their essays to identify the topics in the order in which they will present them.

Ngo's explanation of cannibalism illustrates the importance of a logical plan. The following topical scratch outline of the essay will help you see Ngo's classification and plan:

- Narration of a specific recent incident of cannibalism (paragraphs 1–4)
- Context for the concept (5)
- Definition of cannibalism and introduction of its two main categories and three types (6)

- Definition of survival cannibalism, with two brief examples (7)
- Definition of dietary cannibalism (8)
- Two extended examples of dietary cannibalism (9–10)
- Definition of ritual cannibalism, with one brief example (11)
- Two extended examples of ritual cannibalism (12–13)
- Conclusion (14)

Ngo presents the classification in paragraph 6. It has two levels. On the first level, the information is divided into exocannibalism and endocannibalism. On the second level, each of the first two divisions is divided into three parts: survival, dietary, and ritual cannibalism. That is, either outsiders or members of one's own group can be eaten in each type of cannibalism. Ngo relies on the three types of cannibalism to create a plan for his essay. First he explains survival cannibalism, then dietary cannibalism, and finally, ritual cannibalism. This plan may be considered logical in at least two ways: It moves from most to least familiar and from least to most complex. Perhaps Ngo assumes that his readers will know about the Donner Party, an unfortunate group of 1846 immigrants to California who were trapped high in the Sierra Nevada Mountains by early, heavy snowstorms and ended up practicing survival endocannibalism. Therefore, Ngo explains this type of cannibalism first and then moves on to the less familiar types, whose complex practice takes different forms around the world. Ngo devotes two or three times more space to explaining dietary and ritual cannibalism than he does to explaining survival cannibalism, and he presents detailed examples of these forms.

Ngo does more than adopt a classification and use it to plan his essay. He helps readers anticipate and follow the plan by forecasting it and then providing cues to the steps in the plan. At the end of paragraph 6, Ngo forecasts the types of cannibalism he will focus on: survival cannibalism, dietary cannibalism, and religious and ritual cannibalism. This forecast introduces the names or terms that Ngo will use consistently throughout the explanation and presents the types of cannibalism in the order that Ngo will discuss them. Readers are thereby prepared for the step-by-step plan of the explanation.

Ngo lets readers know when he is leaving one type of cannibalism and addressing the next type by constructing visible transitions at the beginnings of paragraphs. Here are the three key transition sentences:

> Survival cannibalism occurs when people trapped without food have to decide "whether to starve or to eat fellow humans...." (paragraph 7)

> Unlike survival cannibalism, in which human flesh is eaten as a last resort after a person has died, in dietary cannibalism humans are purchased or trapped for food and then eaten as a part of a culture's traditions. (8)

> Religious or ritual cannibalism is different from survival and dietary cannibalism in that it has a ceremonial purpose rather than one of nourishment. (11)

You can feature these types of cues—forecasts and transitions—in your essay explaining a concept. Whereas forecasting is optional, transitions are essential; without them, your readers will struggle to follow your explanation and may throw up their hands in confusion and irritation.

Considering Topics for Your Own Essay

Consider writing about some other well-established religious or cultural taboo such as murder, incest, or pedophilia. Or you might consider writing about a concept that tells something about current or historical social values, practices, or attitudes. To look at changing attitudes toward immigration, for example, think about concepts like assimilation, multiculturalism, the melting pot, and race. To look at changing attitudes toward dating, consider concepts like courtship, calling, and flirting.

■ PURPOSE AND AUDIENCE

Though it often seeks to engage readers' interests, explanatory writing gives prominence to facts about a subject. It aims to engage readers' intellects rather than their imaginations, to instruct rather than entertain or argue.

Setting out to teach readers about a concept is no small undertaking. To succeed, you must know the concept so well that you can explain it simply, without jargon or other confusing language. You must be authoritative without showing off or talking down. You must also estimate what your readers already know about the concept to decide which information will be truly new to them. You want to define unfamiliar words and pace the information carefully so that your readers are neither bored nor overwhelmed.

This assignment requires a willingness to cast yourself in the role of expert, which may not come naturally to you at this stage in your development as a writer. Students are most often asked to explain things in writing to readers who know more than they do—their instructors. When you plan and draft this essay, however, you will be aiming at readers who know less—maybe much less—than you do about the concept you will explain. Like Toufexis and Angier, you could write for a general audience of adults who regularly read a newspaper and subscribe to a few magazines. Even though some of them may be highly educated, you can readily and confidently assume the role of expert after a couple of hours of research into your concept. Your purpose may be to deepen your readers' understanding of a concept they may already be familiar with. If you choose to write for upper elementary or secondary school students, you could introduce them to an unfamiliar concept, or if you write for your classmates, you could demonstrate to them that a concept in an academic discipline that they find forbidding can actually be made both understandable and interesting. Even if you are told to consider your instructor your sole reader, you can assume that your instructor is eager to be informed about nearly any concept you choose.

You have spent many years in school reading explanations of concepts: Your textbooks in every subject have been full of concept explanations. Now, instead of receiving these explanations, you will be delivering one. To succeed, you will have to accept your role of expert. Your readers will expect you to be authoritative and well informed; they will also expect that you have limited the focus of your explanation but that you have not excluded anything essential to their understanding.

BASIC FEATURES: EXPLAINING CONCEPTS

A Focused Concept

The primary purpose for explaining a concept is to inform readers, but writers of explanatory essays do not hope to communicate everything that is known about a concept. Instead, they make choices about what to include, what to emphasize, and what to omit. Most writers focus on one aspect of the concept. Anastasia Toufexis focuses on the neurochemistry of love, Natalie Angier focuses on girls' preference for indirect aggression, and Linh Kieu Ngo focuses on three specific types of cannibalism.

An Appeal to Readers' Interests

Most people read explanations of concepts for work or study. Consequently, they expect the writing to be simply informative and not necessarily entertaining. Yet readers appreciate explanations that both identify the concept's importance and engage them with lively writing and vivid detail. The essays in this chapter show some of the ways in which writers may appeal to readers. For example, Toufexis uses humor and everyday language to attract readers' attention. She opens her essay with this direct address to readers: "O.K., let's cut out all this nonsense about romantic love." Calling romantic love "nonsense" arrests readers' attention as they thumb through the magazine in which the essay originally appeared. An opening strategy like this can do much to interest readers in the concept.

A Logical Plan

Since concept explanations present information that is new to readers and can therefore be hard to understand, writers need to develop a plan that presents new material step by step in a logical order. The most effective explanations are carefully organized and give readers all the obvious cues they need, such as forecasting statements, topic sentences, transitions, and summaries. In addition, the writer may try to frame the essay for readers by relating the ending to the beginning. We have seen these features repeatedly in the readings in this chapter. For example, Toufexis frames her essay with references to Ph.D.'s, forecasts the three sciences from which she has gleaned her information about the neurochemistry of love, and begins nearly all of her paragraphs with a transition sentence.

Good writers never forget that their readers need clear signals. Because writers already know the information and are aware of how their essays are organized, they can find it difficult to see the essay the way someone reading it for the first time would. That is precisely how it should be seen, however, to be sure that the essay includes all the necessary cues.

Clear Definitions

Essays explaining concepts depend on clear definitions. To relate information clearly, a writer must be sensitive to readers' knowledge; any key terms that are likely to be unfamiliar or misunderstood must be explicitly defined, as Toufexis defines *attraction junkies* (paragraph 12) and *endorphins* (paragraph 13) and as Ngo defines the *categories* of cannibalism (paragraph 6) and *types* of cannibalism (at the beginnings of paragraphs where he illustrates them). In a sense, all the readings in this chapter are extended definitions of concepts, and all the authors offer relatively concise, clear definitions of their concepts at some point in their essays.

Appropriate Writing Strategies

Many writing strategies are useful for presenting information. The strategies that a writer uses are determined by the way he or she focuses the essay and the kind of information available. The following strategies are particularly useful in explaining concepts:

Classification. One way of presenting information is to divide it into groups and discuss the groups one by one. For example, Toufexis divides the chemicals she discusses into those associated with falling in love and those associated with lasting relationships. Ngo divides cannibalism into three types.

Process Narration. Process narration typically explains how something is done. Many concepts involve processes that unfold over time, such as the geologic scale, or over both time and space, such as bird migration. Process narration involves some of the basic storytelling strategies covered in Chapter 2: narrative time signals, actors and action, and connectives showing temporal relationships. For example, Ngo briefly narrates one process of ritual cannibalism (paragraph 12).

Comparison and Contrast. The comparison/contrast strategy is especially useful for explaining concepts because it helps readers understand something new by showing how it is similar to or different from things they already know. Every essayist in this chapter makes use of comparison and contrast. For example, Angier compares indirect aggression with physical and verbal aggression, girls with boys, and different age groups with one another. Ngo compares the three types of cannibalism as well as different cultures.

Cause and Effect. Another useful strategy for explaining a concept is to report its causes or effects. Toufexis explains the evolutionary benefits of romantic love, and Angier reports the causes established by research to explain why adolescent girls rely on indirect aggression. Note that writers of explanatory essays ordinarily either report established causes or effects or report others' speculated causes or effects as if they were established facts. They usually do not themselves speculate about possible causes or effects.

Careful Use of Sources

To explain concepts, writers usually draw on information from many different sources. Although they often draw on their own experiences and observations, they almost always do additional research into what others have to say about their subject. Referring to expert sources always lends authority to an explanation.

How writers treat sources depends on the writing situation. Certain formal situations, such as college assignments or scholarly papers, have rules for citing and documenting sources. Students and scholars are expected to cite their sources formally because readers judge their work in part by what the writers have read and how they have used their reading. Ngo's essay illustrates this academic form of citing sources. For more informal writing — magazine articles, for example — readers do not expect or want page references or publication information, but they do expect sources to be identified. This identification often appears within the text of the article, as illustrated in the selection by Toufexis, which was originally published in a magazine. Other nonacademic writing — popular books, for example — may be based on research, but those authors may choose not to impose on readers the formal documentation style of academic writing. Angier, for example, mentions in her preface that she interviewed hundreds of experts. She also includes a list of sources at the end of the book and identifies most of them in the text — such as Björkqvist in paragraphs 4 and 12 — so that her readers can find their names in the alphabetical list at the end.

GUIDE TO WRITING
Explaining Concepts

THE WRITING ASSIGNMENT

Write an essay about a concept that interests you and that you want to study further. When you have a good understanding of the concept, explain it to your readers, considering carefully what they already know about it and how your essay might add to what they know.

THE WRITING ASSIGNMENT

INVENTION & RESEARCH

Finding a Concept to Write About

Surveying Information about the Concept

Focusing the Concept

Testing Your Choice

Researching Your Topic Focus

Considering Explanatory Strategies

Considering Document Design

Defining Your Purpose for Your Readers

Formulating a Tentative Thesis Statement

INVENTION AND RESEARCH

PLANNING & DRAFTING

Seeing What You Have

Setting Goals

Outlining

Drafting

PLANNING AND DRAFTING

CRITICAL READING GUIDE

First Impression

Clear Focus and Explanation of Concept

Appropriate Content

Organization

Clarity of Definitions

Use of Sources

Effectiveness of Visuals

Final Thoughts

CRITICAL READING GUIDE

REVISING

A Focused Concept

An Appeal to Readers' Interests

A Logical Plan

Clear Definitions

Appropriate Writing Strategies

Careful Use of Sources

REVISING

EDITING & PROOFREADING

Checking the Punctuation of Adjective Clauses

Checking for Commas around Interrupting Phrases

EDITING AND PROOFREADING

GUIDE TO WRITING

■ THE WRITING ASSIGNMENT

Write an essay about a concept that interests you and that you want to study further. When you have a good understanding of the concept, explain it to your readers, considering carefully what they already know about it and how your essay might add to what they know.

■ INVENTION AND RESEARCH

The following guidelines will help you find a concept, understand it fully, select a focus that is appropriate for your readers, test your choice, and devise strategies for presenting your discoveries in a way that will be truly informative for your particular readers. Each activity is easy to do and takes only a few minutes. If you can spread out the activities over several days, you will have adequate time to understand the concept and decide how to present it. Keep a written record of your invention work to use when you draft the essay and later when you revise it. If you write on the computer, you may be able to copy and paste into your draft material from your invention and research notes.

Finding a Concept to Write About

Even if you already have a concept in mind, completing the following activities will help you to be certain of your choice.

Listing Concepts. *Make a list of concepts you could write about.* The longer your list, the more likely you are to find just the right concept for you. And should your first choice not work out, you will have a ready list of alternatives. Include concepts you already know something about as well as some you know only slightly and would like to research further. Also include concepts suggested by the Considering Topics for Your Own Essay activities following each reading in this chapter.

Your courses provide many concepts you will want to consider. Here are some typical concepts from a number of academic and other subjects. Your class notes or textbooks will suggest many others.

- *Literature:* irony, metaphysical conceit, semiotics, hero, dystopian novel, humanism, picaresque, the absurd, canon, representation, figurative language, modernism, identity politics, queering
- *Philosophy:* existentialism, nihilism, logical positivism, determinism, metaphysics, ethics, natural law, Zeno's paradox, epistemology, ideology
- *Business management:* autonomous work group, quality circle, cybernetic control system, management by objectives, zero-based budgeting, liquidity gap

- *Psychology:* metacognition, Hawthorne effect, assimilation/accommodation, social cognition, moratorium, intelligence, divergent/convergent thinking, operant conditioning, short-term memory, the Stroop effect, sleep paralysis
- *Government:* majority rule, minority rights, federalism, popular consent, exclusionary rule, political party, political machine, interest group, hegemony
- *Biology:* photosynthesis, mitosis, karyotype analysis, morphogenesis, ecosystem, electron transport, plasmolysis, phagocytosis, homozygosity, diffusion
- *Art:* cubism, Dadaism, surrealism, expressionism
- *Math:* polynomials, boundedness, null space, permutations and combinations, factoring, Rolle's theorem, continuity, derivative, indefinite integral
- *Physical sciences:* matter, mass, weight, energy, gravity, atomic theory, law of definite proportions, osmotic pressure, first law of thermodynamics, entropy
- *Public health:* alcoholism, seasonal affective disorder, contraception, lead poisoning, prenatal care, toxicology
- *Environmental studies:* acid rain, recycling, ozone depletion, toxic waste, endangered species
- *Sports:* squeeze play, hit and run (baseball); power play (hockey); nickel defense, wishbone offense (football); serve and volley offense (tennis); setup (volleyball); pick and roll, inside game (basketball)
- *Personal finance:* mortgage, budget, insurance, deduction, revolving credit, interest rates, dividend, bankruptcy
- *Law:* tort, contract, garnishment, double indemnity, reasonable doubt, class-action suits, product liability, lemon law
- *Sociology:* norm, deviance, role conflict, ethnocentrism, class, social stratification, conflict theory, action theory, acculturation, Whorf-Sapir hypothesis, machismo

Listing Concepts Related to Identity and Community. Many concepts are important in understanding identity and community. As you consider the following concepts, try to think of others in this category: self-esteem, character, personality, autonomy, individuation, narcissism, multiculturalism, ethnicity, race, racism, social contract, communitarianism, community policing, social Darwinism, identity politics, special-interest groups, diaspora, colonialism, public space, the other, agency, difference, yuppie, generation X.

Listing Concepts Related to Work and Career. Concepts like the following enable you to gain a deeper understanding of your work experiences and career aspirations: free enterprise, minimum wage, affirmative action, stock option, sweatshop, glass ceiling, downsizing, collective bargaining, service sector, market, entrepreneur, bourgeoisie, underclass, working class, middle class, division of labor, monopoly, automation, robotics, management style, deregulation, multinational corporation.

Choosing a Concept. *Look over your list of possibilities, and select one concept to explore.* Pick a concept that interests you, one you feel eager to learn more about. Consider also whether it might interest others. You may know very little about the concept now, but the guidelines that follow will help you research it and understand it fully.

Surveying Information about the Concept

Your research efforts for a concept essay must be divided into two stages. First, you want to achieve quickly a far-reaching survey or overview of information about the concept you have chosen. Your goal in this first stage is to learn as much as you can from diverse sources so that you may decide whether you want to write about this topic and whether you can identify an aspect of it to focus on.

In the second stage, when you know what your focus will be, you begin in-depth research for information that will educate you about this focus. When Natalie Angier arrived at this stage, she would have been learning as much as possible about indirect aggression between girls, not aggression in general. When Linh Kieu Ngo arrived at this stage, he would have been digging for information on ways to classify the different types of cannibalism.

The activities that follow will guide you through this two-stage research process.

Discovering What You Already Know. *Before doing any research on your concept or even looking at any handy references, take a few minutes to write about what you already know about the concept.* Also say why you have chosen the concept and why you find it interesting and worth knowing about. Write quickly, without planning or organizing. Write phrases or lists as well as sentences. You could even add drawings or quick sketches or write down questions about the concept, questions that express your curiosity or uncertainty. If you find that you know very little about the concept, you still might want to write about it—out of personal motivation, which is not a bad reason to commit yourself to the study of an unfamiliar concept.

Sorting Through Your Personal Resources. *Check any materials you already have at hand that explain your concept.* If you are considering a concept from one of your academic courses, you will find explanatory material in your textbook or perhaps your lecture notes.

To acquire a comprehensive, up-to-date understanding of your concept, however, you will need to know how experts other than your textbook writer and instructor define and illustrate it. To find this information, you might locate relevant articles or books in the library, search for resources or make inquiries on the Internet, or consult experts on campus or in the community.

Going Online. *Keep a list of Web sites you find that invite more than a quick glance, sites that hold your attention and inform you about your concept. Bookmark each site, or record its name and URL. You might make a few brief notes about key contents or features of sites from which you learn the most. Also keep a list of possible focuses you discover.*

Keep your goal for this stage in mind: to educate yourself quickly about the concept and look for a possible focus for your essay. It is too early to begin downloading a lot of material.

Going to the Library.   *Keep a list of the most promising materials you discover in the library. Continue your other list of possible focuses, trying to come up with at least two or three possibilities.* Besides taking a quick look at relevant encyclopedias and disciplinary guides, look for your concept name in the subject headings of the *Library of Congress Subject Headings* and also in the library catalog, using the keyword search option. The library can give you access to special online resources; ask a librarian for advice. Remember that moving through your search quickly will give you a good overview of information about your concept.

Researching Concepts: An Online Activity   One way to get a quick initial overview of the information available on a concept is to search for the concept online. You can do this in several ways:

- Enter the name of your concept in a search tool such as Google (www.google.com) or Yahoo! Directory (http://dir.yahoo.com) to discover possible sources of information about the concept.
- Check an online encyclopedia in the field to which the concept belongs. Here are a few specialized encyclopedias that may be helpful:
  - *Encyclopedia of Psychology* www.psychology.org/
  - *The Internet Encyclopedia of Philosophy* www.utm.edu/research/iep/
  - *Webopedia* www.webopedia.com

  Bookmark or keep a record of promising sites. When you proceed to a narrower search for information about your topic focus, you could then download any materials, including visuals, that you might consider including in your own essay.

Focusing the Concept

Once you have an overview of your concept, you must choose a focus for your essay. More is known about most concepts than you can include in an essay, and concepts can be approached from many perspectives (for example, history, definition, significance), so you must limit your explanation. Doing this will help you avoid the common problem of trying to explain too much. Because the focus must reflect both your special interest in the concept and your readers' likely knowledge and interest, you will want to explore both.

Exploring Your Own Interests. *Make a list of two or three aspects of the concept that could become a focus for your essay, and evaluate what you know about each focus. Leave some space after each item in the list.* Under each possible focus in your list, make notes about why it interests you and why it seems just the right size (not so small that it is trivial and not so large that it is overwhelming). Indicate whether you know enough to begin writing about that aspect of the concept, what additional questions you would need to answer, and what is important or interesting to you about that particular aspect.

Analyzing Your Readers. *Take a few minutes to analyze in writing your readers.* To decide what aspect of the concept to focus on, you also need to think about who your prospective readers are likely to be and to speculate about their knowledge of and interest in the concept. Even if you are writing only for your instructor, you should give some thought to what he or she knows and thinks about the concept.

The following questions are designed to help you with your analysis:

- Who are my readers, and what are they likely to know about this concept?
- What, if anything, might they know about the field of study to which this concept applies?
- What could I point out that would be useful for them to know about this concept, perhaps something that could relate to their life or work?
- What connections could I make between this concept and others that my readers are likely to be familiar with?

Choosing a Focus. *With your interests and those of your readers in mind, choose an aspect of your concept on which to focus, and write a sentence justifying its appropriateness.*

Testing Your Choice

Pause now to test whether you have chosen a workable concept and focused it appropriately. As painful as it may be to consider, starting fresh with a new concept is better than continuing with an unworkable one. The following questions can help you test your choice:

- Do I understand my concept well enough to explain it?
- Have I discovered a focus for writing about this concept?
- Do I think I can find enough information for an essay with such a focus?
- Do I see possibilities for engaging my readers' interest in this aspect of my concept?

If you cannot answer yes to all four questions, consider choosing another focus or selecting another concept to write about.

| **Testing Your Choice: A Collaborative Activity** | Get together with two or three other students to find out what your readers are likely to know about your subject and what might interest them about it. Your instructor may ask you to complete this activity in class or online in a chat room. |

Presenters: Take turns briefly explaining your concept, describing your intended readers, and identifying the aspect of the concept that you will focus on.

Listeners: Briefly tell the presenter whether the focus sounds appropriate and interesting for the intended readers. Share what you think readers are likely to know about the concept and what information might be especially interesting and memorable for them.

Researching Your Topic Focus

Now begins stage two of your research process. With a likely focus in mind, you are ready to mine both the Internet and the library for valuable nuggets of information. Your research becomes selective and deliberate, and you will now want to keep careful records of all sources you believe will contribute in any way to your essay. If possible, make photocopies of print sources, and print out sources you download from CD-ROMs or the Internet. If you must rely on notes, be sure to copy any quotations exactly and enclose them in quotation marks so that later you can quote sources accurately.

Since you do not know which sources you will ultimately use, keep a careful record of the author, title, publication information, page numbers, and other required information for each source you gather. Check with your instructor about whether you should follow the Modern Language Association (MLA) or American Psychological Association (APA) style of acknowledging sources. In this chapter, the Ngo essay follows the MLA style.

Going Online.   *Return to online searching, with your focus in mind. Download and print out essential material if possible, or take careful notes. Record all of the details you will need to acknowledge sources in your essay, should you decide to use them.*

Going to the Library.   *Return to the library to search for materials relevant to your focus. Photocopy, print out, or take notes on promising print and electronic materials. Keep careful records so that you can acknowledge your sources.*

Considering Explanatory Strategies

Before you move on to plan and draft your essay, consider some possible ways of presenting the concept. Try to answer each of the following questions in a sentence or two.

Questions that you can answer readily may identify strategies that can help you explain your concept.

- What term is used to name the concept, and what does it mean? (definition)
- How is this concept like or unlike related concepts? (comparison and contrast)
- How can an explanation of this concept be divided into parts? (classification)
- How does this concept happen, or how does one go about doing it? (process narration)
- What are this concept's known causes or effects? (cause and effect)

Considering Document Design

Think about whether visual elements—tables, graphs, drawings, photographs—would make your explanation clearer. These are not a requirement of an essay explaining a concept, but they could be helpful. Consider also whether your readers might benefit from design features such as headings, bulleted or numbered lists, or other elements that would present information efficiently or make your explanation easier to follow. You could construct your own graphic elements, download materials from the Internet, copy images from television or other sources, or scan into your document visuals from books and magazines. Remember that you should cite the source of any visual you do not create yourself, and you should also request permission from the source of the visual if your paper is going to be posted on the Web.

Defining Your Purpose for Your Readers

Write a few sentences that define your purpose in writing about this particular concept for your readers. Remember that you have already identified and analyzed your readers and that you have begun to research and develop your explanation with these readers in mind. Given these readers, try now to define your purpose in explaining the concept to them. Use these questions to focus your thoughts:

- Are my readers familiar with the concept? If not, how can I overcome their resistance or puzzlement? Or, if so, will my chosen focus allow my readers to see the familiar concept in a new light?
- If I suspect that my readers have misconceptions about the concept, how can I correct the misconceptions without offending readers?
- Do I want to arouse readers' interest in information that may seem at first to be less than engaging?
- Do I want readers to see that the information I have to report is relevant to their lives, families, communities, work, or studies?

Formulating a Tentative Thesis Statement

Write one or more sentences that could serve as a thesis statement. State your concept and focus. You might also want to forecast the topics you will use to explain the concept.

Anastasia Toufexis begins her essay with this thesis statement:

> O.K., let's cut out all this nonsense about romantic love. Let's bring some scientific precision to the party. Let's put love under a microscope.
> When rigorous people with Ph.D.s after their names do that, what they see is not some silly, senseless thing. No, their probe reveals that love rests firmly on the foundations of evolution, biology and chemistry.

Toufexis's concept is love, and her focus is the scientific explanation of love—specifically the evolution, biology, and chemistry of love. In announcing her focus, she forecasts the order in which she will present information from the three most relevant academic disciplines—anthropology (which includes the study of human evolution), biology, and chemistry. These discipline names become her topics.

In his essay on cannibalism, Linh Kieu Ngo offers his thesis statement in paragraph 6:

> Cannibalism can be broken down into two main categories: exocannibalism, the eating of outsiders or foreigners, and endocannibalism, the eating of members of one's own social group (Shipman 70). Within these categories are several functional types of cannibalism, three of the most common being survival cannibalism, dietary cannibalism, and religious and ritual cannibalism.

Ngo's concept is cannibalism, and his focus is on three common types of cannibalism. He carefully forecasts how he will divide the information to create topics and the order in which he will explain each of the topics, the common types of cannibalism.

As you draft your own tentative thesis statement, take care to make the language clear and unambiguous. Although you may want to revise your thesis statement as you draft your essay, trying to state it now will give your planning and drafting more focus and direction. Keep in mind that the thesis in an explanatory essay merely announces the subject; it never asserts a position that requires an argument to defend it.

■ PLANNING AND DRAFTING

The following guidelines will help you get the most out of your invention notes, determine specific goals for your essay, and write a first draft.

Seeing What You Have

Reread everything you have written so far. This is a critically important time for reflection and evaluation. Before beginning the actual draft, you must decide whether your subject is worthwhile and whether you have sufficient information for a successful essay.

It may help, as you read, to annotate your invention writings. Look for details that will help you explain the concept in a way that your readers can grasp. Highlight key words, phrases, or sentences; make marginal notes or electronic annotations of any material you think could be useful. If you have done your invention writing on the computer, you may have sentences or whole paragraphs that can be copied and pasted into your draft.

Be realistic. If at this point your notes do not look promising, you may want to choose a different focus for your concept or select a different concept to write about. If your notes seem thin but promising, do further research to find more information before continuing.

Setting Goals

Successful writers are always looking beyond the next sentence to larger goals. Indeed, the next sentence is easier to write if you keep larger goals in mind. The following questions can help you set these goals. Consider each one now, and then return to them as necessary while you write.

Your Purpose and Readers

- How can I build on my readers' knowledge?
- What new information can I present to them?
- How can I organize my essay so that my readers can follow it easily?
- What tone would be most appropriate? Would an informal tone like Toufexis's or a formal one like Ngo's be more appropriate to my purpose?

The Beginning

- How shall I begin? Should I open with a provocative quotation, as Toufexis does? With an incident illustrating the concept, as Angier and Ngo do? With an explanation of why readers need to understand the concept? With a question?
- How can I best forecast the plan that my explanation will follow? Should I offer a detailed forecast, as Toufexis and Ngo do?

Writing Strategies

- What terms do I need to define? Can I rely on brief sentence definitions, or will I need to write extended definitions? Should I give a history of the concept term?
- Are there ways to classify the information?
- What examples can I use to make the explanation more concrete?
- Would any comparisons or contrasts help readers understand the information?
- Do I need to explain any processes or known causes or effects?

The Ending

- Should I frame the essay by relating the ending to the beginning, as Toufexis does?
- Should I end by suggesting what is special about the concept, as Angier does?
- Should I end with a speculation about the past, as Ngo does?
- Should I end by suggesting how my readers can apply the concept to their own lives?

Outlining

The goals that you have set should help you draft your essay, but first you might want to make a quick scratch outline to refocus on the basic story line. You could use the outlining function of your word processing program. In your outline, list the main topics into which you have divided the information about your concept. Use this outline to guide your drafting, but do not feel tied to it. As you draft, you may find a better way to sequence the action and integrate these features.

An essay explaining a concept is made up of four basic parts:

- An attempt to engage readers' interest
- The thesis statement, announcing the concept, its focus, and its topics
- An orientation to the concept, which may include a description or definition of the concept
- Information about the concept

Here is a possible outline for an essay explaining a concept:

An attempt to gain readers' interest in the concept

Thesis statement

Definition of the concept

Topic 1 with illustration

Topic 2 with illustration

(etc.)

Conclusion

An attempt to gain readers' interest could take as little space as two or three sentences or as much as four or five paragraphs. The thesis statement and definition are usually quite brief—sometimes only a few sentences. A topic illustration may occupy one or several paragraphs, and there can be few or many topics, depending on how the information has been divided up. A conclusion might summarize the information presented, give advice about how to use or apply the information, or speculate about the future of the concept.

Consider any outlining that you do before you begin drafting to be tentative. As you draft, be ready to revise your outline, shift parts around, or drop or add parts. If you use the outlining function of your word processing program, changing your outline will be simple, and you may be able to write the essay simply by expanding the outline.

Drafting

General Advice.   Start drafting your essay, keeping in mind the goals you set while you were planning. Remember also the needs and expectations of your readers; organize, define, and explain with them in mind. Work to increase readers' understanding of your concept. Turn off your grammar checker and spelling checker at this stage if you find them distracting. Do not be afraid to skip around in your document. Jump back and fill in a spontaneous idea, or leap ahead and write a later section first if you find that easier. If you get stuck while drafting, try using some of the writing activities in the Invention and Research section of this chapter.

Sentence Strategies.   As you draft an essay explaining a concept, you must introduce library and Internet research sources and their authors within your sentences. You must also devise sentences that allow you to subordinate some information to other information and to introduce many examples or illustrations for readers to understand the concept. Precise verbs and a versatile sentence modifier called an *appositive* can help you achieve these goals.

Use informative, precise verbs to introduce sources and authors. Experienced writers of all kinds of explanatory and informational writing take great care in choosing verbs to introduce sources and authors, as these examples illustrate (the verbs are in italics):

> Lovers...are literally flooded by chemicals, research *suggests.* (Anastasia Toufexis, paragraph 9)

> The scientists *found* that boys and girls were equally likely to use verbal aggression against their cohorts....(Natalie Angier, paragraph 6)

> In one incident, Japanese troops *were reported* to have sacrificed the Arapesh people of northeastern New Guinea for food in order to avoid death by starvation. (Linh Kieu Ngo, paragraph 7)

When you explain a concept to readers unfamiliar with it, you usually are presenting information that is well established and currently considered reliable by experts on your topic. Because you are not making an argument either for or against your sources or authors, you need to introduce them to readers using somewhat neutral language — like the italicized verbs *suggests, found,* and *were reported* in the preceding examples. Yet there are important distinctions in meaning among these three verbs. *Found* connotes that Natalie Angier is merely reporting a research discovery or an earlier discovery newly confirmed. *Suggests* may indicate that Anastasia Toufexis is referring to broad implications of research rather than to findings. Paraphrasing a source with *were reported,* Linh Kieu Ngo makes clear to readers that the writer relied on second-hand information.

As you refer to sources in your concept explanation, you will be able to choose carefully among a wide variety of precise verbs. Every writer in this chapter uses a great variety of verbs for this purpose — sometimes for the sake of variety, no doubt, but usually in an effort to help readers better understand how the writer is using a source. As you draft your essay, you may find this partial list of verbs from the readings helpful in selecting precisely the right verbs to introduce your sources:

reveals	contends	questions
explains	brings into focus	tells

observes	pulls together	reports
notes	documents	finds
shows	warns	according to [name of
speculates	mounts	author or source]
rejects	tries to understand	

Use appositives to identify people, define terms, and give examples and specifics. An appositive can be defined as a group of words, usually based on a noun or pronoun, that identifies or gives more information about another noun or pronoun just preceding it. Appositives come in many forms, as shown in these examples (the appositives are in italics):

> Says Michael Mills, *a psychology professor at Loyola Marymount University in Los Angeles:* "Love is our ancestors whispering in our ears." (Anastasia Toufexis, paragraph 2)

> Cannibalism, *the act of human beings eating human flesh* (Sagan 2), has a long history and continues to hold interest and create controversy. (Linh Kieu Ngo, paragraph 5)

In this chapter's three readings, appositives appear frequently. Writers explaining concepts rely to such an extent on appositives because they serve so many purposes. Among the most common are the following:

- Identifying a thing or person, often to establish a source's authority

  > "Love is a natural high," observes Anthony Walsh, *author of* The Science of Love: Understanding Love and Its Effects on Mind and Body. (Anastasia Toufexis, paragraph 10)

- Giving examples or more specific information

  > Girls who become good friends feel a compulsion to define the friendship, *to stamp it and name it*....(Natalie Angier, paragraph 10)

- Introducing a new term

  > Each person carries in his or her mind a unique subliminal guide to the ideal partner, *a "love map."*...(Anastasia Toufexis, paragraph 17)

Appositives accomplish these and other purposes very efficiently by enabling the writer to put related bits of information next to each other in the same sentence, thereby merging two potential sentences into one or shrinking a potential clause to a phrase. For example, Ngo, instead of making use of the appositive, could have written either of the following:

> Cannibalism can be defined as the act of human beings eating human flesh. It has a long history and continues to hold interest and create controversy.

> Cannibalism, which can be defined as the act of human beings eating human flesh, has a long history and continues to hold interest and create controversy.

Both of these versions are readable and clear. By using an appositive, however, Ngo saves four or five words, subordinates the definition of cannibalism to his main idea about history and controversy, and yet locates the definition exactly where readers need to see it.

In addition to using precise verbs to introduce sources and examples and to relying on appositives, you can strengthen your concept explanation with other kinds of sentences as well, and you may want to turn to the information about sentences that express comparison and contrast (pp. 293–94) and sentences that use conjunctions and phrases to indicate the logical relationships between clauses and sentences (pp. 198–99).

CRITICAL READING GUIDE
Now is the time to get a good critical reading of your draft. Your instructor may arrange such a reading as part of your coursework—in class or online. If not, you can ask a classmate, friend, or family member to read your draft using this guide. If your campus has a writing center, you might ask a tutor there to read and comment on your draft. (If you are unable to have someone else review your draft, turn ahead to the Revising section on p. 154, where you will find guidelines for reading your own draft critically.)

If you read another student's draft online, you may be able to use a word processing program to insert suggested improvements directly into the text of the draft or to write them out at the end of the draft. If you read a printout of the draft, you may write brief comments in the margins and lengthier suggestions on a separate page. When the writer sits down to revise, your thoughtful, extended suggestions written at the end of the draft or on separate pages will be especially helpful.

If You Are the Writer. To provide focused, helpful comments, your reader must know your essay's intended audience, your purpose, and a problem in the draft that you need help solving. Briefly write out this information at the top of your draft.

- *Readers:* To whom are you directing your concept explanation? What do you assume they know about the concept? How do you plan to engage and hold their interest?
- *Purpose:* What do you hope to achieve with your readers?
- *Problem:* Ask your reader to help you solve the most important problem you see in the draft. Describe this problem briefly.

If You Are the Reader. Use the following guidelines to help you give constructive, helpful comments to others on essays explaining concepts.

1. *Read for a First Impression.* Read first to get a sense of the concept. Then briefly write out your impressions. What in the draft do you think will especially interest the intended readers? Where might they have difficulty in following the explanation? Next, consider the problem the writer identified, and respond briefly to that concern now. (If you find that the problem is covered by one of the other guidelines listed below, respond to it in more detail there if necessary.)

2. *Assess Whether the Concept Is Clearly Explained and Focused.* Restate, in one sentence, what you understand the concept to mean. Indicate any confusion or uncertainty you have about its meaning. Given the concept, does the focus seem appropriate, too broad, or too narrow for the intended readers? Can you think of a more interesting aspect of the concept on which to focus the explanation?

3. *Consider Whether the Content Is Appropriate for the Intended Readers.* Does it tell them all that they are likely to want to know about the concept? Can you suggest additional information that should be included? What unanswered questions might readers have about the concept? Point out any information that seems either superfluous or too predictable.

4. *Evaluate the Organization.* Look at the way the essay is organized by making a scratch outline. Does the information seem to be logically divided? If not, suggest a better way to divide it. Also consider the order or sequence of information. Can you suggest a better way of sequencing it?

   - *Look at the beginning.* Does it pull readers into the essay and make them want to continue? Does it adequately forecast the direction of the essay? If possible, suggest a better way to begin.

   - *Look for obvious transitions in the draft.* Tell the writer how they are helpful or unhelpful. Try to improve one or two of them. Look for additional places where transitions would be helpful.

   - *Look at the ending.* Explain what makes it particularly effective or less effective than it might be, in your opinion. If you can, suggest a better way to end.

5. *Assess the Clarity of Definitions.* Point out any definitions that may be unclear or confusing to the intended readers. Identify any other terms that may need to be defined.

6. *Evaluate the Use of Sources.* If the writer has used sources, review the list of sources cited. Given the purpose, readers, and focus of the essay, does the list seem balanced, and are the selections appropriate? Try to suggest concerns or questions about sources that readers knowledgeable about the concept might raise. Then consider the use of sources within the text of the essay. Are there places where summary or paraphrase would be preferable to quoted material or vice versa? Note any places where the writer has

placed quotations awkwardly into the text, and recommend ways to smooth them out.

7. *Evaluate the Effectiveness of Visuals.* If charts, graphs, tables, or other visuals are included, let the writer know whether they help you understand the concept. Suggest ideas you have for changing, adding, moving, or deleting visuals.

8. *Give the Writer Your Final Thoughts.* Which part needs the most work? What do you think the intended readers will find most informative or memorable? What do you like best about the draft essay?

■ REVISING

Now you are ready to revise your essay. Your instructor or other students may have given you advice on improving your draft. Nevertheless, you may have begun to realize that your draft requires not so much revision as rethinking. For example, you may recognize that the focus you chose is too broad to be explained adequately in a few pages, that you need to make the information more engaging or interesting for your intended readers, or that you need substantially more information to present the concept adequately. Consequently, instead of working to improve parts of the draft, you may need to write a new draft that radically reenvisions your explanation. It is not unusual for students—and professional writers—to find themselves in this situation. Seek your instructor's advice if you must plan a radical revision.

On the other hand, you may feel quite satisfied that your draft achieves most, if not all, of your goals. In that case, you can focus on refining specific parts of your draft. Very likely you have thought of ways to improve your draft, and you may even have begun improving it. This section will help you get an overview of your draft and revise it accordingly.

Getting an Overview

Consider your draft as a whole. It may help to do so in two steps:

1. *Reread.* If at all possible, put the draft aside for a day or two before rereading it. When you return to it, start by reconsidering your readers and purpose. Then read the draft straight through, trying to see it as your intended readers will.

2. *Outline.* Make a scratch outline to get an overview of the essay's development. Consider using the headings and outline/summary functions of your word processor.

Planning for Revision.   Resist the temptation to dive in and start changing your text until after you have a clear view of the big picture. Using your outline as a guide, move through the document, using the highlighting or commenting tools of your word processor to note comments received from others and problems you want to solve (or mark on a hard copy if you prefer).

Analyzing the Basic Features of Your Own Draft.   Using the Critical Reading Guide on the preceding pages, reread the draft to identify problems you need to solve. Note the problems on your draft.

Studying Critical Comments.   Review all of the comments you have received from other readers, and add to your notes any that you intend to act on. Try not to react defensively. For each comment, look at the draft to determine what might have led the reader to make the comment. By letting you see how others respond to your draft, these comments provide valuable information about how you might improve it.

Carrying Out Revisions

Having identified problems in your draft, you now need to come up with solutions and—most important—to carry them out. Basically, there are three ways to find solutions:

1. Review your invention and planning notes and your sources for information and ideas to add to the draft.
2. Do further invention or research to answer questions your readers raised.
3. Look back at the readings in this chapter to see how other writers have solved similar problems.

The following suggestions, which are organized according to the basic features of explanatory essays, will get you started solving some writing problems common to them.

A Focused Concept

- **Is the focus too broad?** Consider limiting it further so that you can explain one part of the concept in more depth. If readers were uninterested in the aspect you focused on, consider focusing on some other aspect.
- **Is the focus too narrow?** You may have isolated too minor an aspect. Go back to your invention and research notes, and look for larger or more significant aspects.

An Appeal to Readers' Interests

- **Do you fail to connect to readers' interests and engage their attention throughout the essay?** Help readers see the significance of the information to them personally. Eliminate superfluous or too-predictable content. Open with an unusual piece of information that catches readers' interest.
- **Do you think readers will have unanswered questions?** Review your invention writing and sources for further information to answer them.

A Logical Plan

- **Does the beginning successfully orient readers to your purpose and plan?** Try making your focus obvious immediately. Forecast the plan of your essay.

- **Is the explanation difficult to follow?** Look for a way to reorder the parts so that the essay is easier to follow. Try constructing an alternative outline. Add transitions or summaries to help keep readers on track. Or consider ways you might classify and divide the information to make it easier to understand or provide a more interesting perspective on the topic.

- **Is the ending inconclusive?** Consider moving important information there. Try summarizing highlights of the essay or framing it by referring to something in the beginning. Or you might speculate about the future of the concept or assert its usefulness.

Clear Definitions

- **Do readers need a clearer or fuller definition of the concept?** Add a concise definition early in your essay, or consider adding a brief summary that defines the concept later in the essay (in the middle or at the end). Remove any information that may blur readers' understanding of the concept.

- **Are other key terms inadequately defined?** Supply clear definitions, searching your sources or checking a dictionary if necessary.

Appropriate Writing Strategies

- **Does the content seem thin or the definition of the concept blurred?** Consider whether any other writing strategies would improve the presentation.

  - Try comparing or contrasting the concept with a related one that is more familiar to readers.
  - Add some information about its known causes or effects.
  - See whether adding examples enlivens or clarifies your explanation. Remember that appositive phrases are a good way to introduce brief examples.
  - Tell more about how the concept works or what people do with it.
  - Add design features or visuals such as charts, headings, drawings, or photographs.

Careful Use of Sources

- **Do readers find your sources inadequate?** Return to the library or the Internet to find additional ones. Consider dropping weak or less reliable sources. Make sure that your sources provide coverage in a comprehensive, balanced way.

- **Do you rely too much on quoting, summarizing, or paraphrasing?** Change some of your quotations to summaries or paraphrases, or vice versa.

- **Does quoted material need to be more smoothly integrated into your own text?** Revise to make it so. Remember to use precise verbs to introduce sources and authors.

- *Are there discrepancies between your in-text citations and the entries in your list of sources?* Compare each citation and entry against the examples given in your writing handbook for the documentation style you are using. Be sure that all of the citations and entries follow the style exactly. Check to see that your list of sources has an entry for each source that you cite in the text.

Checking Sentence Strategies Electronically. To check your draft for a sentence strategy especially useful in explaining concepts, use your word processor's highlighting function to mark places where you refer to sources and their authors. Then look at the verbs that you use to introduce each source or author, and think about whether changing any of them to a more precise, informative verb would help your readers understand better how you are using the source. For more on using informative, precise verbs to introduce sources, see p. 150.

■ EDITING AND PROOFREADING

Now is the time to check your revised draft carefully for errors in usage, punctuation, and mechanics and to consider matters of style. Our research on students' writing has identified several errors that are especially common in writing that explains concepts. The following guidelines will help you check and edit your essay for these errors. This book's Web site also provides interactive online exercises to help you learn to identify and correct each of these errors; to access the exercises for a particular error, go to the URLs listed after each set of guidelines.

Checking the Punctuation of Adjective Clauses. Adjective clauses include both a subject and a verb. They give information about a noun or a pronoun. They often begin with *who, which,* or *that*. Here is an example from a student essay explaining the concept of schizophrenia, a type of mental illness:

> It is common for schizophrenics to have delusions *that they are being persecuted.*

Because adjective clauses add information about the nouns they follow — defining, illustrating, or explaining — they can be useful in writing that explains a concept. Adjective clauses may or may not need to be set off with a comma or commas. To decide, first you have to determine whether the clause is essential to the meaning of the sentence. Clauses that are essential to the meaning of a sentence should not be set off with a comma; clauses that are not essential to the meaning must be set off with a comma. Here are two examples from the student essay about schizophrenia:

ESSENTIAL   It is common for schizophrenics to have delusions *that they are being persecuted.*

The adjective clause defines and limits the word *delusions*. If the clause were removed, the basic meaning of the sentence would change, saying that schizophrenics commonly have delusions of all sorts.

NONESSENTIAL   Related to delusions are hallucinations, *which are very common in schizophrenics.*

The adjective clause gives information that is not essential to understanding the main clause *(Related to delusions are hallucinations)*. Taking away the adjective clause *(which are very common in schizophrenics)* in no way changes the basic meaning of the main clause.

To decide whether an adjective clause is essential or nonessential, mentally delete the clause. If taking out the clause changes the basic meaning of the sentence or makes it unclear, the clause is probably essential and should not be set off with commas. If the meaning of the main part of the sentence or the main clause does not change enormously, the clause is probably nonessential and should be set off with commas.

▶ Postpartum neurosis, which can last for two weeks or longer, can adversely affect a mother's ability to care for her infant.

▶ The early stage starts with memory loss, which usually causes the patient to forget recent life events.

▶ Seasonal affective disorders are mood disturbances, that occur with a change of season.

▶ The coaches, who do the recruiting should be disciplined.

Adjective clauses following proper nouns always require commas.

▶ Nanotechnologists defer to K. Eric Drexler, who speculates imaginatively about the uses of nonmachines.

For practice, go to bedfordstmartins.com/conciseguide/comma and bedfordstmartins .com/conciseguide/uncomma.

Checking for Commas around Interrupting Phrases.   When writers are explaining a concept, they need to supply a great deal of information. They add much of this information in phrases that interrupt the flow of a sentence. Words that interrupt are usually set off with commas. Be especially careful with interrupting phrases that fall in the middle of a sentence. Such phrases must be set off with two commas, one at the beginning and one at the end:

▶ People on the West Coast, especially in Los Angeles, have always been receptive to new ideas.

▶ Alzheimer's disease, named after the German neuropathologist Alois Alzheimer, is a chronic degenerative illness.

▶ These examples, though simple, present equations in terms of tangible objects.

For practice, go to bedfordstmartins.com/conciseguide/comma and bedfordstmartins .com/conciseguide/uncomma.

A Note on Grammar and Spelling Checkers. These tools are good at catching certain types of errors, but currently there's no replacement for a good human proofreader. Grammar checkers in particular are extremely limited in what they can usually find, and often they only give you summary information that isn't helpful if you don't already understand the rule in question. They are also prone to give faulty advice for fixing problems and to flag correct items as wrong. Spelling checkers cause fewer problems but can't catch misspellings that are themselves words, such as *to* for *too*.

REFLECTING ON YOUR WRITING

Now that you have read and discussed several essays that explain concepts and written one of your own, take some time for reflection. Reflecting on your writing process will help you gain a greater understanding of what you learned about solving the problems you encountered in explaining a concept.

Write a one-page explanation, telling your instructor about a problem you encountered in writing your essay and how you solved it. Before you begin, gather all of your writing—invention and planning notes, drafts, critical comments, revision notes and plans, and final revision. Review these materials, and refer to them as you complete this writing task.

1. *Identify one writing problem you had to solve as you worked to explain the concept in your essay.* Do not be concerned with grammar and punctuation; concentrate instead on problems unique to developing a concept explanation. For example: Did you puzzle over how to focus your explanation? Did you worry about how to appeal to your readers' interests or how to identify and define the

terms that your readers would need explained? Did you have trouble integrating sources smoothly?

2. ***Determine how you came to recognize the problem.*** When did you first discover it? What called it to your attention? If you did not become aware of the problem until someone else pointed it out, can you now see hints of it in your invention writings? If so, where specifically? How did you respond when you first recognized the problem?

3. ***Reflect on how you went about solving the problem.*** Did you work on the wording of a particular passage, cut or add information, move paragraphs or sentences around, add transitions or forecasting statements, experiment with different writing strategies? Did you reread one of the essays in this chapter to see how another writer handled the problem, or did you look back at the invention suggestions? If you talked about the writing problem with another student, a tutor, or your instructor, did talking about it help? How useful was the advice you received?

4. ***Write a brief explanation of how you identified the problem and how you solved it.*** Be as specific as possible in reconstructing your efforts. Quote from your invention notes and draft essay, others' critical comments, your revision plan, or your revised essay to show the various changes your writing underwent as you tried to solve the problem. If you are still uncertain about your solution, say so. Thinking in detail about how you identified a particular problem, how you went about solving it, and what you learned from this experience can help you solve future writing problems more easily.

Arguing a Position

5

You may associate arguing with quarreling or with the in-your-face debating we hear so often on radio and television talk shows. These ways of arguing may let us vent strong feelings, but they seldom lead us to consider seriously other points of view or to look critically at our own thinking.

This chapter presents a more deliberative way of arguing that we call *reasoned argument* because it depends on giving reasons rather than raising voices. It demands that positions be supported rather than merely asserted. It also commands respect for the right of others to disagree with you as you may disagree with them. Reasoned argument requires more thought than quarreling but no less passion or commitment, as you will see when you read the essays in this chapter arguing about controversial issues.

Controversial issues are, by definition, issues about which people may have strong feelings. The issue may involve a practice that has been accepted for some time, like fraternity hazing, or it may concern a newly proposed or recently instituted policy, like the Peacekeepers school program. People may agree about goals but disagree about the best way to achieve them, as in the perennial debate over how to guarantee adequate health care for all citizens. Or they may disagree about fundamental values and beliefs, as in the debate over euthanasia or abortion.

As you can see from these examples, controversial issues have no obvious right answer, no truth that everyone accepts, no single authority on which everyone relies. Writers cannot offer absolute proof in debates about controversial issues because such issues are matters of opinion and judgment. Simply gathering information—finding the facts or learning from experts—will not settle disputes like these, although the more that is known about an issue, the more informed the positions will be.

Although it is not possible to prove that a position on a controversial issue is right or wrong, it is possible through reasoned argument to convince others to accept or reject a particular position. To be convincing, not only must an argument present convincing reasons and plausible support for its position, but it also should anticipate readers' likely objections and opposing arguments, conceding those that are reasonable and refuting those that are not. Vigorous debate that sets forth arguments and counterarguments on all sides of an issue can advance everyone's thinking.

Learning to make reasoned arguments on controversial issues and to think critically about our own as well as others' arguments is not a luxury; it is a necessity if our increasingly diverse society is to survive and flourish. As citizens in a democracy, we have a special duty to inform ourselves about pressing issues and to participate constructively in the public debate. Honing our thinking and arguing skills also has practical advantages in school, where we often are judged by our ability to write convincingly, and in the workplace, where we often need to recommend or defend controversial policy decisions.

You will encounter writing that argues a position in many different contexts, as the following examples suggest.

Writing in Your Other Courses

- For a sociology class, a student writes an essay on surrogate mothering. She finds several newspaper and magazine articles and checks the Internet for surrogate mothering Web sites. In her essay, she acknowledges that using *in vitro* fertilization and a surrogate may be the only way some couples can have their own biological children. Although she respects this desire, she argues that from a sociological perspective surrogate mothering does more harm than good. She gives two reasons: that the practice has serious emotional consequences for the surrogates and their families and that it exploits poor women by creating a class of professional breeders. She supports her argument with anecdotes from surrogates and their families as well as with quotations from sociologists and psychologists who have studied surrogate mothering.

- For a business course, a student writes an essay arguing that the glass ceiling that prevents women from advancing up the corporate ladder still exists at the highest executive levels. She acknowledges that in the nearly twenty years after the phrase "glass ceiling" was coined by a writer at the *Wall Street Journal* in 1986, the percentage of corporate officers who are women has grown. Nevertheless, she argues, the statistics are misleading. Because it is good business to claim gender equity, many companies define to their own advantage the positions counted as corporate officers. The student cites statistics from the Catalyst research group indicating that only 7 percent of the corporate officers in line positions—those responsible for the bottom line and therefore most likely to be promoted to chief executive positions—are women.

Writing in the Community

- For the campus newspaper, a student writes an editorial condemning the practice of fraternity hazing. He acknowledges that most hazing is harmless but argues that hazing can get out of hand and even be lethal. He refers specifically to two incidents reported in the national news in which one student died of alcohol poisoning after being forced to drink too much liquor and another student had a heart attack after being made to run too many laps around the school's track. To show that the potential for a similar tragedy exists on his campus, the writer recounts several anecdotes told to him by students there about their experiences pledging for fraternities. He concludes with a plea to the fraternities on campus to radically change—or at least, curtail—their hazing practices before someone is seriously hurt or killed.

- In a letter to the school board, parents protest a new Peacekeepers program that is being implemented at the local middle school. The writers acknowledge that the aim of the program—to teach students to avoid conflict—is worthwhile. But they argue that the program's methods unduly restrict students' freedoms. Moreover, they claim that the program teaches children to become passive and submissive rather than thinking adults who are willing and able to fight for what is right. To support their argument, they list some of the rules that have been instituted at the middle school: Students must wear uniforms to school, must keep their hands clasped behind their backs when walking down the halls, may not raise their voices in anger or use obscenities, and cannot play aggressive games like dodge ball or contact sports like basketball and football.

Writing in the Workplace

- For a business magazine, a corporate executive writes an essay arguing that protecting the environment is not only good citizenship, but also good business. She supports her position with examples of two companies that became successful by developing innovative methods of reducing hazardous wastes. She also reminds readers of the decisive actions taken in the late 1980s by established corporations to help solve the problem of ozone depletion, such as DuPont's decision to discontinue production of chlorofluorocarbons (CFCs) and McDonald's elimination of styrofoam cartons. Finally, she points out that *Fortune* magazine agrees with her position, noting that the eight deciding factors in its annual ranking of America's Most Admired Corporations include community and environmental responsibility alongside financial soundness.

- In a memo to the director of personnel, a loan company manager argues that written communication skills should be a more important factor in hiring. He acknowledges that math skills are necessary but tries to convince the director that mistakes in writing are too costly to ignore. To support his argument, he cites examples of bad writing in letters and memos that cost the company money and time. For additional examples and suggestions on solving the problem, he refers the personnel director to an ongoing discussion about writing on a listserv to which the manager subscribes.

| **Practice Arguing a Position: A Collaborative Activity** | The preceding scenarios suggest some occasions for arguing a position. Your instructor may schedule this collaborative activity as a face-to-face in-class discussion or ask you to conduct an online real-time discussion in a chat room. Whatever the medium, here are some guidelines to follow: |

To construct an effective argument, you must assert a position and offer support for it. This activity gives you a chance to practice constructing an argument with other students.

Part 1. Get together with two to three other students, and choose an issue. You do not have to be an expert on the issue, but you should be familiar with some of the arguments people typically make about it. If you do not have an issue in mind, the following list might help you think of possibilities.

- Should all students be required to wear uniforms in school?
- Should college athletes be paid a portion of the money the school gains from sports events?
- Should community service be a requirement for graduation from high school or college?

In your group, spend two to three minutes quickly exchanging your opinions, and then agree together to argue for the same position on the issue, whether you personally agree with the position or not. Also decide who you would want to read your argument and what you expect these readers to think about the issue. Choose someone in the group to write down the results of your discussion like this:

Issue: Should grades in college be abolished?

Position: Grades should be abolished.

Readers: Teachers who think grades measure learning accurately and efficiently.

Take another ten to fifteen minutes to construct an argument for your position, giving several reasons and noting the kinds of support you would need. Also try to anticipate one or two objections you would expect from readers who disagree with your position. Write down what you discover under the following headings: Reasons, Support Needed, and Likely Objections. Following is an example of this work for the position that grades should be abolished.

Reasons

1. Tests are not always the best way to judge students' knowledge because some students do poorly on tests even though they know the material.
2. Tests often evaluate only what is easily measurable, such as whether students remember facts, rather than whether students can use facts to support their ideas.

Support Needed

1. Research on testing anxiety
2. Anecdotes from students' experience with testing anxiety
3. Teachers' comments on why they rely on tests and how they feel about alternatives to testing (such as group projects)

Likely Objections

1. Tests are efficient for teachers and for students, especially in comparison with research papers.

2. Tests are evaluated strictly on what students have learned about the subject, not on how well they write or how well a group collaborates.

Part 2. Discuss for about five minutes what you did as a group to construct an argument:

Reasons: What did you learn about giving reasons? If you thought of more reasons than you needed, how did you choose? If you had difficulty thinking of reasons, what could you do?

Support: What did you learn about supporting an argument? How many different kinds of support (such as quotations, examples, or anecdotes) did you consider? Which reasons seemed the easiest to support? Which the hardest?

Objections: What did you learn about anticipating objections to your argument? How did you come up with these objections? Given your designated readers, was it easy or hard to think of their likely objections? How could you learn more about your readers' likely objections?

READINGS

No two essays taking a position are alike, and yet they share defining features. Together, the three readings in this chapter reveal a number of these features, so you will want to read as many of them as possible. If time permits, complete the activities in the Analyzing Writing Strategies section that follows each selection, and read the Commentary. Following the readings is a section called Basic Features: Arguing Positions (p. 182), which offers a concise description of the features of writing that takes a position and provides examples from the three readings.

Richard Estrada *was the associate editor of the* Dallas Morning News *editorial page and a syndicated columnist whose essays appeared regularly in the* Washington Post, *the* Los Angeles Times, *and other major newspapers. He was best known as a thoughtful, independent-minded commentator on immigration and social issues. Before joining the* Dallas Morning News *in 1988, Estrada worked as a congressional staff member and as a researcher at the Center for Immigration Studies in Washington, D.C. In the 1990s, he was appointed to the U.S.*

Commission on Immigration Reform. Following his death at the age of forty-nine in 1999, the Richard Estrada Fellowship in Immigration Studies was established in his honor.

Estrada wrote this essay during the 1995 baseball World Series in which the Atlanta Braves played the Cleveland Indians. The series drew the public's attention to the practice of dressing team mascots like Native Americans on the warpath and encouraging fans to rally their team with gestures like the "tomahawk chop" and pep yells like the "Indian chant." The controversy over these practices revitalized a longstanding debate over naming sports teams with words associated with Native Americans. Several high schools and at least one university, Stanford, have changed the names of their sports teams because of this ongoing controversy. A coworker remarked that in his newspaper columns, Estrada "firmly opposed separating the American people into competing ethnic and linguistic groups." As you read this essay, think about his purpose in writing this position essay and how it seeks to bring different groups together.

Sticks and Stones and Sports Team Names

Richard Estrada

When I was a kid living in Baltimore in the late 1950s, there was only one professional sports team worth following. Anyone who ever saw the movie *Diner* knows which one it was. Back when we liked Ike, the Colts were the gods of the gridiron and Memorial Stadium was their Mount Olympus.   1

Ah, yes: The Colts. The Lions. Da Bears. Back when defensive tackle Big Daddy Lipscomb was letting running backs know exactly what time it was, a young fan could easily forget that in a game where men were men, the teams they played on were not invariably named after animals. Among others, the Packers, the Steelers and the distant 49ers were cases in point. But in the roll call of pro teams, one name in particular always discomfited me: the Washington Redskins. Still, however willing I may have been to go along with the name as a kid, as an adult I have concluded that using an ethnic group essentially as a sports mascot is wrong.   2

The Redskins and the Kansas City Chiefs, along with baseball teams like the Atlanta Braves and the Cleveland Indians, should find other names that avoid highlighting ethnicity.   3

By no means were such names originally meant to disparage Native Americans. The noble symbols of the Redskins or college football's Florida State Seminoles or the Illinois Illini are meant to be strong and proud. Yet, ultimately, the practice of using a people as mascots is dehumanizing. It sets them apart from the rest of society. It promotes the politics of racial aggrievement at a moment when our storehouse is running over with it.   4

The World Series between the Cleveland Indians and the Atlanta Braves re-ignited the debate. In the chill night air of October, tomahawk chops and war chants suddenly became far more familiar to millions of fans, along with the ridiculous and offensive cartoon logo of Cleveland's "Chief Wahoo."   5

The defenders of team names that use variations on the Indian theme argue that tradition should not be sacrificed at the altar of political correctness. In truth, the nation's No. 1 P.C. [politically correct] school, Stanford University, helped matters some when it   6 changed its team nickname from "the Indians" to "the Cardinals." To be sure, Stanford did the right thing, but the school's status as P.C. without peer tainted the decision for those who still need to do the right thing.

Another argument is that ethnic group leaders are too inclined to cry wolf in alleging   7 racial insensitivity. Often, this is the case. But no one should overlook genuine cases of political insensitivity in an attempt to avoid accusations of hypersensitivity and political correctness.

The real world is different from the world of sports entertainment. I recently heard a   8 father who happened to be a Native American complain on the radio that his child was being pressured into participating in celebrations of Braves baseball. At his kid's school, certain days are set aside on which all children are told to dress in Indian garb and celebrate with tomahawk chops and the like.

That father should be forgiven for not wanting his family to serve as somebody's   9 mascot. The desire to avoid ridicule is legitimate and understandable. Nobody likes to be trivialized or deprived of their dignity. This has nothing to do with political correctness and the provocations of militant leaders.

Against this backdrop, the decision by newspapers in Minneapolis, Seattle and Port-   10 land to ban references to Native American nicknames is more reasonable than some might think.

What makes naming teams after ethnic groups, particularly minorities, reprehen-   11 sible is that politically impotent groups continue to be targeted, while politically powerful ones who bite back are left alone. How long does anyone think the name "Washington Blackskins" would last? Or how about "the New York Jews"?

With no fewer than 10 Latino ballplayers on the Cleveland Indians' roster, the team   12 could change its name to "the Banditos." The trouble is, they would be missing the point: Latinos would correctly object to that stereotype, just as they rightly protested against Frito-Lay's use of the "Frito Bandito" character years ago.

It seems to me that what Native Americans are saying is that what would be intoler-   13 able for Jews, blacks, Latinos and others is no less offensive to them. Theirs is a request not only for dignified treatment, but for fair treatment as well. For America to ignore the complaints of a numerically small segment of the population because it is small is neither dignified nor fair.

Connecting to Culture and Experience: Name-Calling

As children, we may say, "Sticks and stones will break my bones, but words will never hurt me." Most children, however, recognize the power of words, especially words that make them feel different or inferior.

Make a list of derogatory words that are used to refer to groups with which you identify. Try to think of words associated with your ethnicity, religion, gender, interests, geographic region, or any other factor. (Are you perhaps a redneck Okie good ole boy religious fanatic?) Which of the words on your list, if any, do you consider insulting? Why? Would you consider someone who called you these names insensitive?

With two or three other students, discuss your name-calling lists, giving examples from your list. Tell when, where, and by whom you or others in your group have been called these names. Speculate about motives of the name callers, and describe your reactions.

Analyzing Writing Strategies

1. At the beginning of this chapter, we discuss several features of essays that argue a position. Consider which of these is true of Estrada's essay:

   - It presents a controversial issue.
   - It asserts a clear position on the issue.
   - It argues for the position by presenting plausible reasons and support.
   - It anticipates readers' objections and arguments, either conceding or refuting them.

2. Reread paragraphs 11–13, where Estrada offers hypothetical examples of team names for ethnic groups, such as the "Washington Blackskins" and "the New York Jews." How do these examples support Estrada's argument? Given his readers, how convincing do you think they are likely to be? How effective are they for you, as one reader?

Commentary: Presenting the Issue and Plausible Reasons

Although the title of his essay implies its subject, Estrada does not identify the issue explicitly until the end of the second paragraph. He begins the essay by remembering his childhood experience as a football fan and explaining that, even as a child, he was made uncomfortable by the practice of naming sports teams for Native Americans. In paragraphs 2–4, he lists team names (Washington Redskins, Kansas City Chiefs, Atlanta Braves, Cleveland Indians, Florida State Seminoles, Illinois Illini) to remind readers how common the practice is. Then, in paragraph 8, he relates an anecdote about a father who not only feels uncomfortable but also feels personally ridiculed as a Native American when his son's school celebrates Braves' victories with Indian costumes and tomahawk chops. Estrada uses this anecdote to demonstrate that the issue is important and worth taking seriously.

Estrada presents the issue in this way to appeal to the readers of his column in the politically conservative *Dallas Morning News*. He apparently assumes that unless he can convince his readers that the issue of sports teams' names is significant, many readers would dismiss it as unimportant or as advancing a liberal agenda. Therefore, Estrada tries to make his readers empathize with what he calls a real-world issue, one that actually hurts kids (paragraph 8). When you present the issue in your own essay, you also may need to help readers understand why it is important and for whom. In the next reading, for example, you will notice that the primary purpose of Barbara Ehrenreich's essay is to make readers appreciate the seriousness of the issue she is addressing.

Presenting the issue is just a beginning. To convince readers, Estrada has to give the reasons that he believes naming sports teams for ethnic groups is detrimental. He gives two: because it treats people like team mascots and it singles out a politically weak group. Moreover, to be convincing, the reasons have to seem plausible to readers. The position (naming sports teams for Native Americans is wrong) has to follow logically from the reason: If readers accept the reason, then they also should accept the position. In other words, if readers are convinced by the support Estrada provides to show the effects of treating people like mascots, then they will be inclined to agree with Estrada that the practice is wrong. Similarly, if readers are convinced also that naming sports teams for Native Americans unfairly singles out a politically weak group, then they would be even more likely to agree with Estrada's conclusion.

Considering Topics for Your Own Essay

List some issues that involve what you believe to be unfair treatment of a marginalized minority group. For example, should a law be passed to make English the official language in this country, requiring that ballots and drivers' tests be printed only in English? Should elementary schools continue bilingual education to help non-English-speaking students learn subjects like math, science, and history while they are learning to read and write fluently in English? What is affirmative action, and should it be used in college admissions for underrepresented groups?

Barbara Ehrenreich published her first article in a science journal when she was a graduate student in biology. After earning her Ph.D., she chose a career as a writer instead of as a research scientist, but Ehrenreich believes that her science background has helped her to look at things both analytically and systematically, seeing the "ways things fit together." A prolific author, she has published essays in such journals as Time, the Atlantic Monthly, the New York Times Magazine, the Nation, and Harper's, for which she is also a contributing editor. Ehrenreich has researched and written more than a dozen books, including The American Health Empire: Power, Profits, and Politics (1970); Fear of Falling: The Inner Life of the Middle Class (1989), which was nominated for a National Book Critics' Award; and Blood Rites: Origins and History of the Passions of War (1997). For the critically acclaimed Nickel and Dimed: On (Not) Getting By in America (2001), from which this reading comes, Ehrenreich went "undercover" as a waitress, a maid, a nursing home aide, and a Wal-Mart sales associate. A chapter from Nickel and Dimed published in Harper's won the Sydney Hillman Award for Journalism, and Ehrenreich has also received a National Magazine Award for Excellence in Reporting, a Ford Foundation Award for Humanistic Perspectives on Contemporary Society, a Guggenheim Fellowship, and a John D. and Catherine T. MacArthur Foundation grant.

At the time Ehrenreich began her research in 1998, most Americans were enjoying unprecedented economic prosperity stimulated by the dot-com bubble that burst by the time her book was published in 2001. Controversial welfare reform that required single mothers to find jobs was considered a success because more than half of former welfare recipients were employed and the unemployment rate in general was at an all-time low. Nevertheless, reports like that of the Economic Policy Institute, which Ehrenreich refers to in the first paragraph of this reading, indicated that the working poor were struggling just to keep their heads above water. Of course, economic conditions change, and when you read this essay, the situation for the working poor may be better or worse than it was when Ehrenreich completed her research. As you read the essay, think about your own economic situation and that of your family and friends.

Nickel and Dimed

Barbara Ehrenreich

Many people earn far less than they need to live on. How much is that? The Economic Policy Institute recently reviewed dozens of studies of what constitutes a "living wage" and came up with an average figure of $30,000 a year for a family of one adult and two children, which amounts to a wage of $14 an hour. This is not the very minimum such a family could live on; the budget includes health insurance, a telephone, and child care at a licensed center, for example, which are well beyond the reach of millions. But it does not include restaurant meals, video rentals, Internet access, wine and liquor, cigarettes and lottery tickets, or even very much meat. The shocking thing is that the majority of American workers, about 60 percent, earn less than $14 an hour. Many of them get by by teaming up with another wage earner, a spouse or grown child. Some draw on government help in the form of food stamps, housing vouchers, the earned income tax credit, or — for those coming off welfare in relatively generous states — subsidized child care. But others — single mothers, for example — have nothing but their own wages to live on, no matter how many mouths there are to feed.

Employers will look at that $30,000 figure, which is over twice what they currently pay entry-level workers, and see nothing but bankruptcy ahead. Indeed, it is probably impossible for the private sector to provide everyone with an adequate standard of living through wages, or even wages plus benefits, alone: too much of what we need, such as reliable child care, is just too expensive, even for middle-class families. Most civilized nations compensate for the inadequacy of wages by providing relatively generous public services such as health insurance, free or subsidized child care, subsidized housing, and effective public transportation. But the United States, for all its wealth, leaves its citizens to fend for themselves — facing market-based rents, for example, on their wages alone. For millions of Americans, that $10 — or even $8 or $6 — hourly wage is all there is.

It is common, among the nonpoor, to think of poverty as a sustainable condition — austere, perhaps, but they get by somehow, don't they? They are "always with us." What is harder for the nonpoor to see is poverty as active distress: The lunch that consists of Doritos or hot dog rolls, leading to faintness before the end of the shift. The "home" that is also a car or a van. The illness or injury that must be "worked through," with gritted teeth, because there's no sick pay or health insurance and the loss of one day's pay will mean no groceries for the next. These experiences are not part of a sustainable lifestyle, even a lifestyle of chronic deprivation and relentless low-level punishment. They are, by almost any standard of subsistence, emergency situations. And that is how we should see the poverty of so many millions of low-wage Americans — as a state of emergency....

Some odd optical property of our highly polarized and unequal society makes the   4
poor almost invisible to their economic superiors. The poor can see the affluent easily
enough—on television, for example, or on the covers of magazines. But the affluent
rarely see the poor or, if they do catch sight of them in some public space, rarely know
what they're seeing, since—thanks to consignment stores and, yes, Wal-Mart—the
poor are usually able to disguise themselves as members of the more comfortable
classes. Forty years ago the hot journalistic topic was the "discovery of the poor" in their
inner-city and Appalachian "pockets of poverty." Today you are more likely to find commentary on their "disappearance," either as a supposed demographic reality or as a
shortcoming of the middle-class imagination.

In a 2000 article on the "disappearing poor," journalist James Fallows reports that,   5
from the vantage point of the Internet's nouveaux riches, it is "hard to understand people
for whom a million dollars would be a fortune . . . not to mention those for whom $246 is a
full week's earnings."[1] Among the reasons he and others have cited for the blindness of
the affluent is the fact that they are less and less likely to share spaces and services with
the poor. As public schools and other public services deteriorate, those who can afford to
do so send their children to private schools and spend their off-hours in private spaces—
health clubs, for example, instead of the local park. They don't ride on public buses and
subways. They withdraw from mixed neighborhoods into distant suburbs, gated communities, or guarded apartment towers; they shop in stores that, in line with the prevailing
"market segmentation," are designed to appeal to the affluent alone. Even the affluent
young are increasingly unlikely to spend their summers learning how the "other half"
lives, as lifeguards, waitresses, or housekeepers at resort hotels. The *New York Times*
reports that they now prefer career-relevant activities like summer school or interning in
an appropriate professional setting to the "sweaty, low-paid and mind-numbing slots that
have long been their lot."[2]

Then, too, the particular political moment favors what almost looks like a "conspiracy   6
of silence" on the subject of poverty and the poor. . . . Welfare reform itself is a factor
weighing against any close investigation of the conditions of the poor. Both parties
heartily endorsed it, and to acknowledge that low-wage work doesn't lift people out of
poverty would be to admit that it may have been, in human terms, a catastrophic mistake.
In fact, very little is known about the fate of former welfare recipients because the 1996
welfare reform legislation blithely failed to include any provision for monitoring their post-
welfare economic condition. Media accounts persistently bright-side the situation, highlighting the occasional success stories and downplaying the acknowledged increase in
hunger.[3] And sometimes there seems to be almost deliberate deception. In June 2000,
the press rushed to hail a study supposedly showing that Minnesota's welfare-to-work
program had sharply reduced poverty and was, as *Time* magazine put it, a "winner."[4]
Overlooked in these reports was the fact that the program in question was a pilot project
that offered far more generous child care and other subsidies than Minnesota's actual
welfare reform program. Perhaps the error can be forgiven—the pilot project, which
ended in 1997, had the same name, Minnesota Family Investment Program, as Minnesota's much larger, ongoing welfare reform program.[5]

You would have to read a great many newspapers very carefully, cover to cover, to   7
see the signs of distress. You would find, for example, that in 1999 Massachusetts food
pantries reported a 72 percent increase in the demand for their services over the previous year, that Texas food banks were "scrounging" for food, despite donations at or above
1998 levels, as were those in Atlanta.[6] You might learn that in San Diego the Catholic
Church could no longer, as of January 2000, accept homeless families at its shelter, which
happens to be the city's largest, because it was already operating at twice its normal
capacity.[7] You would come across news of a study showing that the percentage of Wis-
consin food-stamp families in "extreme poverty"—defined as less than 50 percent of the
federal poverty line—has tripled in the last decade to more than 30 percent.[8] You might
discover that, nationwide, America's food banks are experiencing "a torrent of need which
[they] cannot meet" and that,[9] according to a survey conducted by the U.S. Conference of
Mayors, 67 percent of the adults requesting emergency food aid are people with jobs.[10]

One reason nobody bothers to pull all these stories together and announce a wide-   8
spread state of emergency may be that Americans of the newspaper-reading professional middle class are used to thinking of poverty as a consequence of unemployment.
During the heyday of downsizing, in the Reagan years, it very often was, and it still is for
many inner-city residents who have no way of getting to the proliferating entry-level jobs
on urban peripheries. When unemployment causes poverty, we know how to state the
problem—typically, "the economy isn't growing fast enough"—and we know what the
traditional liberal solution is—"full employment." But when we have full or nearly full
employment, when jobs are available to any job seeker who can get to them, then the
problem goes deeper and begins to cut into that web of expectations that make up the
"social contract." According to a recent poll conducted by Jobs for the Future, a Boston-
based employment research firm, 94 percent of Americans agree that "people who work
fulltime should be able to earn enough to keep their families out of poverty."[11] I grew up
hearing over and over, to the point of tedium, that "hard work" was the secret of success:
"Work hard and you'll get ahead" or "It's hard work that got us where we are." No one ever
said that you could work hard—harder even than you ever thought possible—and still
find yourself sinking ever deeper into poverty and debt.

When poor single mothers had the option of remaining out of the labor force on wel-   9
fare, the middle and upper middle class tended to view them with a certain impatience, if
not disgust. The welfare poor were excoriated for their laziness, their persistence in
reproducing in unfavorable circumstances, their presumed addictions, and above all for
their "dependency." Here they were, content to live off "government handouts" instead of
seeking "self-sufficiency," like everyone else, through a job. They needed to get their act
together, learn how to wind an alarm clock, get out there and get to work. But now that
government has largely withdrawn its "handouts," now that the overwhelming majority of
the poor are out there toiling in Wal-Mart or Wendy's—well, what are we to think of
them? Disapproval and condescension no longer apply, so what outlook makes sense?

Guilt, you may be thinking warily. Isn't that what we're supposed to feel? But guilt   10
doesn't go anywhere near far enough; the appropriate emotion is shame—shame at our
own dependency, in this case, on the underpaid labor of others. When someone works

for less pay than she can live on—when, for example, she goes hungry so that you can eat more cheaply and conveniently—then she has made a great sacrifice for you, she has made you a gift of some part of her abilities, her health, and her life. The "working poor," as they are approvingly termed, are in fact the major philanthropists of our society. They neglect their own children so that the children of others will be cared for; they live in substandard housing so that other homes will be shiny and perfect; they endure privation so that inflation will be low and stock prices high. To be a member of the working poor is to be an anonymous donor, a nameless benefactor, to everyone else. As Gail, one of my restaurant coworkers put it, "you give and you give."

Someday, of course—and I will make no predictions as to exactly when—they are   11
bound to tire of getting so little in return and to demand to be paid what they're worth. There'll be a lot of anger when that day comes, and strikes and disruption. But the sky will not fall, and we will all be better off for it in the end.

Notes

1. "The Invisible Poor," *New York Times Magazine,* March 19, 2000.

2. "Summer Work Is out of Favor with the Young," *New York Times,* June 18, 2000.

3. The *National Journal* reports that the "good news" is that almost six million people have left the welfare rolls since 1996, while the "rest of the story" includes the problem that "these people sometimes don't have enough to eat" ("Welfare Reform, Act 2," June 24, 2000: 1,978–93).

4. "Minnesota's Welfare Reform Proves a Winner," *Time,* June 12, 2000.

5. Center for Law and Social Policy, "Update," Washington, D.C., June 2000.

6. "Study: More Go Hungry since Welfare Reform," *Boston Herald,* January 21, 2000; "Charity Can't Feed All while Welfare Reforms Implemented," *Houston Chronicle,* January 10, 2000; "Hunger Grows as Food Banks Try to Keep Pace," *Atlanta Journal and Constitution,* November 26, 1999.

7. "Rise in Homeless Families Strains San Diego Aid," *Los Angeles Times,* January 24, 2000.

8. "Hunger Problems Said to Be Getting Worse," *Milwaukee Journal Sentinel,* December 15, 1999.

9. Deborah Leff, the president and CEO of the hunger-relief organization America's Second Harvest, quoted in the *National Journal,* "Welfare Reform, Act 2."

10. "Hunger Persists in U.S. despite the Good Times," *Detroit News,* June 15, 2000.

11. "A National Survey of American Attitudes toward Low-Wage Workers and Welfare Reform," Jobs for the Future, Boston, May 24, 2000.

Connecting to Culture and Experience: The American Dream

In paragraph 8, Barbara Ehrenreich writes about "that web of expectations that make up the 'social contract.'" She explains the essential feature of this social contract in these terms: "'hard work' was the secret of success: 'Work hard and you'll get ahead.'" What she is referring to here is the ideology of the American dream, a set of beliefs and values held by people in the United States and around the world. The American dream assumes that if you work hard enough, you—or at least your children—will be better off financially.

Make a list of the values and beliefs that you associate with the American dream. Then get together with two or three other students, and compare your lists. What do your lists say about the value and rewards of hard work?

Analyzing Writing Strategies

1. In arguing a position on a controversial issue, writers usually state their position in a thesis statement. At the end of paragraph 3, Ehrenreich asserts her thesis: "And that is how we should see the poverty of so many millions of low-wage Americans—as a state of emergency." For a position to be effective, it must be arguable. That is, it should not be a simple statement of fact that can be proven true or false. Nor should a thesis be a matter of faith. Instead, it should be an opinion about which others disagree. It also should be clear and unambiguous as well as appropriately qualified. Use these criteria—that the position be arguable, clear, and appropriately qualified—to decide how effectively Ehrenreich states her position.

2. Ehrenreich sprinkles her argument with statistics. For example, in the opening paragraph, she specifies $14 an hour as the "living wage" that a family of one adult and two children needs. In the same paragraph, she also writes that 60 percent of American workers earn less than this hourly wage. Statistics like these can carry a lot of weight if readers are confident that they come from a reliable source that collects data objectively and professionally. Writers usually cite their sources so that readers can decide for themselves whether the statistics can be believed. For example, if you did a Google search on the Economic Policy Institute, you would find the institute's Web site and learn about EPI's purpose; its corporate, academic, or other affiliations; and its membership. This information could help you judge with some confidence the source's credibility and whether you can count on its statistics.

   Underline the statistics Ehrenreich presents in paragraphs 7 and 8, and put brackets around the sources. Then check Ehrenreich's notes to see what information she gives about each source that could help you determine its credibility.

   (Notice that Ehrenreich does not follow either the MLA or APA formal style of documentation; instead she uses a modified form of the *Chicago Manual of Style* system that is often used in books for a general audience. Instead of giving parenthetical citations in the text that are keyed to a list of works cited, she provides notes and does not include a list of works cited. She also does not systematically include page references. When you write a research paper for any of your classes, be sure to ask your instructor what documentation style you should use.)

Commentary: Supporting Examples

In the book from which this selection comes, Ehrenreich has the luxury of space to present extended examples to show how particular individuals struggle every day to make ends meet. In this selection from the book's conclusion, however, she needs to make her point quickly with a few brief examples.

Notice how she gives examples in paragraph 3. She provides a list of three examples, and the list is framed by introductory and concluding sentences:

> It is common, among the nonpoor, to think of poverty as a sustainable condition—austere, perhaps, but they get by somehow, don't they? They are "always with us." What is harder for the nonpoor to see is poverty as active distress: The lunch that consists of Doritos or hot dog rolls, leading to faintness before the end of the shift. The "home" that is also a car or a van. The illness or injury that must be "worked through," with gritted teeth, because there's no sick pay or health insurance and the loss of one day's pay will mean no groceries for the next. These experiences are not part of a sustainable lifestyle, even a lifestyle of chronic deprivation and relentless low-level punishment. They are, by almost any standard of subsistence, emergency situations.

This set of examples provides vivid images of the "active distress" Ehrenreich is trying to help her readers to see. Each example refers to a fundamental human need: food, shelter, and health. By emphasizing needs such as these, she reinforces a point she makes at the beginning of her essay: The working poor lack basic necessities, not luxuries. Examples like these help readers to understand what Ehrenreich means by "active distress," and they can also help to convince readers that the problem she is trying to call attention to is serious indeed.

As a writer, you will want to notice not only that Ehrenreich uses examples to support her argument but also that she uses punctuation and sentence structure to present the examples in a way that emphasizes her point:

> What is harder for the nonpoor to see is poverty as active distress: The lunch that.... The "home" that.... The illness or injury that....

Notice that she introduces the list with a colon, a punctuation mark that often precedes a series of examples. Notice also that Ehrenreich uses the same sentence structure for each example: beginning with *the* and a noun (*lunch, home, illness*) followed by a clause beginning with *that*. By consistently beginning each clause with a noun—*lunch, home,* and *illness*—Ehrenreich focuses readers' attention on the basic necessities that many of the working poor lack, thereby repeatedly stressing the point she is making in the paragraph. You might also note that the examples are not full sentences in themselves but are grammatical because they complete the first part of the sentence ("What is harder...is").

When you are writing your own argument, you may want to provide examples for your readers to help them appreciate your point. Following Ehrenreich, try to arrange your sentences in a way that will draw your readers' attention to what you think is most important for them to notice.

Considering Topics for Your Own Essay

You might want to write an essay arguing your own position on the issue that Ehren-reich addresses. If you agree with her that the working poor need help, you might want to argue that the minimum wage should be raised. (The federal minimum wage is currently $5.85 an hour, although some states have higher rates. The minimum wage for employees who earn tips is $2.13 an hour.) Or you might want to argue that citizens should be provided a better social safety net that guarantees quality health care, food stamps, housing subsidies, child care, or other support services. Consider any other social issues you might want to write about. Identify an issue on which you have a position, and think about how you would gather information to construct an argument for your position.

Jessica Statsky wrote the following essay about children's competitive sports for her college composition course. Before reading, recall your own experiences as an elementary student playing competitive sports, either in or out of school. If you were not actively involved yourself, did you know anyone who was? Looking back, do you think that winning was unduly empha-sized? What value was placed on having a good time? On learning to get along with others? On developing athletic skills and confidence?

Children Need to Play, Not Compete

Jessica Statsky

Over the past three decades, organized sports for chil-dren have increased dramatically in the United States. And though many adults regard Little League Baseball and Peewee Football as a basic part of childhood, the games are not always joyous ones. When overzealous parents and coaches impose adult standards on children's sports, the result can be activ-ities that are neither satisfying nor beneficial to children. 1

I am concerned about all organized sports activities for children between the ages of six and twelve. The damage I see results from noncontact as well as contact sports, from sports organized locally as well as those organized nationally. Highly organized competi-tive sports such as Peewee Football and Little League Baseball are too often played to adult standards, which are developmentally inappropriate for children and can be both physically and psychologically harmful. Furthermore, because they eliminate many chil-dren from organized sports before they are ready to compete, they are actually counter-productive for developing either future players or fans. Finally, because they emphasize competition and winning, they unfortunately provide occasions for some parents and coaches to place their own fantasies and needs ahead of children's welfare. 2

One readily understandable danger of overly competitive sports is that they entice children into physical actions that are bad for growing bodies. Although the official Little League Web site acknowledges that children do risk injury playing baseball, they insist that severe injuries are infrequent, "far less than the risk of riding a skateboard, a bicycle, or even the school bus" ("What about My Child?"). Nevertheless, Leonard Koppett in 3

Sports Illusion, Sports Reality claims that a twelve-year-old trying to throw a curve ball, for example, may put abnormal strain on developing arm and shoulder muscles, sometimes resulting in lifelong injuries (294). Contact sports like football can be even more hazardous. Thomas Tutko, a psychology professor at San Jose State University and coauthor of the book *Winning Is Everything and Other American Myths,* writes:

> I am strongly opposed to young kids playing tackle football. It is not the right stage of development for them to be taught to crash into other kids. Kids under the age of fourteen are not by nature physical. Their main concern is self-preservation. They don't want to meet head on and slam into each other. But tackle football absolutely requires that they try to hit each other as hard as they can. And it is too traumatic for young kids. (qtd. in Tosches A1)

As Tutko indicates, even when children are not injured, fear of being hurt detracts from their enjoyment of the sport. The Little League Web site ranks fear of injury as the seventh of seven reasons children quit ("What about My Child?"). One mother of an eight-year-old Peewee Football player explained, "The kids get so scared. They get hit once and they don't want anything to do with football anymore. They'll sit on the bench and pretend their leg hurts . . ." (qtd. in Tosches). Some children are driven to even more desperate measures. For example, in one Peewee Football game, a reporter watched the following scene as a player took himself out of the game:

> "Coach, my tummy hurts. I can't play," he said. The coach told the player to get back onto the field. "There's nothing wrong with your stomach," he said. When the coach turned his head the seven-year-old stuck a finger down his throat and made himself vomit. When the coach turned back, the boy pointed to the ground and told him, "Yes there is, coach. See?" (Tosches A33)

Besides physical hazards and anxieties, competitive sports pose psychological dangers for children. Martin Rablovsky, a former sports editor for the *New York Times,* says that in all his years of watching young children play organized sports, he has noticed very few of them smiling. "I've seen children enjoying a spontaneous pre-practice scrimmage become somber and serious when the coach's whistle blows," Rablovsky says. "The spirit of play suddenly disappears, and sport becomes joblike" (qtd. in Coakley 94). The primary goal of a professional athlete—winning—is not appropriate for children. Their goals should be having fun, learning, and being with friends. Although winning does add to the fun, too many adults lose sight of what matters and make winning the most important goal. Several studies have shown that when children are asked whether they would rather be warming the bench on a winning team or playing regularly on a losing team, about 90 percent choose the latter (Smith, Smith, and Smoll 11).

Winning and losing may be an inevitable part of adult life, but they should not be part of childhood. Too much competition too early in life can affect a child's development. Children are easily influenced, and when they sense that their competence and worth are based on their ability to live up to their parents' and coaches' high expectations—and on their ability to win—they can become discouraged and depressed. Little League advises parents to "keep winning in perspective" ("Your Role"), noting that the most common reasons children give for quitting, aside from change in interest, are lack of playing time, failure and fear of failure, disapproval by significant others, and psychological stress ("What about My Child?"). According to Dr. Glyn C. Roberts, a professor of kinesiology at the Institute of Child Behavior and Development at the University of Illinois, 80 to 90 percent of children who play competitive sports at a young age drop out by sixteen (Kutner).

This statistic illustrates another reason I oppose competitive sports for children: because they are so highly selective, very few children get to participate. Far too soon, a few children are singled out for their athletic promise, while many others, who may be on the verge of developing the necessary strength and ability, are screened out and discouraged from trying out again. Like adults, children fear failure, and so even those with good physical skills may stay away because they lack self-confidence. Consequently, teams lose many promising players who with some encouragement and experience might have become stars. The problem is that many parent-sponsored, out-of-school programs give more importance to having a winning team than to developing children's physical skills and self-esteem. 7

Indeed, it is no secret that too often scorekeeping, league standings, and the drive to win bring out the worst in adults who are more absorbed in living out their own fantasies than in enhancing the quality of the experience for children (Smith, Smith, and Smoll 9). Recent newspaper articles on children's sports contain plenty of horror stories. *Los Angeles Times* reporter Rich Tosches, for example, tells the story of a brawl among seventy-five parents following a Peewee Football game (A33). As a result of the brawl, which began when a parent from one team confronted a player from the other team, the teams are now thinking of hiring security guards for future games. Another example is provided by an *L.A. Times* editorial about a Little League manager who intimidated the opposing team by setting fire to one of their team's jerseys on the pitching mound before the game began. As the editorial writer commented, the manager showed his young team that "intimidation could substitute for playing well" ("The Bad News"). 8

Although not all parents or coaches behave so inappropriately, the seriousness of the problem is illustrated by the fact that Adelphi University in Garden City, New York, offers a sports psychology workshop for Little League coaches, designed to balance their "animal instincts" with "educational theory" in hopes of reducing the "screaming and hollering," in the words of Harold Weisman, manager of sixteen Little Leagues in New York City (Schmitt). In a three-and-one-half-hour Sunday morning workshop, coaches learn how to make practices more fun, treat injuries, deal with irate parents, and be "more sensitive to their young players' fears, emotional frailties, and need for recognition." Little League is to be credited with recognizing the need for such workshops. 9

Some parents would no doubt argue that children cannot start too soon preparing to live in a competitive free-market economy. After all, secondary schools and colleges require students to compete for grades, and college admission is extremely competitive. And it is perfectly obvious how important competitive skills are in finding a job. Yet the ability to cooperate is also important for success in life. Before children are psychologi- 10 cally ready for competition, maybe we should emphasize cooperation and individual performance in team sports rather than winning.

Many people are ready for such an emphasis. In 1988, one New York Little League official who had attended the Adelphi workshop tried to ban scoring from six- to eight-year-olds' games — but parents wouldn't support him (Schmitt). An innovative children's sports program in New York City, City Sports for Kids, emphasizes fitness, self-esteem, and sportsmanship. In this program's basketball games, every member on a team plays at least two of six eight-minute periods. The basket is seven feet from the floor, rather than ten feet, and a player can score a point just by hitting the rim (Bloch). I believe this kind of local program should replace overly competitive programs like Peewee Football and Little League Baseball. As one coach explains, significant improvements can result from a few simple rule changes, such as including every player in the batting order and giving every player, regardless of age or ability, the opportunity to play at least four innings a game (Frank). 11

Authorities have clearly documented the excesses and dangers of many competitive sports programs for children. It would seem that few children benefit from these programs and that those who do would benefit even more from programs emphasizing fitness, cooperation, sportsmanship, and individual performance. Thirteen- and fourteen-year-olds may be eager for competition, but few younger children are. These younger children deserve sports programs designed specifically for their needs and abilities. 12

Works Cited

Bloch, Gordon B. "Thrill of Victory Is Secondary to Fun." *New York Times* 2 Apr. 1990, late ed.: C12.

"The Bad News Pyromaniacs?" Editorial. *Los Angeles Times* 16 June 1990: B6.

Coakley, Jay J. *Sport in Society: Issues and Controversies.* St. Louis: Mosby, 1982.

Frank, L. "Contributions from Parents and Coaches." Online posting. 8 July 1997. CYB Message Board. 14 May 1999 <http://members.aol.com/JohnHoelter/b-parent .html>.

Koppett, Leonard. *Sports Illusion, Sports Reality.* Boston: Houghton, 1981.

Kutner, Lawrence. "Athletics, through a Child's Eyes." *New York Times* 23 Mar. 1989, late ed.: C8.

Schmitt, Eric. "Psychologists Take Seat on Little League Bench." *New York Times* 14 Mar. 1988, late ed.: B2.

Smith, Nathan, Ronald Smith, and Frank Smoll. *Kidsports: A Survival Guide for Parents.* Reading: Addison, 1983.

Tosches, Rich. "Peewee Football: Is It Time to Blow the Whistle?" *Los Angeles Times* 3 Dec. 1988: A1+.

"What about My Child?" *Little League Online.* 1999. Little League Baseball, Inc. 30 June 1999 <http://www.littleleague.org/about/parents/yourchild.htm>.

"Your Role as a Little League Parent." *Little League Online.* 1999. Little League Baseball, Inc. 30 June 1999 <http://www.littleleague.org/about/parents/yourrole.htm>.

Connecting to Culture and Experience: Competition versus Cooperation

Statsky makes the point that competition is highly valued in our culture and that cooperation tends to be downplayed. With two or three other students, discuss some of the ways in which schools encourage competition, especially through courses, instruction, and testing; tutoring and counseling; and sports or other activities. Consider also how cooperation is encouraged. Think about whether, in your own experience, the schools you attended encouraged one more than the other.

If you believe that your schools preferred either competition or cooperation, reflect on why they might have done so. Who in society might benefit most from such a preference — men or women, the poor or the middle class or upper class, your school's administrators or teachers or students? Who loses most?

Analyzing Writing Strategies

1. Anecdotes can provide convincing support if they are clearly relevant to the point they support, believable, and vivid enough to enable readers to imagine what happened. In paragraph 4, Statsky presents one fully developed anecdote that includes dialogue and a detailed narrative. In paragraph 8, she offers two brief anecdotes that summarize rather than detail the events: One is about a brawl among parents, and the other about a team manager who set fire to a jersey of the opposing team. Locate and reread these anecdotes to find out what each one contributes to Statsky's argument and to judge how convincing they are likely to be for her readers.

2. To support her argument, Statsky repeatedly quotes authorities, experts who agree with her position. Skim the essay, underlining each authority she cites. Note where she quotes whole sentences or individual words and phrases. Then pick one source you think adds something important to her argument, and briefly explain what it adds.

3. Several times in her argument, Statsky adopts a strategy that is favored by writers taking positions on issues and that you can identify. To analyze two examples of the strategy, underline the second and third sentences of paragraph 1 and the first sentence of paragraph 9. What do these two examples have in common? Begin by thinking about the relation of the opening "though" and "although" clauses to what follows in the sentences. For more on sentence strategies important to writers taking positions, turn to Sentence Strategies, p. 196.

Commentary: A Clear Position

Writers arguing a position must state their position clearly, but they also try not to overstate it. By avoiding absolute, unconditional language and carefully qualifying her position, Statsky makes clear her concerns without making enthusiasts of competitive sports overly defensive. Throughout the essay, she qualifies with words like *not always, can, maybe,* and *it would seem*—words that potentially have a major effect on readers, making Statsky's position seem reasonable without making her seem indecisive. Similarly, Statsky qualifies her position by focusing on a particular age group. To ensure that readers know the particular kind of sports she is talking about, she gives two familiar examples: Peewee Football and Little League Baseball.

Statsky's unambiguous word choice and appropriate qualification satisfy two of the three requirements for an effective thesis. The third requirement, that the position be arguable, is indicated clearly in paragraph 2, where Statsky forecasts the three reasons for opposing organized competitive sports for young children that she develops later in the essay:

1. Such sports are "both physically and psychologically harmful" (developed in paragraphs 3–6)

2. They are "counterproductive for developing either future players or fans" (developed in paragraph 7)

3. They allow adults "to place their own fantasies and needs ahead of children's welfare" (developed in paragraphs 8–9)

Inexperienced writers are sometimes reluctant to state a thesis and forecast their reasons as clearly and directly as Statsky does. They fear that being direct will oversimplify or give away their whole argument. But we can see from Statsky's essay that the effectiveness of her argument is enhanced, not diminished, by her directness. Nor does directness prevent her from advancing a complex and thoughtful argument on an issue that is certain to arouse strong feelings in many readers.

Considering Topics for Your Own Essay

Make a list of issues related to childhood and adolescence. For example, should elementary and secondary schools be on a year-round schedule? Should children have the right to divorce their parents? Should adolescents who commit serious crimes be tried as adults? Then choose an issue that you think you could write about. What position would you take?

■ PURPOSE AND AUDIENCE

Purpose and audience are closely linked when you write an essay arguing a position. In defining your purpose, you also need to anticipate your readers. Most writers compose essays arguing for a position because they care deeply about the issue. As they develop an argument with their readers in mind, however, writers usually feel challenged to think critically about their own as well as their readers' feelings and thoughts about the issue.

Writers with strong convictions seek to influence their readers. Assuming that logical argument will prevail over prejudice, they try to change readers' minds by presenting compelling reasons and support based on shared values and principles. Nevertheless, they also recognize that in cases where disagreement is profound, it is highly unlikely that a single essay will be able to change readers' minds, no matter how well written it is. When they are addressing an audience that is completely opposed to their position, most writers are satisfied if they can simply win their readers' respect for a different point of view. Often, however, all that they can do is to sharpen the differences.

BASIC FEATURES: ARGUING POSITIONS

A Focused Presentation of the Issue

Writers use a variety of strategies to present the issue and prepare readers for their argument. For current, hotly debated issues, the title may be enough to identify the issue. Estrada's allusion to the familiar children's chant in his title "Sticks and Stones and Sports Team Names" is enough to identify the issue for many readers. Statsky gives a brief history of the debate about competitive sports for children. Many writers provide concrete examples early on to make sure that readers can understand the issue. Statsky mentions Peewee Football and Little League Baseball as examples of the kind of organized sports she opposes. Ehrenreich opens her essay by detailing what would constitute a "living wage," noting how few American workers earn that amount.

How writers present the issue depends on what they assume readers already know and what they want readers to think about the issue. Therefore, they try to define the issue in a way that promotes their position. Estrada defines the issue of naming sports teams after Native Americans in terms of how it affects individuals, especially children, rather than in terms of liberal or conservative politics. Similarly, Ehrenreich presents the issue of a living wage in terms of its practical impact on society.

A Clear Position

Very often writers declare their position in a thesis statement early in the essay. This strategy has the advantage of letting readers know right away where the writer stands. Statsky places her thesis in the opening paragraph, whereas Estrada puts his in the second paragraph. Moreover, all of the writers in this chapter restate the thesis at places in the argument where readers could lose sight of the central point. And they reiterate the thesis at the end.

In composing a thesis statement, writers try to make their position unambiguous, appropriately qualified, and clearly arguable. For example, to avoid ambiguity, Estrada uses common words like *wrong*. But because readers may differ on what they consider to be wrong, Estrada demonstrates exactly what he thinks is wrong about naming teams for ethnic groups. To show readers he shares their legitimate concerns about hypersensitivity, Estrada qualifies his thesis to apply only to genuine cases of political insensitivity. Finally, to show that his position is not based solely on personal feelings, Estrada appeals to readers' common sense of right and wrong.

Plausible Reasons and Convincing Support

To argue for a position, writers must give reasons. Even in relatively brief essays, writers sometimes give more than one reason and state their reasons explicitly. Estrada, for instance, gives two reasons for his position that naming sports teams for ethnic groups is detrimental: It treats people like team mascots, and it singles out politically weak groups. Statsky gives three reasons for her opposition to competitive sports for children: They are harmful to the children, discourage most from participating, and encourage adults to behave badly.

Writers know they cannot simply assert their reasons. They must support them with examples, statistics, authorities, or anecdotes. We have seen all of these kinds of support used in this chapter. For instance, Statsky uses all of them in her essay—giving examples of common sports injuries that children incur, citing statistics indicating the high percentage of children who drop out of competitive sports, quoting authorities on the physical and psychological hazards of competitive sports for young children, and relating an anecdote of a child vomiting to show the enormous psychological pressure competitive sports put on some children. Ehrenreich depends primarily on examples and statistics to support her position that the working poor are living in a perpetual state of emergency that must be acknowledged and remedied.

An Anticipation of Opposing Positions and Objections

Writers also try to anticipate other widely held positions on the issue as well as objections and questions readers might raise to an argument. The writers in this chapter counterargue by either accommodating or refuting opposing positions and objections. Estrada does both, implying that he shares his readers' objection to political correctness but arguing that naming sports teams after ethnic groups is a genuine case of political insensitivity and not an instance of hypersensitivity.

Anticipating readers' positions and objections can enhance the writer's credibility and strengthen the argument. When readers holding an opposing position recognize that the writer takes their position seriously, they are more likely to listen to what the writer has to say. It can also reassure readers that they share certain important values and attitudes with the writer, building a bridge of common concerns among people who have been separated by difference and antagonism.

GUIDE TO WRITING
Arguing Positions

THE WRITING ASSIGNMENT

Write an essay on a controversial issue. Learn more about the issue, and take a position on it. Present the issue to readers, and develop an argument for the purpose of confirming, challenging, or changing your readers' views on the issue.

THE WRITING ASSIGNMENT

INVENTION & RESEARCH

Finding an Issue to Write About

Exploring the Issue

Analyzing Potential Readers

Testing Your Choice

Developing Your Argument

Anticipating Readers' Objections and Questions

Anticipating Opposing Positions

Considering Document Design

Defining Your Purpose for Your Readers

Formulating a Tentative Thesis Statement

INVENTION AND RESEARCH

PLANNING & DRAFTING

Seeing What You Have

Doing Further Research

Setting Goals

Outlining

Drafting

PLANNING AND DRAFTING

CRITICAL READING GUIDE

First Impression

Presentation of the Issue

Clear Statement of the Position

Reasons and Support

Treatment of Opposing Positions, Likely Objections

Effectiveness of Organization

Final Thoughts

CRITICAL READING GUIDE

REVISING

A Focused Presentation of the Issue

A Clear Position

Plausible Reasons and Convincing Support

An Anticipation of Opposing Positions and Objections

The Organization

REVISING

EDITING & PROOFREADING

Checking for Commas before Coordinating Conjunctions

Checking the Punctuation of Conjunctive Adverbs

A Common ESL Problem: Subtle Differences in Meaning

EDITING AND PROOFREADING

GUIDE TO WRITING

■ THE WRITING ASSIGNMENT

Write an essay on a controversial issue. Learn more about the issue, and take a position on it. Present the issue to readers, and develop an argument for the purpose of confirming, challenging, or changing your readers' views on the issue.

■ INVENTION AND RESEARCH

The following activities will help you find an issue, explore what you know about it, and do any necessary research to develop an argument and counterargument. Each activity is easy to do and in most cases takes only a few minutes. Spreading the activities over several days will help you think critically about your own as well as other people's positions on the issue. Keep a written record of your invention and research to use when you draft and revise your essay.

Finding an Issue to Write About

To find the best possible issue for your essay, list as many possibilities as you can. The following activities will help you make a good choice.

Listing Issues. *Make a list of issues you might consider writing about.* Begin your list now, and add to it over the next few days. Include issues on which you already have a position and ones you do not know much about but would like to explore further. Do not overlook the issues suggested by the Considering Topics for Your Own Essay activities following each reading in this chapter.

Put the issues you list in the form of questions, like the following examples:

- Should local school boards be allowed to ban books (like *The Adventures of Huckleberry Finn* and *Of Mice and Men*) from school libraries?
- Should teenagers be required to get their parents' permission to obtain birth-control information and contraceptives?
- Should public libraries and schools be allowed to block access to selected Internet sites?
- Should undercover police officers be permitted to pose as high school students to identify sellers and users of drugs?
- Should training in music performance or art (drawing, painting, sculpting) be required of all high school students?
- Should college admission be based solely on academic achievement in high school?
- Should colleges be required to provide child-care facilities for children of students taking classes?

- Should students attending public colleges be required to pay higher tuition fees if they have been full-time students but do not graduate within four years?
- Should elected state or national representatives vote primarily on the basis of their individual conscience, their constituents' interests, or the general welfare?
- Should scientists attempt to clone human beings as they have done with animals?
- Should more money be directed into research to cure [any disease you want to name]?

Listing Issues Related to Identity and Community.   As the following suggestions indicate, many controversial issues will enable you to explore your understanding of identity and community. List issues that interest you.

- Should student athletes be required to maintain a certain grade point average to participate in college sports?
- Should parents be held responsible legally and financially for crimes committed by their children under age eighteen?
- Should students choose a college or courses that would confirm or challenge their beliefs and values?
- Should high schools or colleges require students to perform community service as a condition for graduation?
- Should children of immigrants who do not speak English be taught in their native language while they are learning English?
- Should all materials related to voting, driving, and income-tax reporting be written only in English or in other languages read by members of the community?
- Should the racial, ethnic, or gender makeup of a police force parallel the makeup of the community it serves?

Listing Issues Related to Work and Career.   Many current controversial issues will allow you to explore work and career topics. Identify issues that you would consider writing about.

- Should businesses remain loyal to their communities, or should they move to wherever labor costs, taxes, or other conditions are more favorable?
- When they choose careers, should people look primarily for jobs that are well paid or for jobs that are personally fulfilling, morally acceptable, or socially responsible?
- Should the state or federal government provide job training or temporary employment to people who are unemployed but willing to work?
- Should the primary purpose of a college education be job training?
- Should drug testing be mandatory for people in high-risk jobs such as bus drivers, heavy-equipment operators, and airplane pilots?

Choosing an Interesting Issue.   *Select an issue from your list that you think would be interesting to explore further.* You may already have an opinion on the issue, or you may have chosen it because you want to learn more about it.

Your choice may be influenced by whether you have time for research or whether your instructor requires you to do research. Issues that have been written about extensively make excellent topics for extended research projects. In contrast, you may feel confident writing about a local community or campus issue without doing much, if any, research.

Exploring the Issue

To explore the issue, you need to define it, determine whether you need to do research, and decide tentatively on your position.

Defining the Issue.   *To begin thinking about the issue, write for a few minutes explaining how you currently understand it.* If you have strong feelings about the issue, briefly explain why, but do not try to present your argument at this time. Focus on clarifying the issue by considering questions like these:

- Who has taken a position on this issue, and what positions have they taken?
- How does the issue affect different groups of people? What is at stake for them?
- What is the issue's history? How long has it been an issue? Has it changed over time? What makes it important now?
- How broad is the issue? What other issues are related to it?

Doing Research.   *If you do not know very much about the issue or the different views people have taken on it, do some research before continuing.* You can gather information by talking to others and by reading what others have written. Choosing one or two key terms of your issue, look for them in the subject headings of the *Library of Congress Subject Headings* and also in the library catalog, using the keyword search option. The library can also give you access to special online resources; check the library's Web site or ask a librarian for advice. Keep a list of the most promising materials you discover.

If you do not have time for research and lack confidence in your knowledge of the issue, you should switch to another issue about which you are better informed. Return to your list of possible issues, and start over.

Exploring Your Opinion.   *Write for a few minutes exploring your current thinking on the issue.* What is your current position? Why do you hold this position? What other positions on the issue do you know about? As you develop your argument and learn more about the issue, you may change your mind. Your aim now is merely to record your thinking as of this moment.

Analyzing Potential Readers

Write several sentences describing the readers to whom you will be addressing your argument. Begin by briefly identifying your readers; then use the following questions to help you describe them.

- What position or positions will my readers take on this issue? How entrenched are these positions likely to be?

- What do my readers know about the issue? In what contexts are they likely to have encountered it? In what ways might the issue affect them personally or professionally?

- How far apart on the issue are my readers and I likely to be? What fundamental differences in worldview or experience might keep us from agreeing? Which of my readers' values might most influence their view of the issue?

- Why would I want to present my argument to these particular readers? What could I realistically hope to achieve—convincing them to adopt my point of view, getting them to reconsider their own position, confirming or challenging some of their underlying beliefs and values?

Testing Your Choice

Decide whether you should proceed with this particular issue. Review your invention notes to see whether you understand the issue well enough to continue working with it and whether you can feel confident that you will be able to construct a convincing argument for your prospective readers. To make these decisions, ask yourself the following questions:

- Have I begun to understand the issue and my own position well enough to begin constructing a well-reasoned, well-supported argument?

- Do I have a good enough sense of how my readers view this issue to begin formulating an argument that is appropriate for them?

- Do I now know enough about the issue, or can I learn what I need to know in the time I have remaining?

If you cannot answer these questions affirmatively at this point in the process, it might be wise to consider a different issue. Giving up on a topic after you have worked on it is bound to be frustrating, but if you have little interest in the issue and do not have any idea how you could address your readers, starting over may be the wisest course of action. The following collaborative activity may help you decide whether to go on with this issue or to begin looking for an alternative.

Testing Your Choice: A Collaborative Activity

At this point in your invention work, you will find it helpful to get together with two or three other students to discuss the issue you have tentatively chosen.

Arguers: In turn, each of you identify the issue you are planning to write about. Explain briefly why you care about it personally and why you think your intended readers might see it as important. Then tell the most important reason that you have taken your position on the issue.

Listeners: Tell the arguer what you know about the issue and what you think makes it worth arguing about. Then try to suggest one thing the arguer could say to make the favored reason most convincing to the intended readers.

Developing Your Argument

To construct a convincing argument, you need to list reasons for your position, choose the most plausible ones, and support them.

Listing Reasons. *Write down every reason you can think of for why you have taken your position.* You can discover reasons for your position by trying to come up with "because" statements—for example, "I believe that my college should provide day care for the young children of full-time students *because these students are most likely to drop out if they cannot count on reliable day care.*" Given that few convincing arguments rely on only one reason, try to come up with at least two or three.

Choosing the Most Plausible Reasons. *Write several sentences on each reason to determine which reasons seem most plausible—that is, most likely to be convincing to your particular readers. Then identify your most plausible reasons.* If you decide that none of your reasons seems very plausible, you might need to reconsider your position, do some more research, or choose another issue.

Anticipating Readers' Objections and Questions

To construct a convincing argument, you also need to anticipate and decide how you will counterargue readers' objections and questions.

Listing Your Most Plausible Reasons. *Review the choices you made at the end of the preceding activity, and list your two or three most plausible reasons.*

Listing Objections and Questions. *Under each reason, list one or more objections to or questions about it that readers could raise.* You may know how readers will respond to some of your reasons. For others, you may need to be inventive. Imagining yourself as a critical reader, look for places where your argument is vulnerable to criticism. For example, think of an assumption that you are making that others might not accept or a value others might not share. Imagine how people in different situations—different neighborhoods, occupations, age groups, living arrangements—might react to your argument.

Accommodating a Legitimate Objection or Question. *Choose one objection or question that makes sense to you, and write for a few minutes on how you could accommodate it into your argument.* You may be able simply to acknowledge an objection or answer a question and explain why you think it does not negatively affect your argument. If the criticism is more serious, try not to let it shake your confidence. Instead, consider how you can accommodate it, perhaps by conceding the point and qualifying your position or changing the way you argue for it.

If the criticism seems so damaging that you cannot accommodate it into your argument, however, you may need to rethink your position or even consider writing on a different issue. If you arrive at such an impasse, discuss the problem with your instructor; do not abandon your issue unless it is absolutely necessary.

Refuting an Illegitimate Objection or Question. *Choose one objection or question that seems to challenge or weaken your argument, and write for a few minutes on how you could refute it.* Do not choose to refute only the weakest objection (to make what is sometimes called a *straw-man argument*) while ignoring the strongest one. Consider whether you can show that an objection is based on a misunderstanding or that it does not really damage your argument.

Anticipating Opposing Positions

Now that you have planned your argument and counterargument, you need to consider how you can respond to the arguments for other positions on the issue.

Considering Other Positions. *Identify one or more widely held positions other than your own that people take on the issue.* If you can, identify the individuals or groups who support the positions you list.

Researching Opposing Positions: An Online Activity To learn more about opposing positions, search for your issue online. To do so, enter a key term—a word or brief phrase—of your issue into a search tool such as Google (www.google.com) or Yahoo! Directory (http://dir.yahoo.com). If possible, identify at least two positions different from your own. No matter how well argued, they need not weaken your confidence in your position. Your purpose is to understand opposing positions so well that you can represent one or more of them accurately and counterargue them effectively.

Bookmark or keep a record of promising sites. Download any materials that may help you represent and counterargue opposing positions.

Listing Reasons for the Opposing Position. *Choose the opposing position you think is likely to be most attractive to your particular readers, and list the reasons people give for it.* Given what you now know, try to represent the argument accurately and fairly. Later, you may need to do some research to find out more about this opposing position.

Accommodating a Plausible Reason. *Choose one reason that makes sense to you, and write for a few minutes on how you could accommodate it into your argument.* Consider whether you can accommodate the point and put it aside as not really damaging to your central argument. You may also have to consider qualifying your position or changing the way you argue for it.

Refuting an Implausible Reason. *Choose one reason that you do not accept, and write for a few minutes on how you will plan your refutation.* Do not choose to refute a position no one really takes seriously. Also be careful not to misrepresent other people's positions or to criticize people personally (sometimes called an *ad hominem attack*). Do try to get at the heart of your disagreement.

You may want to argue that the values on which the opposing argument is based are not widely shared or are just plain wrong. Or perhaps you can point out that the reasoning is flawed (for instance, showing that an example applies only to certain people in certain situations). Or maybe you can show that the argument lacks convincing support (for instance, that the opposition's statistics can be interpreted differently or that quoted authorities do not qualify as experts). If you do not have all the information you need, make a note of what you need and where you might find it. Later, you can do more research to develop this part of your argument.

Considering Document Design

Think about whether including visual or audio elements—cartoons, photographs, tables, graphs, or snippets from films, television programs, or songs—would strengthen your argument. These are not a requirement of an effective essay arguing a position, but they could be helpful. Consider also whether your readers might benefit from design features such as headings, bulleted or numbered lists, or other elements that would make your essay easier to follow. You could construct your own graphic elements, download materials from the Internet, tape images and sounds from television or other sources, or scan into your document visuals from books and magazines. If you do use visual or audio materials you did not create yourself, be sure to acknowledge your sources in your essay (and request permission from the sources if the essay will be posted on the Web).

Defining Your Purpose for Your Readers

Write a few sentences, defining your purpose in writing about your position on this issue for your particular readers. Remember that you already have analyzed your potential readers and developed your argument with these readers in mind. Given these readers, try now to define your purpose by considering the following possibilities and any others that might apply to your writing situation:

- If my readers are likely to be sympathetic to my point of view, what do I hope to achieve—give them reasons to commit to my position, arm them with ammunition to make their own arguments, or win their respect and admiration?

- If my readers are likely to be hostile to my point of view, what do I hope to accomplish—get them to concede that other points of view must be taken seriously, make them defend their reasons, show them how knowledgeable and committed I am to my position, or show them how well I can argue?

- If my readers are likely to take an opposing position but are not staunchly committed to it, what should I try to do—make them think critically about the reasons and the kinds of support they have for their position, give them reasons to change their minds, show them how my position serves their interests better, appeal to their values and sense of responsibility, or disabuse them of their preconceptions and prejudices against my position?

Formulating a Tentative Thesis Statement

Write several sentences that could serve as a thesis statement. Assert your position carefully. You might also forecast your reasons, listing them in the order in which you will take them up in your argument. In other words, draft a thesis statement that tells your readers simply and directly what you want them to think about the issue and why.

Estrada states his thesis at the end of the second paragraph: "Still, however willing I may have been to go along with the name as a kid, as an adult I have concluded that using an ethnic group essentially as a sports mascot is wrong." Perhaps the most explicit and fully developed thesis statement in this chapter's readings is Jessica Statsky's. She asserts her thesis at the end of the first paragraph and then qualifies it and forecasts her reasons in the second paragraph:

> When overzealous parents and coaches impose adult standards on children's sports, the result can be activities that are neither satisfying nor beneficial to children.
>
> I am concerned about all organized sports activities for children between the ages of six and twelve. The damage I see results from noncontact as well as contact sports, from sports organized locally as well as those organized nationally. Highly organized competitive sports such as Peewee Football and Little League Baseball are too often played to adult standards, which are developmentally inappropriate for children and can be both physically and psychologically harmful. Furthermore, because they eliminate many children from organized sports before they are ready to compete, they are actually counterproductive for developing either future players or fans. Finally, because they emphasize competition and winning, they unfortunately provide occasions for some parents and coaches to place their own fantasies and needs ahead of children's welfare.

As you formulate your own tentative thesis statement, pay attention to the language you use. It should be clear and unambiguous, emphatic but appropriately qualified, as well as arguable and based on plausible reasons. Although you will most probably refine this thesis statement as you work on your essay, trying now to articulate it will help give your planning and drafting direction and impetus.

■ PLANNING AND DRAFTING

You should now review what you have learned about the issue, do further research if necessary, and plan your first draft by setting goals and making an outline.

Seeing What You Have

Pause now to reflect on your invention and research notes. Reread everything carefully to decide whether you have enough plausible reasons and convincing support to offer readers and whether you understand the debate well enough to anticipate and respond to your readers' likely objections. It may help, as you read, to annotate your invention writings. If you have done your invention writing on the computer, you may have sentences or whole paragraphs that can be copied and pasted into your draft. Reread what you have written so far to identify the potentially useful material. Look for details that will help you clarify the issue for readers, present a strong argument for your position, and counterargue possible objections and alternative positions. Highlight key words, phrases, or sentences; make marginal notes or electronic annotations.

If your invention notes are skimpy, you may not have given enough thought to the issue or know enough at this time to write a convincing argument about it. You can do further research at this stage or begin drafting and later do research to fill in the blanks.

If you fear that you are in over your head, consult your instructor to determine whether you should make a radical change. For example, your instructor might suggest that you tackle a smaller, more doable aspect of the issue, perhaps one with which you have firsthand experience. It is also possible that your instructor will advise you to give up on this topic for the time being and to try writing on a different issue.

Doing Further Research

If you think you lack crucial information that you will need to plan and draft your essay, this is a good time to do some further research. Consider possible sources, including people you could interview as well as library materials and Internet sites. Then do your research, making sure to note down all the information you will need to cite your sources.

Setting Goals

Before you begin writing your draft, consider some specific goals for your essay. The draft will be easier to write and more focused if you have some clear goals in mind. The following questions will help you set them. You may find it useful to return to them while you are drafting, for they are designed to help you look at specific features and strategies of an essay arguing a position on a controversial issue.

Your Purpose and Readers

- Who are my readers, and what can I realistically hope to accomplish by addressing them?
- Should I write primarily to change readers' minds, to get them to consider my arguments seriously, to confirm their opinions, to urge them to do something about the issue, or to accomplish some other purpose?
- How can I present myself so that my readers will consider me informed, knowledgeable, and fair?

The Beginning

- What opening would capture readers' attention?
- Should I begin as if I were telling a story, with phrases like "When I was" (Estrada) or "Over the past three decades" (Statsky)?
- Should I open with a rhetorical question, an arresting quotation, or a surprising statistic? Ehrenreich combines all three in her opening sentences.
- Should I open by summarizing an opposing argument that I will refute?
- Should I make clear at the outset exactly what my concerns are and how I see the issue, as Statsky does?

Presentation of the Issue

- Should I place the issue in a historical context or in a personal context, as Estrada does?
- Should I use examples—real or hypothetical—to make the issue concrete for readers, as Estrada does?
- Should I try to demonstrate that the issue is important by citing statistics, quoting authorities, or describing its negative effects, as Statsky and Ehrenreich do?

Your Argument and Counterargument

- How can I present my reasons so that readers will see them as plausible, leading logically to my position?
- If I have more than one reason, how should I sequence them?
- Should I forecast my reasons or counterarguments early in the essay, as Statsky does?

- Which objections should I anticipate? Can I concede any objections without undermining my argument, as Estrada does?
- Which opposing positions should I anticipate? Can I counterargue by showing that the statistics offered by others are not relevant? Can I support my position with anecdotes, as Estrada does?

The Ending

- How can I conclude my argument effectively? Should I reiterate my thesis?
- Should I try to unite readers with different allegiances by reminding them of values we share, as Estrada and Ehrenreich do?
- Could I conclude by looking to the future or by urging readers to take action or make changes, as Statsky does?

Outlining

An essay arguing a position on a controversial issue contains as many as four basic parts:

1. Presentation of the issue
2. A clear position
3. Reasons and support
4. Anticipation of opposing positions and objections

These parts can be organized in various ways. If you expect some of your readers to oppose your argument, you might try to redefine the issue so that these readers can see the possibility that they may share some common values with you after all. To reinforce your connection to readers, you could go on to concede the wisdom of an aspect of their position before presenting the reasons and support for your position. You would conclude by reiterating the shared values on which you hope to build agreement. In this case, an outline might look like this:

Presentation of the issue

Accommodation of some aspect of an opposing position

Thesis statement

First reason with support

Second reason with support (etc.)

Conclusion

If you have decided to write primarily for readers who agree rather than disagree with you, then you might choose to organize your argument as a refutation of opposing arguments to strengthen your readers' convictions. Begin by presenting the issue, stating your position, and reminding readers of your most plausible reasons. Then take up each opposing argument, and try to refute it. You might conclude by calling your supporters to arms. Here is an outline showing what this kind of essay might look like:

Presentation of the issue

Thesis statement

Your most plausible reasons

First opposing argument with refutation

Second opposing argument with refutation

Conclusion

There are, of course, many other possible ways to organize an essay arguing for a position on a controversial issue, but these outlines should help you start planning your own essay.

Consider tentative any outlining you do before you begin drafting. Never be a slave to an outline. As you draft, you will usually see ways to improve on your original plan. Be ready to revise your outline, shift parts around, or drop or add parts as you draft. If you use the outlining function of your word processing program, changing your outline will be simple, and you may be able to write the essay simply by expanding the outline.

Drafting

General Advice.   Start drafting your essay, keeping in mind the goals you set while you were planning. Remember also the needs and expectations of your readers; organize, define, and explain with them in mind. Turn off your grammar checker and spelling checker at this stage if you find them distracting. Don't be afraid to skip around in your draft; jump back and fill in a spontaneous idea, or leap ahead and write a later section first if you find that easier. If, as you draft, you find that you need more information, just make a note of what you have to find out and go on to the next point. When you are done drafting, you can search for the information you need. If you get stuck while drafting, explore the problem by using some of the writing activities in the Invention and Research section of this chapter.

As you draft, keep in mind that the basis for disagreement about controversial issues often depends on values as much as on credible support. Try to think critically about the values underlying your own as well as others' views so that your argument can take these values into account. Consider the tone of your argument and how you want to come across to readers.

Sentence Strategies.   As you draft, you will need to move back and forth smoothly between direct arguments for your position and counterarguments for your readers' likely objections, questions, and preferred positions on the issue. One useful strategy for making this move is to concede the value of a likely criticism and then to attempt to refute it immediately, either in the same sentence or in the next one. You will also need to use conjunctions and similar phrases to indicate explicitly and precisely the logical relationships between your sentences.

Counterargue by conceding and then immediately refuting. How do you introduce brief concession followed by refutation into your argument? The following sentences from Jessica Statsky's essay illustrate several ways to do so (the concessions are in italics, the refutations in bold):

> The primary goal of professional athletes — winning — is not appropriate for children. Their goals should be having fun, learning, and being with friends. *Although winning does add to the fun,* **too many adults lose sight of what matters and make winning the most important goal.** (paragraph 5)

> *And it is perfectly obvious how important competitive skills are in finding a job.* **Yet the ability to cooperate is also important for success in life.** (10)

In both these examples from different stages in her argument, Statsky concedes the importance or value of some of her readers' likely objections, but then firmly refutes them. (Because these illustrations are woven into an extended argument, you may be better able to appreciate them if you look at them in context by turning to the paragraphs where they appear.) The following example comes from another reading in the chapter:

> *Guilt, you may be thinking warily. Isn't that what we're supposed to feel?* **But guilt doesn't go anywhere near far enough; the appropriate emotion is shame.** . . . (Barbara Ehrenreich, paragraph 10)

This important counterargument strategy sometimes begins not with concession but with acknowledgment; that is, the writer simply accurately restates part of an opponent's argument without conceding the wisdom of it. Here is an example:

> *Another argument is that ethnic group leaders are too inclined to cry wolf in alleging racial insensitivity. Often, this is the case.* **But no one should overlook genuine cases of political insensitivity in an attempt to avoid accusations of hypersensitivity and political correctness.** (Richard Estrada, paragraph 7)

The concession-refutation move, sometimes called the "yes-but" strategy, is important in most arguments; in fact, it usually recurs, as it does in all the readings in this chapter. Following is an outline of some of the other language this chapter's authors rely on to introduce their concession-refutation moves:

Introducing the concession	*Introducing the refutation that follows*
I understand that	What I think is
I can't prove	But I think
I am grateful	But surely
It is true that	But my point is
Another argument	But

And it is not difficult to imagine other concession-refutation pairings:

It has been argued that	Nevertheless,
We are told that	My own belief is

Proponents argue that	This argument, however,
This argument seems plausible	But experience and evidence show
One common complaint is	In recent years, however,
I'm not saying. . . . Nor am I saying	But I am saying
Activists insist	Still, in spite of their good intentions
A reader might ask	But the real issue

Use conjunctions and phrases like them to indicate explicitly and precisely the logical relationships between clauses and sentences. In all writing, conjunctions serve to indicate the specific ways that clauses and sentences relate in meaning to each other, but reasoned arguments are especially dependent on these logical links. There are three main types of conjunctions: coordinating conjunctions like *and, but,* or *so;* subordinating conjunctions like *while, because,* and *although;* and, of special importance in arguments taking a position, conjunctive adverbs like *furthermore, consequently, however, nevertheless,* and *therefore.* Here is an example from a reading in this chapter, with the conjunctive adverb in italics:

> Highly organized competitive sports such as Peewee Football and Little League Baseball are too often played to adult standards, which are developmentally inappropriate for children and can be both physically and psychologically harmful. *Furthermore,* because they eliminate many children from organized sports before they are ready to compete, they are actually counterproductive for developing either future players or fans. (Jessica Statsky, paragraph 2)

Statsky chooses the conjunctive adverb *furthermore* because in the previous sentence she has given one reason that she opposes highly competitive organized sports for children and she wants readers to understand that she is about to give another one. In this situation, she might also have chosen *moreover, in addition,* or *at the same time.*
Now look at this example:

> Like adults, children fear failure, *and so* even those with good physical skills may stay away because they lack self-confidence. *Consequently,* teams lose many promising players who with some encouragement and experience might have become stars. (Jessica Statsky, paragraph 7)

Here Statsky uses *and so* to link the two main clauses in the first sentence and the conjunctive adverb *consequently* to link the second sentence to the first. In both cases, she is arguing that what comes after the conjunction is an unfortunate effect or consequence of what comes before it: Fear of failure causes staying away, which in turn causes the loss of promising players. Instead of *consequently,* she might have chosen *therefore, as a result,* or *in effect* to make this logical relationship explicit.
Notice that conjunctive adverbs seem somewhat formal. This level of formality would be appropriate in most arguments taking positions on public issues. Should you be writing for a familiar audience of peers or a publication aimed at a popular audience, however, you might want to adopt less formal conjunctions or phrases for indicating logical relationships between your clauses and sentences. For example, you could use *but* instead of *however, and* or *in addition* instead of *moreover, still* for *never-*

theless, or *so* instead of *consequently.* In this chapter's readings, Barbara Ehrenreich consistently uses informal conjunctions, and Jessica Statsky mostly uses formal ones.

You might find the following list helpful when you are searching for precisely the right conjunctive adverb or phrase for the logical relationship you want to signal. If you are unsure about which one to choose, look up the most likely one in a dictionary or, better, a dictionary of synonyms. Keep in mind that these useful expressions serve only to *signal* a logical relationship; they cannot *create* such a relationship, which is determined by the content of the clauses or sentences they join. Your readers will not necessarily see the similarities between two things, for example, just because you have joined them with *similarly.*

To expand or add: *moreover, further, furthermore, in addition, at the same time, in the same way, by the same token, that is, likewise*

To reformulate or replace: *in other words, better, rather, again, alternatively, on the other hand*

To exemplify: *for example, as an example, thus, for instance*

To qualify: *however, nevertheless, on the other hand, at the same time*

To dismiss: *in any case, in either case, whichever way it is, anyhow, at any rate, however it is*

To show cause or effect: *therefore, consequently, as a result, in effect, for this reason, otherwise, in that case, accordingly, hence, thus*

To show comparison: *in comparison, by comparison, in the same way, similarly, likewise*

To show contrast: *instead, on the contrary, rather, by contrast, in opposition, on the other hand*

To show emphasis: *indeed, again*

In addition to making the concession-refutation move and using conjunctions to signal logical relationships, you can strengthen your reasoned arguments with other kinds of sentence strategies as well, and you may want to turn to the discussions of sentences that feature appositives to identify or establish the authority of a source (pp. 151–52).

CRITICAL READING GUIDE

Now is the time to get a good critical reading of your draft. Your instructor may arrange such a reading as part of your coursework; if not, you can ask a classmate, friend, or family member to read it over. If your campus has a writing center, you might ask a tutor there to read and comment on your draft using this guide to critical reading. (If you are unable to have someone else review your draft, turn ahead to the Revising section on p. 202, where you will find guidelines for reading your own draft critically.)

If you read another student's draft online, you may be able to use a word processing program to insert suggested improvements directly into the text of the draft or to write them out at the end of the draft. If you read a printout of the draft, you may write brief comments in the margins and lengthier suggestions on a separate page. When the writer sits down to revise, your thoughtful, extended suggestions written at the end of the draft or on separate pages will be especially helpful.

If You Are the Writer.   To provide focused, helpful comments, your critical reader must know your essay's intended audience, your purpose, and a problem in the draft that you need help solving. Briefly write out this information at the top of your draft.

- *Readers:* To whom are you directing your argument? What do you assume they think about this issue? Do you expect them to be receptive, skeptical, resistant, antagonistic?

- *Purpose:* What effect do you realistically expect your argument to have on these particular readers?

- *Problem:* Ask your reader to help you solve the most important problem you see in your draft. Describe this problem briefly.

If You Are the Reader.   Use the following guidelines to help you give constructive, critical comments to others on their position papers.

1. *Read for a First Impression.* Tell the writer what you think the intended readers would find most and least convincing. If you personally think the argument is seriously flawed, share your thoughts. Then try to help the writer improve the argument for the designated readers. Next, consider the problem the writer identified, and respond briefly to that concern now. (If you find that the problem is covered by one of the other guidelines listed below, respond to it in more detail there if necessary.)

2. *Analyze the Way the Issue Is Presented.* Look at the way the issue is presented, and indicate whether you think that most readers would understand the issue differently. If you think that readers will need more information to grasp the issue and appreciate its importance, ask questions to help the writer fill in whatever is missing.

3. *Assess Whether the Position Is Stated Clearly.* Write a sentence or two summarizing the writer's position as you understand it from reading the draft.

Then identify the sentence or sentences in the draft where the thesis is stated explicitly. (It may be restated in several places.) If you cannot find an explicit statement of the thesis, let the writer know. Given the writer's purpose and audience, consider whether the thesis statement is too strident or too timid and whether it needs to be more qualified, more sharply focused, or more confidently asserted. If you think that the thesis, as presented, is not really arguable — for example, if it asserts a fact no one questions or a matter of personal belief — let the writer know.

4. *Evaluate the Reasons and Support.* Identify the reasons given for the writer's position. Have any important reasons been left out or any weak ones overemphasized? Indicate any contradictions or gaps in the argument. Point to any reasons that do not seem plausible to you, and briefly explain why. Then note any places where support is lacking or unconvincing. Help the writer think of additional support or suggest sources where more or better support might be found.

5. *Assess How Well Opposing Positions and Likely Objections Have Been Handled.* Identify places where opposing arguments or objections are mentioned, and point to any where the refutation could be strengthened or where shared assumptions or values offer the potential for accommodation. Also consider whether the writer has ignored any important opposing arguments or objections.

6. *Consider Whether the Organization Is Effective.* Get an overview of the essay's organization, perhaps by making a scratch outline. Point to any parts that might be more effective earlier or later in the essay. Point out any places where more explicit cueing — transitions, summaries, or topic sentences — would clarify the relationship between parts of the essay.

   • *Reread the beginning.* Will readers find it engaging? If not, see whether you can recommend something from later in the essay that might work better as an opening.

   • *Study the ending.* Does the essay conclude decisively and memorably? If not, suggest an alternative. Could something be moved to the end?

   • *Assess the design features and visuals.* Comment on the contribution of any headings, tables, or other design features and illustrations. Help the writer think of additional design features and illustrations that could make a contribution to the essay.

7. *Give the Writer Your Final Thoughts.* What is this draft's strongest part? What part is most in need of further work?

■ REVISING

Now you are ready to revise your essay. Your instructor or other students may have given you advice on improving your draft. Nevertheless, you may have begun to realize that your draft requires not so much revising as rethinking. For example, you may recognize that your reasons do not lead readers to accept your position, that you cannot adequately support your reasons, or that you have been unable to refute damaging objections to your argument. Consequently, instead of working to improve parts of the draft, you may need to write a new draft that radically reenvisions your argument. It is not unusual for students — and professional writers — to find themselves in this situation. Learning to make radical revisions is a valuable lesson for all writers.

On the other hand, you may feel quite satisfied that your draft achieves most, if not all, of your goals. In that case, you can focus on refining specific parts of your draft. Very likely you have thought of ways of improving your draft, and you may even have begun improving it. This section will help you get an overview of your draft and revise it accordingly.

Getting an Overview

Consider your draft as a whole, following these two steps:

1. *Reread.* If at all possible, put the draft aside for a day or two before rereading it. When you return to it, start by reconsidering your purpose. Then read the draft straight through, trying to see it as your intended readers will.

2. *Outline.* Make a scratch outline, indicating the basic features as they appear in the draft. Consider using the headings and outline/summary functions of your word processor.

Planning for Revision.   Resist the temptation to dive in and start changing your text until after you have a clear view of the big picture. Using your outline as a guide, move through the document, using the highlighting or commenting tools of your word processor to note comments received from others and problems you want to solve (or mark on a hard copy if you prefer).

Analyzing the Basic Features of Your Own Draft.   Using the questions presented in the Critical Reading Guide on pp. 199–201, reread your draft to identify specific problems you need to solve. Note the problems on your draft.

Studying Critical Comments.   Review all of the comments you have received from other readers, and add to your notes any suggestions you intend to act on. For each comment, look at the draft to see what might have led the reader to make that particular point. Try to be receptive to any criticism. By letting you see how other readers respond to your draft, these comments provide valuable information about how you might improve it.

Carrying Out Revisions

Having identified problems in your draft, you now need to come up with solutions and—most important—to carry them out. Basically, you have three ways of finding solutions:

1. Review your invention and planning notes for information and ideas to add to your draft.

2. Do additional invention and research to provide material you or your readers think is needed.

3. Look back at the readings in this chapter to see how other writers have solved similar problems.

The following suggestions, which are organized according to the basic features of position papers, will help you get started solving some problems common to them.

A Focused Presentation of the Issue

- *Do readers have difficulty summarizing the issue, or do they see it differently from the way you do?* Try to anticipate possible misunderstandings or other ways of seeing the issue.

- *Do readers need more information?* Consider adding examples, quoting authorities, or simply explaining the issue further.

- *Does the issue strike readers as unimportant?* State explicitly why you think it is important and why you think your readers should think so, too. Try to provide an anecdote, facts, or a quote from an authority that would demonstrate its importance.

A Clear Position

- *Do readers have difficulty summarizing your position or finding your thesis statement?* You may need to announce your thesis statement more explicitly or rewrite it to prevent misunderstanding.

- *Do any words seem unclear or ambiguous?* Use other words, explain what you mean, or add an example to make your position more concrete.

- *Do you appear to be taking a position that is not really arguable?* Consider whether your position is arguable. If you believe in your position as a matter of faith and cannot provide reasons and support, then your position probably is not arguable. Consult your instructor about changing your position or topic.

- *Could you qualify your thesis to account for exceptions or strong objections to your argument?* Add language that specifies when, where, under what conditions, or for whom your position applies.

Plausible Reasons and Convincing Support

- *Do readers have difficulty identifying your reasons?* Announce each reason explicitly, possibly with topic sentences. Consider adding a forecast early in the essay so readers know what reasons to expect.

- *Have you left out any reasons?* Consider whether adding particular reasons would strengthen your argument. To fit in new reasons, you may have to reorganize your whole argument.

- *Do any of your reasons seem implausible or contradictory?* Either delete such reasons, or show how they relate logically to your position or to your other reasons.

- *Does your support seem unconvincing or scanty?* Where necessary, explain why you think the support should lead readers to accept your position. Review your invention notes, or do some more research to gather additional examples, statistics, anecdotes, or quotations from authorities.

An Anticipation of Opposing Positions and Objections

- *Do readers have difficulty finding your responses to opposing arguments or objections?* Add transitions that call readers' attention to each response.

- *Do you ignore any important objections or arguments?* Consider adding to your response. Determine whether you should replace a response to a relatively weak objection with a new response to a more important one.

- *Are there any concessions you could make?* Consider whether you should acknowledge the legitimacy of readers' concerns or accommodate particular objections. Show on what points you share readers' values, even though you may disagree on other points. Remember that all of the authors in this chapter concede and then attempt to refute, relying on useful sentence openers like *I understand that, What I think is,* and *It is true that…, but my point is….*

- *Do any of your attempts at refutation seem unconvincing?* Try to strengthen them. Avoid attacking your opponents. Instead, provide solid support— respected authorities, accepted facts, and statistics from reputable sources—to convince readers that your argument is credible.

The Organization

- *Do readers have trouble following your argument?* Consider adding a brief forecast of your main reasons at the beginning of your essay and adding explicit topic sentences and transitions to announce each reason as it is developed. As all the authors do in this chapter, consider signaling explicitly the logical relations between steps and sentences in your argument. Remember that they use both informal signals like *yet* and *still* and formal signals like *moreover, consequently,* and *therefore.*

- *Does the beginning seem vague and uninteresting?* Consider adding a striking anecdote or surprising quotation to open the essay, or find something in the essay you could move to the beginning.

- *Does the ending seem indecisive or abrupt?* Search your invention notes for a strong quotation, or add language that will reach out to readers. Try moving your strongest point to the ending.

- *Can you add illustrations or any other design features to make the essay more interesting to read and to strengthen your argument?* Consider incorporating a visual you came across in your research or one you can create on your own.

Checking Sentence Strategies Electronically. To check your draft for a sentence strategy especially useful in essays arguing a position, use your word processor's highlighting function to mark places where you are either making concessions or trying to refute opposing arguments or objections that readers might have to your argument. Then look at each place, and think about whether you could strengthen your argument at that point by combining concession and refutation, either by moving or adding a concession just before a refutation or by moving or adding a refutation immediately following a concession. For more on the concession-refutation strategy, see pp. 196–98.

■ EDITING AND PROOFREADING

Now is the time to edit your revised draft for errors in grammar, punctuation, and mechanics and to consider matters of style. Our research has revealed several errors that are especially likely to occur in student essays arguing a position. The following guidelines will help you check and edit your draft for these common errors. This book's Web site also provides interactive online exercises to help you learn to identify and correct some of these errors; to access the exercises for a particular error, go to the URLs listed after each set of guidelines.

Checking for Commas before Coordinating Conjunctions. An independent clause is a group of words that can stand alone as a complete sentence. Writers often join two or more such clauses with coordinating conjunctions *(and, but, for, or, nor, so, yet)* to link related ideas in one sentence. Look at one example from Jessica Statsky's essay:

> Winning and losing may be an inevitable part of adult life, but they should not be part of childhood. (paragraph 6)

In this sentence, Statsky links two ideas: (1) that winning and losing may be part of adult life and (2) that they should not be part of childhood. In essays that argue a position, writers often join ideas in this way as they set forth the reasons and support for their positions.

When you join independent clauses, use a comma before the coordinating conjunction so that readers can easily see where one idea stops and the next one starts:

▶ The new immigration laws will bring in more skilled people; but their presence will take jobs away from other Americans.

▶ Sexually transmitted diseases are widespread; and many students are sexually active.

Do not use a comma when the coordinating conjunction joins phrases that are not independent clauses:

▶ Newspaper reporters have visited pharmacies,/and observed pharmacists selling steroids illegally.

▶ We need people with special talents,/and diverse skills to make the United States a stronger nation.

For practice, go to bedfordstmartins.com/conciseguide/comma and bedfordstmartins .com/conciseguide/uncomma.

Checking the Punctuation of Conjunctive Adverbs. When writers take a position, the reasoning they need to employ seems to invite the use of conjunctive adverbs (*consequently, furthermore, however, moreover, therefore, thus*) to connect sentences and clauses. Conjunctive adverbs that open a sentence should be followed by a comma:

▶ Consequently; many local governments have banned smoking.

▶ Therefore; talented nurses will leave the profession because of poor working conditions and low salaries.

If a conjunctive adverb joins two independent clauses, it must be preceded by a semi-colon and followed by a comma:

▶ The recent vote on increasing student fees produced a disappointing turnout,; moreover; the presence of campaign literature on ballot tables violated voting procedures.

▶ Children watching television recognize violence but not its intention; thus; they become desensitized to violence.

Conjunctive adverbs that fall in the middle of an independent clause are set off with commas:

▶ Due to trade restrictions; however; sales of Japanese cars did not surpass sales of domestic cars.

For practice, go to bedfordstmartins.com/conciseguide/comma, bedfordstmartins .com/conciseguide/uncomma, and bedfordstmartins.com/conciseguide/semi.

A Common ESL Problem: Subtle Differences in Meaning. Because the distinctions in meaning among some common conjunctive adverbs are subtle, nonnative speakers often have difficulty using them accurately. For example, the difference between *however* and *nevertheless* is small; each is used to introduce statements that contrast with what precedes it. But *nevertheless* emphasizes the contrast, whereas *however* softens it. Check usage of such terms in an English dictionary rather than a bilingual one. *The American Heritage Dictionary of the English Language* has special usage notes to help distinguish frequently confused words.

A Note on Grammar and Spelling Checkers. These tools are good at catching certain types of errors, but currently there's no replacement for a good human proofreader. Grammar checkers in particular are extremely limited in what they can usually find, and often they only give you summary information that isn't helpful if you don't already understand the rule in question. They are also prone to give faulty advice for fixing problems and to flag correct items as wrong. Spelling checkers cause fewer problems but can't catch misspellings that are themselves words, such as *to* for *too*.

REFLECTING ON YOUR WRITING

Now that you have read and discussed several essays that argue a position on a controversial issue and written one of your own, take some time for reflection. Reflecting on your writing process will help you gain a greater understanding of what you learned about solving the problems you encountered in writing an argument.

Write a one-page explanation telling your instructor about a problem you encountered in writing your essay and how you solved it. Before you begin, gather all of your invention and planning notes, drafts, critical comments, revision plan, and final revision. Review these materials as you complete this writing task.

1. *Identify one writing problem you needed to solve as you worked on the essay.* Do not be concerned with grammar and punctuation; concentrate instead on problems unique to developing an essay arguing for a position. For example: Did you puzzle over how to convince your readers that the issue is important? Did you have trouble asserting your position forcefully while acknowledging other points

of view? Was it difficult to refute an important objection you knew readers would raise?

2. ***Determine how you came to recognize the problem.*** When did you first discover it? What called it to your attention? If you did not become aware of the problem until someone pointed it out to you, can you now see hints of it in your invention writings? If so, where specifically?

3. ***Reflect on how you went about solving the problem.*** Did you work on the wording of a passage, cut or add reasons or refutations, conduct further research, or move paragraphs or sentences around? Did you reread one of the essays in this chapter to see how another writer handled a similar problem, or did you look back at your invention writing? If you talked about the problem with another student, a tutor, or your instructor, did talking about it help? How useful was the advice you received?

4. ***Write a brief explanation of how you identified the problem and tried to solve it.*** Be as specific as possible in reconstructing your efforts. Quote from your invention notes and draft essay, others' critical comments, your revision plan, or your revised essay to show the various changes your writing—and thinking—underwent as you tried to solve the problem. If you are still uncertain about your solution, say so. Taking time to explain how you identified a particular problem, how you went about solving it, and what you learned from this experience can help you solve future writing problems more easily.

Proposing a Solution

Proposals are vital to a democracy. They inform citizens about problems affecting their well-being and suggest actions that could be taken to remedy these problems. People write proposals every day in business, government, education, and the professions. Proposals are a basic ingredient of the world's work.

As a special form of argument, proposals have much in common with position papers, described in Chapter 5. Both analyze a subject about which there is disagreement and take a definite stand on it. Both make an argument, giving reasons and support and acknowledging readers' likely objections or questions. Proposals, however, go further: They urge readers to take specific action. They argue for a proposed solution to a problem, and they succeed or fail by the strength of that argument.

Problem-solving is basic to most disciplines and professions. For example, scientists use the scientific method, a systematic form of problem-solving; political scientists and sociologists propose solutions to troubling political and social problems; engineers employ problem-solving techniques in building bridges, automobiles, and computers; teachers make decisions about how to help students with learning problems; counselors devote themselves to helping clients solve personal problems; business owners and managers daily solve problems large and small.

Problem-solving depends on a questioning attitude—wondering about alternative approaches to bringing about change, puzzling over how a goal might be achieved, questioning why a process unfolds in a particular way, posing challenges to the status quo. In addition, it demands imagination and creativity. To solve a problem, you need to see it anew, to look at it from new angles and in new contexts.

Because a proposal tries to convince readers that its way of defining and solving the problem makes sense, proposal writers must be sensitive to readers' needs and expectations. Readers need to know details of the solution and to be convinced that it will solve the problem and can be implemented. If readers initially favor a different solution, knowing why the writer rejects it will help them decide whether to support or reject the writer's proposed solution. Readers may be wary of costs, demands on their time, and grand schemes.

As you plan and draft a proposal, you will have to determine whether your readers are aware of the problem and whether they recognize its seriousness, and you will have to consider their views on alternative possible solutions. Knowing what your readers know—their knowledge of the problem and willingness to make changes, their assumptions and biases, the kinds of arguments likely to appeal to them—is a central part of proposal writing.

The writing of proposals occurs in many different contexts, as the following examples suggest.

Writing in Your Other Courses

- For an economics class, a student writes an essay proposing a solution to the problem of inadequate housing for Mexican workers in the nearly three thousand maquiladora factories clustered along the Mexican side of the border with the United States. She briefly describes the binational arrangement that has produced over a million low-paying jobs for Mexican workers and increased profits for American manufacturers who own the assembly plants—along with job losses for thousands of American workers. She sketches the history of maquiladoras since the 1970s and then surveys some of the problems they have spawned. Focusing on inadequate housing, she argues that it, of all the problems, should be addressed first and is most amenable to modest, short-term solutions. The student argues that maquiladora owners must share with Mexican city and state governments the costs of planning and installing water delivery systems and minimal house plumbing installations, and provide low-interest loans to workers who want to buy indoor plumbing fixtures. Recognizing that this is only a first-stage solution to a major problem requiring long-term efforts, the student calls for an international competition to design entire maquiladora workers' communities, along with plans for adequate low-cost houses with plumbing and electricity.

- For an education class, a student researches the history of educational television production and programming for two- to thirteen-year-old children, beginning with the 1969 production of Children's Television Workshop's *Sesame Street*. He also researches children's television in Australia, Great Britain, and Japan and learns that these countries provide much more support for children's television programming than the United States does. For an assignment to write an essay proposing a solution, he proposes a plan to develop government support for children's programming. He presents the problem by comparing other countries' support for children's television to U.S. support. Influenced by a book by the founder of Children's Television Workshop, the student argues that television is the most efficient and effective way to teach preschool-age children basic math and English skills. Arguing to support his proposal, the student concedes that attractive new programs continue to appear—for example, *Bill Nye, the Science Guy*—but argues that these are sporadic and cannot provide the amount or diversity of programming that is needed.

Writing in the Community

- A California high school junior enters an essay contest, "There Ought to Be a Law," sponsored by her state legislator. The goal of the contest is to encourage high school students to propose solutions to community problems. The student wins the contest with a proposal for a state law requiring school districts to replace textbooks every ten years. She presents the problem by describing her own battered, marked-up, dated textbooks, particularly a chemistry text published before she was born. To gain a better understanding of the problems caused by outdated textbooks, she talks with several other students and with teachers. Recognizing that she lacks the expertise to outline a legislative solution, she speculates about the probable obstacles, chief among them the costs of implementing her solution. The legislator drafts a law based on the student's proposal, invites the student to attend the opening of the next legislative session, and introduces the law at that session.

- A social services administrator in a large northeastern city becomes increasingly concerned about the rise in numbers of adolescents in jail for minor and major crimes. From his observations and the research studies he reads, he becomes convinced that a partial solution to the problem would be to intervene at the first sign of delinquent behavior in eight- to twelve-year-olds. In developing a proposal to circulate among influential people in the local police department, juvenile justice system, school system, and business and religious communities, the administrator begins by describing the long-term consequences of jailing young criminals. Trying to make the problem seem significant and worth solving, he focuses mainly on the costs and the high rate of return to criminal activity after release from jail. He then lists and discusses at length the major components of his early intervention program. These components include assigning mentors to young people who are beginning to fail in school, placing social workers in troubled families to help out daily before and after school, hiring neighborhood residents to work full-time on the streets to counter the influence of gangs, and encouraging businesses to hire high school students as paid interns. The administrator acknowledges that early intervention to head off serious criminal activity will require the cooperation of many city agencies. He offers to take the lead in bringing about this cooperation and in launching the program.

Writing in the Workplace

- Frustrated by what they see as the failure of schools to prepare students for the workplace, managers of a pharmaceuticals corporation in the Midwest decide to develop a proposal to move vocational and technical training out of ill-equipped high school vocational programs and onto the plant's floor. Seven division managers meet weekly for four months to develop a proposal for schools in the region. They are joined by one of the firm's experienced technical writers, who takes notes of discussions, writes progress reports, and eventually drafts the proposal. They define the problem as schools being unable to offer the cutting-edge teaching, modern equipment, motivation, or accountability of on-the-job training. They eventually propose a vocational track that would begin in grade 10, with all of the job training taking place in businesses and industries. Each year students would spend more time on the job, and by grade 12 they would work thirty-two hours a week and spend ten hours a week in school, mainly in courses in English (reading and writing) and advanced math. As the managers detail their solution, develop a timetable for implementing it, and speculate about how current school budgets could be reworked to support the program, they seek advice on early drafts of their proposal from business leaders, school board members, school administrators, representatives of teachers' unions, newspaper editorial boards, and key members of the state legislature. The final draft incorporates suggestions from these advisers and attempts to refute known arguments against the proposal.

- A woman in her sixties who has been hauling asphalt and gravel in a double-bottom dump truck for sixteen years writes a proposal for trucking company owners and managers, who face a continual shortage of well-qualified drivers for heavy diesel tractor-and-trailer trucks, suggesting that the companies focus on recruiting more women. As she plans her proposal, she talks to the owner of the company she drives for and to the few women drivers she knows. She begins the proposal by describing her work briefly and explaining how she got a lucky break when her brother taught her how to drive his truck. She then points out the problem: that few women ever get the chance to learn this skill. She proposes her solution to this problem: an in-house training program in which women recruits would be trained by company drivers on the job and after hours. Drivers would be paid for their after-hours training contributions, and the students would be paid a small stipend after agreeing to drive for the company for a certain number of months at a reduced salary. She argues that her proposal would succeed only if trucking companies sponsor a well-designed recruitment program relying on advertisements published on Web sites and in magazines read by working women, and she lists titles of several such publications. She attempts to refute the alternative solution of relying on already established truck-driving schools by arguing that many women cannot afford the tuition. Her proposal is first published in her company's internal newsletter and later, in slightly revised form, in a leading magazine read by trucking company owners and managers.

Practice Proposing a Solution to a Problem: A Collaborative Activity

The preceding scenarios suggest some occasions for writing proposals to solve problems. To get a sense of the complexities and possibilities involved in proposing solutions, think through a specific problem, and try to come up with a feasible proposal. Your instructor may schedule this collaborative activity as a face-to-face in-class discussion or ask you to conduct an online real-time discussion in a chat room. Whatever the medium, here are some guidelines to follow:

Part 1. Form a group with two or three other students, and select one person to take notes during your discussion.

- First, identify two or three problems within your college or community, and select one that you all recognize and agree needs to be solved.

- Next, consider possible solutions to this problem, and identify one solution that you can all support. You need not all be equally enthusiastic for this solution.

- Finally, determine which individual or group has the authority to take action on your proposed solution and how you would go about convincing this audience that the problem is serious and must be solved and that your proposed solution is feasible and should be supported. Make notes also about questions this audience might have about your proposal and what objections the audience might raise.

Part 2. As a group, discuss your efforts at proposing a solution to a problem. What surprised or pleased you most about this activity? What difficulties did you encounter in coming up with arguments that the problem must be solved and that your proposed solution would solve it? How did the objections you thought of influence your confidence in your proposed solution?

READINGS

The three readings in this chapter illustrate a number of the features of essays that propose solutions to problems and many of the strategies that writers rely on to realize the features. No two proposals are alike, and yet they share defining features. Together, the three essays cover many of the possibilities of proposals, so you will want to read as many of them as possible. If time permits, complete the activities in the Analyzing Writing Strategies section that follows each selection, and read the Commentary. Following the readings is a section called Basic Features: Proposing Solutions (p. 233), which offers a concise description of the features of proposals and provides examples from the three readings.

Mark Hertsgaard *is a journalist and a regular contributor to National Public Radio. His essays have appeared in numerous newspapers and magazines such as the* New York Times, *the* New Yorker, *the* Atlantic Monthly, Outside, Harper's, *and* Rolling Stone. *He also teaches non-fiction writing at Johns Hopkins University and has written five books, including* Nuclear, Inc.: The Men and Money behind Nuclear Energy *(1983),* A Day in the Life: The Music and Artistry of the Beatles *(1995), and* The Eagle's Shadow: Why America Fascinates and Infuriates the World *(2002). This proposal was originally published in* Time *magazine's special Earth Day edition in 2000, and it reflects the extensive research he did for his 1999 book* Earth Odyssey: Around the World in Search of Our Environmental Future.

Hertsgaard probably titled his proposal "A Global Green Deal" to remind readers of President Franklin D. Roosevelt's New Deal, which helped the United States recover from the Great Depression of the 1930s. Hertsgaard proposes that government encourage businesses to develop and use new, more efficient and environmentally friendly technologies. You will see that toward the end of his essay, Hertsgaard admits that his proposal is "no silver bullet" but argues that it will take us in the right direction and "buy us time to make the more deep-seated changes" that are needed (paragraph 16). As you read, notice how sensitive he is to readers who fear the problem is too daunting. Pay attention to the ways he tries to bolster readers' confidence that the problem can be solved while at the same time trying to be realistic about what his proposed solution can accomplish.

A Global Green Deal

Mark Hertsgaard

The bad news is that we have to change our ways—and fast. Here's the good news: it could be a hugely profitable enterprise. 1

So what do we do? Everyone knows the planet is in bad shape, but most people are resigned to passivity. Changing course, they reason, would require economic sacrifice and provoke stiff resistance from corporations and consumers alike, so why bother? It's easier to ignore the gathering storm clouds and hope the problem magically takes care of itself. 2

Such fatalism is not only dangerous but mistaken. For much of the 1990s I traveled the world to write a book about our environmental predicament. I returned home sobered by the extent of the damage we are causing and by the speed at which it is occurring. But there is nothing inevitable about our self-destructive behavior. Not only could we dramatically reduce our burden on the air, water and other natural systems, we could make money doing so. If we're smart, we could make restoring the environment the biggest economic enterprise of our time, a huge source of jobs, profits and poverty alleviation. 3

What we need is a Global Green Deal: a program to renovate our civilization environmentally from top to bottom in rich and poor countries alike. Making use of both market incentives and government leadership, a twenty-first-century Global Green Deal would do for environmental technologies what government and industry have recently done so well for computer and Internet technologies: launch their commercial takeoff. 4

Getting it done will take work, and before we begin we need to understand three facts about the reality facing us. First, we have no time to lose. While we've made progress in certain areas—air pollution is down in the U.S.—big environmental problems like climate change, water scarcity and species extinction are getting worse, and faster than ever. Thus we have to change our ways profoundly—and very soon. 5

Second, poverty is central to the problem. Four billion of the planet's 6 billion people face deprivation inconceivable to the wealthiest 1 billion. To paraphrase Thomas Jefferson, nothing is more certainly written in the book of fate than that the bottom two-thirds of humanity will strive to improve their lot. As they demand adequate heat and food, not to mention cars and CD players, humanity's environmental footprint will grow. Our challenge is to accommodate this mass ascent from poverty without wrecking the natural systems that make life possible. 6

Third, some good news: we have in hand most of the technologies needed to chart a   7
new course. We know how to use oil, wood, water and other resources much more efficiently than we do now. Increased efficiency—doing more with less—will enable us to
use fewer resources and produce less pollution per capita, buying us the time to bring
solar power, hydrogen fuel cells and other futuristic technologies on line.

Efficiency may not sound like a rallying cry for environmental revolution, but it packs   8
a financial punch. As Joseph J. Romm reports in his book *Cool Companies*, Xerox, Com-
paq and 3M are among many firms that have recognized they can cut their greenhouse-
gas emissions in half—and enjoy 50 percent and higher returns on investment through
improved efficiency, better lighting and insulation and smarter motors and building
design. The rest of us (small businesses, homeowners, city governments, schools) can
reap the same benefits.

Super-refrigerators use 87% less electricity than older, standard models while cost-   9
ing the same (assuming mass production) and performing better, as Paul Hawken and
Amory and L. Hunter Lovins explain in their book *Natural Capitalism*. In Amsterdam the
headquarters of ING Bank, one of Holland's largest banks, uses one-fifth as much energy
per square meter as a nearby bank, even though the buildings cost the same to construct. The ING center boasts efficient windows and insulation and a design that enables
solar energy to provide much of the building's needs, even in cloudy Northern Europe.

Examples like these lead even such mainstream voices as AT&T and Japan's energy   10
planning agency, NEDO, to predict that environmental restoration could be a source of
virtually limitless profit. The idea is to retrofit our farms, factories, shops, houses, offices
and everything inside them. The economic activity generated would be enormous. Better
yet, it would be labor intensive; investments in energy efficiency yield two to 10 times
more jobs than investments in fossil fuel and nuclear power. In a world where 1 billion
people lack gainful employment, creating jobs is essential to fighting the poverty that
retards environmental progress.

But this transition will not happen by itself—too many entrenched interests stand in   11
the way. Automakers often talk green but make only token efforts to develop green cars
because gas-guzzling sport-utility vehicles are hugely profitable. But every year the U.S.
government buys 56,000 new vehicles for official use from Detroit. Under the Global
Green Deal, Washington would tell Detroit that from now on the cars have to be hybrid-
electric or hydrogen-fuel-cell cars. Detroit might scream and holler, but if Washington
stood firm, carmakers soon would be climbing the learning curve and offering the com-
petitively priced green cars that consumers say they want.

We know such government pump-priming works; it's why so many of us have com-   12
puters today. America's computer companies began learning to produce today's affordable systems during the 1960s while benefiting from subsidies and guaranteed markets
under contracts with the Pentagon and the space program. And the cyberboom has
fueled the biggest economic expansion in history.

The Global Green Deal must not be solely an American project, however. China and   13
India, with their gigantic populations and ambitious development plans, could by themselves doom everyone else to severe global warming. Already, China is the world's

second largest producer of greenhouse gases (after the U.S.). But China would use 50% less coal if it simply installed today's energy-efficient technologies. Under the Global Green Deal, Europe, America and Japan would help China buy these technologies, not only because that would reduce global warming but also because it would create jobs and profits for workers and companies back home.

Governments would not have to spend more money, only shift existing subsidies away from environmentally dead-end technologies like coal and nuclear power. If even half the $500 billion to $900 billion in environmentally destructive subsidies now offered by the world's governments were redirected, the Global Green Deal would be off to a roaring start. Governments need to establish "rules of the road" so that market prices reflect the real social costs of clearcut forests and other environmental abominations. Again, such a shift could be revenue neutral. Higher taxes on, say, coal burning would be offset by cuts in payroll and profits taxes, thus encouraging jobs and investment while discouraging pollution. A portion of the revenues should be set aside to assure a just transition for workers and companies now engaged in inherently anti-environmental activities like coal mining. 14

All this sounds easy enough on paper, but in the real world it is not so simple. Beneficiaries of the current system—be they U.S. corporate-welfare recipients, redundant German coal miners, or cutthroat Asian logging interests—will resist. Which is why progress is unlikely absent a broader agenda of change, including real democracy: assuring the human rights of environmental activists and neutralizing the power of Big Money through campaign-finance reform. 15

The Global Green Deal is no silver bullet. It can, however, buy us time to make the more deep-seated changes—in our often excessive appetites, in our curious belief that humans are the center of the universe, in our sheer numbers—that will be necessary to repair our relationship with our environment. 16

None of this will happen without an aroused citizenry. But a Global Green Deal is in the common interest, and it is a slogan easily grasped by the media and the public. Moreover, it should appeal across political, class and national boundaries, for it would stimulate both jobs and business throughout the world in the name of a universal value: leaving our children a livable planet. The history of environmentalism is largely the story of ordinary people pushing for change while governments, corporations and other established interests reluctantly follow behind. It's time to repeat that history on behalf of a Global Green Deal. 17

Connecting to Culture and Experience: Acting to Create a More Livable Planet

Hertsgaard acknowledges in this proposal that his solution is "no silver bullet," but he hopes it will "buy us time to make the more deep-seated changes" that are needed (paragraph 16).

With two or three other students, discuss other actions that can be taken to buy us time and possibly also help to repair the environment. Begin by telling each other about conservation efforts you have made. For example, you may buy recycled paper, or your family may compost food remains. What other actions could you take? Then discuss whether helping the environment is a high priority for you. If you were buying a car, for instance, would getting an energy-efficient car be a high priority? If you have a choice between driving a car or taking public transportation to school or work, would you take public transportation to reduce energy costs and air pollution?

Analyzing Writing Strategies

1. At the beginning of this chapter, we make several generalizations about essays that propose solutions to problems. Consider which of these assertions are true of Hertsgaard's proposal:

   - It defines the problem and helps readers realize the seriousness of the problem.
   - It describes the proposed solution.
   - It attempts to convince readers that the solution will help solve the problem and can be implemented.
   - It anticipates readers' likely questions and objections.
   - It evaluates alternative solutions that readers may initially favor.

2. The most important part of a proposal is the solution. To be effective, the proposal has to describe the solution in a way that convinces readers that it can be implemented. Hertsgaard first presents his solution in paragraph 4, where he describes in broad terms the "Global Green Deal" he is proposing. But he does not describe how his solution to renovate the environment can be implemented until paragraphs 11–14. Reread these paragraphs to see how convincing he is in arguing that his solution can and should be implemented. Highlight in paragraphs 11 and 13–14 what would need to be done to implement the solution. Also look closely at paragraph 12 to see what it adds to his argument.

Commentary: Defining the Problem

Every proposal begins with a problem. Writers usually spend some time defining the problem—establishing that the problem exists and is serious enough to warrant action. What writers say about the problem and how much space they devote to it depend on what they assume their readers already know and think about it. In this proposal, Hertsgaard assumes the readers of *Time* magazine's special Earth Day edition know that "the planet is in bad shape," as he puts it in paragraph 2.

He identifies the problem more specifically at various points in the essay: "big environmental problems like climate change, water scarcity and species extinction" (5), "pollution" (7), and "global warming" (13). In paragraphs 5–9, Hertsgaard elaborates further by presenting "three facts about the reality" of the problem (5). The first two facts make the problem seem overwhelming, but the third is a ray of hope. He notes that we have made progress but that time is running out as developing countries become wealthier and place increasing pressures on the environment. The third fact, however, provides the "good news" that is an essential ingredient of his proposed solution: We already have the technological efficiency to make a difference.

Hertsgaard knows that many of his readers feel defeated by the enormity of the problem and that his proposal will fall on deaf ears if his readers do not believe that the steps he is proposing will do any good. Therefore, he tries to allay his readers' fears, in particular their feeling of "fatalism" (3). To reassure readers, he tries to be optimistic yet realistic. He tempers his own enthusiasm with language like this: "If we're smart, we could" (3) and "The Global Green Deal is no silver bullet. It can, however, buy us time to make the more deep-seated changes" (16). Ultimately, Hertsgaard tries to represent the problem as a "challenge" (6), something that "will take work" (5) but that can be done.

As you plan your proposal, you also will need to consider your readers' feelings as well as their knowledge. Remember that defining the problem is part of your argument. It should be designed to convince readers that you know what you are talking about and can be trusted. Hertsgaard builds his credibility with readers in part by referring to his extensive research (3, 8–9) but also by showing readers he understands the complexity of the problem.

Considering Topics for Your Own Essay

Hertsgaard's admittedly limited proposal might suggest to you other proposals to solve environmental problems. For example, you might consider writing a proposal for increasing the use of carpools on campus, reducing energy consumption in dormitories, or instituting a campus recycling program. You might interview people in your community about the feasibility of subsidizing alternative energy sources, such as solar-heating panels that could be installed in public buildings and parks. You might also research promising newer technologies for a proposal addressed to your college administration or local government.

Katherine S. Newman is the Malcolm Wiener Professor of Urban Studies at Harvard University; chair of the joint doctoral program in sociology, government, and social policy at Harvard's Kennedy School of Government; and dean of social science at the Radcliffe Institute for Advanced Studies. She has written many books, including Declining Fortunes: The Withering of the American Dream *(1993),* No Shame in My Game: The Working Poor in the Inner City *(1999), and* A Different Shade of Gray: Mid-Life and Beyond in the Inner City *(2003). Her essays have appeared in popular newspapers and magazines such as the* New York Times *and* Newsweek *as well as in numerous scholarly journals such as the* American Anthropologist, *the* International Journal of Sociology and Social Policy, *and the* Brookings Review, *a journal concerned with public policy, in which "Dead-End Jobs: A Way Out" was originally published.*

This proposal resulted from Newman's research for No Shame in My Game, *a book that was awarded the Sidney Hillman Book Prize and the Robert F. Kennedy Book Award. As you read her proposal, notice her analysis of why the social networks that inner-city fast-food workers belong to fail to lead them to better jobs, and evaluate whether you think the proposed solution—an employer consortium (a group of cooperating employers)—"might re-create the job ladders that have disappeared," as Newman explained in an interview.*

Dead-End Jobs: A Way Out

Katherine S. Newman

Millions of Americans work full-time, year-round in jobs that still leave them stranded in poverty. Though they pound the pavement looking for better jobs, they consistently come up empty-handed. Many of these workers are in our nation's inner cities.

I know, because I have spent two years finding out what working life is like for 200 employees—about half African-American, half Latino—at fast-food restaurants in Harlem. Many work only part-time, though they would happily take longer hours if they could get them. Those who do work full-time earn about $8,840 (before taxes)—well below the poverty threshold for a family of four.

These fast-food workers make persistent efforts to get better jobs, particularly in retail and higher-paid service-sector occupations. They take civil service examinations and apply for jobs with the electric company or the phone company. Sometimes their efforts bear fruit. More often they don't.

A few workers make their way into the lower managerial ranks of the fast-food industry, where wages are marginally better. An even smaller number graduate into higher management, a path made possible by the internal promotion patterns long practiced by these firms. As in any industry, however, senior management opportunities are limited. Hence most workers, even those with track records as reliable employees, are locked inside a low-wage environment. Contrary to those who preach the benefits of work and persistence, the human capital these workers build up—experience in food production, inventory management, cash register operation, customer relations, minor machinery repair, and cleaning—does not pay off. These workers are often unable to move upward out of poverty. And their experience is not unusual. Hundreds of thousands of low-wage workers in American cities run into the same brick wall. Why? And what can we do about it?

Stagnation in the Inner City

Harlem, like many inner-city communities, has lost the manufacturing job base that once sustained its neighborhoods. Service industries that cater to neighborhood consumers, coupled with now dwindling government jobs, largely make up the local economy. With official jobless rates hovering around 18 percent (14 people apply for every minimum-wage fast-food job in Harlem), employers can select from the very top of the preference "queue." Once hired, even experienced workers have virtually nowhere to go.

One reason for their lack of mobility is that many employers in the primary labor market outside Harlem consider "hamburger flipper" jobs worthless. At most, employers credit the fast-food industry with training people to turn up for work on time and to fill out job applications. The real skills these workers have developed go unrecognized. However inaccurate the unflattering stereotypes, they help keep experienced workers from "graduating" out of low-wage work to more remunerative employment. . . .

As Harry Holzer, an economist at Michigan State University, has shown, "central-city" employers insist on specific work experience, references, and particular kinds of formal training in addition to literacy and numeracy skills, even for jobs that do not require a college degree. Demands of this kind, more stringent in the big-city labor markets than in the surrounding suburbs, clearly limit the upward mobility of the working poor in urban areas. If the only kind of job available does not provide the "right" work experience or formal training, many better jobs will be foreclosed. 7

Racial stereotypes also weaken mobility prospects. Employers view ghetto blacks, especially men, as a bad risk or a troublesome element in the workplace. They prefer immigrants or nonblack minorities, of which there are many in the Harlem labor force, who appear to them more deferential and willing to work harder for low wages. As Joleen Kirshenman and Kathryn Neckerman found in their study of Chicago workplaces, stereotypes abound among employers who have become wary of the "underclass." Primary employers exercise these preferences by discriminating against black applicants, particularly those who live in housing projects, on the grounds of perceived group characteristics. The "losers" are not given an opportunity to prove themselves. . . . 8

Social Networks

Social networks are crucial in finding work. Friends and acquaintances are far more useful sources of information than are want ads. The literature on the urban underclass suggests that inner-city neighborhoods are bereft of these critical links to the work world. My work, however, suggests a different picture: the working poor in Harlem have access to two types of occupational social networks, but neither provides upward mobility. The first is a homogeneous *lateral* network of age mates and acquaintances, employed and unemployed. It provides contacts that allow workers to move sideways in the labor market—from Kentucky Fried Chicken to Burger King or McDonald's—but not to move to jobs of higher quality. Lateral networks are useful, particularly for poor people who have to move frequently, for they help ensure a certain amount of portability in the low-wage labor market. But they do not lift workers out of poverty; they merely facilitate "churning" laterally in the low-wage world. 9

Young workers in Harlem also participate in more heterogeneous *vertical* networks with their older family members who long ago moved to suburban communities or better urban neighborhoods to become homeowners on the strength of jobs that were more widely available 20 and 30 years ago. Successful grandparents, great-aunts and uncles, and distant cousins, relatives now in their 50s and 60s, often have (or have retired from) jobs in the post office, the public sector, the transportation system, public utilities, the military, hospitals, and factories that pay union wages. But these industries are now shedding workers, not hiring them. As a result, older generations are typically unable to help job-hunting young relatives. 10

Although little is known about the social and business networks of minority business 11
owners and managers in the inner city, it seems that Harlem's business community, particularly its small business sector, is also walled off from the wider economy of midtown. Fast-food owners know the other people in their franchise system. They do business with banks and security firms inside the inner city. But they appear less likely to interact with firms outside the ghetto.

For that reason, a good recommendation from a McDonald's owner may represent a 12
calling card that extends no farther than the general reputation of the firm and a prospective employer's perception—poor, as I have noted—of the skills that such work represents. It can move someone from an entry-level job in one restaurant to the same kind of job in another, but not into a good job elsewhere in the city.

Lacking personal or business-based ties that facilitate upward mobility, workers in 13
Harlem's fast-food market find themselves on the outside looking in when it comes to the world of "good jobs." They search diligently for them, they complete many job applications, but it is the rare individual who finds a job that pays a family wage. Those who do are either workers who have been selected for internal promotion or men and women who have had the luxury of devoting their earnings solely to improving their own educational or craft credentials. Since most low-wage service workers are under pressure to support their families or contribute to the support of their parents' households, this kind of human capital investment is often difficult. As a result, the best most can do is to churn from one low-wage job to another.

The Employer Consortium

Some of the social ills that keep Harlem's fast-food workers at the bottom of a short job 14
ladder—a poor urban job base, increasing downward mobility, discrimination, structural problems in the inner-city business sector—are too complex to solve quickly enough to help most of the workers I've followed. But the problem of poor social networks may be amenable to solution if formal organizations linking primary and secondary labor market employers can be developed. An "employer consortium" could help to move hard-working inner-city employees into richer job markets by providing the job information and precious referrals that "come naturally" to middle-class Americans.

How would an employer consortium function? It would include both inner-city 15
employers of the working poor and downtown businesses or nonprofit institutions with higher-paid employees. Employers in the inner city would periodically select employees they consider reliable, punctual, hard-working, and motivated. Workers who have successfully completed at least one year of work would be placed in a pool of workers eligible for hiring by a set of linked employers who have better jobs to offer. Entry-level employers would, in essence, put their own good name behind successful workers as they pass them on to their consortium partners in the primary sector.

Primary-sector employers, for their part, would agree to hire from the pool and meet 16
periodically with their partners in the low-wage industries to review applications and follow up on the performance of those hired through the consortium. Employers "up the line"

would provide training or educational opportunities to enhance the employee's skills. These training investments would make it more likely that hirees would continue to move up the new job ladders.

As they move up, the new hirees would clear the way for others to follow. First, their performance would reinforce the reputation of the employers who recommended them. Second, their achievements on the job might begin to lessen the stigma or fear their new employers may feel toward the inner-city workforce. On both counts, other consortium-based workers from the inner city would be more likely to get the same opportunities, following in a form of managed chain migration out of the inner-city labor market. Meanwhile, the attractiveness of fast-food jobs, now no better reputed among inner-city residents than among the rest of society, would grow as they became, at least potentially, a gateway to something better. 17

Advantages for Employers

Fast-food employers in Harlem run businesses in highly competitive markets. Constant pressure on prices and profit discourage them from paying wages high enough to keep a steady workforce. In fact, most such employers regard the jobs they fill as temporary placements: they *expect* successful employees to leave. And despite the simple production processes used within the fast-food industry to minimize the damage of turnover, sudden departures of knowledgeable workers still disrupt business and cause considerable frustration and exhaustion. 18

An employer consortium gives these employers—who *can't* raise wages if they hope to stay in business—a way to compete for workers who will stay with them longer than usual. In lieu of higher pay, employers can offer access to the consortium hiring pool and the prospect of a more skilled and ultimately better-paying job upon graduation from this real world "boot camp." ... 19

Consortiums would also appeal to the civic spirit of minority business owners, who often choose to locate in places like Harlem rather than in less risky neighborhoods because they want to provide job opportunities for their own community. The big franchise operations mandate some attention to civic responsibility as well. Some fast-food firms have licensing requirements for franchisees that require demonstrated community involvement. 20

At a time when much of the public is voicing opposition to heavy-handed government efforts to prevent employment discrimination, employer consortiums have the advantage of encouraging minority hiring based on private-sector relationships. Institutional employers in particular—for example, universities and hospitals, often among the larger employers in East Coast cities—should find the consortiums especially valuable. These employers typically retain a strong commitment to workforce diversity but are often put off by the reputation of secondary-sector workers as unskilled, unmotivated, and less worthy of consideration. 21

The practical advantages for primary-sector managers are clear. Hirees have been vetted and tested. Skills have been assessed and certified in the most real world of settings. A valuable base of experience and skills stands ready for further training and 22 advancement. The consortium assures that the employers making and receiving recommendations would come to know one another, thus reinforcing the value of recommendations — a cost-effective strategy for primary-sector managers who must make significant training investments in their workers.

Minimal Government Involvement

Despite the evident advantages for both primary and secondary labor market employers, it may be necessary for governments to provide modest incentives to encourage wide participation. Secondary-sector business owners in the inner city, for example, might be deterred from participating by the prospect of losing some of their best employees at the end of a year. Guaranteeing these employers a lump sum or a tax break for every worker they promote into management internally or successfully place with a consortium participant could help break down such reluctance. 23

Primary-sector employers, who would have to provide support for training and possibly for schooling of their consortium employees, may also require some kind of tax break to subsidize their efforts at skill enhancement. Demonstration projects could experiment with various sorts of financial incentives for both sets of employers by providing grants to underwrite the costs of training new workers. 24

Local governments could also help publicize the efforts of participating employers. Most big-city mayors, for example, would be happy to shower credit on business people looking to boost the prospects of the deserving (read working) poor. 25

Government involvement, however, would be minimal. Employer consortiums could probably be assembled out of the existing economic development offices of U.S. cities, or with the help of the Chamber of Commerce and other local institutions that encourage private-sector activity. Industry- or sector-specific consortiums could probably be put together with the aid of local industry councils. 26

Moreover, some of the negative effects of prior experiments with wage subsidies for the "hard to employ" — efforts that foundered on the stigma assigned to these workers and the paperwork irritants to employers — would be reversed here. Consortium employees would be singled out for doing well, for being the cream of the crop. And the private-sector domination of employer consortiums would augur against extensive paperwork burdens. 27

Building Bridges

The inner-city fast-food workers that I have been following in Harlem have proven themselves in difficult jobs. They have shown that they are reliable, they clearly relish their economic independence, and they are willing to work hard. Still, work offers them no escape from poverty. Trapped in a minimum-wage job market, they lack bridges to the kind of work that can enable them to support their families and begin to move out of poverty. For reasons I have discussed, those bridges have not evolved naturally in our inner cities. But where they are lacking, they must be created and fostered. And we can begin with employer consortiums, to the benefit of everyone, workers and employers alike. 28

Connecting to Culture and Experience: The Value of Routine, Repetitive Work

Newman explains that one reason fast-food workers cannot find better jobs is that employers believe such workers learn only routine, repetitive skills that do not prepare them for other types of jobs.

With several students, discuss this possible limitation of fast-food jobs and other kinds of routine jobs. You may hold such a job now, or you may have held one in the past. Maybe you parked cars, delivered pizzas, ran a cash register, wiped down cars in a car wash, bagged and carried groceries or other merchandise, wrapped holiday packages, or did cleanup work. Tell each other about the routine jobs you have held. Then consider Newman's criticism of these jobs: that they only teach workers how to show up on time and follow rudimentary directions. Is this a fair criticism, do you think? Have critics overlooked certain important kinds of learning on these jobs? If so, what might these kinds of learning be? Or if you agree that these jobs are as limiting as the critics contend, what other kinds of low-paying work might teach more important skills?

Analyzing Writing Strategies

1. Reread paragraphs 1–8, where Newman defines the problem she believes needs to be solved. In a sentence or two, state what you understand the problem to be.

   At the end of paragraph 4, Newman asks why this problem continues. Underline the main reasons she gives in paragraphs 6–8. For her purpose and readers, how well does she define the problem? What questions might readers have about her presentation of the problem? Finally, how well does her proposed solution (employer consortiums) address the reasons the problem continues?

2. Readers are often aware of previous attempts to solve a problem, or they might think of solutions they believe are better than the one the writer is proposing. Writers who hope to win readers' support must evaluate alternative solutions that readers are likely to be aware of. To evaluate an alternative solution, writers usually either concede that it has some merit or refute it as meritless and not worth further consideration.

   Newman evaluates an alternative solution in paragraphs 9–13. How would you summarize this alternative to Newman's proposed solution of an employer consortium? What are the main reasons Newman gives for not taking this alternative solution seriously and encouraging readers to do the same? How well do you think she refutes this alternative to her proposed solution?

Commentary: Describing the Proposed Solution and Anticipating Objections

The heart of an essay proposing a solution to a problem is the proposed solution and the direct argument supporting the solution. Readers need to know exactly what is being proposed and how it can be implemented before they can decide whether it is feasible—cost-effective and likely to help solve the problem. Newman describes her proposed solution relatively fully. In paragraphs 14–17, she provides many details about the employer consortium. She begins paragraph 14 acknowledging the scope and complexity of the problem and admitting that the solution she is proposing focuses on only one aspect of the problem, "poor social networks." She ends the paragraph by explaining the goal of her proposed solution: to find better jobs for hardworking, ambitious fast-food workers. An "employer consortium," as she envisions it, would provide information about jobs and referrals to specific available jobs—the two main resources that inner-city fast-food employees lack.

Newman then describes in detail how easy it would be to implement or put into effect her solution (15–17). In explaining how an employer consortium would function, she outlines the responsibilities of the two key players in the consortium she envisions: the inner-city fast-food employers and the downtown employers with the better-paying jobs. Notice that she does not hesitate to specify criteria for eligible inner-city employees: They must be "reliable, punctual, hard-working, and motivated," and they must "have successfully completed at least one year of work" (15). To make it clear that inner-city employers will not be doing all the work, she describes how downtown employers would meet with fast-food employers, review workers' job applications, and pay attention to workers once they are on the job. The downtown employers would also be required to offer on-the-job training to prepare the new workers for better jobs (16).

She also points out some of the advantages of her solution for everyone involved. She argues that it offers inner-city employers a competitive edge without requiring them to raise wages (19). For other business owners and institutions, she argues that not only does her plan provide them with new employees who are well-trained, conscientious workers, but it also increases diversity in the workplace without government interference.

In addition to the direct argument for the solution, proposal writers usually try to anticipate readers' likely objections. To respond to the concern of inner-city employers that they would be continually giving up their best workers, Newman suggests that employers' reputations would be enhanced and the image of fast-food work would improve as the jobs came to be seen as a step to better jobs (17). She also argues that fast-food workers would presumably be more committed to doing a good job if the quality of their work could lead to a better job downtown—and their employers would benefit as a result. In addition, she acknowledges both that the loss of experienced workers would be a financial disadvantage to inner-city employers and that the costs of training employees would be an added burden to consortium employers. To accommodate these concerns, she adds to her proposal government subsidies to compensate employers (23–24).

When you plan your essay, you will need to develop an argument with your readers in mind, trying to convince them that your proposed solution makes sense and can be put into effect.

Considering Topics for Your Own Essay

Think of barriers or obstacles you have met or expect to meet in realizing your goals and dreams. You might want to think specifically about obstacles to preparing for and entering the career of your choice, but you need not limit yourself to career goals. Perhaps you are not able to get into an internship program that would give you some experience with the kind of work you hope to do. Perhaps your high school did not offer the courses you needed to prepare for the college major you want to pursue. Perhaps at some crucial point in your life you received inadequate medical care or counseling. Identify an obstacle you faced and think of it as a general problem to be solved; that is, assume that other people have confronted the same obstacle. How would you define the problem? How might you propose to solve it? To be more than a personal complaint about bad luck or mistreatment, your proposal would need to appeal to readers who have experienced a similar obstacle or who would be able to remove the obstacle or give sound advice on getting around it.

Patrick O'Malley wrote the following proposal while he was a first-year college student. He proposes that college professors give students frequent brief examinations in addition to the usual midterm and final exams. After discussing with his instructor his unusual rhetorical situation — a student advising professors — he decided to revise the essay into the form of an open letter to professors at his college, a letter that might appear in the campus newspaper.

O'Malley's essay may strike you as unusually authoritative. This tone of authority is due in large part to what O'Malley learned about the possibilities and problems of frequent exams as he interviewed two professors (his writing instructor and the writing program director) and talked with several students. As you read his essay, notice particularly how he anticipates professors' likely objections to his proposal and evaluates their preferred solutions to the problem he identifies.

More Testing, More Learning

Patrick O'Malley

It's late at night. The final's tomorrow. You got a C on the midterm, so this one will make or break you. Will it be like the midterm? Did you study enough? Did you study the right things? It's too late to drop the course. So what happens if you fail? No time to worry about that now — you've got a ton of notes to go over. 1

Although this last-minute anxiety about midterm and final exams is only too familiar to most college students, many professors may not realize how such major, infrequent, high-stakes exams work against the best interests of students both psychologically and intellectually. They cause unnecessary amounts of stress, placing too much importance on one or two days in the students' entire term, judging ability on a single or dual performance. They don't encourage frequent study, and they fail to inspire students' best performance. If professors gave additional brief exams at frequent intervals, students would 2 be spurred to study more regularly, learn more, worry less, and perform better on midterms, finals, and other papers and projects.

Ideally, a professor would give an in-class test or quiz after each unit, chapter, or focus of study, depending on the type of class and course material. A physics class might require a test on concepts after every chapter covered, while a history class could necessitate quizzes covering certain time periods or major events. These exams should be given weekly or at least twice monthly. Whenever possible, they should consist of two or three essay questions rather than many multiple-choice or short-answer questions. To preserve class time for lecture and discussion, exams should take no more than 15 or 20 minutes.

The main reason professors should give frequent exams is that when they do and when they provide feedback to students on how well they are doing, students learn more in the course and perform better on major exams, projects, and papers. It makes sense that in a challenging course containing a great deal of material, students will learn more of it and put it to better use if they have to apply or "practice" it frequently on exams, which also helps them find out how much they are learning and what they need to go over again. A recent Harvard study notes students' "strong preference for frequent evaluation in a course." Harvard students feel they learn least in courses that have "only a midterm and a final exam, with no other personal evaluation." They believe they learn most in courses with "many opportunities to see how they are doing" (Light, 1990, p. 32). In a review of a number of studies of student learning, Frederiksen (1984) reports that students who take weekly quizzes achieve higher scores on final exams than students who take only a midterm exam and that testing increases retention of material tested.

Another, closely related argument in favor of multiple exams is that they encourage students to improve their study habits. Greater frequency in test taking means greater frequency in studying for tests. Students prone to cramming will be required—or at least strongly motivated—to open their textbooks and notebooks more often, making them less likely to resort to long, kamikaze nights of studying for major exams. Since there is so much to be learned in the typical course, it makes sense that frequent, careful study and review are highly beneficial. But students need motivation to study regularly, and nothing works like an exam. If students had frequent exams in all their courses, they would have to schedule study time each week and gradually would develop a habit of frequent study. It might be argued that students are adults who have to learn how to manage their own lives, but learning history or physics is more complicated than learning to drive a car or balance a checkbook. Students need coaching and practice in learning. The right way to learn new material needs to become a habit, and I believe that frequent exams are key to developing good habits of study and learning. The Harvard study concludes that "tying regular evaluation to good course organization enables students to plan their work more than a few days in advance. If quizzes and homework are scheduled on specific days, students plan their work to capitalize on them" (Light, 1990, p. 33).

By encouraging regular study habits, frequent exams would also decrease anxiety by reducing the procrastination that produces anxiety. Students would benefit psychologically if they were not subjected to the emotional ups and downs caused by major exams, when after being virtually worry-free for weeks they are suddenly ready to check into the psychiatric ward. Researchers at the University of Vermont found a strong relationship among procrastination, anxiety, and achievement. Students who regularly put off studying for exams had continuing high anxiety and lower grades than students who procrastinated less. The researchers found that even "low" procrastinators did not study regularly and recommended that professors give frequent assignments and exams to reduce procrastination and increase achievement (Rothblum, Solomon, & Murakami, 1986, pp. 393–394).

Research supports my proposed solution to the problems I have described. Common sense as well as my experience and that of many of my friends support it. Why, then, do so few professors give frequent brief exams? Some believe that such exams take up too much of the limited class time available to cover the material in the course. Most courses meet 150 minutes a week—three times a week for 50 minutes each time. A 20-minute weekly exam might take 30 minutes to administer, and that is one-fifth of each week's class time. From the student's perspective, however, this time is well spent. Better learning and greater confidence about the course seem a good trade-off for another 30 minutes of lecture. Moreover, time lost to lecturing or discussion could easily be made up in students' learning on their own through careful regular study for the weekly exams. If weekly exams still seem too time-consuming to some professors, their frequency could be reduced to every other week or their length to 5 or 10 minutes. In courses where multiple-choice exams are appropriate, several questions could be designed to take only a few minutes to answer.

Another objection professors have to frequent exams is that they take too much time to read and grade. In a 20-minute essay exam, a well-prepared student can easily write two pages. A relatively small class of 30 students might then produce 60 pages, no small amount of material to read each week. A large class of 100 or more students would produce an insurmountable pile of material. There are a number of responses to this objection. Again, professors could give exams every other week or make them very short. Instead of reading them closely they could skim them quickly to see whether students understand an idea or can apply it to an unfamiliar problem; and instead of numerical or letter grades they could give a plus, check, or minus. Exams could be collected and responded to only every third or fourth week. Professors who have readers or teaching assistants could rely on them to grade or check exams. And the Scantron machine is always available for instant grading of multiple-choice exams. Finally, frequent exams could be given *in place of* a midterm exam or out-of-class essay assignment.

Since frequent exams seem to some professors to create too many problems, however, it is reasonable to consider alternative ways to achieve the same goals. One alternative solution is to implement a program that would improve study skills. While such a program might teach students how to study for exams, it cannot prevent procrastination or reduce "large test anxiety" by a substantial amount. One research team studying anxiety and test performance found that study skills training was not effective in reducing anxiety or improving performance (Dendato & Diener, 1986, p. 134). This team, which also reviewed other research that reached the same conclusion, did find that a combination of "cognitive/relaxation therapy" and study skills training was effective. This possible solution seems complicated, however, not to mention time-consuming and expensive. It seems much easier and more effective to change the cause of the bad habit rather than treat the habit itself. That is, it would make more sense to solve the problem at its root: the method of learning and evaluation.

Still another solution might be to provide frequent study questions for students to 10 answer. These would no doubt be helpful in focusing students' time studying, but students would probably not actually write out the answers unless they were required to. To get students to complete the questions in a timely way, professors would have to collect and check the answers. In that case, however, they might as well devote the time to grading an exam. Even if it asks the same questions, a scheduled exam is preferable to a set of study questions because it takes far less time to write in class, compared to the time students would devote to responding to questions at home. In-class exams also ensure that each student produces his or her own work.

Another possible solution would be to help students prepare for midterm and final 11 exams by providing sets of questions from which the exam questions will be selected or announcing possible exam topics at the beginning of the course. This solution would have the advantage of reducing students' anxiety about learning every fact in the textbook, and it would clarify the course goals, but it would not motivate students to study carefully each new unit, concept, or text chapter in the course. I see this as a way of complementing frequent exams, not as substituting for them.

From the evidence and from my talks with professors and students, I see frequent, 12 brief in-class exams as the only way to improve students' study habits and learning, reduce their anxiety and procrastination, and increase their satisfaction with college. These exams are not a panacea, but only more parking spaces and a winning football team would do as much to improve college life. Professors can't do much about parking or football, but they can give more frequent exams. Campus administrators should get behind this effort, and professors should get together to consider giving exams more frequently. It would make a difference.

References

Dendato, K. M., & Diener, D. (1986). Effectiveness of cognitive/relaxation therapy and study-skills training in reducing self-reported anxiety and improving the academic performance of test-anxious students. *Journal of Counseling Psychology, 33,* 131–135.

Frederiksen, N. (1984). The real test bias: Influences of testing on teaching and learning. *American Psychologist, 39,* 193–202.

Light, R. J. (1990). *Explorations with students and faculty about teaching, learning, and student life.* Cambridge, MA: Harvard University Graduate School of Education and Kennedy School of Government.

Rothblum, E. D., Solomon, L., & Murakami, J. (1986). Affective, cognitive, and behavioral differences between high and low procrastinators. *Journal of Counseling Psychology, 33,* 387–394.

Connecting to Culture and Experience: Experience with Frequent Exams

O'Malley advocates frequent brief exams as a solution to the problems of midterm- and final-exam anxiety, poor study habits, and disappointing exam performance. With two or three other students, discuss O'Malley's proposal in light of your own experience. To what extent do your courses without frequent exams produce the problems he identifies? Which of your high school or college courses included frequent exams? Describe these courses and the kinds of exams they offered. When you were taking these courses, what effect did the frequent exams have on your study habits, anxiety level, and mastery of the coursework?

Analyzing Writing Strategies

1. O'Malley devotes almost a third of his essay to anticipating readers' likely objections to his proposal. This section of the essay begins in the middle of paragraph 5 (with the sentence "It might be argued...") and then resumes in paragraphs 7 and 8. Begin by underlining the three objections, one each in paragraphs 5, 7, and 8. Then make notes about how O'Malley counterargues these objections. Finally, evaluate how successful each counterargument seems to be for its intended readers—college professors. What seems most and least convincing in each counterargument?

2. Readers of proposals are nearly always aware of solutions different from the one the writer is proposing. Readers may know of alternatives to the writer's solution—a solution someone has already proposed or one that has been tried with mixed results. Or—as readers have a tendency to do—they may think of an alternative solution after learning about the writer's preferred one. Consequently, effective proposals try to evaluate one or more likely alternative solutions. O'Malley evaluates alternative solutions in paragraphs 9–10, a different one in each paragraph. Reread these counterarguments and notice two things: the strategies and resources that O'Malley relies on and the extent to which he either concedes that some good ideas can be found in each alternative or refutes alternatives as unworkable. How do you think his intended readers will react to these paragraphs? What might they find most and least convincing?

Commentary: Supporting the Proposed Solution

O'Malley's essay demonstrates the importance of taking readers seriously. Not only does he interview both those who would carry out his proposal (professors) and those who would benefit from it (students), but he also features in his essay what he has learned from these interviews. Paragraphs 7–11 directly acknowledge professors' objections, their questions, and the alternative solutions they would probably prefer. These counterarguments, which may be essential to convincing readers to support a proposal, are only part of the overall argument, which centers on the writer's direct support of the proposed solution. Most of O'Malley's direct argument can be found in paragraphs 4–6, in which O'Malley presents three reasons that professors should give frequent exams: Students will (1) learn more and perform better on major exams, projects, and essays; (2) acquire better study habits; and (3) experience decreased anxiety and improved performance. He supports each reason with a combination of assertions based on his own experience and references to reputable research studies carried out at three universities. He quotes and paraphrases these studies.

Argument and counterargument can be woven together in many different ways in an essay proposing a solution to a problem. Because O'Malley succeeds at balancing argument and counterargument, the organization of his proposal is worth noting. The following is a scratch outline of his essay:

opening: a scenario to introduce the problem (paragraph 1)

presentation of the problem and introduction of the solution (2)

details of the solution (3)

reason 1: improved learning and performance (4)

reason 2: improved study habits (5)

refutation of objection 1: students as adults (5)

reason 3: less procrastination and anxiety (6)

accommodation of objection 2: limited class time (7)

accommodation of objection 3: too much work (8)

refutation of alternative solution 1: study-skills training (9)

refutation of alternative solution 2: study questions (10)

accommodation of alternative solution 3: sample exam questions (11)

closing: reiteration of the proposed solution and advice on implementing it (12)

Except for a brief refutation in paragraph 5, O'Malley first presents the direct argument for frequent exams (paragraphs 4–6) and then counterargues (paragraphs 7–11). The outline reveals that counterargument takes up most of the space, not an unusual balance in proposals to solve problems. O'Malley might have counterargued first or counterargued as he presented his direct argument, as he does briefly in paragraph 5. The approach you take depends on what your readers know about the problem and their experience with other proposed solutions to it.

Considering Topics for Your Own Essay

Much of what happens in high school and college is predictable and conventional. Examples of conventional practices that have changed very little over the years are exams, group instruction, graduation ceremonies, required courses, and lowered admission requirements for athletes. Think of additional examples of established practices in high school or college; then select one that you believe needs to be improved or refined in some way. What changes would you propose? What individual or group might be convinced to take action on your proposal for improvement? What questions or objections should you anticipate? How could you discover whether others have previously proposed improvements in the practice you are concerned with? Whom might you interview to learn more about the practice and the likelihood of changing it?

■ PURPOSE AND AUDIENCE

Most proposals are calls to action. Because of this clear purpose, a writer must anticipate readers' needs and concerns more when writing a proposal than in any other kind of writing. The writer attempts not only to convince readers but also to inspire them, to persuade them to support or implement the proposed solution. What your particular readers know about the problem and what they are capable of doing to solve it determine how you address them.

Readers of proposals are often unaware of the problem. In this case, your task is clear: to present them with evidence that will convince them of its existence. This evidence may include statistics, testimony from witnesses or experts, and examples, including the personal experiences of people involved with the problem. You can also speculate about the cause of the problem and describe its ill effects.

Sometimes readers recognize the existence of a problem but fail to take it seriously. When readers are indifferent, you may need to connect the problem closely to their own concerns. For instance, you might show how much they have in common with the people directly affected by it or how it affects them indirectly. However you appeal to readers, you must do more than alert them to the problem; you must also make them care about it. You want to touch readers emotionally as well as intellectually.

At other times, readers concerned about the problem may assume that someone else is taking care of it and that they need not become personally involved. In this situation, you might want to demonstrate that the people they thought were taking care of the problem have failed. Another assumption readers might make is that a solution they supported in the past has already solved the problem. You might point out that the original solution has proved unworkable or that new solutions have become available through changed circumstances or improved technology. Your aim is to rekindle these readers' interest in the problem.

Perhaps the most satisfying proposals are addressed to parties who can take immediate action to remedy the problem. You may have the opportunity to write such a proposal if you choose a problem faced by a group to which you belong. Not only do you have a firsthand understanding of the problem, but you also have a good idea of the kinds of solutions that other members of the group will support. (You might informally survey some of them before you submit your proposal to test your definition of the problem and your proposed solution.) When you address readers who are in a position to take action, you want to assure them that it is wise to do so. You must demonstrate that the solution is feasible — that it can be implemented and that it will work.

BASIC FEATURES: PROPOSING SOLUTIONS

A Well-Defined Problem

A proposal is written to offer a solution to a problem. Before presenting the solution, the writer must be sure that readers know and understand what the problem is. Patrick O'Malley, for example, devotes the first three paragraphs of his essay to defining the problem of infrequent course exams. It is wise to define the problem explicitly, as all the writers in this chapter do.

Stating the problem is not enough, however; the writer also must establish the problem as serious enough to need solving. Sometimes a writer can assume that readers will recognize the problem and its seriousness. For example, Hertsgaard assumes his readers understand the seriousness of the problem; his challenge is to help them overcome their feeling of fatalism so that they will pay attention to the solution he is proposing. At other times, readers may not be aware of the problem and will need to be convinced that it deserves their attention. Katherine S. Newman, for instance, does not assume that her readers will understand how difficult it is for inner-city fast-food workers to find better jobs.

In addition to defining the problem and establishing its seriousness for readers, a proposal writer may have to analyze the problem, exploring its causes, consequences, and history and past efforts at dealing with it.

A Clearly Described Solution

Once the problem is defined and its existence established, the writer must describe the solution so that readers can readily imagine what it would be like. Because O'Malley assumes that his readers know what brief exams are like, he runs little risk in not describing them. He does, however, identify their approximate lengths and possible forms—brief essay, short answer, or multiple choice. In contrast, because Newman cannot assume her readers will know what she means by an employer consortium, she describes it at length, focusing on who would be involved and the roles they would play.

A Convincing Argument in Support of the Proposed Solution

The main purpose of a proposal is to convince readers that the writer's solution will help to solve the problem. To this end, O'Malley gives three reasons why he thinks more brief exams will solve the problem and supports each reason with published research studies as well as his own experience.

Writers must also argue that the proposed solution is feasible—that it can actually be implemented and that it will work. The easier it is to implement, the more likely it is to win readers' support. Therefore, writers sometimes set out the steps required to put the proposed solution into practice, an especially important strategy when the solution might seem difficult, time-consuming, or expensive to enact. All the writers in this chapter offer specific suggestions for implementing their proposals, though none outlines all the steps required. For example, O'Malley offers professors several specific ways to give their students frequent, brief exams; Hertsgaard explains how government pump priming would work; and Newman offers many details about how an employer consortium would function.

An Anticipation of Readers' Objections and Questions

The writer arguing for a proposal must anticipate objections or reservations that readers may have about the proposed solution. Probably the greatest concern Hertsgaard anticipates is his readers' sense that the problem is too overwhelming to be solved. He accommodates or concedes the scope and seriousness of the problem but refutes his readers' hopelessness, arguing that we have already made progress in some areas and we possess the technology to make additional progress.

An Evaluation of Alternative Solutions

Proposal writers sometimes try to convince readers that the proposed solution is preferable to other possible solutions. They may compare the proposed solution to other solutions readers may know about or ones they may think of themselves. O'Malley, for example, evaluates three alternative solutions — study-skills training, study questions, and sample exam questions as alternatives to frequent exams — and demonstrates what is wrong with each one. He rejects study-skills training because it is overly complicated, time-consuming, and expensive. He rejects study questions because, compared with exams, they would not save either students or professors any time or ensure that students each do their own individual work. He rejects sample exam questions by arguing that they solve only part of the problem.

GUIDE TO WRITING
Proposing Solutions

Write an essay proposing a solution to a problem. Choose a problem faced by a community or group to which you belong, and address your proposal to one or more members of the group or to outsiders who might help solve the problem.

◄ **THE WRITING ASSIGNMENT**

INVENTION AND RESEARCH ►

INVENTION & RESEARCH

Finding a Problem to Write About

Analyzing and Defining the Problem

Identifying Your Readers

Finding a Tentative Solution

Defending Your Solution

Testing Your Choice

Offering Reasons for Your Proposal

Considering Alternative Solutions

Doing Research

Considering Document Design

Defining Your Purpose for Your Readers

Formulating a Tentative Thesis Statement

◄ **PLANNING AND DRAFTING**

PLANNING & DRAFTING

Seeing What You Have

Setting Goals

Outlining

Drafting

CRITICAL READING GUIDE ►

CRITICAL READING GUIDE

First Impression

Definition of the Problem

Description of the Solution

Convincing Argument in Support of Proposed Solution

Anticipation of Readers' Objections, Questions

Evaluation of Alternative Solutions

Effectiveness of Organization

Final Thoughts

◄ **REVISING**

REVISING

A Well-Defined Problem

A Clearly Described Solution

A Convincing Argument in Support of the Proposed Solution

An Anticipation of Readers' Objections and Questions

An Evaluation of Alternative Solutions

The Organization

EDITING AND PROOFREADING

EDITING & PROOFREADING ►

Checking for Ambiguous Use of *This* and *That*

Checking for Sentences That Lack an Agent

GUIDE TO WRITING

■ THE WRITING ASSIGNMENT

Write an essay proposing a solution to a problem. Choose a problem faced by a community or group to which you belong, and address your proposal to one or more members of the group or to outsiders who might help solve the problem.

■ INVENTION AND RESEARCH

The following activities will help you prepare to write a proposal. You will choose a problem you can write about, analyze and define the problem, identify your prospective readers, decide on and defend your proposed solution, test your choice, offer reasons and support for adopting your proposal, and consider readers' objections and alternative solutions, among other things. These activities are easy to complete. Doing them over several days will give your ideas time to ripen and grow. Be sure to keep a written record of your invention and research to use later when you draft and revise.

Finding a Problem to Write About

You may have already thought about a problem you could write about. Or you may have been drawn to one of the problems suggested by the Considering Topics for Your Own Essay activities following the readings in this chapter. Even so, you will want to consider several problems that need solving before making your final choice. The following activity will help you get started.

Listing Problems. *Make a list of problems you could write about.* Make a double-column chart like the following one. Divide a piece of paper or your computer screen into two columns. In the left-hand column, list communities, groups, or organizations to which you belong. Include as many communities as possible: college, neighborhood, hometown, and cultural or ethnic groups. Also include groups you participate in: sports, musical, work, religious, political, support, hobby, and so on. In the right-hand column, list any problems that exist within each group. Here is how such a chart might begin:

Community	*Problem*
My college	Poor advising or orientation
	Shortage of practice rooms in music building
	No financial aid for part-time students
	Lack of facilities for disabled students
	Lack of enough sections of required courses

Class scheduling that does not accommodate working
students or students with children

My neighborhood — Need for traffic light at dangerous intersection
Unsupervised children getting into trouble
Megastores driving away small businesses
Lack of safe places for children to play

Listing Problems Related to Identity and Community. Writing a proposal can
give you special insight into issues of identity and community by helping you understand how members of a community negotiate their individual needs and concerns.
You may already have made a chart of communities to which you belong and problems in those communities. The following categories may help you think of additional
problems in those or other communities that you could add to your list:

- Disagreement over conforming to community standards
- Conflicting economic, cultural, or political interests within the community
- Problems with equity or fairness between men and women, rich and poor, differ-
  ent ethnic groups
- Lack of respect or trust among the members of the community
- Struggles for leadership of the community

Listing Problems Related to Work and Career. Proposals are frequently written
on the job and about the work people do. Based on your work experience, make a
double-column chart like the following one. List the places you have worked in the
left column and the problems you encountered on the job in the right column.

Workplace	*Problem*
Restaurant	Inadequate training
	Conflicts with supervisor
	Unfair shift assignments
Department store	Inadequate inventory
	Computer glitches
	Overcomplicated procedures
Office	Unfair workloads
	Changing requirements
	Inflexible work schedules
	Lack of information about procedures
	Difficulty in scheduling vacations
	Outdated technology

Choosing a Problem. *Choose one problem from your list that seems especially important to you, that concerns others in the group or community, and that seems solvable. (You*

need not know the exact solution now.) The problem should also be one that you can explore in detail and are willing to discuss in writing.

Proposing to solve a problem in a group or community to which you belong gives you an inestimably important advantage: You can write as an expert, an insider. You know about the history of the problem, have felt the urgency to solve it, and perhaps have already thought of possible solutions. Equally important, you will know precisely to whom to address the proposal, and you can interview others in the group to get their views of the problem and to understand how they might resist your solution. From such a position of knowledge and authority comes confident, convincing writing.

Should you want to propose a solution for a social problem of national scope, concentrate on one with which you have direct experience and for which you can suggest a detailed plan of action. Even better, focus on unique local aspects of the problem. For example, if you would like to propose a solution to the lack of affordable child care for children of college students or working parents, you have a great advantage if you are a parent who has experienced the frustration of finding professional, affordable child care. Moreover, even though such a problem is national in scope, it may be solvable only campus by campus, business by business, or neighborhood by neighborhood.

Analyzing and Defining the Problem

Before you can begin to consider the best possible solution, you must analyze the problem carefully and then try to define it. Keep in mind that you will have to demonstrate to readers that the problem exists, that it is serious, and that you have a more than casual understanding of its causes and consequences. If you find that you cannot do so, you will want to select some other problem to write about.

Analyzing. *Start by writing a few sentences in response to these questions:*

- Does the problem really exist? How can I tell?
- What caused this problem? Can I identify any immediate causes? Any deeper causes? Is the problem caused by a flaw in the system, a lack of resources, individual misconduct or incompetence? How can I tell?
- What is the history of the problem?
- What are the bad effects of the problem? How does it harm members of the community or group? What goals of the group are endangered by the existence of this problem? Does it raise any moral or ethical questions?
- Who in the community or group is affected by the problem? Be as specific as possible: Who is seriously affected? Minimally affected? Unaffected? Does anyone benefit from its existence?
- What similar problems exist in this same community or group? How can I distinguish my problem from these?

Defining. *Write a definition of the problem, being as specific as possible.* Identify who or what seems responsible for it, and give one recent, telling example.

Identifying Your Readers

In a few sentences, describe your readers, stating your reason for directing your proposal to them. Then take a few minutes to write about these readers. Whom do you need to address — everyone in the community or group, a committee, an individual, an outsider? You want to address your proposal to the person or group who can help implement it. The following questions will help you develop a profile of your readers:

- How informed are my readers likely to be about the problem? Have they shown any awareness of it?
- Why would this problem be important to my readers? Why would they care about solving it?
- Have my readers supported any other proposals to solve this problem? If so, what do those proposals have in common with mine?
- Do my readers ally themselves with any group, and would that alliance cause them to favor or reject my proposal? Do we share any values or attitudes that could bring us together to solve the problem?
- How have my readers responded to other problems? Do their past reactions suggest anything about how they might respond to my proposal?

Finding a Tentative Solution

Solving problems takes time. Apparent solutions often turn out to be impossible. After all, a solution has to be both workable and acceptable to the community or group involved. Consequently, you should strive to come up with several possible solutions whose advantages and disadvantages you can weigh. You may notice that the most imaginative solutions sometimes occur to you only after you have struggled with a number of other possibilities.

Look back at the way you defined the problem and described your readers. Then with these factors in mind, list as many possible solutions to the problem as you can think of. You might come up with only two or three possible solutions; but at this stage, the more the better. To come up with different solutions, use the following problem-solving questions:

- What solutions to this problem have already been tried?
- What solutions have been proposed for related problems? Might they solve this problem as well?
- Is a solution required that would disband or change the community or group in some way?
- What solution might eliminate some of the causes of the problem?
- What solution would eliminate any of the bad effects of the problem?
- Is the problem too big to be solved all at once? Can I divide it into several related problems? What solutions might solve one or more of these problems?
- If a series of solutions is required, which should come first? Second?

- What solution would ultimately solve the problem?
- What might be a daring solution, arousing the most resistance but perhaps holding out the most promise?
- What would be the most conservative solution, acceptable to nearly everyone in the community or group?

Give yourself enough time to let your ideas percolate as you continue to add to your list of possible solutions and to consider the advantages and disadvantages of each one in light of your prospective readers. If possible, discuss your solutions with those members of the community or group who can help you consider the advantages and disadvantages of each one.

Choosing the Most Promising Solution. *In a sentence or two, state what you consider the best possible way of solving the problem.*

Determining Specific Steps. *Write down the major stages or steps necessary to carry out your solution.* This list of steps will provide an early test of whether your solution can, in fact, be implemented.

Defending Your Solution

Proposals have to be feasible—that is, they must be both reasonable and practical. Imagine that one of your readers strongly opposes your proposed solution and confronts you with the following statements. *Write a few sentences refuting each one.*

- It would not really solve the problem.
- I am comfortable with things as they are.
- We cannot afford it.
- It would take too long.
- People would not do it.
- Too few people would benefit.
- I do not even see how to get started on your solution.
- We already tried that, with unsatisfactory results.
- You support this proposal merely because it would benefit you personally.

Answering these questions should help you prepare responses to possible objections. If you feel that you need a better idea of how others are likely to feel about your proposal, talk with a few people who are directly involved with or affected by the problem. The more you know about your readers' concerns, the better you will be able to anticipate their reservations and preferred alternative solutions.

Testing Your Choice

Now examine the problem and your proposed solution to see whether you can write a strong proposal. Start by asking yourself the following questions:

- Is this a significant problem? Do other people in the community or group really care about it, or can they be persuaded to care?
- Will my solution really solve the problem? Can it be implemented?
- Can I answer objections from enough people in the community or group to win support for my solution?

As you plan and draft your proposal, you will probably want to consider these questions again. If at any point you decide that you cannot answer them with a confident yes, you may want to consider proposing a different, more feasible solution to the problem; if none exists, you may need to choose a different problem to write about.

Testing Your Choice: A Collaborative Activity

At this point, you will find it useful to get together with two or three other students and present your plans to one another. This collaborative activity will help you determine whether you can write this proposal in a way that will interest and convince others.

Presenters: Take turns briefly defining the problem you hope to solve, identifying your intended readers, and describing your proposed solution.

Listeners: Tell the presenter whether the proposed solution seems appropriate and feasible for the situation and intended readers. Suggest objections and reservations you believe readers may have.

Offering Reasons for Your Proposal

To make a convincing case for your proposed solution, you must offer your readers good reasons for adopting your proposal.

Listing Reasons. *Write down every plausible reason you could give that might persuade readers to accept your proposal.* These reasons should answer your readers' key question: Why is this the best possible solution?

Choosing the Strongest Reasons. *Put an asterisk next to the strongest reasons — the reasons most likely to be convincing to your intended readers.* If you do not consider at least two or three of your reasons strong, you will probably have difficulty developing a strong proposal and should reconsider your topic.

Evaluating Your Strongest Reasons. *Now look at your strongest reasons and explain briefly why you think each one will be effective with your particular readers, the members of the group or community you are addressing.*

Considering Alternative Solutions

List alternative solutions that members of the group or community might offer when they learn about your solution, and consider the advantages and disadvantages of each one relative to your solution. Even if members are likely to consider your proposal reasonable, they will probably want to compare your proposed solution with other possible solutions. You might find it helpful to chart the information as follows:

Possible Solutions	*Advantages*	*Disadvantages*
My solution		
Alternative solution 1		
Alternative solution 2		
Etc.		

Researching Alternative Solutions: an Online Activity

Searching the Web can be a productive way of learning about solutions other people have proposed or tried out. If possible, use your online research to identify at least two alternative solutions. Your purpose is to gain information about these solutions that will help you evaluate them fairly. Here are some specific suggestions for finding information about solutions:

- Enter keywords—words or brief phrases related to the problem or a solution—into a search tool such as Google (www.google.com) or Yahoo! Directory (http://dir.yahoo.com). For example, if you are concerned that many children in your neighborhood have no adult supervision after school, you could try keywords associated with the problem such as *latchkey kids,* or keywords associated with possible solutions such as *after-school programs.*

- If you think solutions to your problem may have been proposed by a government agency, you could try adding the word *government* to your keywords or searching on FirstGov.gov, the U.S. government's official Web portal. For example, you might explore the problem of latchkey children by following links at the Web site of the U.S. Department of Health & Human Services (www.hhs.gov). If you want to see whether the problem has been addressed in your state or local government, you can go to the Library of Congress Internet Resource Page on State and Local Governments (www.loc.gov/global/state/) and follow the links.

Add to your chart of the advantages and disadvantages of alternative solutions any information you find from your online research. Bookmark or keep a record of promising sites. You may want to download or copy information you could use in your essay, including visuals; if so, remember to record documentation information.

Doing Research

So far you have relied largely on your own knowledge and experience for ideas about solving the problem. You may now feel that you need to do some research to learn more about the causes of the problem and to find more technical information about implementing the solution.

If you are proposing a solution to a problem about which others have written, you will want to find out how they have defined the problem and what solutions they have proposed. You may need to acknowledge these solutions in your essay, either accommodating or refuting them. Now is a good time — before you start drafting — to get any additional information you need. If you are proposing a solution to a local problem, you will want to conduct informal interviews with several people who are aware of or affected by the problem. Find out whether they know anything about its history and current ill effects. Try out your solution on them. Discover whether they have other solutions in mind.

Considering Document Design

Think about whether your readers might benefit from design features, such as headings, numbered lists, or other elements that would make your presentation of the problem easier to follow and your solution more convincing. Earlier in this chapter's readings, for instance, Katherine S. Newman uses headings to introduce the major sections of her proposal. Consider also whether visuals — drawings, photographs, tables, or graphs — would strengthen your argument. These are not required for essays proposing a solution, but they could be helpful. You may come across promising visuals in your research and either download them from the Internet or make photocopies from library materials. When you reproduce visuals, make sure to acknowledge their sources. If you are going to post your essay on the Web, you also need to ask the source for permission.

Defining Your Purpose for Your Readers

Write a few sentences defining your purpose in proposing a solution to a problem of concern to the particular readers you have in mind. Remember that you have already identified your readers in the group or community you are addressing and developed your proposal with these readers in mind. Given these readers, try now to define your purpose by considering the following questions:

- Do I seek incremental, moderate, or radical change? Am I being realistic about what my readers are prepared to do? How can I overcome their natural aversion to change of any kind?

- How can I ensure that my readers will not remain indifferent to the problem?

- Who can I count on for support, and what can I do to consolidate that support? Who will oppose my solution? Shall I write them off or seek common ground with them?

- What exactly do I want my readers to do? To take my proposed solution as a starting point for further discussion about the problem? To take action immediately to implement my solution? To commit themselves to take certain preliminary steps, like seeking funding or testing the feasibility of the solution? To take some other action?

Formulating a Tentative Thesis Statement

Write one or more sentences that could serve as your tentative thesis statement. In most essays proposing solutions to problems, the thesis statement is a concise assertion or announcement of the solution. Think about how emphatic you should make the thesis and whether you should include in it a forecast of your reasons.

Review the readings in this chapter to see how other writers construct their thesis statements. For example, recall that Patrick O'Malley states his thesis early in his essay: "If professors gave additional brief exams at frequent intervals, students would be spurred to study more regularly, learn more, worry less, and perform better on midterms, finals, and other papers and projects" (paragraph 2). O'Malley's thesis announces his solution—brief, frequent exams—to the problems created for students in courses limited to anxiety-producing, high-stakes midterms and finals. The thesis lists the reasons students will benefit from the solution in the order in which the benefits appear in the essay. A forecast is not a requirement of a thesis statement, but it does enable readers to predict the stages of the argument, thereby increasing their understanding.

As you draft your own thesis statement, pay attention to the language you use. It should be clear and unambiguous, emphatic but appropriately qualified. Although you will probably refine your thesis statement as you draft and revise your essay, trying now to articulate it will help give your planning and drafting direction and impetus.

■ PLANNING AND DRAFTING

This section will help you review your invention writing and research notes, determine specific goals for your essay, prepare a rough outline, and get started on your first draft.

Seeing What You Have

You have now produced a lot of writing for this assignment about a problem and why it needs attention, about alternative solutions, and about the solution you want to propose and why it is preferable to the other proposed solutions. If you have done your invention writing on the computer, you may have sentences or whole paragraphs that can be copied and pasted into your draft. Reread what you have written so far to identify the potentially useful material. Look for details that will help you present a convincing argument for your solution and a strong counterargument in response to readers' likely objections to your solution and their preference for alternative solutions. Highlight key words, phrases, or sentences; make marginal notes or electronic annotations.

If at this point you doubt the significance of the problem or question the success of your proposed solution, you might want to consider a new topic. If you are unsure about these basic points, you cannot expect to produce a convincing draft.

However, if your invention material seems thin but promising, you may be able to strengthen it with additional invention writing. Ask yourself the following questions:

- Can I make a stronger case for the seriousness of the problem?
- Can I think of additional reasons for readers to support my solution?
- Are there any other ways of refuting alternative solutions to or troubling questions about my proposed solution?

Setting Goals

Before beginning to draft, think seriously about the overall goals of your proposal. Not only will the draft be easier to write once you have clear goals, but it will almost surely be more convincing as well.

Here are some questions that will help you set goals now. You may find it useful to return to them while drafting, for they are designed to help you focus on exactly what you want to accomplish with this proposal.

Your Purpose and Readers

- What do my readers already know about this problem?
- Are they likely to welcome my solution or resist it?
- How can I anticipate any specific reservations or objections they may have?
- How can I gain readers' enthusiastic support? How can I get them to want to implement the solution?
- How can I present myself so that I seem both reasonable and authoritative?

The Beginning

- How can I immediately engage my readers' interest? Should I open with a dramatic scenario, as O'Malley does? With statistics that highlight the seriousness of the problem, as Newman does? With a recitation of facts or events? Or with a rhetorical question, anecdote, or quotation?
- What information should I give first? Next? Last?

Defining the Problem

- How much do I need to tell about the problem's causes or history?
- How can I show the seriousness of the problem? Should I stress negative consequences, as O'Malley does? Should I cite statistics, as Newman does?

- Is it an urgent problem? Should I emphasize its urgency, as Hertsgaard does?
- How much space should I devote to defining the problem? Only a little space (like O'Malley) or much space (like Hertsgaard and Newman)?

Describing the Proposed Solution

- How can I describe my solution so that it will look like the best way to proceed? Should I show how to implement it, as Hertsgaard and Newman do? Or should I focus on my reasons to support it, as O'Malley does?
- How can I make the solution seem easy to implement? Or should I acknowledge that the solution may be difficult to implement and argue that it will be worth the effort?

Anticipating Readers' Objections

- Should I acknowledge every possible objection to my proposed solution? How might I choose among these objections?
- Has anyone already raised these objections? Should I name the person?
- Should I accommodate certain objections and refute others, as O'Malley does?
- How can I support my refutation? Should I cite an authority my readers are likely to respect?
- How can I refute my readers' objections without seeming to attack anyone? Can I accommodate as well as refute objections, as Hertsgaard and O'Malley do?

Evaluating Alternative Solutions

- How many alternative solutions do I need to mention? Which ones should I discuss at length? Should I indicate where each one comes from?
- How can I support my refutation of the alternative solutions? Can I argue that they are too expensive and time-consuming, as O'Malley does, or that they will not really solve the problem, as Newman does?
- How can I reject these other solutions without seeming to criticize their proponents? Newman and O'Malley, for example, succeed at rejecting other solutions respectfully.

The Ending

- How should I conclude? Should I end by restating the problem or by summarizing my solution and its advantages, as O'Malley and Newman do? Should I end with an inspiring call to action, as Hertsgaard and Newman do?
- Is there something special about the problem that I should remind readers of at the end?
- Should I end with a scenario suggesting the consequences of a failure to solve the problem?
- Might a shift to humor or satire provide an effective way to end?

Outlining

After setting goals for your proposal, you are ready to make a working outline—a scratch outline or a more formal outline using the outlining function of your word processing program. The basic outline for a proposal is quite simple:

> The problem
>
> The solution
>
> The reasons for accepting the solution

This simple plan is nearly always complicated by other factors, however. In outlining your material, you must take into consideration many other details, such as whether readers already recognize the problem, how much agreement exists on the need to solve the problem, how many alternative solutions are available, how much attention must be given to these other solutions, and how many objections should be expected.

Here is a possible outline for a proposal where readers may not understand the problem fully and other solutions have been proposed:

> Presentation of the problem
>> Its existence
>>
>> Its seriousness
>>
>> Its causes
>
> Consequences of failing to solve the problem
>
> Description of the proposed solution
>
> List of steps for implementing the solution
>
> Reasons and support for the solution
>> Acknowledgment of objections
>>
>> Accommodation or refutation of objections
>
> Consideration of alternative solutions and their disadvantages
>
> Restatement of the proposed solution and its advantages

(See p. 231 for another sample outline.)

Your outline will of course reflect your own writing situation. As you develop it, think about what your readers know and feel about your own writing goals. Once you have a working outline, you should not hesitate to change it as necessary while drafting and revising. For instance, you might find it more effective to hold back on presenting your own solution until you have dismissed other possible solutions. Or you might find a better way to order the reasons for adopting your proposal. The purpose of an outline is to identify the basic features of your proposal and to help you organize them effectively, not to lock you into a particular structure. If you use the outlining function of your word processing program, changing your outline will be simple and you may be able to write the essay simply by expanding the outline.

Most of the information you will need to develop each feature of a proposal can be found in your invention writing and research notes. How much space you devote to each feature is determined by the topic, not the outline. Do not assume that each entry on your outline must be given one paragraph. For example, each reason for supporting the solution may require a paragraph, but you might instead present the reasons, objections, and refutations all in one paragraph.

Consider tentative any outlining you do before you begin drafting. Never be a slave to an outline. As you draft, you will usually see ways to improve on your original plan. Be ready to revise your outline, shift parts around, or drop or add parts as you draft.

Drafting

General Advice.   Start drafting your proposal, keeping in mind the goals you set while you were planning and the needs and expectations of your readers; organize, define, and argue with them in mind. Also keep in mind the two main goals of proposals: (1) to establish that a problem exists and is serious enough to require a solution and (2) to demonstrate that your proposed solution is both feasible and the best possible alternative. Use your outline to guide you as you write, but do not hesitate to stray from it whenever you find that drafting takes you in an unexpected direction.

Turn off your grammar checker and spelling checker at this stage if you find them distracting. Don't be afraid to skip around in your document. Jump back and fill in a spontaneous idea, or leap ahead and write a later section first if you find that easier. If you get stuck while drafting, explore the problem by using some of the writing activities in the Invention and Research section of this chapter (p. 236).

Sentence Strategies.   As you draft an essay proposing a solution to a problem, you will want to connect with your readers. You will also want readers to become concerned with the seriousness of the problem and thoughtful about the challenge of solving it. Sentences that take the form of rhetorical questions and sentences that feature either assertive or tentative language can help you achieve these goals.

Use rhetorical questions to engage your readers, orient them to reading a proposal, and forecast the plan of your proposal. A rhetorical question is conventionally defined as a sentence posing a question to which the writer expects no answer from the reader. (Of course, not being face to face with the writer, a reader could not possibly answer.) In proposals, however, rhetorical questions do important rhetorical work—that is, they assist a writer in realizing a particular purpose and they influence readers in certain ways. Here are two examples from Katherine S. Newman's proposal:

> Why? And what can we do about it? (paragraph 4)

> How would an employer consortium function? (15)

These questions help readers understand that they will be reading a proposal: Newman implies through the questions that she will be explaining why inner-city workers are trapped in low-wage jobs and outlining a proposal to solve the problem. In addition, she engages readers by sharing with them the questions behind her research project and voicing one of the specific questions they are likely to have about her proposed solution. Consequently, readers have confidence that she will answer the questions she has posed so boldly.

Here are further examples from the other readings in this chapter:

So what do we do? (Mark Hertsgaard, paragraph 2)

Why, then, do so few professors give frequent brief exams? (Patrick O'Malley, paragraph 7)

All of the authors in this chapter use at least one carefully placed rhetorical question. Nevertheless, rhetorical questions are not a requirement for a successful proposal; and when they are used, they appear only occasionally.

Present the problem assertively, and argue the solution tentatively. To stress the seriousness of the problem and the urgency of solving it, use assertive language freely. In contrast, to convince readers to join you in taking action to solve the problem, use tentative language. These language contrasts—assertiveness versus tentativeness—play out quite predictably in this chapter's readings, as in the following example from Katherine S. Newman's proposal:

- Asserting the seriousness of the problem and the urgency of solving it

  Millions of Americans work full-time, year-round in jobs that leave them *stranded in poverty.* (Newman, paragraph 1)

This sentence features language that is blunt, unqualified, and attention-getting. Newman uses a familiar image of being stranded—isolated, alone, beyond reach of help—to dramatize the plight of low-paid full-time workers. Such language seems chosen to expose the failure of the status quo—of business as usual, of the way things have always been done—and to make clear that the problem is serious and urgently requires a solution. It expresses exasperation, even anger. It expresses a moral judgment: Something is wrong, and it is best to admit it.

- Arguing tentatively for the solution to the problem

  Second, their achievements on the job *might begin to lessen* the stigma or fear their new employers *may feel* toward the inner-city workforce. (Newman, paragraph 17)

This sentence features language that is cautious, provisional, and diffident: *might, begin to, may.* It acknowledges that every proposal is untried, its outcome unknowable. At the same time, it does not give the impression that Newman lacks confidence in her proposal. It simply recognizes that every proposal will inevitably be greeted with skepticism and that proposers must strategically overcome readers' resistance by showing themselves to be tentative, if not cautious, about advocating change, even though they may fervently wish for change.

In addition to using rhetorical questions and sentences that feature assertive or tentative language, you can strengthen your proposal with other kinds of sentences as well; and you may want to turn to the discussions of sentences that introduce concession and refutation (pp. 197–98) and that signal explicitly their logical relationship to a previous sentence (pp. 198–99).

CRITICAL READING GUIDE

Now is the time to get a good critical reading of your draft. Writers usually find it helpful to have someone else read and comment on their drafts, and all writers know how much they learn when they read other writers' drafts. Your instructor may arrange such a reading as part of your coursework—in class or online. If not, you can ask a classmate, friend, or family member to read your draft. You could also seek comments from a tutor at your campus writing center. (If you are unable to have someone else read your draft, turn ahead to the Revising section at p. 252, where you will find guidelines for reading your own draft critically.)

If you read another student's draft online, you may be able to use a word processing program to insert suggested improvements directly into the text of the draft or to write them out at the end of the draft. If you read a printout of the draft, you may write brief comments in the margins and lengthier suggestions on a separate page. When the writer sits down to revise, your thoughtful, extended suggestions written at the end of the draft or on separate pages will be especially helpful.

If You Are the Writer. To provide focused, helpful comments, your reader must know your essay's intended audience, your purpose, and a problem in the draft that you need help solving. Briefly write out this information at the top of your draft.

- *Readers:* Identify the intended readers of your essay. How much do they know about the problem? How will they react to your proposed solution?

- *Purpose:* What do you want your readers to do or think as a result of reading your proposal?

- *Problem:* Ask your reader to help you solve the single most important problem you see with your draft. Describe this problem briefly.

If You Are the Reader. Reading a draft critically means reading it more than once—first to get a general impression and then to analyze its basic features. Use the following guidelines to help you give critical comments to others on essays that propose solutions to problems.

1. *Read for a First Impression.* Read first to get a basic understanding of the problem and the proposed solution to it. After reading the draft, briefly write out your impressions. How convincing do you think the proposal will be for its particular readers? What do you notice about the way the problem is presented and the way the solution is argued for? Next, consider the problem the writer identified, and respond briefly to that concern now. (If you find that the problem is covered by one of the other guidelines listed below, respond to it in more detail there if necessary.)

2. *Evaluate How Well the Problem Is Defined.* Decide whether the problem is stated clearly. Does the writer give enough information about its causes and consequences? What more might be done to establish its seriousness? Is there more that readers might need or wish to know about it?

3. *Consider Whether the Solution Is Described Adequately.* Does the presentation of the solution seem immediately clear and readable? How could the presentation be strengthened? Has the writer laid out steps for implementation? If not, might readers expect or require them? Does the solution seem practical? If not, why?

4. *Assess Whether a Convincing Argument Is Advanced in Support of the Proposed Solution.* Look at the reasons offered for advocating this solution. Are they sufficient? Which are likely to be most and least convincing to the intended readers? What kind of support does the writer provide for each reason? How believable do you think readers will find it? Has the writer argued forcefully for the proposal without offending readers?

5. *Evaluate How Well the Writer Anticipates Readers' Objections and Questions.* Which accommodations and refutations seem most convincing? Which seem least convincing? Are there other objections or reservations that the writer should acknowledge?

6. *Assess the Writer's Evaluation of Alternative Solutions.* Are alternative solutions discussed and either accommodated or refuted? Which are the most convincing reasons given against other solutions? Which are least convincing, and why? Has the writer sought out common ground with readers who may advocate alternative solutions? Are such solutions accommodated or rejected without a personal attack on those who propose them? Try to think of other solutions that readers may prefer.

7. *Consider the Effectiveness of the Organization.* Evaluate the overall plan of the proposal, perhaps by outlining it briefly. Would any parts be more effectively placed earlier or later in the essay?

   • *Look at the beginning.* Is it engaging? If not, how might it be revised to capture readers' attention? Does it adequately forecast the main ideas and the plan of the proposal? Suggest other ways the writer might begin.

   • *Look closely at the way the writer orders the argument* for the solution — the presentation of the reasons and the accommodation or refutation of objections and alternative solutions. How might the sequence be revised to strengthen the argument? Point out any gaps in the argument.

   • *Look at the ending.* Does it frame the proposal by echoing or referring to something at the beginning? If not, how might it do so? Does the ending convey a sense of urgency? Suggest a stronger way to conclude.

- *Look at any design elements and visuals* the writer has incorporated. Assess how well they are incorporated into the essay. Point to any items that do not strengthen either the presentation of the problem or the argument in support of the solution.

8. *Give the Writer Your Final Thoughts.* What is the draft's strongest part? What part is most in need of further work?

■ REVISING

Now you have the opportunity to revise your essay. Your instructor or other students may have given you advice on how to improve your draft. Or you may have begun to realize that your draft requires not so much revising as rethinking. For example, you may recognize that you are no longer convinced that the problem is serious, that you feel it is serious but cannot be solved now or anytime soon, that you cannot decide to whom to address the proposal, that you cannot come up with a set of convincing reasons that readers should support your solution, or that you have been unable to accommodate or refute readers' objections and questions or to evaluate alternative solutions. Consequently, instead of working to improve the various parts of your first draft, you may need to write a new draft that reshapes your argument. Many students—and professional writers—find themselves in this situation. Often a writer produces a draft or two and gets advice on them from others and only then begins to see what might be achieved.

If you feel satisfied that your draft mostly achieves what you set out to do, you can focus on refining the various parts of it. This section will help you get an overview of your draft and revise it accordingly.

Getting an Overview

Consider your draft as a whole, following these two steps:

1. *Reread.* If at all possible, put the draft aside for a day or two before rereading it. When you do go back to it, start by reconsidering your audience and purpose. Then read the draft straight through, trying to see it as your intended readers will.

2. *Outline.* Make a scratch outline, indicating the basic features as they appear in the draft. Consider using the headings and outline or summary functions of your word processor.

Planning for Revision. Resist the temptation to dive in and start changing your text until after you have a clear view of the big picture. Using your outline as a guide, move through the document, using the change-highlighting or commenting tools of your word processor to note comments received from others and problems you want to solve (or mark a hard copy if you prefer).

Analyzing the Basic Features of Your Own Draft. Turn to the Critical Reading Guide that begins on p. 250. Using this guide, reread the draft to identify problems you need to solve. Note the problems on your draft.

Studying Critical Comments. Review all of the comments you have received from other readers. For each comment, look at the draft to determine what might have led the reader to make that particular point. Try to be receptive to constructive criticism. Ideally, these comments will help you see your draft as others see it. Add to your notes any problems readers have identified.

Carrying Out Revisions

Having identified problems in your draft, you now need to find solutions and—most important—to carry them out. You have three ways of finding solutions:

1. Review your invention and planning notes for additional information and ideas.
2. Do further invention writing or research to provide material you or your readers think is needed.
3. Look back at the readings in this chapter to see how other writers have solved similar problems.

The following suggestions, which are organized according to the basic features of essays that propose solutions, will get you started solving some common writing problems. For now, focus on solving the problems identified in your notes. Avoid tinkering with grammar and punctuation; those tasks will come later, when you edit and proofread.

A Well-Defined Problem

- *Is the definition of the problem unclear?* Consider sketching out its history, including past attempts to deal with it, discussing its causes and consequences more fully, dramatizing its seriousness more vividly, or comparing it to other problems that readers may be familiar with. Remember that all the authors of the readings in this chapter use assertive language to stress the seriousness of the problem.

A Clearly Described Solution

- *Is the description of the solution inadequate?* Try outlining the steps or phases involved in its implementation. Help readers see how easy the first step will be, or acknowledge the difficulty of the first step.

A Convincing Argument in Support of the Proposed Solution

- *Does the argument seem weak?* Try to think of more reasons for readers to support your proposal.

- *Is the argument hard to follow?* Try to put your reasons in a more convincing order — leading up to the strongest one rather than putting it first, perhaps.

An Anticipation of Readers' Objections and Questions

- *Does your refutation of any objection or question seem unconvincing?* Consider accommodating it by modifying your proposal.

- *Have you left out any likely objections to the solution?* Acknowledge those objections and either accommodate or refute them. Remember that all the authors of the readings in this chapter use tentative language in arguing to support their solutions.

An Evaluation of Alternative Solutions

- *Have you neglected to mention alternative solutions that some readers are likely to prefer?* Do so now. Consider whether you want to accommodate or refute these alternatives. For each one, try to acknowledge its good points, but argue that it is not as effective a solution as your own. You may in fact want to strengthen your own solution by incorporating into it some of the good points from alternatives.

The Organization

- *Is the beginning weak?* Think of a better way to start. Would an anecdote or an example of the problem engage readers more effectively?

- *Is the ending flat?* Consider framing your proposal by mentioning something from the beginning of your essay or ending with a call for action that expresses the urgency of implementing your solution.

- *Would design elements make the problem or proposed solution easier to understand?* Consider adding headings or visuals.

Checking Sentence Strategies Electronically. To check your draft for a sentence strategy especially useful in proposals, use your word processor's highlighting function to mark specific language where you present the problem and where you propose the solution. Then think about whether you could strengthen your proposal either by making the language about the problem more assertive, so that the problem seems more serious or urgent, or by making the language about the solution more tentative and cautious, so that readers are less likely to resist it. For more on assertive and tentative language in proposals, see p. 249.

◼ EDITING AND PROOFREADING

Now is the time to check your revised draft for errors in grammar, punctuation, and mechanics as well as to consider matters of style. Our research has identified several errors that are especially common in essays that propose solutions. The following guidelines will help you check and edit your essay for these common errors.

Checking for Ambiguous Use of *This* and *That*.   Using *this* and *that* vaguely to refer to other words or ideas can confuse readers. Because you must frequently refer to the problem and the solution in a proposal, you will often use pronouns to avoid the monotony or wordiness of repeatedly referring to them by name. Check your draft carefully for ambiguous use of *this* and *that*. Often the easiest way to edit such usage is to add a specific noun after *this* or *that,* as Patrick O'Malley does in the following example from his essay in this chapter:

> Another possible solution would be to help students prepare for midterm and final exams by providing sets of questions from which the exam questions will be selected or announcing possible exam topics at the beginning of the course. *This solution* would have the advantage of reducing students' anxiety about learning every fact in the textbook. . . .

O'Malley avoids an ambiguous *this* in the second sentence by repeating the noun *solution.* (He might just as well have used *preparation* or *action* or *approach.*)

The following sentences from proposals have been edited to avoid ambiguity:

▶ Students would not resist a reasonable fee increase of about $40 a year.
   increase
This would pay for the needed dormitory remodeling.
   ^

▶ Compared to other large California cities, San Diego has the weakest
   neglect
programs for conserving water. This and our decreasing access to Colorado
   ^
River water give us reason to worry.

                                                                one
▶ Compared to other proposed solutions to this problem, that is clearly the
   ^
most feasible.

Checking for Sentences That Lack an Agent.   A writer proposing a solution to a problem usually needs to indicate who exactly should take action to solve it. Such actors are called "agents." An agent is a person who is in a position to take action. Look at this sentence from O'Malley's proposal:

> To get students to complete the questions in a timely way, professors would have to collect and check the answers.

In this sentence, *professors* are the agents. They have the authority to assign and collect study questions, and they would need to take this action in order for this solution to be successfully implemented. Had O'Malley instead written "the answers would have to be collected and checked," the sentence would lack an agent. Naming an agent makes his argument convincing, demonstrating to readers that O'Malley has thought through one of the key parts of any proposal: who is going to take action.

The following sentences from student-written proposals illustrate how you can edit agentless sentences:

▶ *Your staff should plan a survey*
~~A survey could be planned~~ to find out more about students' problems in scheduling the courses they need.

▶ *The registrar should extend*
~~Extending~~ the deadline to mid-quarter ~~would make sense.~~

Sometimes it is appropriate to write agentless sentences, however. Study the following examples from O'Malley's essay:

These exams should be given weekly, or at least twice monthly.

Exams could be collected and responded to only every third or fourth week.

Still another solution might be to provide frequent study questions for students to answer.

Even though these sentences do not name explicit agents, they are all fine because it is clear from the larger context who will perform the action. In each case, it is obvious that the action will be carried out by a professor.

A Note on Grammar and Spelling Checkers. These tools are good at catching certain types of errors, but currently there's no replacement for a good human proofreader. Grammar checkers in particular are extremely limited in what they can usually find, and often they only give you summary information that isn't helpful if you don't already understand the rule in question. They are also prone to give faulty advice for fixing problems and to flag correct items as wrong. Spelling checkers cause fewer problems but can't catch misspellings that are themselves words, such as *to* for *too*.

REFLECTING ON YOUR WRITING

Now that you have worked extensively with essays that propose solutions to problems—reading them, talking about them, writing one of your own—take some time for reflection. Reflecting on your writing process will help you gain a greater understanding of what you learned about solving the problems you encountered in writing a proposal.

Write a page or two telling your instructor about a problem you encountered in writing an essay that proposes a solution and how you solved it. Before you begin, gather all of your writing—invention and planning notes, drafts, critical comments, revision notes and plans, and final revision. Review these materials as you complete this writing task.

1. *Identify one writing problem you had to solve as you worked on your proposal essay.* Do not be concerned with grammar and punctuation; concentrate instead on problems unique to developing a proposal. For example: Did you puzzle over how to convince readers that your proposed solution would actually solve the problem you identified? Did you find it difficult to support the reasons you gave for recommending the solution? Did you have trouble coming up with alternative solutions that your readers might favor?

2. *Determine how you came to recognize the writing problem.* When did you first discover it? What called it to your attention? If someone else pointed out the problem to you, can you now see hints of it in your invention writings? If so, where specifically? When you first recognized the problem, how did you respond?

3. *Reflect on how you went about solving the problem.* Did you reword a passage, cut or add details about the problem or solution, or move paragraphs or sentences around? Did you reread one of the essays in this chapter to see how another writer handled a similar problem, or did you look back at the invention suggestions? If you discussed the writing problem with another student, a tutor, or your instructor, did talking about it help? How useful was the advice you received?

4. *Write a page or so explaining the problem and your solution.* Be as specific as possible in reconstructing your efforts. Quote from your invention notes, your draft essay, others' critical comments, your revision plan, and your revised essay to show the various changes your writing underwent as you tried to solve the problem. If you are still uncertain about your solution, say so. The point is not to prove that you have solved the problem perfectly but rather to show what you have learned about solving problems when writing proposals. Taking time to explain how you identified a particular problem, how you went about trying to solve it, and what you learned from this experience can help you solve future writing problems more easily.

7

Justifying an Evaluation

Evaluation involves making judgments. Many times each day, we make judgments about subjects as diverse as the weather, food, music, computer programs, sports events, politicians, and films. In everyday conversation, we often express judgments casually ("I like it" or "I don't like it"), only occasionally giving our reasons (for example, "I hate cafeteria food because it is bland and overcooked") or supporting them with specific examples ("Take last night's spaghetti. That must have been a tomato sauce because it was red, but it didn't have the tang of tomatoes. And the noodles were so overdone that they were mushy").

When we write an evaluation, however, we know most readers expect that instead of merely asserting a judgment, we will provide reasons and support for the judgment. We know that unless we argue convincingly, readers who disagree will simply dismiss our judgments as personal preferences.

Evaluators can argue convincingly in several ways. One way is by making the reasons for your judgment explicit and by providing specific examples to support your reasons. You can also demonstrate knowledge of the particular subject being evaluated and the general category to which the subject belongs. For example, in an evaluation of *The Matrix Revolutions,* you would want to reassure readers that you are judging this particular film against other action and science-fiction films, including the first two films in the *Matrix* trilogy, *The Matrix* and *The Matrix Reloaded.* Given the film's genre, readers will expect you to base your judgment on qualities such as special effects, action sequences, and ideas or themes. Showing readers you understand how your particular subject relates to other subjects in the same general category demonstrates that your judgment is based on standards that readers recognize as appropriate for judging that kind of subject. For example, most people would agree that taste and consistency are appropriate standards for judging spaghetti served in the school cafeteria, but they would reject the high noise level and uncomfortable seating in a cafeteria as appropriate reasons for evaluating cafeteria food (although these reasons would be appropriate for judging the cafeteria itself).

As you can see, writing evaluations contributes to your intellectual growth by teaching you to develop reasoned, well-supported arguments for your judgments. Evaluations also require you to look critically at the standards underlying your own judgments as well as those of other people. You will encounter evaluative writing in many different contexts, as the following examples suggest.

Writing in Your Other Courses

- For a film-study course, a student evaluates two films (*Emma* and *Clueless*) based on the Jane Austen novel *Emma*. The student reads the novel, watches both films on videotape, and takes extensive notes. He also does an Internet search for reviews of the films. In his evaluation, the student argues that *Emma*, a period piece that faithfully follows the novel, is less successful than *Clueless*, a loose adaptation set in contemporary Beverly Hills, in capturing the spirit and romance of the novel. He supports his judgment with examples from the films and the novel as well as a few quotations from the movie reviews.

- For a political science course, a student writes a research paper evaluating the two major presidential candidates' performances during the first of their scheduled televised debates. Before watching the debate, she researches newspaper and magazine reports on two previous presidential debates to see what standards others have used to evaluate televised debates. Then she watches the debate and records it so that she can review it later. As she views the debate, she makes notes evaluating each candidate's performance. Afterward, she copies the transcript of the debate from the newspaper and collects published, televised, and online reviews of the debate. She uses this material both to support her own judgment and to respond to opposing judgments. Her final multimedia research paper includes downloaded Internet materials and videotaped excerpts from the debate.

Writing in the Community

- For the travel section of a local newspaper, a motorcycle enthusiast writes an article called "Hog Heaven" evaluating a tour of the Harley-Davidson factory and museum in York, Pennsylvania. He argues that Harley fans will enjoy the two dozen antique bikes on display and that people interested in business will be fascinated by the Harley plant because it includes both a classic assembly line (in which each worker performs an isolated operation on the motorcycles as they move along a conveyor belt) and a Japanese-inspired assembly team (in which three workers assemble an entire motorcycle from beginning to end, following whatever procedure they think works best). He concludes by emphasizing that the free tour offers something for everyone.

- For a campus publication, a college student writes an evaluation of a history course. She explains that the course includes three one-hour lectures per week by the professor plus a one-hour-per-week discussion led by a teaching assistant (TA). She states her judgment that although the lectures are boring, hard to follow, and seemingly unrelated to the assigned reading, the TA-led discussions are stimulating and help students grasp important information in each week's lectures and readings. To support her judgment, she describes a typical lecture and contrasts it to a typical discussion. She praises the TA for his innovative "term game," in which two teams of students compete to identify important concepts brought up in the week's lectures and reading, and for reviewing essay drafts via email. She concludes by recommending the course even though she wishes the TA could conduct the lectures as well as the discussions.

Writing in the Workplace

- In a written review of the work of a probationary employee, a supervisor judges the employee's performance as being adequate overall but still needing improvement in two key areas: completing projects on time and communicating effectively with others. To support his judgment, the supervisor explains that in one instance the employee's lateness derailed a team of workers and tells how the employee's lack of tact and clarity in communicating with coworkers created serious misunderstandings during the six-month probation period.

- For a conference on innovations in education, an elementary school teacher evaluates *Schoolhouse Rock,* an animated educational television series developed in the 1970s and recently reissued in several new formats: books, CD-ROM learning games, and music CDs. She praises the series as an entertaining and inventive way of presenting information, giving two reasons why it is an effective teaching tool: Witty lyrics and catchy tunes make the information memorable, and cartoonlike visuals make the lessons painless. She supports each reason by showing and discussing videotaped examples of popular *Schoolhouse Rock* segments, such as "Conjunction Junction," "We the People," and "Three Is a Magic Number." She ends by expressing her hope that teachers and developers of multimedia educational software will learn from the example of *Schoolhouse Rock.*

Practice Evaluating a Subject: A Collaborative Activity

The preceding scenarios suggest some occasions for evaluating a subject. You can discover how much you already know about evaluating by completing the following collaborative activity. Your instructor may schedule it for an in-class discussion or ask you to conduct an online discussion in a chat room.

Part 1. Get together with two or three other students to choose a reading from an earlier chapter that you have all already read. Review the reading, and decide whether you think the reading was helpful or unhelpful to you in learning to write well in the genre of the reading. Everyone in the group does not have to share the same judgment.

- First, take turns telling the group whether the reading was helpful in learning to write in the genre and giving two reasons for that judgment. Do not try to convince the others that your judgment is right or your reasons are sound; simply state your judgment and reasons.

- Next, after each person gives a judgment and reasons, discuss briefly as a group whether the reasons seem appropriate for judging a reading in a writing course. Again, you do not have to agree about whether the reading was helpful or unhelpful; all you have to do is discover whether you can agree on the kinds of reasons that make sense when evaluating a reading in the context of a writing course.

Part 2. As a group, spend a few minutes discussing what happened when you tried to agree on appropriate reasons for evaluating the reading:

- Begin by focusing on the reasons your group found easiest to agree on. Discuss why your group found these reasons so easy to agree on.
- Then focus on the reasons your group found hardest to agree on. Discuss why your group found these particular reasons so hard to agree on.

What can you conclude about community standards for judging readings in a writing course?

READINGS

No two essays justifying an evaluation are alike, and yet they share defining features. Together, the three readings in this chapter reveal a number of these features, so you will want to read as many of the essays as possible. If time permits, complete the activities in the Analyzing Writing Strategies section that follows each selection, and read the Commentary. Following the readings is a section called Basic Features: Evaluations (p. 280), which offers a concise description of the features of evaluative essays and provides examples from the three readings.

Stephen Holden *is a film reviewer for the* New York Times *and member of the New York Film Critics Circle. He began his writing career as a freelance rock critic, and his music reviews have appeared in* Rolling Stone, *the* Village Voice, *and other major publications. He briefly was a record producer for RCA Records and later wrote a novel about the record industry entitled* Triple Platinum *(1979). Holden still occasionally writes evaluations of musical performances and recordings, but since 2000 he has been one of the* Times*'s primary film reviewers. He also wrote the introduction to a book based on a series of* Times *articles about the cultural significance of the television series* The Sopranos.

Like The Sopranos, *the film* Road to Perdition *is about the psychological and moral angst of mobsters and their families. In his review, "A Hell for Fathers and Sons," Holden mentions* The Sopranos *and argues that* Road to Perdition *is "a period gangster film that achieves the grandeur of a classic Hollywood western." Evaluations, as you will see, often make comparisons of this kind. As you read, notice how Holden develops the comparison, and think about why he uses the writing strategy of comparing and contrasting. What does it add to his evaluation?*

A Hell for Fathers and Sons

Stephen Holden

Early in *Road to Perdition,* a period gangster film that achieves the grandeur of a classic Hollywood western, John Rooney (Paul Newman), the crusty old Irish mob boss in a town somewhere outside Chicago, growls a lament that echoes through the movie like a subterranean rumble: "Sons are put on the earth to trouble their fathers." 1

Rooney is decrying the trigger-happy behavior of his corrupt, hot-headed son, Connor (Daniel Craig), who in a fit of paranoid rage impulsively murdered one of Rooney's loyal lieutenants. The ear into which Rooney pours his frustration belongs to Michael Sullivan (Tom Hanks), his personal hit man, who witnessed the killing. An orphan whom Rooney brought up as a surrogate son and who has married and fathered two boys, Sullivan is in some ways more beloved to Rooney than his own flesh and blood. He is certainly more trustworthy. 2

But as the film shows, Rooney's bitter observation about fathers and sons also works in reverse: fathers are eternal mysteries put on the earth to trouble their sons as well as teach them. The story is narrated by the older of Sullivan's two boys, 12-year-old Michael Jr. (Tyler Hoechlin), who in a prologue establishes the movie's tone and setting (most of the events take place over six weeks in the winter of 1931) and invites us to decide, once his tale has been told, whether his father was "a decent man" or "no good at all." 3

Road to Perdition, which opens today nationwide, is the second feature film directed by Sam Mendes, the British theatrical maestro who landed at the top of Hollywood's A-list with his cinematic debut, *American Beauty.* The new movie reteams him with Conrad L. Hall, the brilliant cinematographer responsible for that film's surreal classicist shimmer. With *Road to Perdition* they have created a truly majestic visual tone poem, one that is so much more stylized than its forerunners that it inspires a continuing and deeply satisfying awareness of the best movies as monumental "picture shows." 4

Because Sullivan is played by Mr. Hanks, an actor who invariably exudes conscientiousness and decency, his son's question lends the fable a profound moral ambiguity. *Road to Perdition* ponders some of the same questions as *The Sopranos,* a comparably great work of popular art, whose protagonist is also a gangster and a devoted family man. But far from a self-pitying boor lumbering around a suburban basement in his undershirt, Mr. Hanks's antihero is a stern, taciturn killer who projects a tortured nobility. Acutely aware of his sins, Sullivan is determined that his son, who takes after him temperamentally, not follow in his murderous footsteps. Yet when driven to the brink, Sullivan gives his son a gun with instructions to use it, if necessary, and enlists him to drive his getaway car. 5

In surveying the world through Michael Jr.'s eyes, the movie captures, like no film I've seen, the fear-tinged awe with which young boys regard their fathers and the degree to 6

E1
B1   NE
FRIDAY, JULY 12, 2002

Weekend

MOVIES
PERFORMING ARTS

The New York Times

FILM REVIEW

A Hell for Fathers and Sons

An epic of
murderous
family
values.

François Duhamel/DreamWorks Pictures and 20th Century Fox

Tom Hanks as Michael Sullivan, a Chicago hit man, ordering Michael Jr. (Tyler Hoechlin) to wait for him while he attends to business in "Road to Perdition," directed by Sam Mendes. The film opens today nationwide.

which that awe continues to reverberate into adult life. Viewed through his son's eyes, Sullivan, whose face is half-shadowed much of the time by the brim of his fedora, is a largely silent deity, the benign but fearsome source of all knowledge and wisdom. An unsmiling Mr. Hanks does a powerful job of conveying the conflicting emotions roiling beneath Sullivan's grimly purposeful exterior as he tries to save his son and himself from mob execution. It's all done with facial muscles.

Yet Sullivan is also beholden to his own surrogate father, who has nurtured and pro-tected him since childhood. Mr. Newman's Rooney, with his ferocious hawklike glare, sepulchral rasp and thunderous temper, has the ultimate power to bestow praise and shame, to bless and to curse. The role, for which the 77-year-old actor adopts a softened Irish brogue, is one of Mr. Newman's most farsighted, anguished performances.

What triggers the movie's tragic chain of events is Michael Jr.'s worshipful curiosity about his father. Desperate to see what his dad actually does for a living, he hides in the back of the car that Sullivan drives to the fatal meeting at which Connor goes haywire.

7

8

After the boy is caught spying, Connor, who hates and envies Sullivan, decides without consulting Rooney that the boy can't be trusted to keep silent and must die. He steals into Sullivan's house and shoots his wife, Annie (Jennifer Jason Leigh), and his other son, Peter (Liam Aiken), mistaking Peter for Michael Jr., who returns on his bicycle as the murders are taking place.

Arriving home, Sullivan finds his surviving son sitting alone in the dark, and as the camera waits downstairs, Sullivan climbs to the second floor and discovers the bodies. As his world shatters, all we hear is a far-off strangled cry of grief and horror. Minutes later he is frantically packing Michael Jr. into a car, and the two become fugitives, making one deadly stop before heading toward Chicago where Sullivan hopes to work for Frank Nitti (Stanley Tucci), Al Capone's right-hand man. For the rest of the movie, Sullivan plots his revenge on Connor, who remains secreted in a Chicago hotel room, protected by Rooney. Sullivan's plan involves a Robin Hood-style scheme of robbing banks but stealing only mob money. 9

The film, adapted from a comic-book novel by Max Allan Collins with illustrations by Richard Piers Rayner, portrays the conflicts as a sort of contemporary Bible story with associations to Abraham and Isaac, and Cain and Abel. The very word *perdition,* a fancy term for hell, is meant to weigh heavily, and it does. 10

True to the austere moral code of classic westerns, the film believes in heaven and hell and in the possibility of redemption. In that spirit its characters retain the somewhat remote, mythic aura of figures in a western, and the movie's stately tone and vision of gunmen striding to their fates through an empty Depression-era landscape seems intentionally to recall *High Noon, Shane* and *Unforgiven.* When the characters speak in David Self's screenplay, their pronouncements often have the gravity of epigraphs carved into stone. 11

A scary wild card slithering and hissing like a coiled snake through the second half of the film is Maguire (Jude Law), a ghoulish hit man and photojournalist with a fanatical devotion to taking pictures of dead bodies. When he opens fire, his cold saucer-eyed leer and bottled-up volatility explode into frenzied seizures that suggest a demonically dancing puppet. And just when you have almost forgotten the character, he reappears like an avenging fury. 12

The look of the film maintains a scrupulous balance between the pop illustration of a graphic novel (Michael Jr. himself is shown reading one, *The Lone Ranger*) and Depression-era paintings, especially the bare, desolate canvases of Edward Hopper. The camera moves with serene, stealthy deliberation (nothing is rushed or jagged), while the lighting sustains a wintry atmosphere of funereal gloom. Mr. Hall embraces shadow as hungrily as Gordon Willis in the *Godfather* movies, but where the ruddy palette of *The Godfather* suggested a hidden, sensual, blood-spattered twilight, *Road to Perdition* comes in shades of gray fading to black. 13

Those shades are matched by Thomas Newman's symphonic score, which infuses a sweeping Coplandesque evocation of the American flatlands with Irish folk motifs. In the flashiest of many visually indelible moments, a cluster of gangsters silhouetted in a heavy rain are systematically mowed down on a Chicago street in a volley of machine-gun flashes that seem to erupt out of nowhere from an unseen assassin. But no shots or voices are heard. The eerie silence is filled by the solemn swell of Mr. Newman's score. It 14 is one of many scenes of violence in which the camera maintains a discreet aesthetic distance from the carnage.

Although *Road to Perdition* is not without gore, it chooses its bloodier moments with   15
exquisite care. The aftermath of another cold-blooded murder is seen only for an instant in the swing of a mirrored bathroom door. Another is shown as a reflection on a window overlooking an idyllic beach on which a boy frisks with a dog. Here the overlapping images evoke more than any words the characters' tragic apprehension of having to choose between two simultaneous, colliding worlds. One is a heaven on earth, the other hell.

Connecting to Culture and Experience: Parables and Fables

In evaluating *Road to Perdition,* Holden seems to think that the moral dilemma the film presents makes it interesting. He characterizes the comic-book novel from which the film is derived as "a sort of contemporary Bible story" (paragraph 10). Bible stories like those of Abraham and Isaac or Cain and Abel, to which Holden refers, are often parables or fables, simple stories that illustrate a moral or religious lesson — for example, "Thou shalt not kill." Holden calls *Road to Perdition* a fable with "a profound moral ambiguity" (paragraph 5).

With two or three other students, try to think of other films or television programs you have seen that also resemble parables or fables. If you can think of several examples, see whether you agree on what lessons they teach. If, on the other hand, you cannot think of any other examples, consider why contemporary media rarely presents moral lessons. Then discuss whether morality should be taken into account when evaluating films in general or only those films that, like *Road to Perdition,* try to make a point about morality.

Analyzing Writing Strategies

1. At the beginning of this chapter, we make several generalizations about evaluative essays. Consider which of these statements is true of Holden's essay:
   - It asserts an overall judgment.
   - It makes explicit the reasons for the judgment.
   - It provides specific support for the judgment.
   - It tries to demonstrate knowledge of the particular subject as well as the general category to which the subject belongs.

2. One reason Holden thinks highly of *Road to Perdition* is what he calls its "look" (paragraph 13), which is created by camera movements, lighting, sound, and silence. Reread paragraphs 13–14 to see how Holden uses comparisons to support his enthusiasm for the look of the film.

   Underline the comparisons. To what does Holden compare *Road to Perdition?* If any of these comparisons are familiar to you and you have seen *Road to*

Perdition, explain how well they help you understand what Holden is saying about the look of the film. Also notice that for many of these comparisons, Holden adds descriptive language. In talking about lighting, for example, he compares the use of shadow and color in *Road to Perdition* to that in the *Godfather* films (13). Explain how adding a little description helps readers, both those who are familiar with the comparison and those who are not.

3. Holden makes good use of another kind of comparison: the simile. There are three of them in paragraph 12, two beginning with *like* and one with *suggest.* Underline these similes. (Holden also uses metaphors: *wild card, ghoulish, saucer-eyed, explode.*) Explain how the similes help you imagine (or remember, if you have seen the film) the character Maguire. To write comparisons and similes, you have to rely on certain kinds of sentences. For more information on the sentences of comparison and contrast, turn to p. 293.

Commentary: Presenting the Subject and the Overall Judgment

Film reviews, like other evaluations, usually begin by presenting the subject and stating the writer's overall judgment. Stephen Holden identifies the movie by name in the first sentence, and in the first four paragraphs he categorizes it ("a period gangster film" [paragraph 1]), and tells where and when it takes place ("a town somewhere outside Chicago" [1], "six weeks in the winter of 1931" [3]), what the story is about, who the actors are and what characters they play, and who the director is.

Because they can usually assume their readers are trying to decide whether to see the film, reviewers have to think carefully about how much plot detail to include and why. At least in the opening paragraphs, Holden chooses to give information that is shown in the trailer used to advertise the film. Later, in paragraphs 8 and 9, he gives additional information but does not reveal the ending. In contrast, your instructor may want you to assume your readers have seen the film.

In addition to presenting the subject, writers of evaluation usually state their overall judgment early in the essay. In the first sentence, for example, Holden indicates his judgment is positive when he describes *Road to Perdition* as achieving "the grandeur of a classic Hollywood western." At the end of paragraph 4, after he has described the film and the people responsible for it, he reiterates this judgment in a clear, definitive thesis statement: "With *Road to Perdition* they have created a truly majestic visual tone poem, one that is so much more stylized than its forerunners that it inspires a continuing and deeply satisfying awareness of the best movies as monumental 'picture shows'" (4). This thesis statement has the three qualities expected of a good thesis: It is clear, arguable, and appropriately qualified. The key words *majestic* and *monumental* in this thesis sentence (like the words *grandeur* and *classic* in the first sentence) clearly express praise. The thesis is also obviously arguable since some viewers would very likely disagree with Holden's judgment.

Because his is a rave review, Holden does not point out weaknesses of any kind. He does not qualify or limit his thesis. Most film reviews as well as other kinds of evaluations, however, combine praise and criticism. Rarely do critics find nothing to criticize. Even in highly positive evaluations, writers often acknowledge minor shortcomings to show readers that their evaluation is fair and balanced. Similarly, in negative reviews, the writer usually finds something to praise. As you read the next selection, you will see how a writer can express a positive overall judgment but still point out shortcomings.

Considering Topics for Your Own Essay

List several movies that you would enjoy reviewing, and choose one from your list that you recall especially well. Of course, if you were actually to write about this movie, you would need to see it at least twice to develop your reasons and find supporting examples. For this activity, however, you do not have to view your film again. Just be sure you have a strong overall judgment about it. Then consider how you would argue for your judgment. Specifically, what reasons do you think you would give your readers? Why do you assume that your readers would accept these reasons as appropriate for evaluating this particular film?

Jonah Jackson evaluates computer games for TechTV. He also writes reviews for Computer Gaming World *and Gamers.com. This evaluation of a game called The Elder Scrolls III: Morrowind was initially published on the TechTV Web site and also aired on the TechTV show* Extended Play. *It was originally posted December 30, 2002, and modified on April 23, 2003, for a "best picks" program. Jackson gives the game five stars, TechTV's highest rating. According to TechTV, "Five-star games are a rarity. This is a landmark title that every gamer should consider owning. Even gamers who aren't fans of the genre will enjoy playing this game. It may have some slight flaws, but the ambition of the title and what the developer was able to successfully pull off more than make up for any shortcomings. If games are indeed art, these are masterpieces." As you read Jackson's review, notice that he points out the game's weaknesses as well as its strengths. Consider whether balancing the good with the bad in a review like this makes his argument more convincing or less so.*

The Elder Scrolls III: Morrowind

Jonah Jackson

Morrowind, the third title in Bethesda Softworks' Elder Scrolls series, has hit the shelves. In this week's episode of *Extended Play* we sink our teeth into one of the largest and most richly detailed fantasy worlds ever to wear a set of polygons.[1] There are literally hundreds of hours of gameplay. A second CD that contains a construction set promises countless more hours of gameplay as gamers all over the world work hard on [your favorite mod here].[2] It's a good time to be a gamer.

1

---

[1] Polygons are used to create virtual three-dimensional space in video games.
[2] *Mod* is a modification of a computer game's technical features.

Outstanding Graphics

Morrowind would be worth the price of admission for the graphics alone. Building on past games, the island of Vvardenfell was meticulously created with dozens of climates and landscapes. Unique architectural detail differentiates cities and towns across the various regions. The sense of scope and grandeur is well maintained from the open canals of Vivec to the modest Ashlander yurt villages. Seeing the ruined ornate spires of an ancient city appear out of the mist as you walk through the countryside is something to behold.

2

Fog enshrouds the mountaintops, the water glistens and reflects landscape features, lightning, rain, and dust storms howl through the land, and night skies shine with stars. The Bethesda team has created a world that pulls you in with wide eyes from the moment you step off the slave boat onto the port of Seyda Neen.

3

Though the game is best played in the first person, there is a third-person camera position that's worth it if for nothing more than checking out the new duds you pick up in town. The few graphical quirks, such as shadows that get cast through walls and robe sleeves that obscure your ranged weapon targeting, are easy to forgive once you see your character reach up and shield his eyes while turning into the teeth of a windstorm.

4

Free to Explore

Morrowind begins with your arrival in Vvardenfell on an Imperial slave ship. After a short and clever character-generation segment disguised as a new-arrival check-in, you're off and running. Though you're given an initial task related to the game's main story, from the very beginning you're given the freedom to explore and adventure at your own pace.

5

Unlike many games that promise you the freedom to play however you want, Morrowind goes a long way toward meeting that promise. There are hundreds of side quests and locations to explore all over the map. You'll visit many of them and have a satisfying experience by simply following the main story. Alternatively, you can head into the countryside and make your way along a story line on your own. The sheer volume of quests and plot lines ensures that independent exploration will not hamper you when you want to return to the more traditional style of RPG[3] play. Plus it's downright fun to head into the nearest ancestral tomb to pick up a few goodies while walking down a nice country road.

Still, the best way to experience Morrowind is to attach yourself to a guild or two and start role-playing the quests you receive. While the ubiquitous fed-ex and find-my-lost-armor quests are well represented, many of your tasks will have more than one solution, depending on your skills, and you'll often find that the overlapping or conflicting interests of the guilds make the plot lines more interesting. The main story follows an engaging plot line as well and includes a huge back story that's interesting on its own. The island of Vvardenfell is a somewhat troubled section of the Empire. The native Dunmers or Dark Elves are at odds among themselves and with the Imperial presence. As the story unfolds you find that you play a larger and more important role in the future of Vvardenfell.

Quests and plots are revealed most often through interaction with the hundreds of characters found throughout Vvardenfell. Conversation is based on keywords and the interface[4] keeps track of questions and responses in a separate journal. Many of the generic townspeople do begin to look and sound alike after a while and the canned responses to certain questions do get old or even nonsensical. More than once townspeople seemed completely oblivious to world-changing events that had just taken place.

Customization

Every part of the game's design is implemented with an eye toward flexibility and customization to the player's desires. There are 10 races and 21 predefined classes, and you can create custom classes by choosing preferences from 27 skills among three specialization categories: Combat, Magic, and Stealth.

---

[3] *RPG* stands for *role-playing game.*
[4] *Interface* is the part of a program that presents information and allows user input.

Skills are improved through training or successful use of the skill. Level advance- 10
ment is based on improving a combination of any skills a total of 10 times. Level advancement brings additional Health and the opportunity to assign additional points to your base
attributes.

Any character class can improve any skill, although advancement is easier in the 11
skills related to your class. The game has no time limit, though, so you can work to create a mighty sorcerer who's also the most skilled swordsman and deft pickpocket in the
land.

With a few exceptions, all skills are useful and the game is well balanced. Playing a 12
skilled orator and acrobat with limited combat skills is just as rewarding as hacking
through the hordes with a barbarian warrior. Bethesda has done an excellent job writing a
story that can be played through with many different character types.

Control

Navigation is similar to many FPS[5] titles and will be familiar to players of the first two 13
Elder Scrolls games. The seamless combat interface is also easy to use, although the
various types of weapon swing (slash, jab, and so on) are awkwardly related to your
movement direction. A group of windowed menus is available with a simple click of the
right mouse button. This pauses the game and lets you access inventory, map, magic
items, and your character's detailed status. Basics such as health, mana, and spell
effects, plus a minimap, are always available on screen. Some of the interface design
is less than optimal. Your inventory, which you can sort by type, can become unwieldy
as you collect a lot of potions or scrolls. It's especially difficult to manage all the potion-
making ingredients if your character has the Alchemy skill.

The many quests you'll receive along the way are recorded in a chronological journal 14
that's autoindexed as you go. This journal manages to record everything of importance,
but it's missing the ability to sort or group items by quest. Nor does it separate completed
quests and ongoing quests. Although the sheer volume of information is a bit much in
later stages, the index feature does prevent the journal from becoming unusable.

Sound

Bethesda gave the music and sound effects the same care it gave the visuals. The 15
grand scope of the story is served well by the basic theme music. Given 50-plus hours of
game time, it was important to produce something that was unobtrusive enough to hear a
few hundred times while still providing atmosphere. The combat music is a little flat, but it
does provide important auditory clues about nearby enemies. The ambiance of the game
is also helped by the carefully crafted sound of footsteps, creaking doors, howling wind,
moaning spirits, unsheathing swords, rippling water, and dozens of other effects that
really pull the game together.

---

[5] *FPS* refers to *first-person shooter* games, a multiplayer genre of computer games.

Summary

Morrowind is a flawed jewel, but flawed only because its scope is so grand. Beautiful graphics, compelling stories, a huge map to explore, engaging quests, and a simple interface all add up to a premier game. Its bugs and design quirks are more than compensated for by a core game that's just fantastic. It may have just missed the center of the bull's eye, but Bethesda gets five stars for hitting a target that no one else even dares aim for.   16

Connecting to Culture and Experience:
Freedom of Play in Computer Games

According to Jonah Jackson, an important attraction of role-playing computer games is the freedom they give players to explore and play in any way they choose. In addition, computer game enthusiasts can also join online "mod communities" to modify their favorite games.

With two or three other students, discuss your experiences with role-playing computer games. Take turns describing what kinds of games you enjoy playing and what you like about playing these particular games. For example, how much do you value the freedom to play as you choose and the opportunity to be creative? Consider also how you feel about the game's rules. Do the rules restrict your enjoyment or contribute in some way to it? Does it matter to you — and do you think it should matter to Jackson — that what he calls freedom is really scripted?

Analyzing Writing Strategies

1. Writers of evaluations give readers a lot of information about the subject in the course of the essay. But they usually present the subject in the opening paragraph by identifying it in certain ways. Reread paragraph 1 to see how Jackson presents the subject he is evaluating. Underline the information he gives readers, and speculate about why you think he begins with this information.

2. Jackson indicates his overall judgment in the opening and then reasserts it as a thesis statement in the concluding paragraph. Reread paragraph 16 to see whether the thesis statement meets the three standards for a good thesis: that it be clear and unambiguous, arguable, and appropriately qualified.

Commentary: Giving Appropriate Reasons

The argument is probably the most important part of an evaluative essay. Writers argue by giving reasons and support for their overall judgment. In addition to this direct argument, writers also usually counterargue, anticipating and responding to readers' objections and alternative judgments. Here we focus on the way writers give reasons for their judgment.

Reasons in evaluative arguments are often statements praising or criticizing particular qualities of the subject. Jackson uses headings to focus attention on qualities such as graphics, customization, and control. Headings make his argument easy for readers to follow. They are especially useful for text posted online, as was the case with Jackson's original review, because reading long stretches of text onscreen can be difficult. Here is a scratch outline of Jackson's essay, including the headings:

Introduces the subject and states the judgment (paragraph 1)

Develops and supports the first reason: "Outstanding Graphics" (2–4)

Develops and supports the second reason: "Free to Explore" (5–8)

Develops and supports the third reason: "Customization" (9–12)

Develops and supports the fourth reason: "Control" (13–14)

Develops and supports the fifth reason: "Sound" (15)

Concludes and reiterates judgment (16)

Under each heading, Jackson presents his reason in topic sentences like these:

Outstanding Graphics: Morrowind would be worth the price of admission for the graphics alone. Building on past games, the island of Vvardenfell was meticulously created with dozens of climates and landscapes. (paragraph 2)

Free to Explore: Though you're given an initial task related to the game's main story, from the very beginning you're given the freedom to explore and adventure at your own pace. (5)

Customization: Every part of the game's design is implemented with an eye toward flexibility and customization to the player's desires. (9)

He does not simply assert his reasons, he supports them with particular examples. Look at the way he specifies in paragraphs 2–4 what makes the graphics good. In his topic sentence, he claims that the graphics are praiseworthy because the island was "meticulously created with dozens of climates and landscapes" (2). He supports this assertion with numerous examples. In paragraph 2, he points out how each city and town—from "the ruined ornate spires of an ancient city" to "the open canals of Vivec" and "the modest Ashlander yurt villages"—is given its own look with "[u]nique architectural detail." In paragraph 3, he illustrates the different climates—fog, lightning, rain, dust storms, night skies—that the player encounters. In addition to praising the good graphics, Jackson points out the bad ones, what he calls a "few graphical quirks" (4). He gives examples of these "quirks": "shadows that get cast through walls and robe sleeves that obscure your ranged weapon targeting" (4). Supporting reasons with this kind of detail helps to convince readers that the writer is making an informed as well as a balanced evaluation. As you plan your argument, make sure that you support your reasons with specific examples.

Writers also sometimes need to argue that their reasons are appropriate because they are based on the kinds of standards that people knowledgeable about the subject normally use. Jackson, however, does not have to make this kind of argument because he can assume that his original TechTV audience of experienced computer game players agree that his reasons for evaluating a game are appropriate because they are based on important aesthetic and technical features of role-playing games. The order in which Jackson presents his reasons suggests that for this particular kind of game, graphics are the most important standard for judgment. Presumably, if something serious was wrong with the control interface, his review would have been much more negative, and he might have made control the first reason. Notice that he devotes eleven paragraphs to the first three reasons and only three paragraphs to the last two reasons. The Guide to Writing in this chapter (beginning on p. 282) will help you decide which reasons to present, how to support them, whether you need to argue for their appropriateness, and how to organize your essay.

Considering Topics for Your Own Essay

Like Jonah Jackson, you might have a favorite computer game. Or you might do a lot of digital photography and be able to evaluate digital cameras or a software program like Photoshop. Alternatively, you might be interested in evaluating a particular Web site you use regularly. Choose one particular game, software program, or Web site, and list its obvious strengths and weaknesses.

Christine Romano wrote the following essay when she was a first-year college student. In it she evaluates an argument essay written by another student, Jessica Statsky's "Children Need to Play, Not Compete," which appears in Chapter 5 of this book (pp. 176-79). Romano focuses not on the writing strategies or basic features of an essay arguing a position but rather on its logic—on whether the argument is likely to convince its intended readers. She evaluates the logic of the argument according to the standards presented in Chapter 10. You might want to review these standards on pp. 356–59 before you read Romano's evaluation. Also, if you have not already read Statsky's essay, you might want to do so now, thinking about what seems most and least convincing to you about her argument that competitive sports can be harmful to young children.

"Children Need to Play, Not Compete," by Jessica Statsky: An Evaluation

Christine Romano

Parents of young children have a lot to worry about and to hope for. In "Children Need to Play, Not Compete," Jessica Statsky appeals to their worries and hopes in order to convince them that organized competitive sports may harm their children physically and psychologically. Statsky states her thesis clearly and fully forecasts the reasons she will offer to justify her position: Besides causing physical and psychological harm, competitive sports discourage young people from becoming players and fans when they are older and inevitably put parents' needs and fantasies ahead of children's welfare. Statsky also carefully defines her key terms. By *sports,* for example, she means to

1

include both contact and noncontact sports that emphasize competition. The sports may be organized locally at schools or summer sports camps or nationally, as in the examples of Peewee Football and Little League Baseball. She is concerned only with children six to twelve years of age.

In this essay, I will evaluate the logic of Statsky's argument, considering whether the support for her thesis is appropriate, believable, consistent, and complete. While her logic *is* appropriate, believable, and consistent, her argument also has weaknesses. I will focus on two: Her argument seems incomplete because she neglects to anticipate parents' predictable questions and objections and because she fails to support certain parts of it fully. 2

Statsky provides appropriate support for her thesis. Throughout her essay, she relies for support on different kinds of information (she cites eleven separate sources, including books, newspapers, and Web sites). Her quotations, examples, and statistics all support the reasons she believes competitive sports are bad for children. For example, in paragraph 3, Statsky offers the reason that "overly competitive sports" may damage children's growing bodies and that contact sports, in particular, may be especially hazardous. She supports this reason by paraphrasing Koppett that muscle strain or even lifelong injury may result when a twelve-year-old throws curve balls. She then quotes Tutko on the dangers of tackle football. The opinions of both experts are obviously appropriate. They are relevant to her reason, and we can easily imagine that they would worry many parents. 3

Not only is Statsky's support appropriate, but it is also believable. Statsky quotes or summarizes authorities to support her argument in paragraphs 3–6, 8, 9, and 11. The question is whether readers would find these authorities credible. Since Statsky relies almost entirely on authorities to support her argument, readers must believe these authorities for her argument to succeed. I have not read Statsky's sources, but I think there are good reasons to consider them authoritative. First of all, the newspaper authors she quotes write for two of America's most respected newspapers, the *New York Times* and the *Los Angeles Times*. These newspapers are read across the country by political leaders and financial experts and by people interested in the arts and popular culture. Both have sports reporters who not only report on sports events but also take a critical look at sports issues. In addition, both newspapers have reporters who specialize in children's health and education. Second, Statsky gives background information about the authorities she quotes, which is intended to increase the person's believability in the eyes of parents of young children. In paragraph 3, she tells readers that Thomas Tutko is "a psychology professor at San Jose State University and coauthor of the book *Winning Is Everything and Other American Myths*." In paragraph 5, she announces that Martin Rablovsky is "a former sports editor for the *New York Times*," and she notes that he has watched children play organized sports for many years. Third, she quotes from two Web sites—the official Little League site and an AOL message board. Parents are likely to accept the authority of the Little League site and be interested in what other parents and coaches (most of whom are also parents) have to say. 4

In addition to quoting authorities, Statsky relies on examples and anecdotes to support the reasons for her position. If examples and anecdotes are to be believable, they 5 must seem representative to readers, not bizarre or highly unusual or completely unpredictable. Readers can imagine a similar event happening elsewhere. For anecdotes to be believable, they should, in addition, be specific and true to life. All of Statsky's examples and anecdotes fulfill these requirements, and her readers would find them believable. For example, early in her argument, in paragraph 4, Statsky reasons that fear of being hurt greatly reduces children's enjoyment of contact sports. The anecdote comes from Tosches's investigative report on Peewee Football as does the quotation by the mother of an eight-year-old player who says that the children become frightened and pretend to be injured in order to stay out of the game. In the anecdote, a seven-year-old makes himself vomit to avoid playing. Because these echo the familiar "I feel bad" or "I'm sick" excuse children give when they do not want to go somewhere (especially school) or do something, most parents would find them believable. They could easily imagine their own children pretending to be hurt or ill if they were fearful or depressed. The anecdote is also specific. Tosches reports what the boy said and did and what the coach said and did.

Other examples provide support for all the major reasons Statsky gives for her position: 6

- That competitive sports pose psychological dangers—children becoming serious and unplayful when the game starts (paragraph 5)
- That adults' desire to win puts children at risk—parents fighting each other at a Peewee Football game and a coach setting fire to an opposing team's jersey (paragraph 8)
- That organized sports should emphasize cooperation and individual performance instead of winning—a coach banning scoring but finding that parents would not support him and a New York City basketball league in which all children play an equal amount of time and scoring is easier (paragraph 11)

All of these examples are appropriate to the reason they support. They are also believable. Together, they help Statsky achieve her purpose of convincing parents that organized, competitive sports may be bad for their children and that there are alternatives.

If readers are to find an argument logical and convincing, it must be consistent and   7
complete. While there are no inconsistencies or contradictions in Statsky's argument, it is seriously incomplete because it neglects to support fully one of its reasons, it fails to anticipate many predictable questions parents would have, and it pays too little attention to noncontact competitive team sports. The most obvious example of thin support comes in paragraph 11, where Statsky asserts that many parents are ready for children's team sports that emphasize cooperation and individual performance. Yet the example of a Little League official who failed to win parents' approval to ban scores raises serious questions about just how many parents are ready to embrace noncompetitive sports teams. The other support, a brief description of City Sports for Kids in New York City, is very convincing but will only be logically compelling to those parents who are already inclined to agree with Statsky's position. Parents inclined to disagree with Statsky would need additional evidence. Most parents know that big cities receive special federal funding for evening, weekend, and summer recreation. Brief descriptions of six or eight noncompetitive teams in a variety of sports in cities, rural areas, suburban neighborhoods—some

funded publicly, some funded privately—would be more likely to convince skeptics. Statsky is guilty here of failing to accept the burden of proof, a logical fallacy.

Statsky's argument is also incomplete in that it fails to anticipate certain objections and questions that some parents, especially those she most wants to convince, are almost sure to raise. In the first sentences of paragraphs 6, 9, and 10, Statsky does show that she is thinking about her readers' questions. She does not go nearly far enough, however, to have a chance of influencing two types of readers: those who themselves are or were fans of and participants in competitive sports and those who want their six- to twelve-year-old children involved in mainstream sports programs despite the risks, especially the national programs that have a certain prestige. Such parents might feel that competitive team sports for young children create a sense of community with a shared purpose, build character through self-sacrifice and commitment to the group, teach children to face their fears early and learn how to deal with them through the support of coaches and team members, and introduce children to the principles of social cooperation and collaboration. Some parents are likely to believe and to know from personal experience that coaches who burn opposing team's jerseys on the pitching mound before the game starts are the exception, not the rule. Some young children idolize teachers and coaches, and team practice and games are the brightest moments in their lives. Statsky seems not to have considered these reasonable possibilities, and as a result her argument lacks a compelling logic it might have had. By acknowledging that she was aware of many of these objections—and perhaps even accommodating more of them in her own argument, as she does in paragraph 10, while refuting other objections—she would have strengthened her argument.

Finally, Statsky's argument is incomplete because she overlooks examples of non-contact team sports. Track, swimming, and tennis are good examples that some readers would certainly think of. Some elementary schools compete in track meets. Public and private clubs and recreational programs organize competitive swimming and tennis competitions. In these sports, individual performance is the focus. No one gets trampled. Children exert themselves only as much as they are able to. Yet individual performances are scored, and a team score is derived. Because Statsky fails to mention any of these obvious possibilities, her argument is weakened.

The logic of Statsky's argument, then, has both strengths and weaknesses. The support she offers is appropriate, believable, and consistent. The major weakness is incompleteness—she fails to anticipate more fully the likely objections of a wide range of readers. Her logic would prevent parents who enjoy and advocate competitive sports from taking her argument seriously. Such parents and their children have probably had positive experiences with team sports, and these experiences would lead them to believe that the gains are worth whatever risks may be involved. Many probably think that the risks Statsky points out can be avoided by careful monitoring. For those parents inclined to agree with her, Statsky's logic is likely to seem sound and complete. An argument that successfully confirms readers' beliefs is certainly valid, and Statsky succeeds admirably at this kind of argument. Because she does not offer compelling counterarguments to the legitimate objections of those inclined not to agree with her, however, her success is limited.

Connecting to Culture and Experience: Competitive Team Sports and Social Cooperation

Romano reasons in paragraph 8 that some parents "feel that competitive team sports for young children create a sense of community with a shared purpose, build character through self-sacrifice and commitment to the group, teach children to face their fears early and learn how to deal with them through the support of coaches and team members, and introduce children to the principles of social cooperation and collaboration."

With two or three other students, discuss this view of the role that sports plays in developing a child's sense of social cooperation by giving children insights into how people cooperate in communities like neighborhoods, schools, workplaces, or even nations. Begin by telling one another about your own, your siblings', or your children's experiences with team sports between the ages of six and twelve. Explain how participating in sports at this young age did or did not teach social cooperation. If you think team sports failed to teach cooperation or had some other effect, explain the effect it did have.

Analyzing Writing Strategies

1. In paragraph 2, Romano presents her overall judgment. Underline the thesis statement, and evaluate it in terms of how well it meets the three standards for a good thesis: that it be clear and unambiguous, arguable, and appropriately qualified.

2. In addition to presenting her judgment in her thesis statement, Romano forecasts her reasons in paragraph 2. Reread Romano's essay, noting in the margin where she addresses each of these reasons. Then explain what you learn from the way Romano presents her reasons. Are they clear and easy to follow? Do you think her intended readers — her instructor and parents of young children (the same audience Statsky is trying to convince) — are likely to consider her reasons plausible? In other words, are these reasons appropriate for evaluating an essay that argues a position, based on standards her readers are likely to share? If you see a potential problem with any of the reasons she uses, explain the problem you see.

3. In paragraph 8, Romano observes that Statsky fails to anticipate certain objections and questions that her readers are almost sure to raise. Romano herself has analyzed her readers and tried to anticipate their likely objections and questions as well as the judgments they may be inclined to make of the subject.

Commentary: Presenting Convincing Support

Because she is evaluating a written text, Romano uses textual evidence to support her argument. To provide textual evidence, writers can quote, paraphrase, or summarize passages from the text. Romano quotes selectively, usually brief phrases. In paragraph 4, for example, Romano supports her argument about the believability of Statsky's sources with a quote showing how Statsky presents authorities:

In paragraph 3, she tells readers that Thomas Tutko is "a psychology professor at San Jose State University and coauthor of the book *Winning Is Everything and Other American Myths.*" In paragraph 5, she announces that Martin Rablovsky is "a former sports editor for the *New York Times.*"

In addition to quoting, Romano paraphrases and summarizes passages from Statsky's essay. A summary—a distillation of the main ideas—tends to be briefer than a paraphrase. Paraphrasing, in contrast, tries to capture the rich detail of the original. A good example of paraphrasing appears in the opening paragraph, where Romano represents Statsky's argument. Compare Romano's paraphrase to the original passage from Statsky's essay:

Statsky's Original Version

Highly organized competitive sports such as Peewee Football and Little League Baseball are too often played to adult standards, which are developmentally inappropriate for children and can be both physically and psychologically harmful. Furthermore, because they eliminate many children from organized sports before they are ready to compete, they are actually counterproductive for developing either future players or fans. (paragraph 2)

Romano's Paraphrase

Besides causing physical and psychological harm, competitive sports discourage young people from becoming players and fans when they are older and inevitably put parents' needs and fantasies ahead of children's welfare. (paragraph 1)

Notice that in the paraphrase, Romano mostly uses her own words, with a few significant exceptions for key terms like *physical* and *psychological, players* and *fans.*

Romano summarizes primarily to present parts of Statsky's argument, as in the following excerpt:

Romano's Summary

[I]n paragraph 3, Statsky offers the reason that "overly competitive sports" may damage children's growing bodies and that contact sports, in particular, may be especially hazardous. She supports this reason by paraphrasing Koppett that muscle strain or even lifelong injury may result when a twelve-year-old throws curve balls. She then quotes Tutko on the dangers of tackle football. (paragraph 3)

If you compare this summary with Romano's paraphrase, you will notice another important distinction between summarizing and paraphrasing. When summarizing, writers usually describe what the author is doing in the passage. In the summarized passage, for instance, Romano uses Statsky's name and the pronoun *she* to relate the different strategic moves Statsky makes in the paragraph being summarized. When paraphrasing, however, writers typically leave out references to the author and his or her moves. Like Romano does in the preceding sample paraphrase, they simply restate what the author has written.

Especially when you write an evaluation of a written document, these are the strategies you need to employ for presenting textual evidence from the document itself.

Considering Topics for Your Own Essay

List several written texts you would consider evaluating. For example, you might include in your list an essay from one of the chapters in this book. If you choose an argument from Chapters 5–7, you could evaluate its logic, its use of emotional appeals, or its credibility. You might prefer to evaluate a children's book that you read when you were young or that you now read to your own children, a magazine for people interested in a particular topic like computers or cars, a scholarly article you read for a research paper, or a short story. You need not limit yourself to texts written on paper; also consider texts available online. Choose one possibility from your list, and come up with two or three reasons why it is a good or bad text.

■ PURPOSE AND AUDIENCE

When you evaluate something, you seek to influence readers' judgments and possibly their actions. Your primary aim is to convince readers that your judgment is well informed and reasonable and therefore that they can feel confident in making decisions based on it. Readers do not simply accept reviewers' judgments, however, especially on important subjects. More likely they read reviews to learn more about a subject so that they can make an informed decision themselves. Consequently, most readers care less about the forcefulness with which you assert your judgment than about the reasons and support you give for it.

Effective writers develop an argument designed for their particular readers. Given what you can expect your readers to know about your subject and the standards they would apply when evaluating this kind of subject, you decide which reasons to use as well as how much and what kind of support to give.

You may want to acknowledge directly your readers' knowledge of the subject, perhaps revealing that you understand how they might judge it differently. You might even let readers know that you have anticipated their objections to your argument. In responding to objections or different judgments, you could agree to disagree on certain points but try to convince readers that on other points you do share the same or at least similar standards.

A Well-Presented Subject

The subject must be clearly identified if readers are to know what is being evaluated. Most writers name it explicitly. When the subject is a film, an essay, a video game, or a Web site, naming it is easy. When it is something more general, naming may require more imagination or just an arbitrary choice.

Evaluations should provide only enough information to give readers a context for the judgment. However, certain kinds of evaluations—such as reviews of films, computer games, television programs, and books—usually require more information than others because reviewers have to assume that readers will be unfamiliar with the subject and are reading in part to learn more about it. Holden tells readers the names of the actors and director of *Road to Perdition*, the place and time in which the film's story unfolds, and a general outline of what happens to the main characters. For a recently released film, the writer must decide how much of the plot to reveal—trying not to spoil the suspense while explaining how well or poorly the suspense is managed. For a classic film or in certain classroom situations, reviewers need not worry about giving anything away.

A Clear Overall Judgment

Evaluation essays are built around an overall judgment—an assertion that the subject is good or bad or that it is better or worse than something else of the same kind. This judgment is the thesis of the essay. The thesis statement may appear in the first sentence or elsewhere in the essay. Romano puts hers in the second paragraph. Holden asserts his thesis in the fourth paragraph. Writers also may restate the thesis at the end of the essay, summarizing their main points, as Jackson does. Wherever the thesis appears, it must satisfy three requirements: that it be clear and unambiguous, arguable, and appropriately qualified.

Although readers expect a definitive judgment, they also appreciate a balanced one. All of the writers in this chapter, except Holden, acknowledge both good and bad qualities of the subject they are evaluating. Romano praises the strengths and criticizes the weaknesses of Statsky's logic. Jackson gives the computer game his show's highest five-star rating, but he points out its shortcomings.

Appropriate Reasons and Convincing Support

Writers assert the reasons for their judgment, often explain their reasons in some detail, and provide support for their reasons.

For an argument to be convincing, readers have to accept the reasons as appropriate for evaluating the subject. Jackson, for example, assumes that his audience of computer game players will agree that his reasons are appropriate because they are based on standards that knowledgeable gamers apply when evaluating a game.

Evaluators not only give reasons but must also support their reasons. They may use various kinds of support. Romano, for example, relies primarily on textual evidence to support her reasons, presenting it in quotations, paraphrases, and summaries. In evaluating a video game, Jackson supports his argument with examples and descriptions.

Many writers also use comparisons to support an evaluative argument. For example, Holden refers to other films (such as *High Noon, Unforgiven,* and the *Godfather* movies), graphic novels *(The Lone Ranger),* Depression-era paintings (by artists like Edward Hopper), and music (by composers like Aaron Copland). Comparisons like these both support the argument and help to convince readers that the writer is an expert who knows the kinds of standards that knowledgeable people normally apply when evaluating this kind of film. Similarly, Jackson compares the video game he is reviewing to other role-playing games.

An Anticipation of Readers' Objections and Alternative Judgments

Sometimes reviewers try to anticipate and respond to readers' possible objections and alternative judgments, but counterarguing is not as crucial for evaluation as is arguing directly for a judgment by giving reasons and support. When they do counterargue, reviewers may simply acknowledge that others perhaps disagree, may accommodate into their argument points others have made, or may try to refute objections and alternative judgments. Romano, in her evaluation of Statsky's essay, accommodates various criticisms she thinks Statsky's readers would have. Thus, her evaluation turns out to be mixed — praising the strengths but also acknowledging the weaknesses of the argument she is evaluating. Evaluation essays often counterargue in just this way.

GUIDE TO WRITING
Justifying an Evaluation

THE WRITING ASSIGNMENT

Write an essay evaluating a particular subject. Examine your subject closely, and make a judgment about it. Give reasons for your judgment, reasons based on widely recognized standards for evaluating a subject like yours. Support your reasons with examples and other details from your subject.

THE WRITING ASSIGNMENT

INVENTION & RESEARCH

Finding a Subject to Write About

Exploring Your Subject and Possible Readers

Testing Your Choice

Testing Your Choice: A Collaborative Activity

Becoming an Expert on Your Subject

Developing Your Evaluation

Considering Document Design

Defining Your Purpose for Your Readers

Formulating a Tentative Thesis Statement

INVENTION AND RESEARCH

PLANNING & DRAFTING

Seeing What You Have

Setting Goals

Outlining

Drafting

PLANNING AND DRAFTING

CRITICAL READING GUIDE

First Impression

Presentation of the Subject

Clear Judgment

Reasons and Support

Treatment of Readers' Objections, Questions, Alternative Judgments

Effectiveness of the Organization

Final Thoughts

CRITICAL READING GUIDE

REVISING

A Well-Presented Subject

A Clear Overall Judgment

Appropriate Reasons and Convincing Support

An Anticipation of Readers' Objections and Alternative Judgments

The Organization

REVISING

EDITING AND PROOFREADING

EDITING & PROOFREADING

Checking Comparisons

Combining Sentences

GUIDE TO WRITING

■ THE WRITING ASSIGNMENT

Write an essay evaluating a particular subject. Examine your subject closely, and make a judgment about it. Give reasons for your judgment, reasons based on widely recognized standards for evaluating a subject like yours. Support your reasons with examples and other details from your subject.

■ INVENTION AND RESEARCH

The following activities will help you choose and explore a subject, consider your judgment, and develop your argument. These activities are easy to complete. Doing them over several days will give your ideas time to ripen and grow. Keep a written record of your invention and research to use later when you draft and revise.

Finding a Subject to Write About

You may already have a subject in mind and some ideas on how you will evaluate it. Even so, it is wise to take a few minutes to consider some other possible subjects. That way you can feel confident not only about having made the best possible choice but also about having one or two alternative subjects in case your first choice does not work. The following activities will help you make a good choice.

Listing Subjects. *Make a list of subjects you might be interested in evaluating.* Make your list as complete as you can, including, for example, the subjects suggested by the Considering Topics for Your Own Essay activity following each reading in this chapter. The following categories may give you some ideas.

- *Culture:* Television program, magazine or newspaper, computer game, band, songwriter, recording, film, actor, performance, dance club, coffeehouse, artist, museum exhibit, individual work of art
- *Written work:* Poem, short story, novel, Web site, magazine article, newspaper column, letter to the editor, textbook, autobiography, essay from this book
- *Education:* School, program, teacher, major department, library, academic or psychological counseling service, writing center, campus publication, sports team
- *Government:* Government department or official, proposed or existing law, agency or program, candidate for public office
- *Leisure:* Amusement park, museum, restaurant, resort, sports team, sports equipment, national or state park

Listing Subjects Related to Identity and Community.   The following are ideas for an evaluative essay on issues of identity and community.

- Evaluate how well one of the following meets the needs of residents of your town or city: a community center, public library, health clinic, college, athletic team, festival, neighborhood watch or block parent program, meals-on-wheels program, theater or symphony, school or school program.
- Evaluate how well one of the following serves the members of your religious community: a religious school, youth or senior group, religious leader, particular sermon, bingo, revival meeting, choir, building and grounds.
- Evaluate how well one of the following aspects of local government serves the needs of the community: mayor, city council, police, courts, social services, park system, zoning commission.

Listing Subjects Related to Work and Career.   Following are some suggestions for an evaluative essay on issues involving work and career.

- Evaluate a job you have had or currently have, or evaluate someone else you have observed closely, such as a coworker or supervisor.
- Evaluate a local job-training program, either one in which you have participated or one where you can observe and interview trainees.

Choosing a Subject.   *Review your list, and choose the one subject that seems most promising.* Your subject should be one that you can evaluate with some authority, either one that you already know quite well or one that you can study closely over the next week or two.

Exploring Your Subject and Possible Readers

To explore the subject, you need to review what you now know about it, become more familiar with it, make a tentative judgment about it, and think seriously about who your readers may be before you proceed to study your subject in depth. You then will be in a good position to decide whether to stick with this subject for your essay or choose a different subject, making this initial brief period of invention work a very good investment of your time.

Reviewing What You Now Know about the Subject.   *Write for a few minutes about what you already know about your subject right at this moment.* Focus your thinking by considering questions like these:

- Why am I interested in this subject?
- What do I like and dislike about this subject?

- What do I usually look for in evaluating a subject of this kind? What do other people look for?
- How can I arrange to become very familiar with my subject over the next week or two?

Familiarizing Yourself with the Subject.   *Take notes about what you observe and learn as you get acquainted with your subject, notes that include the kinds of details that make your subject interesting and special.* Whatever your subject, you must now take the time to experience it. If you are evaluating a one-time performance, it must be scheduled within the next few days, and you must be exceedingly attentive to the one performance and take careful notes. If you plan to evaluate a film, it would be best if you could rent the video so that you can reexamine parts you need to refer to. If you are evaluating an agency, a service, or a program, observe and talk to people and make notes about what you see and hear.

Making a Tentative Judgment.   *Review what you have written as you have been getting to know your subject; then write a few sentences stating your best current overall judgment of the subject.* Your judgment may be only tentative at this stage, or you may feel quite confident in it. Your judgment may also be mixed: You may have a high regard for certain aspects of the subject and, at the same time, a rather low assessment of other aspects. As you consider your overall judgment, keep in mind that readers of evaluative essays expect writers not only to balance their evaluation of a subject (by pointing out things they like as well as things they dislike) but also to state a definitive judgment, not a vague, wishy-washy, or undecided judgment.

Identifying and Understanding Potential Readers.   *Write several sentences about possible readers, with the following questions in mind:*

- For what particular kinds of readers do I want to write this evaluation?
- What are my readers likely to know about my subject? Will I be introducing the subject to them (as in a film or book review)? Or will they already be familiar with it, and if so, how expert on the subject are they likely to be?
- How are my readers likely to judge my subject? What about it might they like, and what might they dislike?
- What reasons might they give for their judgment?
- On what standards is their overall judgment likely to be based? Do I share these standards or at least recognize their appropriateness?

Testing Your Choice

Pause now to decide whether you have chosen a subject about which you can make a convincing evaluative argument. Reread your invention notes to see whether you know enough about your subject or can get the information you need to write a convincing evaluation for the readers you have identified. Also consider whether you feel confident in your judgment.

As you develop your argument, you should become even more confident. If, however, you begin to doubt your choice, consider beginning again with a different subject selected from your list of possibilities. Before changing your subject, however, discuss your ideas with another student or your instructor to see whether they make sense to someone else.

Testing Your Choice: A Collaborative Activity	At this point in your invention work, you will find it helpful to get together with two or three other students to discuss your subjects and test ways of evaluating them. *Presenters:* Each of you in turn briefly describe your subject without revealing your overall judgment.

Evaluators: Explain to each presenter how you would evaluate a subject of this kind. For example, would you judge a science-fiction film by the story, acting, ideas, special effects, or some other aspect of the film? Would you judge a lecture course by how interesting or entertaining the lectures are, how hard the tests are, how well the lectures are organized, or how well it succeeds in some other aspect of the class? In other words, tell the presenter what standards you would apply to his or her particular subject. (Presenters: Take notes about what you hear.)

Becoming an Expert on Your Subject

Now that you are confident about your choice of subject and have in mind some standards for judging it, you can confidently move ahead to become an expert on your subject. Over the next few days, you can immerse yourself in it to prepare to evaluate it confidently.

Immersing Yourself in Your Subject. *Take careful notes at every stage of gradually becoming thoroughly familiar with your subject.* If you are writing about a film, for example, you will need to view the film at least twice by attending screenings or renting a video or DVD. If you are evaluating the effectiveness of a public official, you will need to read recent public statements by the official and perhaps observe the official in action. If you decide to evaluate a local sports team, you will need to study the team, attend a game and if possible a practice, and review films of recent games. Consult with other students and your instructor about efficient strategies for becoming an expert on your subject. Your goal is to gather the details, facts, examples, or stories you will need to write an informative, convincing evaluation.

If you think you will need to do more research than time permits or you cannot view, visit, or research your subject to discover the details needed to support an evaluation of it, then you may need to consider choosing a different, more accessible subject.

Learning More about Standards for Judging Your Subject. *Make a list of prominent, widely recognized standards for judging your subject.* If you do not know the standards usually used to evaluate your subject, you could do some research. For example, if you are reviewing a film, you could read a few recent film reviews online or in the library, noting the standards that reviewers typically use and the reasons that they assert for liking or disliking a film. If you are evaluating a soccer team or one winning (or losing) game, you could read a book on coaching soccer or talk to an experienced soccer coach to learn about what makes an excellent soccer team or winning game. If you are evaluating a civic, governmental, or religious program, look for information online or in the library about what makes a good program of its type. If you are evaluating an essay in this book, you will find standards in the Purpose and Audience section and in the Basic Features section of the chapter where the essay appears.

Developing Your Evaluation

Now you are ready to discover how you might proceed to make a plausible, even convincing, argument to justify your judgment. Each of the following activities requires only a few minutes of your time spread out over a day or two, and they are all essential to your success in organizing and drafting your evaluation.

Listing Reasons. *Write down every reason you can think of to convince readers of your overall judgment.* Try stating your reasons like this: "My judgment is X because . . ." or "A reason I like (or dislike) X is that. . . ." Then look over your list to consider which reasons you regard as most important and likely to be most convincing to your readers. Highlight these reasons.

Finding Support. *Make notes about how to support your most promising reasons.* From your invention notes made earlier, select a few details, facts, comparisons, contrasts, or examples about your subject that might help you support each reason.

Anticipating Readers' Alternative Judgments, Questions, and Objections. *List a few questions your particular readers would likely want to ask you or objections they might have to your argument. Write for a few minutes responding to at least two of these questions or objections.* Now that you can begin to see how your argument might shape up, assume that some of your particular readers would judge your subject differently from the way you do. Remember that your responses—your counterargument— could simply acknowledge the disagreements, accommodate readers' views by conceding certain points, or refute readers' arguments as uninformed or mistaken.

Researching Alternative Judgments: An Online Activity

One way to learn more about judgments of your subject that differ from your own judgment is to search for reviews or evaluations of your subject online. You may even decide to incorporate quotations from or references to alternative judgments as part of your counterargument, although you need not do so in order to write a successful evaluation. Enter the name of your subject, such as a movie title, restaurant name, compact disc title, title of a proposed law, or the name of a candidate for public office, in a search engine such as Google (www.google.com) or Yahoo! Directory (http://dir.yahoo.com). (Sometimes you can narrow the search usefully by including the keyword *review* as well.) Of course, not all subjects are conveniently searchable online, and some subjects—a local concert, a college sports event, a campus student service, a neighborhood program—will likely not have been reviewed by anyone but you.

Bookmark or keep a record of promising sites. Download any materials you might wish to cite in your evaluation, making sure you have all the information necessary to document the source.

Considering Document Design

Think about whether visual or audio elements—cartoons, photographs, tables, graphs, or snippets from films, television programs, or songs—would strengthen your argument. These are not at all a requirement of an effective evaluation essay, but they could be helpful. Consider also whether your readers might benefit by such design features as headings, bulleted or numbered lists, or other elements that would make your essay easier to follow. You could construct your own graphic elements, download materials from the Internet, tape images and sounds from television or other sources, or scan visuals into your document from books and magazines. If you do use visual or audio elements you did not create yourself, remember to document the sources in your essay (and request permission from the sources if the essay will be posted on the Web).

Defining Your Purpose for Your Readers

Write a few sentences defining your purpose in writing this evaluation for your readers. Remember that you already have analyzed your potential readers and developed your argument with these readers in mind. Given these readers, try now to define your purpose by considering the following possibilities and any others that might apply to your writing situation:

- If my readers are likely to agree with my overall judgment, should I try to strengthen their resolve by giving them well-supported reasons, helping them refute others' judgments, or suggesting how they might respond to questions and objections?

- If my readers and I share certain standards for evaluating a subject of this kind but we disagree on our overall judgment of this particular subject, can I build a convincing argument based on these shared standards or at least get readers to acknowledge the legitimacy of my judgment?
- If my readers use different standards of judgment, what should I try to do—urge them to think critically about their own judgment, to consider seriously other standards for judging the subject, or to see certain aspects of the subject they might have overlooked?

Formulating a Tentative Thesis Statement

Write several sentences that could serve as your thesis statement. Think about how you should state your overall judgment—how emphatic you should make it, whether you should qualify it, and whether you should include in the thesis a forecast of your reasons and support. Remember that a strong thesis statement should be clear, arguable, and appropriately qualified.

Review the readings in this chapter to see how other writers construct thesis statements. For example, recall that Holden boldly asserts an overall judgment he knows will not be expected by his readers. His thesis statement is simple and direct: "With *Road to Perdition* they have created a truly majestic visual tone poem, one that is so much more stylized than its forerunners that it inspires a continuing and deeply satisfying awareness of the best movies as monumental 'picture shows'" (paragraph 4).

Romano uses the thesis statement to forecast her reasons as well as to express her overall judgment. She begins by indicating the standards she thinks are appropriate for evaluating her subject. Her thesis statement shows that she bases her reasons on these standards. In addition, it lets readers know in advance what she likes about the subject she is evaluating as well as what she does not like: "While [Statsky's] logic *is* appropriate, believable, and consistent, her argument also has weaknesses" (paragraph 2). Romano makes her thesis statement seem thoughtful and balanced. There is no ambivalence or confusion, however, about Romano's judgment. She is clear and emphatic, not vague or wishy-washy.

As you draft your own tentative thesis statement, think carefully about the language you use. It should be clear and unambiguous, emphatic but appropriately qualified. Although you will most probably refine your thesis statement as you draft and revise your essay, trying now to articulate it will help give direction and impetus to your planning and drafting.

■ PLANNING AND DRAFTING

This section will help you review what you have learned about evaluating your subject, determine specific goals for your essay, make a tentative outline, and get started on your first draft.

Seeing What You Have

Pause now to reread your invention and research notes. Watch for language that describes the subject vividly, states your judgment clearly, presents your reasons and support convincingly, and counterargues objections to your argument or readers' alternative judgments. Highlight key words, phrases, and sentences; make marginal notes or electronic annotations. If you have done your invention writing on the computer, you may have sentences or whole paragraphs that can be copied and pasted into your draft.

If your invention notes seem skimpy, you may need to do further research at this stage, or you could begin drafting now and later do research to fill in the blanks.

If your confidence in your judgment has been shaken or if you are concerned that you will not be able to write an argument to support your judgment, consult your instructor to determine whether you should try evaluating a different subject.

Setting Goals

Before you begin drafting, set some specific goals to guide the decisions you will make as you draft and revise your essay. The draft will be easier to write and more focused if you start with clear goals in mind. The following questions will help you set goals. You may find it useful to return to them while you are drafting, for they are designed to help you focus on specific features and strategies of evaluative essays.

Your Purpose and Readers

- What do I want my readers to think about the subject after reading my essay? Do I want to show them how the subject that I am evaluating fails, how it succeeds (as Holden does), or how it includes both strengths and weaknesses (as Jackson and Romano do)?

- Should I assume that my readers are likely to have read other evaluations of the subject (perhaps like Holden and Jackson) or to have developed their own evaluation of it (like Romano)? Or should I assume that I am introducing readers to the subject?

- How should I present myself to my readers—as knowledgeable, balanced, or impassioned or in some other way?

The Beginning

- What opening would capture readers' attention? Should I open by stating my overall judgment, as Holden and Jackson do? Or should I begin by giving readers a context for my evaluation, as Romano does?

- Should I try to make clear to readers at the outset the standards I will apply, as Romano does? Should I begin by comparing my subject with a subject more familiar to readers, as Jackson and Holden do?

The Presentation of the Subject

- How should I identify the subject? If it doesn't have a specific name, should I name it after something readers will recognize? Should I place it in a recognized category or genre, as Holden does when he refers to period gangster and classic western films or as Romano does by announcing the title of an essay she evaluates?

- What about the subject should I describe? Can I use visuals to illustrate, as Holden and Jackson do?

- If the subject has a story, how much of it should I tell? Should I simply set the scene and identify the characters, or should I give details of the plot, as Holden does?

Your Evaluative Argument

- How should I state my thesis? Should I forecast my reasons early in the essay, as Romano does? Should I place my thesis at the beginning or wait until after I have provided a context?

- How can I convince readers to consider my overall judgment seriously even if they disagree with it? Should I build my argument on shared standards or defend my standards (like Romano)? Should I try to present a balanced judgment by praising some things and criticizing others, as all the writers in this chapter but Holden do?

- How can I present my reasons? Should I explain the standards on which I base my reasons, as Romano does, or can I assume that my readers will share my standards, as Jackson does?

- If I have more than one reason, how should I order them? Should I begin with the ones I think are most important for judging a subject of this kind, as Jackson does? Or should I begin with the strongest and likely most convincing reason?

- How can I support my reasons? Can I find examples from the text to quote, paraphrase, or summarize, as Holden and Romano do? Can I call on authorities and cite statistics? Can I give examples, as Jackson and Romano do?

- What objections or alternative judgments should I anticipate? How should I respond—by merely acknowledging them, by conceding legitimate objections and qualifying my judgment, or by trying to refute objections I consider illegitimate or weak?

The Ending

- How should I conclude? Should I try to frame the essay by echoing something from the opening or from another part of the essay?

- Should I conclude by restating my overall judgment, as Romano and Jackson do?

- Should I end by making a recommendation?

Outlining

An evaluative essay contains as many as four basic parts:

1. A presentation of the subject
2. A judgment of the subject
3. A presentation of reasons and support
4. A consideration of readers' objections and alternative judgments

These parts can be organized in various ways. If, for example, you expect readers to disagree with your judgment, you could show them what you think they have overlooked or misjudged about the subject. You could begin by presenting the subject; then you could assert your thesis, present your reasons and support, and anticipate and refute readers' likely objections.

> Presentation of the subject
>
> Thesis statement (judgment)
>
> First reason and support
>
> Anticipation and refutation of objection
>
> Second reason and support
>
> Anticipation and accommodation of objection
>
> Conclusion

If you expect some of your readers to disagree with your negative judgment even though they base their judgment on the same standard on which you base yours, you could try to show them that the subject really does not satisfy the standard. You could begin by reinforcing the standard you share and then demonstrate how the subject fails to meet it.

> Establish shared standard
>
> Acknowledge alternative judgment
>
> State thesis (judgment) that subject fails to meet shared standard
>
> First reason and support showing how subject falls short of standard
>
> Second reason and support (etc.)
>
> Conclusion

There are, of course, many other possible ways to organize an evaluative essay, but these outlines should help you start planning your own essay.

Consider tentative any outlining you do before you begin drafting. Never be a slave to an outline. As you draft, you will usually see ways to improve your original plan. Be ready to revise your outline, shift parts around, or drop or add parts as you draft. If you use the outlining function of your word processing program, changing your outline will be simple, and you may be able to write the essay simply by expanding the outline.

Drafting

General Advice.   Start drafting your essay, keeping in mind the goals you set while you were planning. Remember also the needs and expectations of your readers; organize, define, and explain with them in mind. Turn off your grammar checker and spelling checker at this stage if you find them distracting. Don't be afraid to skip around in your draft; jump back and fill in a spontaneous idea, or leap ahead and write a later section first if you find that easier. If you discover that you need more information, just make a note of what you have to find out, and go to the next point. When you are done drafting, you can search for the information you need. If you get stuck while drafting, explore the problem by using some of the writing activities in the Invention and Research section of this chapter (pp. 283–89).

In addition, keep in mind that in writing an evaluative argument, you must accept the burden of proof by offering reasons and support for your judgment. Remember, too, that the basis for judgment often depends on standards as much as reasons and support. Try to think critically about the standards on which you base your judgment as well as the standards that others apply to subjects of the kind you are evaluating.

Sentence Strategies.   As you draft an essay evaluating a subject, you may want to compare or contrast your subject with similar subjects to establish your authority with readers to evaluate a subject like yours. In addition, you are likely to want to balance the evaluation of your subject—by criticizing one or more aspects of the subject if you generally praise it or by praising one or more aspects of it if you generally criticize it. To do so, you will need to use sentences that clearly and efficiently express comparisons or contrasts, specifically ones that contrast criticism with praise and vice versa.

Use sentences comparing or contrasting your subject with similar subjects to help convince readers that you are knowledgeable about the kind of subject you are evaluating. These sentences often make use of key comparative terms like *more, less, most, least, as, than, like, unlike, similar,* or *dissimilar,* as readings in this chapter well illustrate:

> The role, for which the 77-year-old actor adopts a softened Irish brogue, is one of Mr. Newman's *most* farsighted, anguished performances. (Stephen Holden, paragraph 7)

In this sentence Holden compares Newman's performance in *Road to Perdition* to his performances in earlier movies, asserting that it is as good and perhaps even superior.

> The film . . . portrays the conflicts *as* a sort of contemporary Bible story with associations to Abraham and Isaac, and Cain and Abel. (Stephen Holden, paragraph 10)

In this sentence Holden compares the conflicts among the characters in the movie to the conflicts between father and son and between brother and brother in two memorable Bible stories: Abraham was willing to kill his son Isaac when commanded by God to do so (but was not required to actually kill the boy), and Cain killed his brother Abel out of jealous anger because God favored Abel's gift over Cain's. (Comparisons introduced by *like* or *as* are called *similes.*)

> *Unlike* many games that promise you the freedom to play however you want, Morrowind goes a long way toward meeting that promise. (Jonah Jackson, paragraph 6)

In this sentence Jackson contrasts one feature of Morrowind with the corresponding feature of other computer games. Some comparisons or contrasts do not rely on an explicitly comparative term:

> *True to the austere moral code of classic westerns,* the film believes in heaven and hell and in the possibility of redemption. (Stephen Holden, paragraph 11)

> *Increase your authority with readers by using certain kinds of sentences to balance criticism and praise.* The sentence strategies are similar for introducing criticism followed by praise and introducing praise followed by criticism, strategies we refer to in this chapter as *counterargument.* In general, these strategies rely on words expressing contrast, like *but, although, however, while,* and so on to set up the shift between the two responses.

- Praise followed by criticism:

  > This journal manages to record everything of importance, *but* it's missing the ability to sort or group items by quest. (Jonah Jackson, paragraph 14)

  > ...Statsky does show that she is thinking about her readers' questions. She does not go nearly far enough, *however,* to have a chance of influencing two types of readers.... (Christine Romano, paragraph 8)

  > The seamless combat interface is also easy to use, *although* the various types of weapon swing (slash, jab, and so on) are awkwardly related to your movement direction. (Jonah Jackson, paragraph 13)

- Criticism followed by praise:

  > The combat music is a little flat, *but* it does provide important auditory clues about nearby enemies. (Jonah Jackson, paragraph 15)

  > Its bugs and design quirks are *more than compensated for* by a core game that's just fantastic. (Jonah Jackson, paragraph 16)

Notice that the last example does not use an explicitly comparative term to set up the contrast.

In addition to using sentences that make comparisons or contrasts with other subjects and sentences that balance criticism and praise, you can strengthen your evaluation with other kinds of sentences as well. You may want to turn to the information about using appositives (pp. 151–52), writing sentences introducing concession and refutation (pp. 197-98), and expressing logical relationships between sentences (pp. 198–99).

CRITICAL READING GUIDE   Now is the time to get a good critical reading of your draft. Writers usually find it helpful to have someone else read and comment on their drafts, and all writers know how much they learn about writing when they read other writers' drafts. Your instructor may arrange such a reading as part of your coursework—in class or online. If not, you can ask a classmate, friend, or family member to read your draft. You could also seek comments from a tutor at your campus writing center. (If you are unable to have someone else read your draft, turn ahead to the Revising section on p. 297, where you will find guidelines for reading your own draft critically.)

If you read another student's draft online, you may be able to use a word processing program to insert suggested improvements directly into the text of the draft or to write them out at the end of the draft. If you read a printout of the draft, you may write brief comments in the margins and lengthier suggestions on a separate page. When the writer sits down to revise, your thoughtful, extended suggestions written at the end of the draft or on separate pages will be especially helpful.

If You Are the Writer.   To provide focused, helpful comments, your reader must know your essay's intended audience, your purpose, and a problem in the draft that you need help solving. Briefly write out this information at the top of your draft.

- *Readers:* Identify the intended readers of your essay. What do you assume that they think about your subject? Do you expect them to be receptive, skeptical, resistant, or antagonistic?

- *Purpose:* What effect do you realistically expect your argument to have on these particular readers?

- *Problem:* Ask your reader to help you solve the most important problem you see in your draft. Describe this problem briefly.

If You Are the Reader.   Use the following guidelines to help you give constructive, critical comments to others on evaluation essays:

1. *Read for a First Impression.* Tell the writer what you think the intended readers would find most and least convincing. If you personally think the evaluation is seriously flawed, share your thoughts. Then try to help the writer improve the argument for the designated readers. Next, consider the problem the writer identified, and respond briefly to that concern now. (If you find that the problem is covered by one of the other guidelines listed below, respond to it in more detail there if necessary.)

2. *Analyze How Well the Subject Is Presented.* Locate where in the draft the subject is presented, and ask questions that will help the writer strengthen

the presentation. If you are surprised by the way the writer has presented the subject, briefly explain how you usually think of this particular subject or subjects of this kind. Also indicate whether any of the information about the subject seems unnecessary. Finally, and most important, let the writer know whether any of the information about the subject seems to you possibly inaccurate or only partly true.

3. *Assess Whether the Judgment Is Stated Clearly.* Write a sentence or two summarizing the writer's judgment as you understand it from reading the draft. Then identify the sentence or sentences in the draft where the judgment is stated explicitly. (It may be restated in several places.) If you cannot find an explicit statement of the judgment, let the writer know. Given the writer's purpose and audience, consider whether the judgment is arguable, clear, and appropriately qualified. If it seems indecisive or too extreme, suggest how the writer might make it clearer or might qualify it by referring at least occasionally to the strengths of a criticized subject or the weaknesses of a praised subject.

4. *Evaluate the Reasons and Support.* Identify the reasons, and look closely at them and the support that the writer gives for them. If anything seems problematic, briefly explain what bothers you. For example, the reason may not seem appropriate for judging this kind of subject, you may not fully understand the reason or how it applies to this particular subject, the connection between a particular reason and its support may not be clear or convincing to you, the support may be too weak, or there may not be enough support to sustain the argument. Be as specific and constructive as you can, pointing out what does not work and also suggesting what the writer might do to solve the problem. For example, if the reason seems inappropriate, explain why you think so, and indicate what kinds of reasons you expect the intended readers to recognize as acceptable for judging this kind of subject. If the support is weak, suggest how it could be strengthened.

5. *Assess How Well Readers' Objections, Questions, and Alternative Judgments Have Been Handled.* Mark where the writer acknowledges, accommodates, or tries to refute readers' objections, questions, or alternative judgments. Point to any places where the counterargument seems superficial or dismissive, and suggest how it could be strengthened. Help the writer anticipate any important objections or questions that have been overlooked, providing advice on how to respond to them. Keep in mind that the writer may choose to acknowledge, accommodate, or refute opposing arguments.

6. *Consider the Effectiveness of the Organization.* Get an overview of the essay's organization, and point out any places where more explicit cueing— transitions, summaries, or topic sentences—would clarify the relationship between parts of the essay.

- *Look at the beginning.* Do you think readers will find it engaging? If not, propose an alternative or suggest moving something from later in the essay that might work as a better opening.
- *Look at the ending.* Does the essay conclude decisively and memorably? If not, suggest an alternative. Could something be moved to the end?
- *Look at the design features.* Comment on the contribution of figures, headings, tables, and other design features. Indicate whether any visual or audio elements that have been included fail to support the evaluation effectively, and offer suggestions for improvement. Help the writer think of additional visual or audio elements that could make a contribution to the essay.

7. *Give the Writer Your Final Thoughts.* What is this draft's strongest part? What part is most in need of further work?

■ REVISING

Now you are ready to revise your essay. Your instructor or other students may have given you advice on improving your draft. Nevertheless, you may have begun to realize that your draft requires more rethinking than revising. For example, you may recognize that your reasons do not lead readers to accept your evaluation, that you cannot adequately support your reasons, or that you are unable to refute damaging objections to your argument. Consequently, instead of working to improve parts of the draft, you may need to write a new draft that radically reenvisions your argument. It is not unusual for students—and professional writers—to find themselves in this situation. Learning to make radical revisions is a valuable lesson for any writer.

If you feel satisfied that your draft achieves most, if not all, of your goals, you can focus on refining specific parts of it. Very likely you have thought of ways of improving your draft, and you may even have begun revising it. This section will help you get an overview of your draft and revise it accordingly.

Getting an Overview

Consider your draft as a whole, following these two steps:

1. *Reread.* If at all possible, put the draft aside for a day or two before rereading it. When you return to it, start by reconsidering your purpose. Then read the draft straight through, trying to see it as your intended readers will.
2. *Outline.* Make a scratch outline, indicating the basic features as they appear in the draft. Consider using the headings and outline/summary functions of your word processor.

Planning for Revision.   Resist the temptation to dive in and start changing your text until after you have a solid grasp of the big picture. Using your outline as a guide, move through the document, using the change-highlighting or commenting tools of your word processor to note useful comments received from others and problems you want to solve (or mark on a hard copy if you prefer).

Analyzing the Basic Features of Your Own Draft.   Using the Critical Reading Guide that begins on p. 295, identify problems that you now see in your draft.

Studying Critical Comments.   Review all of the comments you have received from other readers, and add to your revision plan any that you intend to act on. For each comment, look at the draft to determine what might have led the reader to make that particular point. Try to be objective about any criticism. Ideally, these comments will help you see your draft as others see it, providing valuable information about how you can improve it.

Carrying Out Revisions

Having identified problems in your draft, you now need to come up with solutions and — most important — to carry them out. Basically, you have three ways of finding solutions:

1. Review your invention and planning notes for information and ideas to add to your draft.
2. Do additional invention and research to provide additional material that you or your readers think is needed.
3. Look back at the readings in this chapter to see how other writers have solved similar problems.

The following suggestions, which are organized according to the basic features of evaluation essays, will help you solve some common problems in this genre.

A Well-Presented Subject

- *Is the subject unclear or hard to identify?* Try to give it a name or to identify the general category to which it belongs. If you need more information about the subject, review your invention writing to see if you have left out any details you could now add. You may also need to revisit your subject or do further invention writing to answer questions that your classmates and instructor have raised or your intended readers might have.

- *Is the subject presented in too much detail?* Cut extraneous and repetitive details. If your subject is a film or book, consider whether you are giving away too much of the plot or whether your readers will expect you to give a lot of detail.

- *Is any of the information inaccurate or only partly true?* Reconsider the accuracy and completeness of the information you present. If any of the information will be surprising to readers, consider how you might reassure them that the information is accurate.

A Clear Overall Judgment

- **Is your overall judgment hard to find?** Announce your thesis more explicitly. If your judgment is mixed—pointing out what you like and do not like about the subject—let readers know this from the beginning. Use sentences that balance praise and criticism, as most of the authors of this chapter's readings do.

- **Does your overall judgment seem indecisive or too extreme?** If your readers do not know what your overall judgment is or if they think you are either too positive or too negative, you may need to clarify your thesis statement or qualify it more carefully.

Appropriate Reasons and Convincing Support

- **Do any of the reasons seem inappropriate to readers?** Explain why you think the reason is appropriate, or show that your argument employs a standard commonly used for evaluating subjects of this kind.

- **Is any of the support thin or unconvincing?** To find additional support, review your invention writing, or reexamine the subject. Look closely again at your subject for more details that would support your reasons. As do all the authors of readings in this chapter, consider comparing or contrasting aspects of your subject with those of other subjects like yours.

- **Are any of your reasons and support unclear?** To clarify them, you may need to explain your reasoning in more detail or use examples and comparisons to make your ideas understandable. You may need to do some additional exploratory writing or research to figure out how to explain your reasoning. Consider also whether any of the reasons should be combined, separated, or cut.

An Anticipation of Reader's Objections and Alternative Judgments

- **Do readers fail to recognize your counterargument?** Make your responses to readers' likely questions or objections or alternative judgments more explicit.

- **Are any important objections or questions overlooked?** Revisit your subject or invention notes to think more deeply about why and where readers might resist your argument. Try to imagine how a reader who strongly disagrees with your judgment (praising a movie or college program or restaurant, for example) might respond to your evaluation.

The Organization

- **Does the essay seem disorganized or confusing?** You may need to add a forecasting statement, transitions, summaries, or topic sentences. You may also need to do some major restructuring, such as moving your presentation of the subject or reordering your reasons.

- *Is the beginning weak?* Review your notes to find an interesting quotation, comparison, image, or example to use in your first paragraph.

- *Is the ending weak?* See if you can restate your judgment, summarize your reasoning, or frame the essay by echoing a point made earlier.

- *Can you add any visuals or design features to make the essay more interesting to read and to strengthen your argument?* Consider taking features from your subject or creating visual or audio elements of your own.

Checking Sentence Strategies Electronically. To check your draft for a sentence strategy especially useful in evaluation essays, use your word processor's highlighting function to mark sentences where you praise or criticize various aspects of the subject. Then think about whether you could make your evaluation more authoritative and convincing to readers by making any of the sentences more balanced, either by praising something in an aspect that you have generally criticized or by criticizing something in an aspect that you have generally praised. For more on sentences that balance criticism and praise, see p. 294.

■ EDITING AND PROOFREADING

Now is the time to check your revised draft for errors in grammar, punctuation, and mechanics and to consider matters of style. Our research has identified several errors that are especially likely to occur in evaluative writing. The following guidelines will help you proofread and edit your revised draft for these common errors.

Checking Comparisons. Whenever you evaluate something, you are likely to engage in comparison. You might want to show that a new recording is inferior to an earlier one, that one film is stronger than another, that this café is better than that one. Make a point of checking to see that all comparisons in your writing are complete, logical, and clear.

Editing to Make Comparisons Complete

▶ *Jazz* is as good ^*as*^ , if not better than, Morrison's other novels.

▶ I liked the Lispector story because it's so different. ^*from anything else I've ever read.*^ /

Editing to Make Comparisons Logical

▶ Will Smith's Muhammad Ali is more serious than any ^*other*^ role he's played.

▶ Ohio State's offense played much better than ~~Michigan.~~ *Michigan's did.*

Check also to see that you say *different from* instead of *different than*.

▶ Carrying herself with a confident and brisk stride, Katherine Parker seems different ~~than~~ *from* the other women in the office.

▶ Films like *Pulp Fiction* that glorify violence for its own sake are different *from* ~~than~~ films like *Apocalypse Now* that use violence to make a moral point.

Combining Sentences. When you evaluate something, you generally present your subject in some detail—defining it, describing it, placing it in some context. Inexperienced writers often give such details almost one by one, in separate sentences. Combining closely related sentences can make your writing more readable, helping readers to see how ideas relate.

▶ In paragraph 5, the details provide a different impression. ~~It is~~ a comic or perhaps even pathetic impression. ~~This impression comes from~~ *based on* the boy's attempts to dress up like a real westerner.

From three separate sentences, this writer combines details about the "different impression" into one sentence, using two common strategies for sentence combining:

- Changing a sentence into an appositive phrase (a noun phrase that renames the noun or pronoun that immediately precedes it: "a comic or perhaps even pathetic impression")
- Changing a sentence into a verbal phrase (phrases with verbals that function as adjectives, adverbs, or nouns: "based on the boy's attempts to dress up like a real westerner")

Using Appositive Phrases to Combine Sentences

▶ "Something Pacific" was created by Nam June Paik. ~~He is~~ a Korean artist who is considered a founder of video art.

▶ One of Dylan's songs ridiculed the John Birch Society. *"Talkin' John Birch Paranoid Blues."* ~~This song was called "Talkin' John Birch Paranoid Blues."~~

Using Verbal Phrases to Combine Sentences

▶ Spider-Man's lifesaving webbing sprung from his wristbands. ~~They carried~~ *carrying*
Mary Jane Watson and him out of peril.

▶ The coffee bar flanks the bookshelves. ~~It entices~~ *enticing* readers to relax with a
book.

A Note on Grammar and Spelling Checkers.   These tools are good at catching certain types of errors, but currently there's no replacement for a good
human proofreader. Grammar checkers in particular are extremely limited in
what they can usually find, and often they only give you summary information
that isn't helpful if you don't already understand the rule in question. They are
also prone to give faulty advice for fixing problems and to flag correct items as
wrong. Spelling checkers cause fewer problems but can't catch misspellings that
are themselves words, such as *to* for *too*.

REFLECTING ON YOUR WRITING

Now that you have read and discussed several evaluation essays and written one of
your own, take some time for reflection. Reflecting on your writing process will help
you gain a greater understanding of what you learned about solving the problems you
encountered in writing an evaluation.

   *Write a one-page explanation, telling your instructor about a problem you encoun-
tered in writing your essay and how you solved it.* Before you begin, gather all of your
writing—invention and planning notes, drafts, critical comments, revision plan, and
final revisions. Review these materials as you complete this writing task.

1. *Identify one writing problem you needed to solve as you worked on the essay.* Do
   not be concerned with grammar and punctuation problems; concentrate instead
   on problems unique to developing an evaluation essay. For example: Did you
   puzzle over how to present your subject? Did you have trouble acknowledging
   what you liked as well as what you disliked? Was it difficult to refute an important
   objection or answer a question you knew readers would raise?

2. *Determine how you came to recognize the problem.* When did you first discover
   it? What called it to your attention? If you did not become aware of the problem

until someone else pointed it out to you, can you now see hints of it in your invention writings? If so, where specifically? When you first recognized the problem, how did you respond?

3. *Reflect on how you went about solving the problem.* Did you work on the wording of a passage, cut or add reasons or refutations, conduct further research, or move paragraphs or sentences around? Did you reread one of the essays in this chapter to see how another writer handled a similar problem, or did you look back at your invention writing? If you talked about the problem with another student, a tutor, or your instructor, did talking about it help? How useful was the advice you received?

4. *Write a brief explanation of the problem and your solution.* Be as specific as possible in reconstructing your efforts. Quote from your invention notes or draft essay, others' critical comments, your revision plan, or your revised essay to show the various changes that your writing—and thinking—underwent as you tried to solve the problem. If you are still uncertain about your solution, say so. Taking time to explain how you identified a particular problem, how you went about trying to solve it, and what you learned from this experience can help you solve future writing problems more easily.

Supplementary Readings

Anne Lamott really tells it like it is. She has helped many of us to begin writing even when we weren't sure where we were going or what we had to say, even when we felt blocked and intimidated. Her advice is funny, but it's very serious too. The idea of "down" drafts, "up" drafts, and "dental" drafts is truly liberating. I can't think of any advice for writers that is more useful. —M. R.

Shitty First Drafts

Anne Lamott

Now, practically even better news than that of short assignments is the idea of shitty first drafts. All good writers write them. This is how they end up with good second drafts and terrific third drafts. People tend to look at successful writers, writers who are getting their books published and maybe even doing well financially, and think that they sit down at their desks every morning feeling like a million dollars, feeling great about who they are and how much talent they have and what a great story they have to tell; that they take in a few deep breaths, push back their sleeves, roll their necks a few times to get all the cricks out, and dive in, typing fully formed passages as fast as a court reporter. But this is just the fantasy of the uninitiated. I know some very great writers, writers you love who write beautifully and have made a great deal of money, and not *one* of them sits down routinely feeling wildly enthusiastic and confident. Not one of them writes elegant first drafts. All right, one of them does, but we do not like her very much. We do not think that she has a rich inner life or that God likes her or can even stand her. (Although when I mentioned this to my priest friend Tom, he said you can safely assume you've created God in your own image when it turns out that God hates all the same people you do.)

Very few writers really know what they are doing until they've done it. Nor do they go about their business feeling dewy and thrilled. They do not type a few stiff warm-up sentences and then find themselves bounding along like huskies across the snow. One writer I know tells me that he sits down every morning and says to himself nicely, "It's not like you don't have a choice, because you do—you can either type or kill yourself." We all often feel like we are pulling teeth, even those writers whose prose ends up being the most natural and fluid. The right words and sentences just do not come pouring out like ticker tape most of the time. Now, Muriel Spark is said to have felt that she was taking dictation from God every morning—sitting there, one supposes, plugged into a Dictaphone, typing away, humming. But this is a very hostile and aggressive position. One might hope for bad things to rain down on a person like this.

For me and most of the other writers I know, writing is not rapturous. In fact, the only way I can get anything written at all is to write really, really shitty first drafts.

The first draft is the child's draft, where you let it all pour out and then let it romp all over the place, knowing that no one is going to see it and that you can shape it later. You just let this childlike part of you channel whatever voices and visions come through and onto the page. If one of the characters wants to say, "Well, so what, Mr. Poopy Pants?," you let her. No one is going to see it. If the kid wants to get into really sentimental, weepy, emotional terri-tory, you let him. Just get it all down on paper, because there may be something great in those six crazy pages that you would never have gotten to by more rational, grown-up means. There may be something in the very last line of the very last paragraph on page six that you just love, that is so beautiful or wild that you now know what you're supposed to be writing about, more or less, or in what direction you might go—but there was no way to get to this without first getting through the first five and a half pages.

I used to write food reviews for *California* magazine before it folded. (My writing food   5 reviews had nothing to do with the magazine folding, although every single review did cause a couple of canceled subscriptions. Some readers took umbrage at my comparing mounds of vegetable puree with various ex-presidents' brains.) These reviews always took two days to write. First I'd go to a restaurant several times with a few opinionated, articulate friends in tow. I'd sit there writing down everything anyone said that was at all interesting or funny. Then on the following Monday I'd sit down at my desk with my notes, and try to write the review. Even after I'd been doing this for years, panic would set in. I'd try to write a lead, but instead I'd write a couple of dreadful sentences, xx them out, try again, xx everything out, and then feel despair and worry settle on my chest like an x-ray apron. It's over, I'd think, calmly. I'm not going to be able to get the magic to work this time. I'm ruined. I'm through. I'm toast. Maybe, I'd think, I can get my old job back as a clerk-typist. But probably not. I'd get up and study my teeth in the mirror for a while. Then I'd stop, remember to breathe, make a few phone calls, hit the kitchen and chow down. Eventually I'd go back and sit down at my desk, and sigh for the next ten minutes. Finally I would pick up my one-inch picture frame, stare into it as if for the answer, and every time the answer would come: all I had to do was to write a really shitty first draft of, say, the opening paragraph. And no one was going to see it.

So I'd start writing without reining myself in. It was almost just typing, just making my fin-gers move. And the writing would be *terrible*. I'd write a lead paragraph that was a whole page, even though the entire review could only be three pages long, and then I'd start writing up descriptions of the food, one dish at a time, bird by bird, and the critics would be sitting on my shoulders, commenting like cartoon characters. They'd be pretending to snore, or rolling their eyes at my overwrought descriptions, no matter how hard I tried to tone those descrip-tions down, no matter how conscious I was of what a friend said to me gently in my early days of restaurant reviewing. "Annie," she said, "it is just a piece of *chicken*. It is just a bit of *cake*."

But because by then I had been writing for so long, I would eventually let myself trust the process—sort of, more or less. I'd write a first draft that was maybe twice as long as it should be, with a self-indulgent and boring beginning, stupefying descriptions of the meal, lots of quotes from my black-humored friends that made them sound more like the Manson girls than food lovers, and no ending to speak of. The whole thing would be so long and incoherent and hideous that for the rest of the day I'd obsess about getting creamed by a car before I could write a decent second draft. I'd worry that people would read what I'd written and believe that the accident had really been a suicide, that I had panicked because my talent was waning and my mind was shot.

The next day, though, I'd sit down, go through it all with a colored pen, take out everything I possibly could, find a new lead somewhere on the second page, figure out a kicky place to end it, and then write a second draft. It always turned out fine, sometimes even funny and weird and helpful. I'd go over it one more time and mail it in.

Then, a month later, when it was time for another review, the whole process would start again, complete with the fears that people would find my first draft before I could rewrite it.

Almost all good writing begins with terrible first efforts. You need to start somewhere. 10
Start by getting something—anything—down on paper. A friend of mine says that the first draft is the down draft—you just get it down. The second draft is the up draft—you fix it up. You try to say what you have to say more accurately. And the third draft is the dental draft, where you check every tooth, to see if it's loose or cramped or decayed, or even, God help us, healthy.

What I've learned to do when I sit down to work on a shitty first draft is to quiet the voices in my head. First there's the vinegar-lipped Reader Lady, who says primly, "Well, *that's* not very interesting, is it?" And there's the emaciated German male who writes these Orwellian memos detailing your thought crimes. And there are your parents, agonizing over your lack of loyalty and discretion; and there's William Burroughs, dozing off or shooting up because he finds you as bold and articulate as a houseplant; and so on. And there are also the dogs: let's not forget the dogs, the dogs in their pen who will surely hurtle and snarl their way out if you ever stop writing, because writing is, for some of us, the latch that keeps the door of the pen closed, keeps those crazy ravenous dogs contained.

Quieting these voices is at least half the battle I fight daily. But this is better than it used to be. It used to be 87 percent. Left to its own devices, my mind spends much of its time having conversations with people who aren't there. I walk along defending myself to people, or exchanging repartee with them, or rationalizing my behavior, or seducing them with gossip, or pretending I'm on their TV talk show or whatever. I speed or run an aging yellow light or don't come to a full stop, and one nanosecond later am explaining to imaginary cops exactly why I had to do what I did, or insisting that I did not in fact do it.

I happened to mention this to a hypnotist I saw many years ago, and he looked at me very nicely. At first I thought he was feeling around on the floor for the silent alarm button, but then he gave me the following exercise, which I still use to this day.

Close your eyes and get quiet for a minute, until the chatter starts up. Then isolate one of the voices and imagine the person speaking as a mouse. Pick it up by the tail and drop it into a mason jar. Then isolate another voice, pick it up by the tail, drop it in the jar. And so on. Drop in any high-maintenance parental units, drop in any contractors, lawyers, colleagues, children, anyone who is whining in your head. Then put the lid on, and watch all these mouse people clawing at the glass, jabbering away, trying to make you feel like shit because you won't do what they want—won't give them more money, won't be more successful, won't see them more often. Then imagine that there is a volume-control button on the bottle. Turn it all the way up for a minute, and listen to the stream of angry, neglected, guilt-mongering voices. Then turn it all the way down and watch the frantic mice lunge at the glass, trying to get to you. Leave it down, and get back to your shitty first draft.

A writer friend of mine suggests opening the jar and shooting them all in the head. But I think he's a little angry, and I'm sure nothing like this would ever occur to you. 15

I like horror movies. I like Stephen King's essay "Why We Crave Horror Movies." But I loved the responses from students to King's piece when I asked them to write a straightforward report-inter-pretation-argument.

The assignment was to summarize the essay, explain the author's central message(s), and then discuss "what you believe is the function of the horror genre for individuals and/or society." I also suggested (but did not require) that students consider a few rhetorical questions: "Is King's essay convincing? Are his assertions credible? Do other sources support or contradict him? Do you believe that horror movies serve a function beyond entertainment? Why are horror movies so popular? Are King's interpretations reasonable? based on evidence? outlandish? irrelevant? Do you believe that horror films play a significant cultural role? Is that role positive or negative? Is there a relationship to psychological stability? crime? aggression? Can you think of any movies that illustrate, support, or contradict the claims you have found in your research?"

I used this assignment in two Writing 100 classes at Rhode Island College and was amazed by the outpouring for and against horror movies, monsters, Stephen King, satanic writers, corruption of society, perverted fun, the exhilaration of terror, vampires, clowns, nightmares, good times in the balcony, and the impending fall of Western Civilization. Some agree that "we're all mentally ill," that they relish celluloid blood and gore, that everyone has a dark side, and that fictional violence is a counterbalance to real horrors in the world. "Why We Crave Horror Movies" is a short article that first appeared in Playboy *magazine in 1981. But if my students' discussions and papers are any indication, the topic itself is* The Thing that Will Not Die. *—C. G.*

Why We Crave Horror Movies

Stephen King

I think that we're all mentally ill; those of us outside the asylums only hide it a little better—and maybe not all that much better, after all. We've all known people who talk to themselves, people who sometimes squinch their faces into horrible grimaces when they believe no one is watching, people who have some hysterical fear—of snakes, the dark, the tight place, the long drop . . . and, of course, those final worms and grubs that are waiting so patiently underground.

When we pay our four or five bucks and seat ourselves at tenth-row center in a theater showing a horror movie, we are daring the nightmare.

Why? Some of the reasons are simple and obvious. To show that we can, that we are not afraid, that we can ride this roller coaster. Which is not to say that a really good horror movie may not surprise a scream out of us at some point, the way we may scream when the roller coaster twists through a complete 360 or plows through a lake at the bottom of the drop. And horror movies, like roller coasters, have always been the special province of the young; by the time one turns 40 or 50, one's appetite for double twists or 360-degree loops may be considerably depleted.

We also go to re-establish our feelings of essential normality; the horror movie is innately conservative, even reactionary. Freda Jackson as the horrible melting woman in *Die, Monster, Die!* confirms for us that no matter how far we may be removed from the beauty of a Robert Redford or a Diana Ross, we are still light-years from true ugliness.

And we go to have fun.

5

Ah, but this is where the ground starts to slope away, isn't it? Because this is a very peculiar sort of fun, indeed. The fun comes from seeing others menaced—sometimes killed. One critic has suggested that if pro football has become the voyeur's version of combat, then the horror film has become the modern version of the public lynching.

It is true that the mythic, "fairy-tale" horror film intends to take away the shades of gray. . . . It urges us to put away our more civilized and adult penchant for analysis and to become children again, seeing things in pure blacks and whites. It may be that horror movies provide psychic relief on this level because this invitation to lapse into simplicity, irrationality, and even outright madness is extended so rarely. We are told we may allow our emotions a free rein . . . or no rein at all.

If we are all insane, then sanity becomes a matter of degree. If your insanity leads you to carve up women like Jack the Ripper or the Cleveland Torso Murderer, we clap you away in the funny farm (but neither of those two amateur-night surgeons was ever caught, heh-heh-heh); if, on the other hand, your insanity leads you only to talk to yourself when you're under stress or to pick your nose on your morning bus, then you are left alone to go about your business . . . though it is doubtful that you will ever be invited to the best parties.

The potential lyncher is in almost all of us (excluding saints, past and present; but then, most saints have been crazy in their own ways), and every now and then, he has to be let loose to scream and roll around in the grass. Our emotions and our fears form their own body, and we recognize that it demands its own exercise to maintain proper muscle tone. Certain of these emotional muscles are accepted—even exalted—in civilized society; they are, of course, the emotions that tend to maintain the status quo of civilization itself. Love, friendship, loyalty, kindness—these are all the emotions that we applaud, emotions that have been immortalized in the couplets of Hallmark cards and in the verses (I don't dare call it poetry) of Leonard Nimoy.

When we exhibit these emotions, society showers us with positive reinforcement; we 10 learn this even before we get out of diapers. When, as children, we hug our rotten little puke of a sister and give her a kiss, all the aunts and uncles smile and twit and cry, "Isn't he the sweetest little thing?" Such coveted treats as chocolate-covered graham crackers often follow. But if we deliberately slam the rotten little puke of a sister's fingers in the door, sanctions follow—angry remonstrance from parents, aunts, and uncles; instead of a chocolate-covered graham cracker, a spanking.

But anticivilization emotions don't go away, and they demand periodic exercise. We have such "sick" jokes as, "What's the difference between a truckload of bowling balls and a truckload of dead babies?" (You can't unload a truckload of bowling balls with a pitchfork . . . a joke, by the way, that I heard originally from a ten-year-old.) Such a joke may surprise a laugh or a grin out of us even as we recoil, a possibility that confirms the thesis: If we share a brotherhood of man, then we also share an insanity of man. None of which is intended as a defense of either the sick joke or insanity but merely as an explanation of why the best horror films, like the best fairy tales, manage to be reactionary, anarchistic, and revolutionary all at the same time.

The mythic horror movie, like the sick joke, has a dirty job to do. It deliberately appeals to all that is worst in us. It is morbidity unchained, our most base instincts let free, our nastiest fantasies realized . . . and it all happens, fittingly enough, in the dark. For those reasons, good liberals often shy away from horror films. For myself, I like to see the most aggressive of them—*Dawn of the Dead*, for instance—as lifting a trap door in the civilized forebrain and throwing a basket of raw meat to the hungry alligators swimming around in that subterranean river beneath.

Why bother? Because it keeps them from getting out, man. It keeps them down there and me up here. It was Lennon and McCartney who said that all you need is love, and I would agree with that.

As long as you keep the gators fed.

I like to use this essay by Donna Britt to disrupt my students' assumptions and their reading of the world (and the word). Britt's essay is a postmodern analysis of the famous Life *magazine cover photo of a sailor and nurse kissing in Times Square on VJ Day in 1945. This is an image that many of my students are familiar with; Britt's analysis of the photo—through a feminist lens—challenges students' own reading of the photo and brings to light how we read the world through the lens of our own experience. It also brings to light how time and age can change the way we read the world. As an analytic piece of writing, Britt's essay shows us the difference between simply describing a text and analyzing it. This provides a solid entrée for Writing 100 students to begin to "see" or "look" in different ways and to read texts—both printed and visual—on more than one level. —J. C.*

A Kiss May Not Still Be a Kiss

Donna Britt

As a youngster growing up in the 1960s and '70s, I saw it at least a dozen times—Alfred Eisenstaedt's unforgettable *Life* magazine cover shot, taken 50 years ago this month, of a sailor kissing a nurse on V-J Day in Times Square.

To my teen-age eyes, the uniformed pair's embrace represented the perfect picture of wartime romance: spontaneous, passionate, urgently but innocently sexy. The horrors of war, the photo said, are over. Let the good times begin again.

Eisenstaedt's death last week at 96 gave us another glimpse of what became his signature shot. Once again, I admired its perfect composition, how it captured, through people whose faces we never see, a nation's rekindled joy.

But it sparks something different in me today than it did when I was 15. Some classic images—such as Mathew Brady's bleak Civil War compositions—would seem to have a similar impact on viewers of any era. Others suggest different things to different people at different times.

Now, gazing at the Eisenstaedt photo, I found myself wondering: What was the nurse 5 feeling? For the first time, I noticed that she is bent over backward, at a nearly 45-degree angle, with her leg slightly twisted to help her maintain her balance. Because she isn't returning the sailor's hug—her visible arm hangs at her side—it is inaccurate to describe their connection as an embrace. But neither is she pushing him away. The woman appears as impassive as a rag doll—neither reciprocating nor rejecting the advance.

The sailor's physical intent, however, seems clear. You can read his resolve in the way his whole upper body bends hers back, the way one arm encircles her waist while the other forms a crook perfect for positioning a head for a kiss. The clenched elbow ensures that she's not getting away—though there's no real suggestion that she wants to.

Eisenstaedt said that he happened upon the shot while scouring Times Square on that momentous day. He noticed a sailor grabbing, kissing and hugging every woman in sight. Following him, the photographer waited until he grabbed a slim nurse all in white—and then snapped.

Analyzing the resulting photo, reading the sailor's and the nurse's disparate body languages, I wonder. Is she, as I once assumed, as rapturous as the man holding her? Is she as caught up in this moment of liberation, in the longed-for end to a struggle unimaginable to those of us who never lived through it?

Or is she stunned by an intimate liberty being taken by a stranger before dozens of people? Was her impassivity that of someone caught unawares or that of a woman who'd prepared herself for the offering? Could she have felt some strange combination of all those things?

These may be '90s questions forced on a '40s vision, but I wish I knew. Knowing how   10
time and celebrity can alter people's views, I'm not even sure I'd trust whatever the nurse's stated feelings about that moment were.

But somehow, the photo that once suggested only romance to me now whispers complexity. Because it hasn't changed, my eyes must have. The photo illustrates how an act that is tolerated or even lauded in one era might a generation later be regarded as unacceptable. It shows how 50 years—during which terms such as "date rape" became part of the lexicon, record numbers of women learned self-defense and women became "assertive" while men became "angry"—can alter an outlook.

Or maybe it's personal. In the decades between looking at the photo and seeing something wonderful and looking at it and seeing only questions, I have become a woman like many women. We've experienced enough uninvited touches—some that we pretended didn't matter, others that mattered far too much for pretense—to ask questions that once never would have arisen.

And I've met dozens of men who are sick to death of women's fears and suspicions—who, tired of feeling like the enemy, will wonder why anybody would see anything but joy in Eisenstaedt's still-amazing masterpiece.

While part of me wishes things were as simple—for the nation and for me—as they once seemed, most of me is glad for the questions.

And, because vision never stops evolving, I know this: Fifty years from now, I may look   15
at Eisenstaedt's masterpiece and see something else entirely.

*In the following excerpt, Mike Rose tells us that "books can spark dreams." He then uses anec-
dotes about students he has known, reflections on his own education, and cultural observations
to analyze under what circumstances that spark is likely to ignite as well as to consider what may
prevent ignition. Perhaps what makes this text most powerful is that Rose writes from the context
and perspective, always, of having once been a struggling student, a student who was unlikely to
finish high school but instead, ultimately, became a college professor. By telling his story and the
stories of his students, Rose invites us to consider our own cul-
tures, stories, and literacies, and to acknowledge the complex
connections among them. —K. P.*

Lives on the Boundary

Mike Rose

I have a vivid memory of sitting on the edge of my bed—I
was twelve or thirteen maybe—listening with unease to a
minute or so of classical music. I don't know if I found it as I
was turning the dial, searching for the Johnny Otis Show or the live broadcast from Scrib-
ner's Drive-In, or if the tuner had simply drifted into another station's signal. Whatever happened, the music caught me in a disturbing way, and I sat there, letting it play. It sounded like
the music I heard in church, weighted, funereal. Eerie chords echoing from another world. I
leaned over, my fingers on the tuner, and, in what I remember as almost a twitch, I turned
the knob away from the melody of these strange instruments. My reaction to the other high
culture I encountered—*The Iliad* and Shakespeare and some schoolbook poems by
Longfellow and Lowell—was similar, though less a visceral rejection and more a rejecting
disinterest, a sense of irrelevance. The few Shakespearean scenes I did know—saw on
television, or read or heard in grammar school—seemed snooty and put-on, kind of dumb.
Not the way I wanted to talk. Not interesting to me.

There were few books in our house: a couple of thin stories read to me as a child in
Pennsylvania (*The Little Boy Who Ran Away*, an *Uncle Remus* sampler), the *M* volume of
the *World Book Encyclopedia* (which I found one day in the trash behind the secondhand
store), and the Hollywood tabloids my mother would bring home from work. I started buying
lots of Superman and Batman comic books because I loved the heroes' virtuous omnipo-
tence—comic books, our teachers said, were bad for us—and, once I discovered them, I
began checking out science fiction novels from my grammar school library. Other reading
material appeared: the instructions to my chemistry set, which I half understood and only
half followed, and, eventually, my astronomy books, which seemed to me to be magical
rather than discursive texts. So it was that my early intrigue with literacy—my lifts and
escapes with language and rhythm —came from comic books and science fiction, from the
personal, nonscientific worlds I created with bits and pieces of laboratory and telescopic
technology, came, as well, from the Italian stories I heard my uncles and parents tell. It
came, too, from the music my radio brought me: music that wove in and out of my days,
lyrics I'd repeat and repeat—"gone, gone, gone, jumpin' like a catfish on a pole"—wanting
to catch that sound, seeking other emotional frontiers, other places to go. Like rocker Joe
Ely, I picked up Chicago on my transistor radio.

Except for school exercises and occasional cards my mother made me write to my
uncles and aunts, I wrote very little during my childhood; it wasn't until my last year in high
school that Jack MacFarland sparked an interest in writing. And though I developed into a

good reader, I performed from moderately well to terribly on other sorts of school literacy tasks. From my reading I knew vocabulary words, and I did okay on spelling tests—though I never lasted all that long in spelling bees—but I got C's and D's on the ever-present requests to diagram sentences and label parts of speech. The more an assignment was related to real reading, the better I did; the more analytic, self-contained, and divorced from context, the lousier I performed. Today some teachers would say I was a concrete thinker. To be sure, the development of my ability to decode words and read sentences took place in school, but my orientation to reading—the way I conceived of it, my purpose for doing it—occurred within the tight and untraditional confines of my home. The quirks and textures of my immediate environment combined with my escapist fantasies to draw me to books. "It is what we are excited about that educates us," writes social historian Elizabeth Ewen. It is what taps our curiosity and dreams. Eventually, the books that seemed so distant, those Great Books, would work their way into my curiosity, would influence the way I framed problems and the way I wrote. But that would come much later—first with Jack MacFarland (mixed with his avant-garde countertradition), then with my teachers at Loyola and UCLA—an excitement and curiosity shaped by others and connected to others, a cultural and linguistic heritage received not from some pristine conduit, but exchanged through the heat of human relation.

A friend of mine recently suggested that education is one culture embracing another. It's interesting to think of the very different ways that metaphor plays out. Education can be a desperate, smothering embrace, an embrace that denies the needs of the other. But education can also be an encouraging, communal embrace—at its best an invitation, an opening. Several years ago, I was sitting in on a workshop conducted by the Brazilian educator Paulo Freire. It was the first hour or so and Freire, in his sophisticated, accented English, was establishing the theoretical base of his literacy pedagogy—heady stuff, a blend of Marxism, phenomenology, and European existentialism. I was two seats away from Freire; in front of me and next to him was a younger man, who, puzzled, finally interrupted the speaker to ask a question. Freire acknowledged the question and, as he began answering, he turned and quickly touched the man's forearm. Not patronizing, not mushy, a look and a tap as if to say: "You and me right now, let's go through this together." Embrace. With Jack MacFarland it was an embrace: no-nonsense and cerebral, but a relationship in which the terms of endearment were the image in a poem, a play's dialogue, the winding narrative journey of a novel.

More often than we admit, a failed education is social more than intellecutal in origin. 5 And the challenge that has always faced American education, that it has sometimes denied and sometimes doggedly pursued, is how to create both the social and cognitive means to enable a diverse citizenry to develop their ability. It is an astounding challenge: the complex and wrenching struggle to actualize the potential not only of the privileged but, too, of those who have lived here for a long time generating a culture outside the mainstream and those who, like my mother's parents and my father, immigrated with cultural traditions of their own. This painful but generative mix of language and story can result in clash and dislocation in our communities, but it also gives rise to new speech, new stories, and once we appreciate the richness of it, new invitations to literacy.

*　　*　　*

Pico Boulevard, named for the last Mexican governor of California, runs an immense stretch west to east: from the wealth of the Santa Monica beaches to blighted Central Avenue, deep in Los Angeles. Union Street is comparatively brief, running north to south, roughly from Adams to Temple, pretty bad off all the way. Union intersects Pico east of Vermont Avenue and too far to the southwest to be touched by the big-money development that is turning downtown Los Angeles into a whirring postmodernist dreamscape. The Pico-Union District is very poor, some of its housing as unsafe as that on Skid Row, dilapidated, overcrowded, rat-infested. It used to be a working-class Mexican neighborhood, but for about ten years now it has become the concentrated locale of those fleeing the political and economic horror in Central America. Most come from El Salvador and Guatemala. One observer calls the area a gigantic refugee camp.

As you move concentrically outward from Pico-Union, you'll encounter a number of other immigrant communities: LittleTokyo and Chinatown to the northeast, Afro-Caribbean to the southwest, Koreatown to the west. Moving west, you'll find Thai and Vietnamese restaurants tucked here and there in storefronts. Filipinos, Southeast Asians, Armenians, and Iranians work in the gas stations, the shoe-repair stores, the minimarts. A lawnmower repair shop posts its sign in Korean, Spanish, and English. A Korean church announces "Jesus Loves You" in the same three languages. "The magnitude and diversity of immigration to Los Angeles since 1960," notes a report from UCLA's Graduate School of Architecture and Urban Planning, "is comparable only to the New York-bound wave of migrants around the turn of the century." It is not at all uncommon for English composition teachers at UCLA, Cal-State L.A., Long Beach State—the big urban universities and colleges—to have, in a class of twenty-five, students representing a dozen or more linguistic backgrounds: from Spanish and Cantonese and Farsi to Hindi, Portuguese, and Tagalog. Los Angeles, the new Ellis Island.

On a drive down the Santa Monica Freeway, you exit on Vermont and pass Rick's Mexican Cuisine, Hawaii Discount Furniture, the Restaurant Ecuatoriano, Froggy's Children's Wear, Seoul Autobody, and the Bar Omaha. Turn east on Pico, and as you approach Union, taking a side street here and there, you'll start seeing the murals: the Virgin of Guadalupe, Steve McQueen, a scene resembling Siqueiros's heroic workers, the Statue of Liberty, Garfield the Cat. Graffiti are everywhere. The dreaded Eighteenth Street gang—an established Mexican gang—has marked its turf in Arabic as well as Roman numerals. Newer gangs, a Salvadoran gang among them, are emerging by the violent logic of territory and migration; they have Xed out the Eighteenth Street *placas* and written their own threatening insignias in place. Statues of the Blessed Mother rest amid potted plants in overgrown front yards. There is a rich sweep of small commerce: restaurants, markets, bakeries, legal services ("Income Tax y Amnestia"), beauty salons ("Lolita's Magic Touch—Salon de Belleza—Unisex"). A Salvadoran restaurant sells teriyaki burgers. A "Discoteca Latina" advertises "great rap hits." A clothing store has a Dick Tracy sweatshirt on a half mannequin; a boy walks out wearing a blue T-shirt that announces "Life's a Beach." Culture in a Waring blender.

There are private telegram and postal services: messages sent straight to "domicilio a CentroAmerica." A video store advertises about immigration: *Ni de Aqui/Ni de Alia*, "Neither from Here nor from There." The poster displays a Central American Indian caught on a wild freeway ride: a Mexican in a sombrero is pulling one of the Indian's pigtails, Uncle Sam pulls the other, a border guard looks on, ominously suspended in air. You see a lot of street vending, from oranges and melons to deco sunglasses: rhinestones and plastic swans and lenses shaped like a heart. Posters are slapped on posters: one has rows of faces of the disappeared. Santa Claus stands on a truck bumper and waves drivers into a ninety-nine cent outlet.

Families are out shopping, men loiter outside a cafe, a group of young girls collectively count out their change. You notice, even in the kaleidoscope you pick out his figure, you notice a dark-skinned boy, perhaps Guatemalan, walking down Pico with a cape across his shoulders. His hair is piled in a four-inch rockabilly pompadour. He passes a dingy apartment building, a *pupuseria*, a body shop with no name, and turns into a storefront social services center. There is one other person in the sparse waiting room. She is thin, her gray hair pulled back in a tight bun, her black dress buttoned to her neck. She will tell you, if you ask her in Spanish, that she is waiting for her English class to begin. She might also tell you that the people here are helping her locate her son—lost in Salvadoran resettlement camps— and she thinks that if she can learn a little English, it will help her bring him to America.

The boy is here for different reasons. He has been causing trouble in school, and arrangements are being made for him to see a bilingual counselor. His name is Mario, and he immigrated with his older sister two years ago. His English is halting, unsure; he seems simultaneously rebellious and scared. His caseworker tells me that he still has flashbacks of Guatemalan terror: his older brother taken in the night by death squads, strangled, and hacked apart on the road by his house. Then she shows me his drawings, and our conversation stops. Crayon and pen on cheap paper; blue and orange cityscapes, eyes on billboards, in the windshields of cars, a severed hand at the bus stop. There are punks, beggars, piñatas walking the streets—upright cows and donkeys—skeletal homeboys, corseted girls carrying sharpened bones. "He will talk to you about these," the caseworker tells me. "They're scary, aren't they? The school doesn't know what the hell to do with him. I don't think he really knows what to do with all that's in him either."

In another part of the state, farther to the north, also rich in immigration, a teacher in a basic reading and writing program asks his students to interview one another and write a report, a capsule of a classmate's life. Caroline, a black woman in her late forties, chooses Thuy Anh, a Vietnamese woman many years her junior. Caroline asks only five questions— Thuy Anh's English is still difficult to understand—simple questions: What is your name? Where were you born? What is your education? Thuy Anh talks about her childhood in South Vietnam and her current plans in America. She is the oldest of nine children, and she received a very limited Vietnamese education, for she had to spend much of her childhood caring for her brothers and sisters. She married a serviceman, came to America, and now spends virtually all of her time pursuing a high school equivalency, struggling with textbook descriptions of the American political process, frantically trying to improve her computational skills. She is not doing very well at this. As one of her classmates observed, she might be trying too hard.

Caroline is supposed to take notes while Thuy Anh responds to her questions, and then use the notes to write her profile, maybe something like a reporter would do. But Caroline is moved to do something different. She's taken by Thuy Anh's account of watching over babies. "Mother's little helper," she thinks. And that stirs her, this woman who has never been a mother. Maybe, too, Thuy Anh's desire to do well in school, her driven eagerness, the desperation that occasionally flits across her face, maybe that moves Caroline as well. Over the next two days, Caroline strays from the assignment and writes a two-and-a-half page fiction that builds to a prose poem. She recasts Thuy Anh's childhood into an American television fantasy.

Thuy Anh is "Mother's little helper." Her five younger sisters "are happy and full of laughter . . . their little faces are bright with eyes sparkling." The little girls' names are "Hellen, Ellen, Lottie, Alice, and Olie" — American names — and they "cook and sew and make pretty doll dresses for their dolls to wear." Though the family is Buddhist, they exchange gifts at Christmas and "gather in the large living room to sing Christmas carols." Thuy Anh "went to school every day she could and studied very hard." One day, Thuy Anh was "asked to write a poem and to recite it to her classmates." And, here, Caroline embeds within her story a prose poem — which she attributes to Thuy Anh:

> My name is Thuy Anh I live near the Ocean. I see the waves boisterous and impudent bursting and splashing against the huge rocks. I see the white boats out on the blue sea. I see the fisher men rapped in heavy coats to keep their bodys warm while bringing in large fishes to sell to the merchants, Look! I see a big white bird going on its merry way. Then I think of how great God is for he made this great sea for me to see and yet I stand on dry land and see the green and hillie side with flowers rising to the sky. How sweet and beautiful for God to have made Thuy Anh and the sea.

I interview Caroline. When she was a little girl in Arkansas, she "would get off into a room by myself and read the Scripture." The "poems in King Solomon" were her favorites. She went to a segregated school and "used to write quite a bit" at home. But she "got away from it" and some years later dropped out of high school to come west to earn a living. She's worked in a convalescent hospital for twenty years, never married, wishes she had, comes, now, back to school and is finding again her love of words. "I get lost . . . I'm right in there with my writing, and I forget all my surroundings." She is classified as a basic student — no diploma, low-level employment, poor test scores — had been taught by her grandmother that she would have to earn her living "by the sweat of my brow." 15

Her work in the writing course had been good up to the point of Thuy Anh's interview, better than that of many classmates, adequate, fairly free of error, pretty well organized. But the interview triggered a different level of performance. Caroline's early engagement with language reemerged in a lyrical burst: an evocation of an imagined childhood, a curious overlay of one culture's fantasy over another's harsh reality. Caroline's longing reshaped a Vietnamese girlhood, creating a life neither she nor Thuy Anh ever had, an intersection of biblical rhythms and *Father Knows Best*.

Over Chin's bent head arches a trellis packed tight with dried honeysuckle and chrysanthemum, sea moss, mushrooms, and ginseng. His elbow rests on the cash register — quiet now that the customers have left. He shifts on the stool, concentrating on the writing before him: "A young children," he scribbles, and pauses. "Young children," that doesn't sound good, he thinks. He crosses out "children" and sits back. A few seconds pass. He can't think of the right way to say it, so he writes "children" again and continues: "a young children with his grandma smail . . . " "Smail." He pulls a Chinese-English dictionary from under the counter.

In front of the counter and extending down the aisle are boxes of dried fish: shark fins, mackerel, pollock. They give off a musky smell. Behind Chin are rows of cans and jars: pickled garlic, pickled ginger, sesame paste. By the door, comic books and Chinese weeklies lean dog-eared out over the thin retaining wire of a dusty wooden display. Chin has found his word: It's not *smail*, it's *smile*. "A young children with his grandma smile. . . . " He reaches in the pocket of his jeans jacket, pulls out a piece of paper, and unfolds it. There's a word copied on it he has been wanting to use. A little bell over the door jingles. An old man comes in, and Chin moves his yellow pad aside.

Chin remembers his teacher in elementary school telling him that his writing was poor, that he didn't know many words. He went to middle school for a few years but quit before completing it. Very basic English—the ABCs and simple vocabulary—was, at one point, part of his curriculum, but he lived in a little farming community, so he figured he would never use it. He did, though, pick up some letters and a few words. He immigrated to America when he was seventeen, and for the two years since has been living with his uncle in China-town. His uncle signed him up for English classes at the community center. He didn't like them. He did, however, start hanging out in the recreation room, playing pool and watching TV. The English on TV intrigued him. And it was then that he turned to writing. He would "try to learn to speak something" by writing it down. That was about six months ago. Now he's enrolled in a community college literacy program and has been making strong progress. He is especially taken with one tutor, a woman in her mid-thirties who encourages him to write. So he writes for her. He writes stories about his childhood in China. He sneaks time when no one is in the store or when customers are poking around, writing because he likes to bring her things, writing, too, because "sometime I think writing make my English better."

The old man puts on the counter a box of tea guaranteed to help you stop smoking. 20 Chin rings it up and thanks him. The door jingles and Chin returns to his writing, copying the word from his folded piece of paper, a word he found in *People* magazine: "A young children with his grandma smile *gleefully*."

Frank Marell, born Meraglio, my oldest uncle, learned his English as Chin is learning his. He came to America with his mother and three sisters in September 1921. They came to join my grandfather who had immigrated long before. They joined, as well, the millions of Italian peasants who had flowed through Customs with their cloth-and-paper suitcases, their strange gestural language, and their dark, empty pockets. Frank was about to turn eight when he immigrated, so he has faint memories of Calabria. They lived in a one-room stone house. In the winter, the family's scrawny milk cow was brought inside. By the door there was a small hole for a rifle barrel. Wolves came out of the hills. He remembers the frost and burrs stinging his feet as he foraged the countryside for berries and twigs and fresh grass for the cow. *Chi esce riesce*, the saying went—"he who leaves succeeds"—and so it was that my grandfather left when he did, eventually finding work amid the metal and steam of the Penn-sylvania Railroad.

My uncle remembers someone giving him bread on the steamship. He remembers being very sick. Once in America, he and his family moved into the company housing projects across from the stockyard. The house was dirty and had gouges in the wood. Each morning his mother had to sweep the soot from in front of the door. He remembers rats. He slept huddled with his father and mother and sisters in the living room, for his parents had to rent out the other rooms in order to buy clothes and shoes and food. Frank never attended school in Italy. He was eight now and would enter school in America. America, where eugenicists were attesting, scientifically, to the feeblemindedness of his race, where the popular press ran articles about the immorality of these swarthy exotics. Frank would enter school here. In many ways, you could lay his life like a template over a current life in the Bronx, in Houston, in Pico-Union.

He remembers the embarrassment of not understanding the teacher, of not being able to read or write. Funny clothes, oversize shoes, his hair slicked down and parted in the middle. He would lean forward—his assigned seat, fortunately, was in the back—and ask other Italian kids, ones with some English, to tell him what for the love of God was going on. He had big, sad eyes, thick hands, skin dark enough to yield the nickname Blacky. Frank remembers other boys—Carmen Santino, a kid named Hump, Bruno Tucci—who couldn't catch on to this new language and quit coming to school. Within six months of his arrival, Frank would be going after class to the back room of Pete Mastis's Dry Cleaners and Shoeshine Parlor. He cleaned and shined shoes, learned to operate a steam press, ran deliveries. He listened to the radio, trying to mimic the harsh complexities of English. He spread Pete Mastis's racing forms out before him, copying words onto the margins of newsprint. He tried talking to the people whose shoes he was shining, exchanging tentative English with the broken English of Germans and Poles and other Italians.

Eventually, Frank taught his mother to sign her name. By the time he was in his teens, he was reading flyers and announcements of sales and legal documents to her. He was also her scribe, doing whatever writing she needed to have done. Frank found himself immersed in the circumstance of literacy.

With the lives of Mario and Caroline and Chin and Frank Marell as a backdrop, I want to consider a current, very powerful set of proposals about literacy and culture. 25

There is a strong impulse in American education—curious in a country with such an ornery streak of antitraditionalism—to define achievement and excellence in terms of the acquisition of a historically validated body of knowledge, an authoritative list of books and allusions, a canon. We seek a certification of our national intelligence, indeed, our national virtue, in how diligently our children can display this central corpus of information. This need for certification tends to emerge most dramatically in our educational policy debates during times of real or imagined threat: economic hard times, political crises, sudden increases in immigration. Now is such a time, and it is reflected in a number of influential books and commission reports. E. D. Hirsch argues that a core national vocabulary, one oriented toward the English literate tradition—Alice in Wonderland to zeitgeist—will build a knowledge base that will foster the literacy of all Americans. Diane Ravitch and Chester Finn call for a return to a traditional historical and literary curriculum: the valorous historical figures and the classical literature of the once-elite course of study. Allan Bloom, Secretary of Education William Bennett, Mortimer Adler and the Paideia Group, and a number of others have affirmed, each in their very different ways, the necessity of the Great Books: Plato and Aristotle and Sophocles,

Dante and Shakespeare and Locke, Dickens and Mann and Faulkner. We can call this orientation to educational achievement the canonical orientation.

At times in our past, the call for a shoring up of or return to a canonical curriculum was explicitly elitist, was driven by a fear that the education of the select was being compromised. Today, though, the majority of the calls are provocatively framed in the language of democracy. They assail the mediocre and grinding curriculum frequently found in remedial and vocational education. They are disdainful of the patronizing perceptions of student ability that further restrict the already restricted academic life of disadvantaged youngsters. They point out that the canon—its language, conventions, and allusions—is central to the discourse of power, and to keep it from poor kids is to assure their disenfranchisement all the more. The books of the canon, claim the proposals, the Great Books, are a window onto a common core of experience and civic ideals. There is, then, a spiritual, civic, and cognitive heritage here, and all our children should receive it. If we are sincere in our desire to bring Mario, Chin, the younger versions of Caroline, current incarnations of Frank Marell, and so many others who populate this book—if we truly want to bring them into our society—then we should provide them with this stable and common core. This is a forceful call. It promises a still center in a turning world.

I see great value in being challenged to think of the curriculum of the many in the terms we have traditionally reserved for the few; it is refreshing to have common assumptions about the capacities of underprepared students so boldly challenged. Many of the people we have encountered in these pages have displayed the ability to engage books and ideas thought to be beyond their grasp. There were the veterans: Willie Oates writing, in prison, ornate sentences drawn from *The Mill on the Floss*. Sergeant Gonzalez coming to understand poetic ambiguity in "Butch Weldy." There was the parole aide Olga who no longer felt walled off from *Macbeth*. There were the EOP students at UCLA, like Lucia who unpackaged *The Myth of Mental Illness* once she had an orientation and overview. And there was Frank Marell who, later in his life, would be talking excitedly to his nephew about this guy Edgar Allan Poe. Too many people are kept from the books of the canon, the Great Books, because of misjudgments about their potential. Those books eventually proved important to me, and, as best I know how, I invite my students to engage them. But once we grant the desirability of equal curricular treatment and begin to consider what this equally distributed curriculum would contain, problems arise: If the canon itself is the answer to our educational inequities, why has it historically invited few and denied many? Would the canonical orientation provide adequate guidance as to how a democratic curriculum should be constructed and how it should be taught? Would it guide us in opening up to Olga that "fancy talk" that so alienated her?

Those who study the way literature becomes canonized, how linguistic creations are included or excluded from a tradition, claim that the canonical curriculum students would most likely receive would not, as is claimed, offer a common core of American experience. Caroline would not find her life represented in it, nor would Mario. The canon has tended to push to the margin much of the literature of our nation: from American Indian songs and chants to immigrant fiction to working-class narratives. The institutional messages that students receive in the books they're issued and the classes they take are powerful and, as I've witnessed since my Voc. Ed. days, quickly internalized. And to revise these messages and redress past wrongs would involve more than adding some new books to the existing canon — the very reasons for linguistic and cultural exclusion would have to become a focus of study in order to make the canon act as a democratizing force. Unless this happens, the democratic intent of the reformers will be undercut by the content of the curriculum they propose.

And if we move beyond content to consider basic assumptions about teaching and 30 learning, a further problem arises, one that involves the very nature of the canonical orientation itself. The canonical orientation encourages a narrowing of focus from learning to that which must be learned: It simplifies the dynamic tension between student and text and reduces the psychological and social dimensions of instruction. The student's personal history recedes as the what of the classroom is valorized over the how. Thus it is that the encounter of student and text is often portrayed by canonists as a transmission. Information, wisdom, virtue will pass from the book to the student if the student gives the book the time it merits, carefully traces its argument or narrative or lyrical progression. Intellectual, even spiritual, growth will *necessarily* result from an encounter with Roman mythology, *Othello*, and "I heard a Fly buzz — when I died — ," with biographies and historical sagas and patriotic lore. Learning is stripped of confusion and discord. It is stripped, as well, of strong human connection. My own initiators to the canon — Jack MacFarland, Dr. Carothers, and the rest — knew there was more to their work than their mastery of a tradition. What mattered most, I see now, were the relationships they established with me, the guidance they provided when I felt inadequate or threatened. This mentoring was part of my entry into that solemn library of Western thought — and even with such support, there were still times of confusion, anger, and fear. It is telling, I think, that once that rich social network slid away, once I was in graduate school in intense, solitary encounter with that tradition, I abandoned it for other sources of nurturance and knowledge.

The model of learning implicit in the canonical orientation seems, at times, more religious than cognitive or social: Truth resides in the printed texts, and if they are presented by someone who knows them well and respects them, that truth will be revealed. Of all the advocates of the canon, Mortimer Adler has given most attention to pedagogy — and his Paideia books contain valuable discussions of instruction, coaching, and questioning. But even here, and this is doubly true in the other manifestos, there is little acknowledgment that the material in the canon can be not only difficult but foreign, alienating, overwhelming.

We need an orientation to instruction that provides guidance on how to determine and honor the beliefs and stories, enthusiasms, and apprehensions that students reveal. How to build on them, and when they clash with our curriculum — as I saw so often in the Tutorial Center at UCLA — when they clash, how to encourage a discussion that will lead to reflection on what students bring and what they're currently confronting. Canonical lists imply canonical answers, but the manifestos offer little discussion of what to do when students fail. If students have been exposed to at least some elements of the canon before — as many have — why didn't it take? If they're encountering it for the first time and they're lost, how can we determine where they're located — and what do we do then?

Each member of a teacher's class, poor or advantaged, gives rise to endless decisions, day-to-day determinations about a child's reading and writing: decisions on how to tap strength, plumb confusion, foster growth. The richer your conception of learning and your understanding of its social and psychological dimensions, the more insightful and effective your judgments will be. Consider the sources of literacy we saw among the children in El Monte: shopkeepers' signs, song lyrics, auto manuals, the conventions of the Western, family stories and tales, and more. Consider Chin's sources—television and *People* magazine—and Caroline's oddly generative mix of the Bible and an American media illusion. Then there's the jarring confluence of personal horror and pop cultural flotsam that surfaces in Mario's drawings, drawings that would be a rich, if volatile, point of departure for language instruction. How would these myriad sources and manifestations be perceived and evaluated if viewed within the framework of a canonical tradition, and what guidance would the tradition provide on how to understand and develop them? The great books and central texts of the canon could quickly become a benchmark against which the expressions of student literacy would be negatively measured, a limiting band of excellence that, ironically, could have a dispiriting effect on the very thing the current proposals intend: the fostering of mass literacy.

To understand the nature and development of literacy we need to consider the social context in which it occurs—the political, economic, and cultural forces that encourage or inhibit it. The canonical orientation discourages deep analysis of the way these forces may be affecting performance. The canonists ask that schools transmit a coherent traditional knowledge to an ever-changing, frequently uprooted community. This discordance between message and audience is seldom examined. Although a ghetto child can rise on the lilt of a Homeric line—books *can* spark dreams—appeals to elevated texts can also divert attention from the conditions that keep a population from realizing its dreams. The literacy curriculum is being asked to do what our politics and our economics have failed to do: diminish differences in achievement, narrow our gaps, bring us together. Instead of analysis of the complex web of causes of poor performance, we are offered a faith in the unifying power of a body of knowledge, whose infusion will bring the rich and the poor, the longtime disaffected and the uprooted newcomers into cultural unanimity. If this vision is democratic, it is simplistically so, reductive, not an invitation for people truly to engage each other at the point where cultures and classes intersect.

I worry about the effects a canonical approach to education could have on cultural dia- 35 logue and transaction—on the involvement of an abandoned unclerclass and on the movement of immigrants like Mario and Chin into our nation. A canonical uniformity promotes rigor and quality control; it can also squelch new thinking, diffuse the generative tension between the old and the new. It is significant that the canonical orientation is voiced with most force during times of challenge and uncertainty, for it promises the authority of tradition, the seeming stability of the past. But the authority is fictive, gained from a misreading of American cultural history. No period of that history was harmoniously stable; the invocation of a golden age is a mythologizing act. Democratic culture is, by definition, vibrant and dynamic, discomforting and unpredictable. It gives rise to apprehension; freedom is not always calming. And, yes, it can yield fragmentation, though often as not the source of fragmentation is intolerant misunderstanding of diverse traditions rather than the desire of members of those traditions to remain hermetically separate. A truly democratic vision of knowledge and social structure would honor this complexity. The vision might not be soothing, but it would provide guidance as to how to live and teach in a country made up of many cultural traditions.

We are in the middle of an extraordinary social experiment: the attempt to provide education for all members of a vast pluralistic democracy. To have any prayer of success, we'll need many conceptual blessings: A philosophy of language and literacy that affirms the diverse sources of linguistic competence and deepens our understanding of the ways class and culture blind us to the richness of those sources. A perspective on failure that lays open the logic of error. An orientation toward the interaction of poverty and ability that undercuts simple polarities, that enables us to see simultaneously the constraints poverty places on the play of mind and the actual mind at play within those constraints. We'll need a pedagogy that encourages us to step back and consider the threat of the standard classroom and that shows us, having stepped back, how to step forward to invite a student across the boundaries of that powerful room. Finally, we'll need a revised store of images of educational excellence, ones closer to egalitarian ideals — ones that embody the reward and turmoil of education in a democracy, that celebrate the plural, messy human reality of it. At heart, we'll need a guiding set of principles that do not encourage us to retreat from, but move us closer to, an understanding of the rich mix of speech and ritual and story that is America.

Student Essays

As the earlier sections of faculty and student voices might indicate, different instructors bring different styles and emphases to this course. Yet, in the over seventy sections of *Writing and Rhetoric* offered within the year, all instructors are working to create those challenges that will help students extend the range and flexibility of their voices as writers. We hope that students will discover, if they have not already done so, that writing is an indispensable aid to thinking, that writing enables us to explore, clarify, and even learn for the first time what we think and feel.

In this section we have included some of the essays that appealed to us as interesting, lively, and thoughtful efforts by students in the first-year course. We are very grateful to the students who have shared their work (even the essays that we did not finally choose for publication) and to the industrious faculty members who have gathered so many wonderful samples for us to look at. This is the first edition of this customized text. We hope in subsequent editions to publish more examples of strong student writing. Please help us by submitting essays throughout the year that might enlarge our pool of examples for the next edition.

In the following pages you will see five sample papers: Cassandra Lucena's essay, "Drawing the Line at Family," comes from Connie Campana's class and is an example of an essay written from remembered experience. Leslie Kennedy's essay, "Anxiety Awareness," also was written for Connie Campana's course and is a sample of an essay of explanation. From Cathryn Molloy-Raisch's class comes Lorin Kinney's essay, "The Culturally Intact World of Hookah," an example of a profile that depends on observation and description and some supplementary research. Scott Abramson's "Journal Entry" comes from an English 010 class taught by Claudine Griggs. It is a sample of a more whimsical assignment: a speculative journal entry regarding "what you plan to be doing in the year 2015." It was offered as an alternate assignment in the course. Finally, we have included the first eight pages of a long piece by Melissa Brown, "Thursday Nite Madness." This essay (all 31 pages of it!) grew out an ethnography assignment in Meg Carroll's Writing 100 Honors section. The piece weaves together observation, description, interviews, narrative, and reflection.

We hope you find these essays inspiring and encouraging. Please help us add more samples in our next edition!

—Marjorie Roemer
Director of Composition

Cassandra Lucena

Writing 100

Professor Campana

July 22, 2007

Drawing the Line at Family

For as long as I can remember my brother and I were complete opposites. He loved to play baseball. I was much happier watching it on television. My parents' weekends were spent sweating in the bleachers of Bentley field, watching my brother live his dream. Our family vacations consisted of traveling to New York to see the Baseball Hall of Fame and sitting at Fenway Park eating cracker jacks. I learned to love that dirty water, if you know what I mean.

I always thought it was something he would outgrow, a phase maybe, but baseball was the one thing he put before anything else. He played for the town from the age of five, made the middle school team two years out of three, and was picked for the all star team that beat every town in the state two years in a row. He was the best third basemen around and I didn't have an athletic bone in my body. We were siblings, we shared the same parents, we shared the same food, we even shared the same blood, yet it was amazing how different the two of us actually were.

Mom signed me up for the town recreational soccer league when I was about nine in hopes of digging up some kind of athletic ability, which I knew from the start wasn't in me. I was the creative one, the artsy one, the one who couldn't do numbers in her head if her life depended on it. I liked musicals and painting, I liked being alone and writing poems. I was messy and unorganized. I was, in fact, the exact opposite of my brother.

Putting baseball aside, my brother loved socializing. Being with his friends and meeting new people was a high for him. I, on the other hand, would rather be left alone with my thoughts than sit and talk to someone who wasn't going to tell me anything important. He loved slapstick movies, I couldn't see the point in them. He was, and I quote him, "the president of the anal club," his room was organized and neat, his shirts hung by color in his closet. He hated to read when it's what I lived for. He was the math wiz and I was nothing like him.

We lived under the same roof, our bedrooms separated only by a flight of stairs. Yet, if someone walked into my room and then walked into his, they would wonder if they had suddenly stepped into another world. My room had a tie-dye theme. Posters with famous quotes and Johnny Depp's face hung on the sky blue walls. My clothes were scattered all over my floor. My bed was half made, and papers from important events and places were thrown all over my very messy desk. My drawers were overflowing with objects I no longer needed, and my closet was filled with stuffed animals I hadn't slept with since puberty. I was a packrat, and good at it.

My brother's room was a sports theme, obviously. Clean as a whistle, not a thing on the floor. His bed was nicely made, and his drawers were labeled so he could find things easily. His desk had a container for pens and pencils on it and some paper to write on. His bedside table contained a bobble head of David Ortiz, his cordless phone, and a box of tissues. His walls were a dark blue with framed photos of Fenway Park and Gillette Stadium. He had a shelf coming out of the wall that held every trophy he'd ever received from every sport he ever played. I think my one trophy was at the bottom of one of my many piles somewhere in my room. I just didn't see why it was important to look for it.

Believe it or not, my brother and I are related. We share DNA, we share mom and dad, we share the television set, and we share a love for each other. We also share the same zodiac sign, causing us to be stubborn. Which means, neither one of us will ever change. I've come to live with the way he is and he's able to tolerate my mess. We were raised the same way, grew up around the same things, and look exactly alike, but once one of us opens our mouth, none of that matters.

Leslie Kennedy
March 1, 2008
WRTG-100-15

Anxiety Awareness

When I was in elementary school, I remember always feeling extremely anxious about school. I was shy and developed a phobia about becoming sick at school. I remember being in a first grade math group, sitting at a long table, and all of a sudden, Julie was sick. From that day on, I was afraid that *I* would be sick at school. For the rest of the school year, every morning before school, I would have a stomachache and be upset because I was afraid I would become sick at school, even though there was nothing wrong with me. The teacher called my mother to have a conference about all the stomachaches. None of these stomachaches existed on the weekends or during vacations. My mother took me to the doctor to convince me that I was not sick. I needlessly worried about things that may or may not happen. It was a long six years, especially for my mother. The nurse and office staff knew me well. I stopped in nearly every morning with an actual stomachache, especially during the long, dreary winter months. They quickly realized that more than anything, I just wanted to phone home for that final reassurance to get through the day.

Anxiety can be hard to understand by people who have not experienced it themselves because it is not easy to explain. Anxiety is defined in Merriam-Webster dictionary as "an abnormal and overwhelming sense of apprehension and fear often marked by physiological signs (as sweating, tension, and increased pulse), by doubt concerning the reality and nature of the threat, and by self-doubt about one's capacity to cope with it." The situations and events that trigger these feelings, as well as the symptoms, differ by individual. Anxiety affects both children and adults. Family and friends may be very patient and consoling but not truly understand the behavior associated with anxiety. While most people may feel a little jittery or anxious before they make a presentation or take an exam, some people actually become paralyzed with fear at the thought of having to do either. To people with anxiety, their fear, no matter how irrational it seems, is very real and can be quite frightening. People who do not understand anxiety need to recognize the symptoms and be aware of the condition.

It was many years later that I realized that the feelings I had about school as a child were anxiety. I thought that my stomachaches and need to call home were just a phase. My mother told me that she had short-lived anxiety issues about going to school when she was young, too. As I neared the end of sixth grade, I became social and enjoyed playing on a softball team, and my feelings of anxiety were less frequent. In junior high, I played on the softball and basketball teams and ran for student council representative for my class, which required me to get up at school assembly to make a speech. In both junior high and high school, I would get a little apprehensive if I had presentation for class. My hands would be sweaty and tremble at first, along with my voice, but I would eventually calm down. Anxiety seemed to be a problem of the past, until my younger son was born.

My older son was a happy baby. When he started school, he was looking forward to getting on the bus and going to school with the older kids on our street. He never worried about anything. My younger son is very different. He showed signs of anxiety as a baby. He would hold his breath while he was crying; his bottom lip turned bluish-purple. This would happen while at the doctor's office, if he got hurt, or if he stayed with a grandparent while we went out, which was not very often. He had separation anxiety. Once he started preschool, he cried every morning. He would start sniffling and crying on the ride to school. By the time we got to the door, he was sobbing uncontrollably and trembling. We would ask him why he was crying. He always said, "I'm really going to miss you." It was so difficult for me to go through this each morning before work that I would have my husband bring him to school most of the time. Because my son told everyone that he "missed us," teachers asked us if there was anything going on at home. My son's behavior would upset me so much that I would feel sick. My stomach would be in a knot all morning, worrying how my son was doing at school.

Kindergarten and first grade were not much better for him, or me. I was in close contact with my son's teachers. The teachers contacted me if he had a particularly bad day. I felt so bad for my son because I truly understood his feelings and felt I needed to help him, so much that some of my anxiety symptoms resurfaced in my everyday life. Along with stomachaches, I had heart palpitations, shortness of breath, trembling, and elevated blood pressure. I remember pacing the floors, unable to sit down, when both of our children were sick with the flu.

My son and I both found coping mechanisms over the years that help ease our anxieties. When I feel anxious, I need to talk to my husband or mother. Though my husband does not have anxiety, he has developed quite an understanding and patience for it. My mother has sympathy for anxiety because she has dealt with it occasionally. Both can reason with me and calm me down. By discussing any worries with them, I become less anxious, even at an event that triggers anxiety. Now that my son is nearly eleven years old, he and I are having fewer episodes of anxiety. He now plays basketball and participates in more classroom and school activities. His anxiety will show privately at home rather than publicly. If he is worried about something at school, he will have a hard time getting to sleep. He talks to us to get whatever is bothering him off his mind and is fine in the morning. We find that routine is very important to him. The more consistency and structure he has, the better his day will be.

People do not always have obvious anxiety symptoms. Just as there are many causes for anxiety, there are many different ways to manage anxiety. Some people may require counseling. Others may need to be put on medication. Some find ways to control their anxiety, sometimes by avoiding situations that are triggers for anxiety. For some, this may mean getting to social gatherings, classes, or meetings early instead of being the last one to enter a crowded room. For others, they may avoid movie theaters, public

Kennedy 4

transportation, or other places that they feel they cannot escape from should their anxiety get the best of them. Understanding and patience with those who have anxiety has a positive effect on those coping with anxiety.

Lorin Kinney
November 27, 2007

The Culturally Intact World of Hookah

There may be something naturally alluring to college students in the aroma and exotic appearance of a tall, slender hookah. It may be a desire to rebel or to find something by which to separate one generation of American students from all others. Whatever the reason may be, young adults are turning the taboo of smoking hookahs trendy inside smoke filled lounges across the nation. Local hookah lounge Providence Byblos is no exception in terms of surprise success. Hookahs are now one of the most popular aspects of Middle Eastern culture in the urban West, second perhaps only to falafel wraps.

As one sucks in, bubbles form in the base of the tall slender object. Smoke enters the chamber as one inhales deeper. The coals at the top burn hotter, until one pulls away to exhale. The taste is sweet, or maybe spicy depending on the selection of the smoker. The exhale is pleasant, and much less harsh than traditional Western tobacco smoking methods. Hookahs are not typically associated with legal substances, possibly due to the caterpillar in Alice in Wonderland. In actuality, they are intended for use with tobacco products. This tobacco, referred to as shisha, is mixed with molasses and various ingredients to reach a desired flavor (Fifield). The result is a relaxing social activity and a room filled with interesting smells.

The tradition of smoking hookah long predates the length of time it has been popular among Americans. According to Michel Feriani, the manager of the Casbah Rouge in New York City, the hookah has a 3,500-year-long cultural and religious legacy (Lewin). It is only natural that America, in its attempts to be multicultural, would be interested in experiencing something with such a rich history.

The phenomenon of hookah lounges in college areas is relatively recent. According to Lewin, two to three hundred hookah bars have sprung up nationwide since 2000. Quite possibly this could be something unique to this generation of young people, since trends do come and go. However, it is still too soon to know if the popularity of hookah bars will wane and go the way of Members Only jackets. It could also remain popular, but become Americanized similar to the way Chinese restaurants have become in the last century. What is certain is that college students have brought the activity out of Middle Eastern enclaves such as Little Egypt in Queens, New York, into venues throughout the country.

Providence Byblos, located on Angell Street in the city's East Side, is a favorite among college students as a place to go during the week or whenever they want to get out of their dorm or apartment. The guests attempt to preserve and respect the culture they are sampling for the evening; however, it is unclear to many researchers if these attempts are at best respectful or at worst damaging to the authenticity of the experience (Schneider 215). Are American college students looking at the experience as an imperialist looks down upon his colonies? Do the customers value the tradition, or are they merely aiming to experience Middle Eastern culture like tourists. There is always the risk of implicit cultural appropriation involved with exposing any clashing cultures to one another. It does appear from the perspective of a frequenting guest that some do not respect the hookah lounge, while others see it as more than just a place that is trendy or relaxing. With the rich history, music, traditional service, and familial environment, it is difficult to overlook the hookah as merely just a way to escape from stress at work and school.

Byblos is a comfortable place to sit and relax, filled with more pillows than anyone needs, and offering foods such as shawarma and falafel, as well as many flavors of tobacco. Lights remain dim and traditional music remains at a volume just low enough for conversation. The crowded upstairs lounge is alive and throbbing with a beat and chatter between guests. It can be overwhelming; claustrophobics be warned. It is not uncommon to find the place so busy one cannot outstretch his or her arms.

A narrow stairway divides the lounge from the rest of the city. It is apparent from the structure itself and the inside architecture that the building was once a two family apartment. Where the bar is now located, remnants of a kitchen remain. The space is cramped, but this does not seem to lessen the popularity of Byblos at all. The waiting time for a seat ranges from up to an hour on a busy Friday night to no wait at all on some weeknights. Tuesday and Thursday night seem busy, perhaps because they are popular nights for alternative clubs and bars in the city, and Byblos always remains an option for those who have grown weary of dancing and colliding with strangers. The experience of Byblos after a few visits is much like visiting the apartment of an old friend who is popular enough to throw parties every night of the week. In a way, this secluded spot could seem unwelcoming to newcomers, but only after a few visits the staff will know you by name and maybe even remember your preferences for food and flavor of tobacco.

The lounge is separate from the deli portion, located on a part of the first floor. Food and drinks are prepared at the deli for people in the lounge upstairs, and waiters rush up and down a set of service steps in the back of the building to keep up with the demands of the customers. At times, television sets will be on playing music videos that coincide with the music in the room. The music ranges from slow to fast in tempo and seems to remain enjoyable throughout an entire night. It seems that no song is played more than once, although it could just be my unfamiliarity with the music preventing my ears from detecting repeating songs. Occasionally waitresses will begin dancing unexpectedly, and sometimes guests will dance along with them. There is a particular air of liberation that looms amidst the smoke inside the lounge.

Many hookah lounges follow the same format, as both a restaurant and a smoking lounge, and sometimes serve alcohol to those old enough to purchase it. The interiors usually reflect the design and furniture found in genuine Persian lounges. Byblos feels like stepping into a bubble where only those inside it are aware of its existence. Not only does it appear entirely different from any other environment most Americans experience, but there is something hidden and mysterious about a dark, smoke-filled room in a small building off of the main street. The spice and smell of the smoke are unfamiliar in the nostrils of

Kinney 4

the newcomer. The atmosphere is so alluring that it is no surprise that it could become so successful in such a short time.

It is not only the hookah and hot chickpea dishes that bring customers back. It is also the sense of familial connection that one feels with their fellow hookah enthusiasts, as well as the staff. It is customary in Middle Eastern culture to be very generous and congenial toward guests. Shuman Ahmed of Shisha Café in Sterling, Virginia, is no stranger to this obligation of hospitality. He greets returning guests with hugs (Chandler). Byblos's employees and its owners have been known to be so generous as to charge nothing for the bills of friends who are celebrating a birthday. This attitude alone could contribute to the success of these lounges, and their place in the hearts of college students who may feel like strangers if they are in school far from home.

Works Cited

Fifield, Adam. "Smoking Sensation." The Philadelphia Inquirer. Feb 22, 2006. D01.

Chandler, Michael. "Hookah Bar Becomes the 'Anti-Loudon': Young People Flock to Café for Tobacco, Camaraderie." The Washington Post. Jan 17, 2006. B01.

Lewin, Tamar. "Collegians Smoking Hookahs Filled with Tobacco." The New York Times. Apr 19, 2006. B09.

Schneider, Arnd. "On 'Appropriation': A Critical Reappraisal of the Concept and Its Application in Global Art Practices." Anthropologie Sociale. Vol 11(2). Jun 2003. 215-229.

Scott Abramson
February 28, 2008
English 010-03

Journal Entry

The year and date is Thursday, September 24, 2015. Location is Mission Viejo, California.

6:45 am   Just woke up. I am alone in the house. Thank god. Today is my day to do nothing. No obligations, no kids, no wife. It's all just me.

6:47 am   The satellite is ringing. I am not answering. It's Alisha. Message: Remember to pick up the kids from the Collaborative (school) at 5:30. They're staying later today. One for art, the other for shuttle training. Fine with me. Going back to sleep.

6:59 am   Alarm goes off. It's the 2nd green house out back. Jump out of bed. The CO_2 levels are way too high. That's my fault. Forgot to vent the roof the night before. Vegetables look fine and the hemp looks good too. *Note to self: Thank god they legalized marijuana. The vegetables can rot for all I care . . . well . . . not really.*

7:25 am   Make breakfast. Have organic, free-range eggs with red peppers, goat cheese and granola. Not sure about those eggs. They say organic but Alisha got them from a guy in the desert. *Note to self: When you get a chance, go take a look at where this guy lives. Otherwise the eggs are pretty good.*

8:00 am   Went back to sleep. Alisha keeps popping up on the tele-screen but I have turned off the two way camera. She's probably really pissed.

Abramson 2

8:30 am   I'm in the garage and I can't believe my eyes. The new Prius-E is not plugged in. I thought I did this the night before. Oh well. It takes two hours to get it charged anyway. They say it will go 150 mpu (miles per electrical unit) but so far we have only gotten 120 mpu on the average. I miss gasoline.

8:45 am   Watching Apple news. Apparently the fabled oxygen supply on the moon is for real. We knew it all along. The 14 acres we bought six years before are about to become a gold mine. Thank Buddha we have little Chad in shuttle training. *Note to self: Tom Cruise bought 1,800 acres. No doubt TomKat will get up there before we do. Famous people always get to do everything first.*

8:47 am   My good news about the moon has been ruined. The Hills, my favorite show of all time is being cancelled. Apparently Heidi had the wedding all set but Spencer did not show for the eighth time. Unbelievable! What a prick. I'm glad it's cancelled. Doesn't matter anyway. I heard Survivor is on Mars this year. Works for me.

11:25 am   Replacing the worms in the compost can. These worms are much better than the last ones. They eat everything. Even plastic! Can't remember the last time we had trash. Trash is a funny word to my kids.

12:00 pm   Having lunch. Three super nutra-vitamins and one can Pepsi-Coke. Side note: In 2012 it was discovered that one can of Coke per day plus a hefty dose of blue green algae retards aging by three minutes per can. We live on the stuff. Got a call from Uncle Larry. He is "sailing out of Oxnard this weekend down to Catalina." Wants know if the "kiddies" can come along.

Abramson 3

12:55 pm   My neighbor is knocking on the door. It's Rishad. His roof is leaking under the new solar panel I recently installed. A few years ago
I would have been hesitant to help because he is a member of Al-
Qaeda but all that changed when they incorporated in 2011. Now,
they not only employ many writers in Hollywood but have an
excellent merchandising plan specifically targeting the MMLC
(Mid-Mid-Life-Crisis) demographic or 28–35 age range. A tough
market to tap. Rish and I are good friends and it doesn't hurt that
he can get me in to the best hotels in Dubai so of course I go
over to help him.

2:00 pm   There is no leaking solar panel at Rishad's house. What a bastard.
He just wanted me to sample his best Northern Lights (which in
the old days meant an exemplary form of marijuana) but now
means hemp grown at the North Pole under the Aurora Borealis or
Northern Lights. *Question to self: Were the polar caps melting
really such a bad thing?*

4:00 pm   The collaborative called. Our oldest, Eurasia, has passed all of her
exams early and will be ready for early enrollment at Brown or
Berkeley as a late entrant in October. I would be overjoyed save
for the fact that this kid has been a real hassle. Alisha has nicknamed her "The Brain." I have secretly nicknamed her "The
Mouth." Mostly because she acts likes she knows everything. The
problem is, she does literally know everything. *Note to self: Stop
modifying your kids' genetics.*

4:30 pm   I'm starting out to pick up the kids but the day was overcast and
hardly any wind. The solar panels and wind generators didn't quite
kick in so the Prius-E is dead. I have to charter a hovercraft for

Abramson 4

five hundred dollars and, of course, the driver doesn't speak English. Who does these days? Fortunately Spanish is my second language. Thank you, Rhode Island College.

5:30 pm   I pick up the kids from school. Right out of the gate I am
           informed by our youngest that he will be cleared to pilot a shuttle
           to the moon in two years. He's only six. This bothers me because
           we haven't even included him on our car insurance as they won't
           allow him a driver's permit until he's twenty-five. Insurance com-
           panies are always sticking it to the liberal left wing, conservative,
           lower, upper, middle class. *Note to Self: Start affiliating with Inde-
           Obama Party.*

7:00 pm   Alisha arrives home. Will be leaving for Providence the next day
           for her job for the next two weeks. I inform her that we did every-
           thing we could to get out of Rhode Island and here she is flying
           back. We start fighting which automatically activates the mute
           chip in both kids' brains. I tried getting one for myself. Appar-
           ently not going to happen.

8:00 pm   Lights out. We can hear the rain skidding off of the wind turbines.
           It's a nice sound. Hopefully this is a clean rain.

Melissa Brown
Honors Writing 100
Meg Carroll
December 9, 2004

Thursday Nite Madness

When I was growing up, I didn't think much about the fact that I didn't have a typical family when it came to cars. I accepted it as a normal part of life when my parents would occasionally forget what car they had been driving when they came back to the parking lot after shopping. I never really stopped to think about how often our family outings turned into an opportunity to pick up a car at a dealership, the auction, or the detailing shop. Other people didn't have strangers frequently wandering around their yards or constantly calling their homes, but we did—they were just "car people," checking out the prospects. People would think it was strange that our cars never seemed to have more than a quarter of a tank of gas; it seemed obvious to me—when it's time to sell a car, there's no sense in giving away a full tank of gas if we don't have to.

I may not have been conscious of how my dad's line of work affected me when I was younger, but I started to be more aware of my unique position in high school. People noticed that I never drove the same car for very long, and among my friends it became quite the joke: "What car do you have today?" From the time I got my license to the time I graduated, I drove around thirty-five different cars to school. These included everything from a turbo-charged Saab and a classy Mustang to a beat-up gray station wagon and an embarrassing teal Suzuki Sidekick. "A used car dealer has to be humble," my dad would jokingly tell me when I had a particularly awful car. In spite of the humbling moments, I enjoyed the experience. I liked the attention, and I felt a certain thrill in not knowing what I was going to drive next.

The fact that my dad is a used car dealer from Rhode Island just added to the joke for my friends from Massachusetts (where I attended high school).

Brown 2

Used car dealers definitely have a reputation. People seem to view them as smooth and calculating, bent on squeezing every last penny out of their sweet-talked victims. I went along with this characterization for the humor value at school, even though I knew my dad wasn't like that. I couldn't speak for other dealers though, and didn't know if the stereotypes were based on real character traits or not. It wasn't until I began attending car auctions that I was able to observe the culture of car dealers and to begin to understand the world that had shaped my life growing up.

• • •

It's Thursday evening, and I drive confidently up to the entrance lanes where my dad and I leave our cars to be assigned numbers and driven into the auction. We unscrew the dealer plates and walk to the main auction building. Since my dad has his own business now and I am an employee, I am an official dealer. No more driver stickers for me. I swipe my auction card into a machine, and it prints out a colored sticker with my name, business, and bidding number for the evening.

As I walk through the office section of the auction complex, I grab a booklet listing the cars being sold tonight. Before I open it, I smile at the apparently half-hearted attempt of the designers to make the cover attractive. I can see that graphic design isn't a strong point here. Every pixel is visible in the black and white clip-art American flag at the top of the page, as well as in the "Manheim's American Auto Auction" logo, in which an antique car forms the cross bar of a giant "A." The car dominates the image; I almost forget to read the words.

I know why no one spent very long on the cover; the important information is on the inside. As I head for the doors to the auction floor, I scan through the pages, each containing eleven columns of information, including the lane, run number, seller name (businesses with names ranging from "Bobby Jean Auto" to "Stateline Auto Brokers"), year, make, model, body, engine, miles, color, and VIN of many of the cars being sold tonight. It takes me a little while to figure out some of the abbreviations I see. "TK" is clearly "truck" from the context, while things like "4DSN," "2DCP," and "SW4D" pose more of a challenge. They look like some sort of automotive personal ad. My best guess tells me that these abbreviations stand for "4-door sedan," "2-door coupe," and "station wagon 4-door." Though I struggle somewhat, I'm sure that for experienced dealers it takes only a glance to find all the information they need in this crammed table.

The pamphlet reflects the theme of efficiency here at the auction. It gets the point across—no frills, no wasted words, no glitz. People are here to buy cars. If the dealer knows his stuff, the auctioneer can say what needs to be said, sell the car as quickly as possible, and move onto the next one. I close the pamphlet and reread the big black letters emblazoned across the cover page: "WELCOME TO THE THURSDAY NITE MADNESS SALE." Tonight, I'm ready for what's waiting behind the double glass doors in front of me. However, I do remember when this was all very new and unfamiliar territory.

I was a senior in high school when I went to my first car auction. It was quite thrilling to walk in with my dad, get my driver sticker, and suddenly be "on the inside." I suppose I was proud of the fact that I had access to something that the average person did not. People buy cars every day, but rarely think about the circuitous route their vehicles may have taken to get to them. The auction is the background world that most people never see or hear about, and I was there.

The sights and sounds were exciting. For a while I couldn't even tell when a car had been sold as I struggled to follow the auctioneer's flow of babble. The sounds that escaped him were like a kid mimicking the sound of a telephone ring, punctuated by shouted numbers here and there. The car dealers also intrigued me. I was curious about this cross section of our culture, but while I watched them with wide-eyed curiosity, I also felt a certain kinship with them. I realized that the way of life I had grown up with was the way these people made a living.

I've come to be much more comfortable in these surroundings, but I still have a lot to learn. I know as well as those around me that I'm not here as a seasoned dealer. "Can I see your identification?" Case in point. The security guard in front of me, whom I recognize (he always reminds me of Pedro Martinez), obviously doesn't remember me and doesn't think I look like a dealer. To prove that I'm the minimum age of 18 and legitimate, I pull out my auction card and driver's license. Satisfied, he thanks me, and I open the double glass doors and enter the world of car sales.

• • •

Right now, there aren't many signs of the "Thursday Nite Madness." The auction won't start for another half an hour or so. My dad heads outside to make sure his cars are where they are supposed to be. Knowing he'll be busy for most of the evening, I head over to the refreshment stand, where two older ladies are spooning out that night's conglomeration of food. The meals on Thursday nights are free, but also a source of humor for many of the dealers, since much of what is served is somewhat hard to identify. I get my food and head over to a couple of picnic tables set up between two of the auction lanes.

As I look around me, I notice once again what a broad spectrum of people are represented: older Italian men (some in shorts, black socks and loafers), Dominicans yelling to each other in Spanish, a few women—mostly dressed to attract attention from the mobs of men, it seems. The vast majority of auction attendees are male. Whites (particularly Italians) and Latinos seem to make up most of the group, but I also see several African Americans and some Asians. I catch snatches of conversations in Portuguese and others in Arabic. The auction brings all kinds of people together under the same roof in such a unique way. Right now it almost feels like a family picnic. Dealers are sitting together, eating, laughing, and giving each other a hard time. Everyone seems to be in a good mood. I settle down and take a few bites of my meal (which is some sort of pasta and chicken combination piled into a paper soup cup).

At the other end of the table, two men are talking and laughing together as they eat. One is a big, red-haired man with purple tinted glasses, and the other is a smaller middle-aged guy wearing a light jacket. Seeing that I'm enjoying the auction food, they put in their two cents about what it contains.

Brown 5

"It's really not steak; that's for sure," says the red-haired man, who I see is a dealer based on his sticker. The other man, his driver, comments on a meal he had earlier. "I didn't know [it] was potatoes," he comments wryly. I point out that whatever I'm eating really doesn't taste that bad. "Red" laughs and exclaims loudly, "The only other person I've heard say the food wasn't bad was a guy who just got out of prison!" We continue to joke about the food for a while. I'm enjoying the low-key conversation with these two characters, but I'm also glad one of our drivers is nearby. I get the impression that part of the reason they're so friendly is because I'm female.

Eventually Red asks, "You buying? Selling? Watching?" I explain that I'm here with my dad, mostly driving (although I *could* bid, I make sure to add with an air of false pride). Realizing this is a good opportunity to get some insider input on the auction's culture, I take the plunge and say, "I'm writing a paper, to be honest." They seem surprised but appreciative, and I briefly explain the project, asking jokingly if they have any good quotes for me. The driver interrupts me and points out to his friend that the first thing I had said was, "to be honest with you." "That means just the opposite," he declares, and is obviously quite amused with my stereotypically salesman lingo.

Soon I'm engaged in a lighthearted exchange about the ethics of car sales. The driver informs me (as his personal opinion and not as a car salesman, he clarifies) that "people don't want to be told the truth." He explains that if a dealer tells a customer something's wrong with a car, that person is much less likely to buy it than if the car is presented as being perfect (even if it's not). I'm surprised to hear this attitude defended, and I play the devil's advocate, arguing that a customer might appreciate an honest approach and be more likely to come back to him than to the dealer who was dishonest with him, but he disagrees. "You'll find another guy who'll con ya," he says.

I ask Red what he does. "I don't do anything," he jokes. He then goes on to complain about all the people he has to put up with, from the customers to the mechanics. His driver jumps in, adding that customers say they'll come back—they "just need to talk to their mother, or husband, or girlfriend—" but then don't. These two sound pretty impatient with all the flak they have to deal with, and I am amused by the irony of this perspective. Do they justify their dishonesty by pointing to inconsistencies in their customers' statements?

Red goes on to give me some inside tips. "I'll tell you what you can do if you're a dealer," he confides, and then launches into a couple of stories. He once had a guy come to look at a van. The man didn't have all the money, so he put a down payment on it with Red's assurance that he'd hold it for him. Later a second guy came and had a little more money to put down, so Red promised him he'd hold the same van for him. Finally, a third customer came who had the money on him, so Red sold the van to him on the spot. When the first guy came back, he wondered what had happened to his van. Red told him he'd had it checked out and it had ended up having some problems, but informed him he had an even better van for him. He ended up selling three vans instead of one.

Red goes on to tell me a similar story involving another customer who put a deposit on a car. A second man came in who looked so similar that Red thought it was the original customer (at least this is the excuse Red wants me to believe), so Red sold him the car. When the first customer came back, Red had a problem. He suddenly asks me, "So, maybe you'll know; you seem like a smart girl. What did I do?" I guess correctly that he's here at the auction to find the same car for the first customer. He and his friend laugh heartily. "Exactly!" Red says. "My mother taught me well —'take the money'." He chuckles. "Take the money—we'll figure something out."

As we continue to talk about car sales, the driver declares, "It's the worst occupation there is." He adds that it's "the lowest form of life," although he concedes, "it's a lot better than the lawyer." When I ask Red why he does it for a living, he laughingly concludes, "I've lost it." I'm having a good time joking with these guys, and I know that their comments aren't completely serious, but the conversation raises some interesting points. From what I can gather, they are aware that stereotypes of dealers do exist, and they seem to get an ironic joy out of the negative label. I have to admit that some of their business tactics make me wonder if these are the type of dealers who generate such stereotypes.

• • •

Saying goodbye to my new friends, I head out to the lot to look at some of the cars. I'm thankful for my light jacket. It's not too cold yet, but the warm summer auction nights are definitely over, and there's a feeling of fall in the air. It's misty and rainy outside as the final minutes of daylight slip away. I walk past cars of all descriptions. Dealers are sitting in some of them, starting the engine and checking to make sure things work. I remember some of the tips my dad has given me: make sure to test all the gears on 5-speeds, check the power windows, radio, air-conditioning, and power steering. Rev the engine to check for weird noises, including those that would indicate a bad exhaust system. Check the tires to make sure they're worn evenly—if not, the car probably isn't aligned properly.

The quality of the cars at the auction varies. Many of the trade-ins are perfectly good vehicles that the new dealers just don't want on their lots, but there are the other cars, too. My dad says it's a known fact that if you buy a problem car and you don't want to put the time and money into fixing it for a customer to buy, it's easiest to just dump it at the auction. I get the impression that since this is the case, dealers just get used to looking for problems. My dad has learned which dealers have good reputations—and which ones he would never buy from.

There are some sketchy business dealings at the auction. There are dealers who will go to all lengths to get the car they want, including switching wires on good cars to make them run rough going into the block (so that other potential buyers will be scared away), or disconnecting wires to make the check-engine light come on. My dad says these people represent a very small percentage of the dealers at the auction, and that most of the crowd views them with disgust. "The same jerk who's messing up wires at the auction," he says, "is the same guy who, when he's selling the car, is a jerk and gives the rest of us a bad reputation."

There seems to be an understanding about the balance between these underhanded methods and the common tricks utilized by dealers to present

Brown 8

their cars in the best light. For example, my dad might wait until a rainy day to sell a car with a bad paint job. Some other common practices that he wouldn't participate in are to patch a leaky exhaust to make it temporarily quiet or to make sure there's hardly any oil in a car that is known to burn oil. These are things that seasoned dealers are aware of, realizing that the cars may be presented as better than they actually are. My dad cuts sellers some slack, saying, "These guys are trying to make a living too—they're not lying."

• • •

Acknowledgments

AGREEMENT FORM

I hereby assign to Rhode Island College ("RIC) all of my right, title and interest throughout the world, including without limitation, all copyrights, in and to my essay, _____, and any notes and drafts pertaining to it (the sample essay and such materials being referred to as the "Essay").

I understand that RIC in its discretion has the right but not the obligation to publish the Essay in any form(s) or format(s) that it may desire; that Bedford/St.Martin's ("Bedford") may edit, revise, condense, or otherwise alter the Essay as it deems appropriate in order to prepare the same for publication; and that RIC and Bedford are under no obligation to publish the Essay. I understand that RIC and Bedford have the right, but not the obligation, to use and to authorize the use of my name as author of the Essay in connection with any work that contains the Essay (or a portion of it).

I represent that the Essay is wholly original and was completely written by me, that publication of it will not infringe upon the rights of any third party, and that I have not granted any rights in it to any third party.

In the event Bedford determines to include any part of the Essay in the Rhode Island College edition of *Axelrod & Cooper's Concise Guide to Writing* or any other RIC custom textbook, I will receive one free copy of that work on publication.

This Agreement constitutes the entire agreement between us concerning its subject matter and shall inure to the benefit of the successors, assignees and licensees of Bedford.

Student's signature _____

Name_____ Date _____

Permanent address _____

_____

Phone number(s) _____

Email address(es) _____

A Note to the Student:
When a writer creates something—a story, an essay, a poem—he or she automatically possesses all of the rights to that piece of writing, no trip to the U.S. Copyright Office needed. When a writer—a historian, a novelist, a sportswriter—publishes his or her work, he or she normally transfers some or all of those rights to the publisher, by formal agreement. The form above is one such formal agreement. By entering into this agreement, you are engaging in a modern publishing ritual—the transfer of rights from writer to publisher. If this is your first experience submitting something for publication, you should know that every student who has published an essay in a Bedford/St. Martin's textbook entered into this agreement, and just about every published writer entered into a similar one.

Thank you for submitting your essay.